OCEANS ODYSSEY

OCEANS ODYSSEY

Deep-Sea Shipwrecks in the English
Channel, Straits of Gibraltar
& Atlantic Ocean

Edited by
Greg Stemm & Sean Kingsley

Odyssey Marine Exploration
Reports 1

Oxbow Books
Oxford and Oakville

Published by
Oxbow Books, Oxford, UK

© Oxbow Books and Odyssey Marine Exploration, 2010

ISBN 978-1-84217-415-9

This book is available direct from:

Oxbow Books, Oxford, UK
(Phone: 01865-241249; Fax: 01865-794449)

and

The David Brown Book Company
PO Box 511, Oakville, CT 06779, USA
(Phone: 860-945-9329; Fax: 860-945-9468)

or from our website

www.oxbowbooks.com

A CIP record for this book is available from the British Library

Library of Congress Cataloging-in-Publication Data

Oceans odyssey : deep-sea shipwrecks in the English Channel, Straits of Gibraltar & Atlantic Ocean /
edited by Greg Stemm & Sean Kingsley.
   p. cm.
 ISBN 978-1-84217-415-9
 1. Underwater archaeology--English Channel. 2. Underwater archaeology--Gibraltar. 3. Underwater
archaeology--Atlantic Ocean. 4. Shipwrecks--English Channel. 5. Shipwrecks--Gibraltar. 6. Ship-
wrecks--Atlantic Ocean. I. Stemm, Greg. II. Kingsley, Sean A.
 CC77.U5O24 2010
 930.1028'04--dc22
             2009050937

Printed and bound in Great Britain by
Butler Tanner & Dennis, Frome

Contents

Preface

I clearly recall the bright April morning in 1989, sitting on the deck of our research vessel in the luminous green Gulf Stream waters between Cuba and Florida. My business partner John Morris, my brother Scott, Graham Hawkes and I were still trying to get our arms around our recent shipwreck find. We were preparing to steam home, elated at having just found the first colonial Spanish shipwreck ever discovered in the deep ocean – using one of Graham's Phantom Remotely-Operated Vehicles (ROV) that we had recently purchased.

The long-term implications of our discovery were not yet clear, and all of us viewed the next step in dealing with this amazing site from significantly different perspectives. John looked at the economic issues, Graham and Scott looked at the technical challenges and I was wondering how we would conduct an archaeological excavation at a depth of 500m using robotics.

During the following year I met with many different archaeologists and deep-ocean technicians in an attempt to develop a system that could replicate best practice shallow-water fieldwork using a deep-ocean robot. The process was complex, yet we were fortunate enough to be at a place in history where billions of dollars were being spent by oil companies and the military to improve the capabilities of deep-ocean technology.

After the better part of a year, our team had developed a framework for employing a work-class ROV with some newly developed manipulators, advanced optics and long baseline acoustic technology that we felt would be able to accomplish what no one else had ever tried – the complete archaeological excavation of a shipwreck using robotic technology. Lost in 1622, the Tortugas shipwreck, as it came to be known, was a technical success that proved it was possible to conduct archaeology remotely. A comprehensive report on this groundbreaking project is currently being prepared for publication by Odyssey.

It was a very expensive endeavor – far beyond the budgets of academic archaeological institutions. To meet the financial requirements of deep-ocean archaeology, we developed a business plan that featured a new model for funding and managing shipwreck resources. We planned to adhere to the most stringent archaeological protocols, respecting full documentation, contexts and sampling. However, we also allowed for generating profits by either making large quantities of duplicate artifacts – such as coins – available to the public after thorough study and documentation or by charging governments a fee based on the value of what we discovered, excavated, conserved and documented on their behalf.

Looking forward optimistically, we felt that we would find many well-preserved shipwrecks in the deep oceans of the world, that governments would be pleased with a model that allowed underwater cultural heritage to be protected and documented without any cost to the taxpayer, and that archaeologists would be delighted that the long-lost knowledge of shipwrecks in the deep ocean would finally see the light of the day.

Reality did not quite work out like that. We found that even in deep water, shipwrecks were being destroyed at an alarming rate and that the politics of underwater cultural heritage were so complex that some government bureaucrats were happier to see shipwrecks being destroyed *in situ* than to consider a new private sector model for managing cultural heritage. In addition, a handful of archaeologists in positions of power were dead set against the private sector coming into 'their' territory, a perceived threat to their funding sources and monopoly on underwater archaeology. In short, our concept for a new model for the management of shipwreck resources came face to face with the real world, where reason and reality do not always go hand in hand.

Fast forward nearly two decades to 2008 and Odyssey's discovery of Admiral Sir John Balchin's HMS *Victory* in the English Channel. After nearly 20 years of perfecting our deep-water survey and archaeological techniques, we were able to locate and thoroughly document the surface features of the shipwreck site and thus identify the *Victory*. In the process we solved one of the greatest mysteries in maritime history. Sadly, this discovery was accompanied by the reality that the site had already been severely damaged – clearly by trawling activities, but also as a result of natural causes. Our preliminary observation of the damage was the catalyst to undertake a massive study of all the sites that we had discovered in the English Channel and Western Approaches – some 267 shipwrecks – and to conduct an investigation into the impacts we observed, layered on fishery data in order to correlate this information and try to make sense of the destruction of what were once believed to be potentially intact sites.

Interestingly, while some specialists with a vested interest in the 'in situ preservation model' initially questioned our research about natural and man-made damage to shipwrecks in the Channel, they found it increasingly difficult to argue with the clear, unbiased hard data – the verdict was obvious. All the sites in the English Channel are without doubt in danger, and the notion of a pristine collection of shipwrecks awaiting study by future generations was a pipe dream.

So, where do we go from here? For Odyssey's part, an important initiative in our mission statement is to share the knowledge gained from our finds with the public. In the past, we have achieved this through hundreds of popular articles, our television series and documentaries, our traveling exhibits and popular books. With the first volume of OME Reports, we have taken this a step further and are specifically addressing the interests of the archaeological and academic community. We are pleased to present a detailed archaeological analysis of some of our projects from a broad range of perspectives, reflecting the many different disciplines that we bring to bear in our study of shipwrecks.

We are already well underway in planning our 2010 publication schedule. Our archaeologists, technicians and historians continue to tease fascinating information from our finds – and we welcome researchers of all types to access the voluminous data that we have obtained through our investigations of hundreds of shipwrecks.

In an ironic turn of events, we go to press with this first volume of Odyssey's scientific reports just as some government bureaucrats are stepping up their efforts to prevent private companies like Odyssey from conducting archaeological work on shipwrecks. Their stated position is that any company with a profit motive could not possibly be concerned with science. But does that argument really hold up under scrutiny?

I propose that many of the great scientific advances of our time are made with a profit motive in mind. Certainly this is the case in medicine, geology, biology, computer sciences and even palaeontology and genetic research. Rewarding shareholders for underwriting risk capital in exchange for advances in knowledge is a system that requires careful monitoring because there are possibilities of shortcuts in the pursuit of profits. However, I do not think anyone in their right mind would honestly propose eliminating any for-profit company from engaging in medical research. Is archaeology so much more critical to

society than medicine? Fossils are bought and sold every day. Has the study of palaeontology really suffered or have private collectors promoted interest in the field?

Our belief is that cultural resources belong to everyone. If the public wants to own a piece of history, it has been shown time and time again that the private sector is an excellent caretaker of the past. Whether it is the study of coins, stamps, fine art of the masters or antiques, it is clear that knowledge is not lost when the public is invited to collect and study cultural artifacts. Quite the contrary: interest is generated through and by the public and the study of artifacts is promoted by private owners.

Enlightened self-interest has been proven to be a firm foundation on which to build our modern culture, and in the case of managing, protecting and preserving our underwater cultural heritage the 'in situ preservation model' being promoted by some is clearly not working or appropriate universally. A review of studies about the preservation and protection of underwater cultural heritage by national heritage bodies shows that a huge amount of information of economic, archaeological and historical value is being lost every year.

At Odyssey, we believe that we have developed a private sector model that accomplishes our stated mission of discovering, protecting and gaining knowledge from shipwreck sites – while encouraging participation from the public and at no cost to the taxpayer. This book is an important step in proving that our model works and that it should be considered as a viable option for managing underwater cultural heritage throughout the world.

Greg Stemm
Co-Founder & CEO
Odyssey Marine Exploration
Tampa, 2009

Introduction

OME Reports 1 is an important step in Odyssey Marine Exploration's mission to bridge the chasm between perception and reality by familiarizing the public, as well as the scientific and academic communities, with the company's projects, methodology and results. Deep-sea shipwreck survey and archaeological excavation is extremely expensive, time-consuming and technologically complex. It requires an unusual inter-disciplinary blend of personnel, from archaeologists to marine engineers and experts in robotics – the high-tech skills of Formula 1 car racing meets academia.

In many ways just positively locating and documenting a target beyond the sight of land at a depth of hundreds of meters, before the surveying or excavation begins, is an art unto itself. Even with the field's most advanced technology, it takes years of experience and expertise developed through monitoring thousands upon thousands of hours of acoustic and magnetometer records to give the technicians subtle clues that lead to the detection of deep-sea wrecks. The technological challenges have been, and will continue to be, highly testing.

After the headlines and media fascination of discovery, however, Odyssey treats sites selected for study as an archaeologist treats any other shallow-water shipwreck. An interlocking set of questions is demanded of the data in order to reconstruct the history of the ship's final voyage, typically:

- What types of cargo was it transporting?
- To what extent does this correspond with or diverge from the historical record?
- What trade route was the ship sailing and what was its destined final port of call?
- How does the domestic assemblage reflect the origins and cultural hierarchy of the captain and crew?
- How has the wreck formed on the seabed?
- What post-depositional impacts has the ship experienced?
- Do the structural remains of the vessel and its navigational equipment provide significant information about shipbuilding and sailing?
- What sample of artifacts needs to be examined as representative of the wreck site and the commercial or military history of the ship's final voyage?
- To what degree are deep-sea wrecks comparable or dissimilar to site formations in shallow waters?
- Finally, is the site at risk and what action should be taken to preserve it or at least to rescue elements of the wreck and the knowledge it holds?

The ten papers in this book, derived from five major sites and projects, address various elements of these questions. They are presented thematically in chronological order from the date when the fieldwork was conducted.

1. *SS Republic*
- A side-wheel steamer wrecked in the Atlantic Ocean on 25 October 1865 en route from New York to New Orleans.
- Discovered by Odyssey at a depth of 500m, some 150km off Georgia, south-eastern America.
- Surveyed and excavated between October 2003 and February 2005.

2. *The Jacksonville 'Blue China' Shipwreck*
- A small merchant vessel carrying a cargo of pottery wares and glass bottles.
- Discovered by Odyssey in early 2003 at a depth of 370m in the Atlantic Ocean, some 120km off Jacksonville, south-east America.
- Briefly surveyed in 2003 and more substantially in early 2005.

3. *HMS Sussex (Site E-82)*
- The possible wreck of the third-rate, 80-gun Royal Navy warship lost in the Straits of Gibraltar on 19 February 1694 en route from Spithead to Cadiz.
- Discovered by Odyssey in the western Mediterranean Sea at a depth of 821m.
- Surveyed and excavated by limited trial trench between December 2005 and January 2006.

4. *The Atlas Shipwreck Survey Project*
- 267 shipwrecks dating between *c.* mid-17th century and the modern day.
- Recorded by Odyssey in depths of 40-190m during a 4,725 square nautical mile survey of the western English Channel and its Western Approaches.
- Survey period 2005-2008.

5. *HMS Victory*
- The wreck of Admiral Sir John Balchin's first-rate Royal Navy warship returning from Gibraltar to Spithead after a military mission and with a commercial cargo.
- Discovered by Odyssey in April 2008 at a depth of about 100m, some 100km west of the Casquets in the western English Channel.
- Surveyed with highly limited trial trenches between June and October 2008.

The wreck of the SS *Republic* served as a site for Odyssey to test numerous deep-sea recording and recovery technologies and techniques exclusively using a Remotely-Operated Vehicle (ROV), the eyes and the hands of the archaeologist working in depths beyond diving capabilities. The pre-disturbance photographic survey of all surface features, in conjunction with the production of a spatially-correct photomosaic, enabled the wreck's cargo and stowage disposition to be characterized and the site formation to be defined (Chapter 1).

In the absence of records detailing the cargo's origins, volume and destination, the archaeological study of the commercial consignments on the *Republic* provides a unique window into life in the American South just five months after the end of the Civil War. The cargo symbolizes the hopes and dreams of the people of New Orleans, intent on replenishing their shelves and kick-starting the urban economy. The sample of 14,414 artifacts recovered from the wreck is a cross-section of the humble and luxury goods that the city needed to resurrect its former glory. Glass bottles filled with gooseberries and rhubarb (Chapter 4) were found next to more decadent beauty products and patent medicines strongly infused with alcohol and opiates. Damming the pain of war with sham remedies in this golden age of quackery created a generation of addicts. The wreck also yielded glass and stoneware ink bottles and children's writing slates for administrators to take stock of the city's economic position and to encourage literacy amongst the younger population. Alongside a major shipment of British ironstone china wares were recorded everything from clock parts to ceramic figurines, door knobs, dominoes, harmonicas and ladies vulcanite combs (Chapter 2).

Historical records describe the *Republic* as transporting an extensive consignment of coins to get the wheels of New Orleans's commerce turning once more. Some 4,135 gold and 47,263 silver coins were recovered from the wreck, literally one by one using the ROV Zeus' delicate limpet suction device or in concreted clumps. This cargo, fully quantified by date and mint (Chapter 3), and with the obverse and reverse of every example photographed individually, constitutes the largest collection of 19th-century American coins found at sea. Indeed, the *Republic* collection is more extensive than the American coins recovered from all other known wrecks combined. These $20 gold, $10 gold and half-dollar silver issues illuminate the styles and mediums of currency in circulation, while imprints of canvas bags and preserved sections of wooden kegs reveal their mode of seaborne transport.

Although the gold and silver coins generated the headlines at the time of discovery, the otherwise historically unattested commercial cargo, and the fresh information it divulges about economic life in the immediate wake of the American Civil War, is without doubt the star find of the *Republic* shipwreck project. Nowhere is this better exemplified than in the single crate of 96 religious objects excavated forward of the steamer's starboard paddlewheel. The consignment includes green and white glass cruciform-shaped candlesticks manufactured by the Boston & Sandwich Glass Company and unglazed porcelain candlesticks, water fonts and figurines in the form of the Virgin and Child, St. Joseph and a host of angels almost certainly produced in and imported from Limoges in France. Such cheap and thus highly accessible and egalitarian religious products are tangible memories of the strength of Christianity and Catholicism that endured during the Civil War and that the Church fiercely promoted amongst soldiers (Chapter 5).

Whereas the *Republic* site consisted of a coherent structure and a largely continuous distribution of cargo, albeit partly propelled off-site by strong bottom currents, Odyssey's discovery of the wreck of a small wooden merchant vessel in the same search zone reveals the clear and present danger to which many sites have been and continue to be subjected. Typical of mid-19th century maritime trade within American waters, and for this reason of pivotal importance to the socio-economic history of America, the Jacksonville 'Blue China' wreck is associated with a primary cargo of blue shell-edged ceramic plates, bowls and platters and slip-ware jugs imported from England, alongside a few pieces of upmarket ginger jars from Canton. An additional cargo consisted of dark green glass beer bottles.

The site initially came to Odyssey's attention after a trawl fisherman inadvertently snagged artifacts in his nets. Following a brief and highly limited photographic survey of the site in 2003, a monitoring project in 2005 was shocked to realize that trawlers had heavily impacted it in the interim years. What had been a well-preserved, continuous wreck mound was being heavily flattened and artifacts dragged, scattered and destroyed. A photographic survey, the creation of a photomosaic and select excavation and recovery are enabling the story of this wreck to be rescued and preserved (Chapter 6).

The HMS *Sussex* shipwreck project has attracted extensive media interest because of this Royal Navy warship's legendary association with a vast cargo of coins. Following labyrinthine negotiations with Her Majesty's Government of Britain, finally at the end of 2005 fieldwork commenced. No other project pursued to date reflects the stark contrast between the public and academic perception of how Odyssey designs and directs its projects and the scientific reality.

The inter-disciplinary *Sussex* (site E-82) survey and preliminary excavation project assembled a skilful and well-respected set of scholars from many fields (Chapter 7). The wide suite of non-disturbance studies pursued included an extensive environmental coring program and an analysis of the biological oasis effect on the wreck through quantification of the distribution of sea urchins on the site's surface. This was complemented by pre-disturbance bathymetric surveys, multiple photomosaics and site plan production. The complex archaeological reality and contextual recording formulated and implemented for this project serves as the template for Odyssey's shipwreck studies. It has also set a new benchmark for the young discipline of deep-sea shipwreck archaeology as a whole.

Since 2005, the Atlas Shipwreck Survey Project has seen Odyssey's research ships relocate to the western English Channel and its infamously moody Western Approaches. With 267 shipwrecks identified across 4,725 square nautical miles, it is the most extensive offshore archaeological survey conducted in the world. After detailed analysis of data from the survey, the extremely disturbing realization has dawned that the rich maritime heritage of the Narrow Seas – as perceived in historical sources – is not reflected in the archaeological record. Site after site exhibited the tell-tale signs of impacts from fishing trawlers, nets and scallop dredges – side-scan imagery with linear furrows running through sites, snagged nets, beam bars and hopper-rubbers (Chapter 8).

Regrettably, it seems to be already too late to rescue the original cultural identity of many shipwrecks in this offshore area. It is hoped that the Atlas survey will serve as a wake-up call to formulate means of rescuing elements of the endangered past. Now that Odyssey and Wreck Watch have acted as underwater cultural heritage 'whistle blowers' in these seas, the responsibility must shift and shift swiftly to heritage organizations to introduce strategies to sample and save elements of this vanishing past. The logical solution would be to create an alliance to promote cooperation between archaeologists, private sector explorers and fishermen to ensure that a structure is created to monitor, survey and, where appropriate, excavate wrecks at risk. Rather than merely lobbying for change, an industry-wide levy on the fishing industry, modeled on the Aggregates Levy Sustainability Fund, would provide it with teeth to act.

The threat of trawling and scallop dredges is global. The UK and France have now been furnished with data by Odyssey relevant to the western English Channel and Western Approaches and so are in a unique position to promote understanding of the challenges of managing this fast-disappearing heritage and to create policies that will set standards for the wider world.

Amongst hundreds of shipwrecks of 19th- and 20th-century fishing boats and 18th-century wooden merchant

vessels, Odyssey's discovery of Admiral Sir John Balchin's first-rate, 100-gun warship HMS *Victory* is the company's most important historical find so far in the Atlas survey zone. The wreck site was formerly England's greatest unsolved maritime mystery. Found in 2008 over 100km west of where the Admiralty concluded she foundered in 1744, and where untold divers have sought her remains down the years, *Victory* lies within one of the most densely fished seas in the world. Odyssey has hardly started to scratch the surface of this wreck site but, following the company's positive identification of the ship, it formally presented the discovery to the UK Ministry of Defense. The two bronze cannon recovered in agreement with the MOD and two bricks lifted to make an Admiralty arrest were declared to the Receiver of Wreck. Under agreement with the MOD, all surface features were photographed and plotted in 2008, an enormous photomosaic of the 61 x 22m site produced, and a site plan generated. Analysis of the bronze cannon on the site in relation to historical records of Royal Navy warship losses in the vicinity are discussed alongside the rationale underlying the wreck's identification (Chapter 9).

Having experienced Odyssey's operations first-hand and having had the fortunate opportunity to be part of the archaeological team that identified the ship and solved the mystery behind *Victory*'s disappearance, as an Englishman it remains a matter of personal discomfort that Odyssey has not received the recognition it deserves for the discovery and, more importantly, for professionally and transparently declaring the find and interpretation to the UK heritage establishment. The concern about the fate of the artifacts on the *Victory* is a genuine dilemma within a moral maze. It currently costs about £20,000 or more a day to mobilize a research ship and team capable of conducting offshore wreck studies in deep waters to high archaeological standards. Currently, in the absence of private patronage, university funding or military support it is difficult to predict where the tens of millions of pounds needed to excavate, conserve and study the wreck of the *Victory* will come from unless Odyssey's realistic commercial model is strongly considered.

Some heritage managers feel passionately that the wreck should be left untouched in line with the preferences currently promoted by the UNESCO Convention on the Protection of the Underwater Cultural Heritage, which seems to me unworkable and anti-intellectual in the case of Balchin's *Victory*. Study of the language and history of this Convention actually clarifies that it only intends *in situ* preservation to be the first option considered, not the preferred option.

The Convention has subsequently been hijacked in some

quarters to promote a solution that better fits many archaeologists' budgets and ideology. During the Convention's negotiation, however, the concept of *in situ* preservation was emphatically designed with language that directly corresponded to the medical precept of *primum nil nocere*, 'first, do not harm'. This concept does not mean that a patient is never to be treated of course, but that all options should be carefully evaluated prior to any treatment. Applying the analogy to the UNESCO Convention, its negotiators intended the proposition to ensure that all options pertinent to a specific shipwreck site – not just intrusive excavation – should be objectively considered prior to fieldwork.

In terms of mainstream public education and scholarly consciousness, the wreck of Balchin's *Victory* holds vast riches of knowledge. If left untouched *in situ*, it remains unexplained who is going to fund and enforce her ongoing remote monitoring to guarantee fishing trawlers do not continue to impact her tired hull. Who will respond with rapidity to treasure hunters trying to grab finds or to nature's relentless assault on her remains? We inhabit a world that promotes plastic surgery and Botox, where society pretends that the aging process can be avoided. This is a vain illusion: decay is the natural state of the planet and unavoidable, except in rare anaerobic conditions.

One final point of consideration keeps me awake at night: a very real nightmare. Odyssey has identified, but left *in situ*, human bones and one human skull in four areas of the wreck of the *Victory* (Chapter 10). These are so close to the surface that they are in danger of ending up in a fisherman's trawl net – to be dumped unceremoniously on deck with a load of fish and then to who knows what fate? I feel that we owe the memory of Admiral Sir John Balchin, a servant of the Royal Navy for 58 years, and his faithful sailors who died for the cause of British military security, the respect that careful study and perhaps eventual re-burial on dry land entails.

Dr Sean A. Kingsley
Director, Wreck Watch Int.
London, 2009

The Shipwreck of the SS *Republic* (1865).
Experimental Deep-Sea Archaeology.
Part 1: Fieldwork & Site History

Neil Cunningham Dobson, Ellen Gerth & J. Lange Winckler
Odyssey Marine Exploration, Tampa, USA

Between October 2003 and February 2005, Odyssey Marine Exploration surveyed and conducted an extensive excavation on the shipwreck of the 19th-century sidewheel steamer the SS *Republic* at a depth of approximately 500m in the Atlantic Ocean, over 150km off the southeastern coast of the United States. The *Republic* was en route from New York to New Orleans with passengers and a composite commercial and monetary cargo when she foundered during a hurricane on 25 October 1865.

Some 262 ROV dives took place on the *Republic*, accumulating approximately 3,500 hours of bottom time on the seabed. 16,000 digital still photographs were taken and over 3,000 hours of video footage recorded. During the archaeological excavation 14,414 artifacts and 51,404 coins were recovered, recorded and conserved. These assemblages have produced a unique image of daily life in post-Civil War America, unparalleled in scale and diversity on any wreck of a steamship. The project provided an opportunity to develop and experiment with advanced robotics, navigation, photographic and excavation methods and techniques on a Remotely-Operated Vehicle (ROV) for the nascent discipline of deep-sea shipwreck archaeology. Part 1 of the report focuses on fieldwork, the wreck's site formation and the history of the *Republic*.

1. Introduction:
The SS *Republic* Project

Between October 2003 and February 2005, Odyssey Marine Exploration (OME) investigated the shipwreck of the SS *Republic*, a 19th-century sidewheel steamer lost in a storm in the Gulf Stream of the Atlantic Ocean off southeastern America on 25 October 1865. This previously undiscovered deep-sea shipwreck, located at a depth of around 500m, was investigated using remote techniques in order to fulfil an interlocking set of scientific, archaeological, technical and commercial objectives:

1. To assess the archaeological level of preservation, the character and site formation of the vessel and cargo.
2. To develop new technology and techniques for the survey and excavation of a shipwreck in deep water through the exclusive use of a Remotely-Operated Vehicle (ROV).
3. To produce non-disturbance photomosaics of the shipwreck site.
4. To systematically excavate and recover a sample of the ship's unique commercial cargo, including a major consignment of coins.

5. To reconstruct the commercial orbit of the SS *Republic*'s final voyage through reference to the wreck's historically unattested cargo and in relation to economic life in New Orleans in the immediate aftermath of the American Civil War.

In the 30 years since scientists and marine archaeologists realized that deep-water technology exploited by the petroleum/gas and sub-sea cable industry – manned submersibles, ROV's and electronic survey/navigation systems – could be adapted for scientific and archaeological investigation (Bascom, 1976), progress has been continuous. Significant deep-sea archaeological investigations have included wreck surveys and excavations in the Florida Strait (Kingsley, 2003), conducted in the Mediterranean and Black Sea (Ballard *et al.*, 2000; Delaporta *et al.*, 2006; McCann, 2001), the Norwegian Sea (Sóreide and Jasinski, 1998) and the Gulf of Mexico (Ford *et al.*, 2008). These successes were rooted in interdisciplinary collaborative initiatives between archaeologists, scientists, the commercial sector and engineers familiar with the latest underwater systems and available technology.

During the summer of 2003, the *Odyssey Explorer* discovered a target believed to be the SS *Republic*. A side-scan image clearly depicted two paddlewheels flanking the sides of a vessel, a walking beam engine standing proud of the seabed, two boilers and remains of a wooden hull (Fig. 1). The absence of sharp contours suggested that the target was not a steel wreck. The image was closely analyzed and compared against the known historical record for ship losses in the area. The dimensions and features visible on the side-scan sonar very closely matched those of the *Republic*, as documented through historical research (Fig. 2). A visual survey of the site was conducted by an inspection ROV and an Admiralty arrest claim sought to protect the wreck. A project plan was then developed for the investigation of the target and an initial pre-disturbance survey initiated to attempt to identify the site conclusively.

The shipwreck is located approximately 150km off the coast of Georgia on a deep shelf of the Gulf Stream's North American continental shelf. The *Republic* settled on a southeast to northwest axis at an average depth of approximately 500m. The seabed sediments are composed of terrigenous particles formed by the weathering of rock once situated on land and the remains of calcareous and siliceous shells. The site retains the classic elliptical shape of a ship (Fig. 4).

The observed shipwreck measures 65.5 x 30.0m within a principal wreck area of 1,965m². Including the surrounding debris field to the north and south of the stern section of the wreck, the site extends across 56,726m² (Fig. 9). It can be characterized as a continuous and coherent wreck, with articulated structural remains and cargo and a large debris field to the north and south of the stern half of the wreck. However, the upper layers of sediment and the strong 1-5 knot currents crossing the seabed have caused considerable abrasion, erosion and destabilization. The swift, deep currents present in the lower depths of the Gulf Stream have displaced part of the cargo and the wooden and metallic ship structure across the debris field.

More than 262 ROV dives took place on the *Republic*, accumulating some 3,500 hours of bottom time. Some 16,000 digital still photographs were taken and over 3,000 hours of video footage recorded. During the archaeological excavation, 14,414 artifacts were recovered, recorded, logged and conserved. A further 51,404 coins were recovered.

The platform used for the project was the 76m-long, 1,431-gross-ton dynamically positioned ship the *Odyssey Explorer*. For this project, the vessel was re-fitted to accommodate an ROV system, while working space was altered to support archaeology, data acquisition, logging and first-aid conservation. The vessel held accommodation for a crew and staff of 40 people. For the *Republic* project Odyssey modified a state-of-the-art ROV, manufactured by Soil Machine Dynamics Ltd. and renamed Zeus. This system

Fig. 1. Side-scan image of the wreck of the SS Republic.

Fig. 2. Reconstruction of the sidewheel steamer Republic *based on a painting of the SS* Tennessee *in the Peabody Essex Museum, Salem, Massachusetts. Painting: by John Batchelor.*

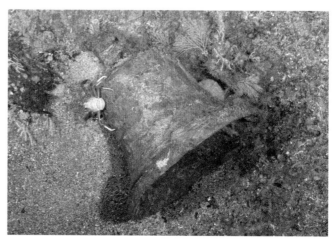

Fig. 3. The bell of the Republic *in situ still retained its former name, the SS* Tennessee.

Fig. 4. Photomosaic of the wreck of the Republic.

Fig. 5. The 7.26-ton, 3.7m-long ROV Zeus used during the survey and excavation of the Republic.

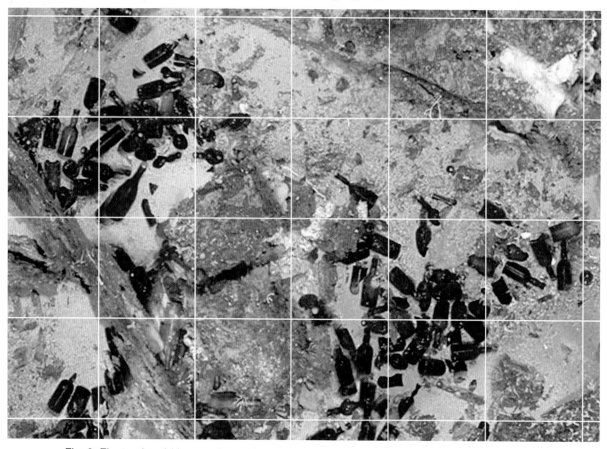

Fig. 6. Electronic grid imposed over the wreck site for contextual recording during excavation.

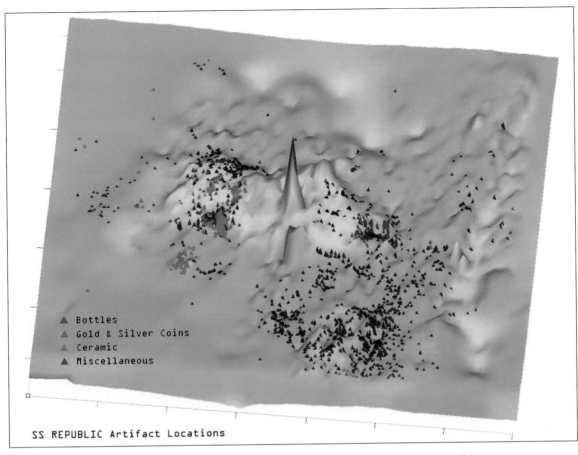

Fig. 7. Bathymetric site plan and scatter plot of artifacts (stern at right).

Fig. 8. The starboard paddlewheel in situ.

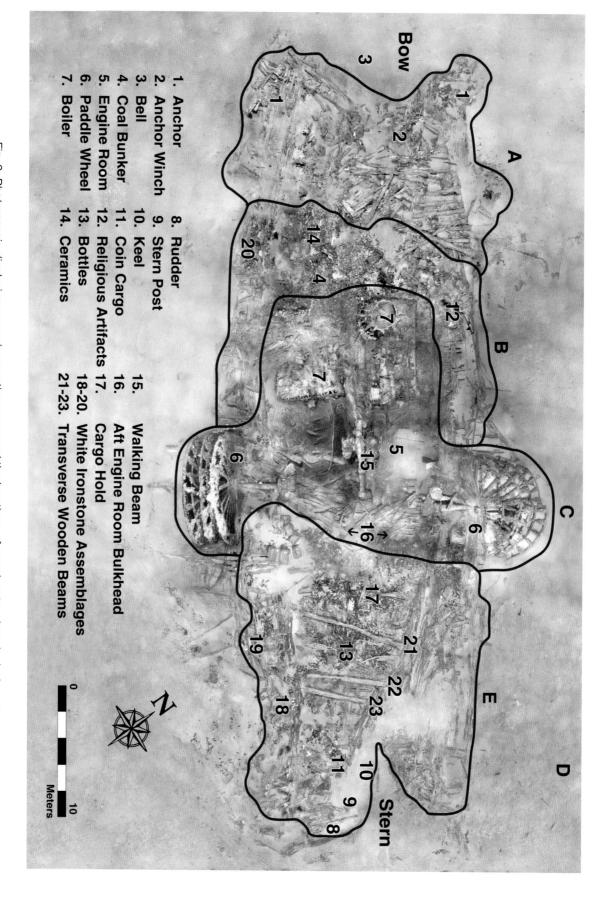

1. Anchor
2. Anchor Winch
3. Bell
4. Coal Bunker
5. Engine Room
6. Paddle Wheel
7. Boiler

8. Rudder
9. Stern Post
10. Keel
11. Coin Cargo
12. Religious Artifacts
13. Bottles
14. Ceramics

15. Walking Beam
16. Aft Engine Room Bulkhead
17. Cargo Hold
18-20. White Ironstone Assemblages
21-23. Transverse Wooden Beams

Fig. 9. Photomosaic displaying survey/excavation areas and the locations of prominent archaeological contexts.

was adapted for survey measurement, photography, manipulation and excavation. The 3.7 x 3.1 x 2.38m, 7.26 metric ton ROV was capable of operations of sustained duration down to depths of 2,000m (Fig. 5).

Zeus was fitted with two Schilling Conan seven-function master/slave manipulator arms on either side of the front of the vehicle. The manipulator arms had a reach of 1.79m, a working arc of 120° and a lifting capacity of 170kg at full extension. The master/slave feature enabled the manipulator arms to duplicate in seabed operations the movements of the operator based in the research ship. Tools were deployed from stowage positions in various points on the vehicle.

For excavation and artifact recovery, the ROV was fitted with a venturi-effect suction device, a limpet suction device and a specialized sediment sifting and collection unit (for more details of this technology, see Cunningham Dobson *et al.*, 2009: 3-6). The nozzle end of the venturi is operated by the starboard manipulator arm, allowing controlled excavation, and sediment is ejected through a hose at the rear of the ROV. Delicate artifacts were retrieved using a silicone rubber limpet suction device, which consisted of a soft bellows-shaped tube with a small suction pad at its end available in different sizes from pads of 2-10cm in diameter (Figs. 10-11).

On the wreck of the *Republic* Odyssey conducted a phase of developmental deep-sea shipwreck archaeology using the ROV Zeus, experimenting with new systems, techniques and equipment to assess a work ROV's capability to perform archaeological surveys and excavations remotely at depth to acceptable comparative archaeological practices and standards. It is important to bear in mind that no guides existed, or have any been formulated to date, for this field of archaeological science. Research was conducted as 24-hour operations for 21-28 days at a time (weather permitting), before returning to port for fuel and water. Personnel typically worked 12-hour shifts on a two-month on, one-month off rotation.

Alongside developing technology and methods for deep-sea shipwreck archaeology, an important research objective of the excavation was to recover an extensive collection of artifacts – undocumented in any cargo manifest – to permit a comprehensive interpretation of the material culture onboard this ship. Study of the cargo was expected to provide primary data about daily life and commerce in immediate post-Civil War America and to contribute to historical knowledge of life at sea aboard 19th-century paddlewheel vessels (cf. Corbin, 2006; Kane, 2004).

2. History of the SS *Republic*

The SS *Republic* was commissioned by the President of the Baltimore and Southern Packet Company, James Hooper & Co., from the John A. Robb shipyard of Fells Point, Baltimore, for the Baltimore-Charleston route. The wooden-hulled sidewheel steamship was 64m long, 10.43m wide and 5.15m deep. When she was launched on 31 August 1853, the ship was rated at 1,149 tons. The *Republic* was equipped with a vertical walking-beam steam engine, twin return-flue boilers and machinery supplied by Charles Reeder and Sons of Baltimore (*Baltimore Sun,* 29 January, 1867; Heyl, 1953: 419; *New York Marine Register,* 1857; Ridgely-Nevitt, 1981: 272). Reeder was a noted pioneering firm in steam engine development that had previously built several famous railroad locomotives and steamship engines. Former ships constructed by Robb, and for which Reeder built engines, included the *Georgia* (1836), *Palmetto* (1851) and *Mosswood* (1863) (Brantz, 1871: 435-36; Kelly, 1961: 10, 30-32; Ridgely-Nevitt, 1981: 272; Scharf, 1881: 427).

Intended for passenger and general cargo merchant service, the *Republic* was originally named the SS *Tennessee*. After being fitted out and her machinery installed, she made her inaugural commercial trip from Baltimore to Charleston on 14 March 1854 with both Hooper and Reeder aboard. During her lifetime, the *Tennessee* enjoyed a colorful service career. In June 1855 she made the first Atlantic crossing by a Baltimore steamship between Baltimore and Southampton, England. In January 1856, under the new ownership of S. de Agreda and Company, she became the first steamship to commence scheduled service between New York and South America. The *Tennessee* changed hands yet again, and by the end of 1856 was making trips to Nicaragua from both New York and New Orleans, on occasion transporting recruits for William Walker's Nicaraguan army and, in the summer of 1857, returning to New York with 275 defeated soldiers (Heyl, 1953: 419; Kelly, 1961: 11). In 1860 a new set of boilers was installed in the ship (Ridgely-Nevitt, 1981: 273-74).

By the outbreak of the American Civil War in April 1861, the *Tennessee* found herself trapped in harbor at New Orleans.[1] Early the next year she was purchased for service in the Confederate navy, but failed to penetrate the Federal blockade of the Gulf of Mexico. After the Union captured New Orleans on 25 April 1862, the *Tennessee* was seized and converted into a powerful gunboat, and was also employed as a troop transport, supply and dispatch vessel (Kelly, 1961: 11). After the battle of Mobile Bay, the

Fig. 10. A Drake's Plantation Bitters bottle being recovered by the
ROV Zeus' pressurized limpet suction device.

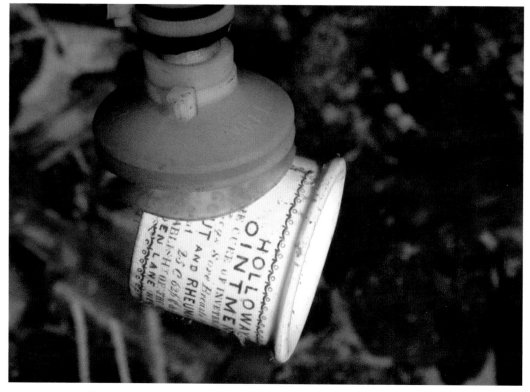

Fig. 11. A Holloway's Ointment medicinal pot being recovered by the
ROV Zeus' pressurized limpet suction device.

Tennessee was renamed the USS *Mobile* to avoid confusion with the captured Confederate ironclad *Tennessee* (Ridgely-Nevitt, 1981: 274). The ship was decommissioned at Brooklyn Naval Yard on 4 December 1864 and in March 1865 was sold out of military service to Russell Sturgis, a merchant whose family had made its fortune from the opium trade with China (Vesilind, 2005: 85). At this stage of her life she was christened the SS *Republic* (Heyl, 1953: 419; Kelly, 1961: 11; Ridgely-Nevitt, 1981: 274).[2]

Quickly repaired and re-fitted, the ship was chartered to William H. Robson's passenger line operating between New York and New Orleans (Heyl, 1953: 420; Ridgely-Nevitt, 1981: 274). On her fifth voyage along this line, the SS *Republic* sailed with 80 passengers and crew, a composite cargo and extensive specie probably destined for use by banks and investors in cash-deprived New Orleans and perhaps even by Yankee businessmen who had financed commercial operations with the enemy as early as 1862 following the Union capture of the city (Capers, 1965: 161, 169-171).

On the morning of 24 October 1865, while battling a hurricane in the Atlantic off Savannah, the SS *Republic's* steam engine failed. Battered by wind and waves, her paddle boxes and deck fittings were swept off deck and the ship rolled and tossed throughout the night. Cargo was jettisoned overboard and a donkey boiler labored to keep the pumps working (*Charleston Daily Courier*, 30 and 31 October 1865; Heyl, 1953: 420; *New York Times*, 3 November 1865; Ridgely-Nevitt, 1981: 274).

On 25 October the auxiliary engine failed. Helpless to stop water rising in the hold, the crew and passengers abandoned ship in two lifeboats, the captain's gig and the ship's dinghy, plus a makeshift raft. The steamer sank at 4pm. All four boats and the raft were eventually picked up at sea. Of the 14 to 18 people aboard the raft, only two survived (*Charleston Daily Courier*, 30, 31 October 1865; Heyl, 1953: 420; *Log of the US Str. Tioga*, 2 November 1865; *New York Herald*, 4 November 1865; Ridgely-Nevitt, 1981: 274). The performance of Captain Edward Young and crew in removing all passengers from the ship during a hurricane was both a remarkable demonstration of good seamanship and an act of exceptional heroic selflessness (*Charleston Daily Courier*, 30 and 31 October 1865; *New York Times*, 3 and 8 November 1865).

The construction details of the *Republic* are historically attested. She was a typical cargo/passenger ship of her day. She was of the average length for a ship of her type and her hull was of a common design. Measuring 210ft long and with a beam of 33ft 11in, she was built of wood and fastened with iron/copper nails/spikes reflecting the refits she was subjected to during her colorful life. Her floor

timbers at throats were moulded 13.5in and sided 8in. Center-to-center frame distances were 26in. She had a solid floor, 13in wide, side and bilge keelsons. The iron lattice was braced, square-fastened throughout and coppered (*Journal of The Franklin Institute* 27.3, 1854: 199). The paddle-wheels had a diameter of 28ft. The 24 blades were 9ft long with a depth of 26in. Power was provided by a vertical walking beam engine located in an engine and boiler space of 55ft. Some 150 tons of coal were stowed in her iron coal bunkers.

3. Survey Results – Phase 1

The archaeological investigation and excavation of the SS *Republic* was divided into two phases: a pre-disturbance survey (Phase 1) and excavation (Phase 2). The first dives of Phase 1 were dedicated to ROV tests, which were conducted off-site to evaluate the functionality of all systems on the ROV and the research vessel. The objective of the initial survey dives was to determine the dimensions of the coherent wreck structures and the extent of the debris field and to characterize the archaeological deposits.

Conditions on-site were generally acceptable for ROV operations. A current of up to 1.0 knot was observed on the seabed. At times, however, 10m above in the water column currents of 3-5 knots were recorded. An understanding of the bottom currents and their direction and speed determined the best headings for the ROV to maintain good visibility through the cameras and to ensure that sediment was cleared downstream of the ROV's heading during the excavation (Phase 2). The initial ROV survey determined that the surface features of the site consist of a hull lying relatively upright, with the metal framework of both paddlewheels slightly canted outwards by 10° (Fig. 8).

The structural remains of the bow (Area A; Fig. 9) are relatively flat, but seem to reveal that the vessel settled on the seabed at an angle on her starboard bow. A very hard and cemented pan area is stratified less than 20-30cm below the sea bottom, composed of hard-packed shell and concreted, calcareous growth. The structural remains of the bow suggest that the *Republic* impacted with this hard surface at the time of wrecking, damaging the hull's sides. The starboard side is more extensively broken up than the port side, possibly indicating that the starboard bow area struck first. Unsupported by sediment, the port side then flattened out over time.

The heavily graphitized starboard anchor is located 9.5m (at right-angles) from the starboard bow (Fig. 12), and the port anchor was identified 16m aft of the port bow at a bearing of 30° (taken from the position of the postulated stem post). Sections of chain associated with both anchors appear to lead towards the chain locker remains.

Fig. 12. The starboard anchor in situ.

Fig. 13. The copper-sheathed rudder in situ.

Fig. 14. Vertical view of the bottom of the copper-sheathed rudder.

Fig. 15. Gudgeon/pintle detail of the copper-sheathed rudder in situ.

Fig. 16. Bronze pintle attached to part of the wooden sternpost.

*Fig. 17. The coal pile in Area A intermixed with J.B. Thorn/James Tarrant
ceramic medicine pots and lids and glass patent medicine bottles.*

Fig. 18. Welsh writing slates alongside glass preserve bottles in situ *in Area A.*

Fig. 19. Glass and porcelain religious artifacts from a decomposed wooden crate in situ *(Area B).*

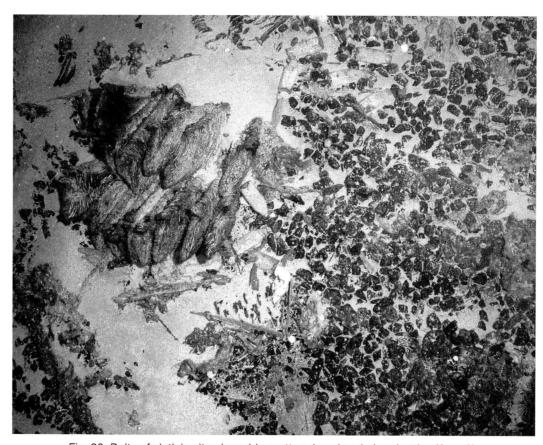

Fig. 20. *Bolts of cloth* in situ *alongside scattered coal and glass bottles (Area A).*

Fig. 21. *Mixed glass bottles, many still containing their original contents, in situ (Area E).*

Fig. 22. *A glass and bronze porthole on top of glass champagne-style bottles* in situ *in Area D.*

Fig. 23. *Brass clock parts* in situ *in the bows.*

Fig. 24. Iron files in situ *(Area B)*.

Fig. 25. Section of rectangular copper hull sheathing alongside glass
bitters, patent medicine and champagne-style bottles in Area C.

The anchor winch may have been dislodged when the bow hit the seabed: it was observed lying on the starboard bow at almost 90° to its original position in its hawse pipe.

Heavily broken and displaced sections of hull timbers and framing, along with sections of deck planking, are scattered across the bow area. Parts of the outer hull planking are still covered with 0.52cm-thick protective copper sheathing. Although launched in 1853, it was not until 1860 that the hull was 'metaled', meaning copper sheathed (*American Lloyd's Registry of American and Foreign Shipping*, 1865: 627). During preliminary inspections of the site while flying the ROV at a distance of about 5-6m off the port bow, the ship's bell was detected lying on its side and partly buried (Fig. 3). Clearly displaying the letters 'SSEE', part of the original name of the ship (the *Tennessee*), this discovery confirmed the identity of the vessel.

Moving astern, a relatively flat area sloping upwards towards the forward bulkhead of the engine room was investigated (Area B; Fig. 9). Covering an area of approximately 280m², it is dominated by a mound of coal protruding some 3.5m above the base of the stempost and up to 1.5m deep in places. Artifacts are dispersed throughout the coal pile, including large groups of small ceramic containers of J.B. Thorn/James Tarrant ceramic medicine pots and lids and glass wine and beer bottles (Fig. 28). Various crates lie adjacent to the port and starboard hull, some broken and their contents spilled (Fig. 19), while others are scattered and displaced from their original stowage positions.

This pattern indicates that the cargo derived from the forward cargo hold in Area B and that the coal originated in the thwart-ship coal bunker situated forward of the boiler. A wooden bulkhead would have separated the cargo hold in Area B from the engine space (Area C). The distribution of the coal suggests that when the bow and the forward section of the ship struck the seabed, the force broke the bulkhead; coal was ejected forward out of the bunker and into the cargo hold. As the ship's sides and decks deteriorated over time, crates of cargo ended up on top of – and partly buried in – the coal in Area B. Close visual inspection of the broken crates and the cargo hold area identified a wide range of merchandise and materials.

Directly aft of this area, the ship's engine room was located, consisting of two boilers, a walking beam engine, paddlewheels and associated fittings and machinery (Area C). Covering an area of approximately 482m², most of the engine room had collapsed inwards. The two boilers had been displaced forward of their mountings and were in a state of poor preservation. The walking beam was fairly intact and vertically preserved to a height of 4m. The rods connecting the walking beam to the paddle wheels were also still whole, and both paddlewheels remained almost vertical, yet canted outwards, even though only their iron framework was preserved. No associated wooden fittings have survived, and all iron on the ship more generally is in an advanced state of deterioration.

The aft engine room bulkhead towards the stern and rudder is broken and the cargo that had been stowed against this bulkhead – largely glass beer and wine bottles – is scattered across the surface of the cargo hold. The stern area has collapsed, exposing the lower port-side hull and a 13m-long section of copper-sheathed keel timber (Area E; Figs. 26-27, 31).

The ship's rudder, 5m long, 2m wide maximum and 30cm thick, lies parallel to the keel timber and is about three-quarters complete, covering an area of 11m² (Fig. 13). Only the top section has broken off and is missing. However, the rudder timber is in an advanced state of degradation. The lower pintle and gudgeon were visible attached to the rudder and sternpost (Figs. 14-15), while a few brass draft numbers were identifiable on the surface of the rudder. Further investigation revealed that the rudder was fitted with four sets of gudgeons and pintles. The upper set was discovered on the seabed below the point where the top of the rudder had broken. One recovered pintle is 43cm long, 31cm wide and 19.6cm high (Fig. 16). After removal of the top layer of fine sediment overlying the rudder and sternpost, it was observed that both were entirely copper sheathed. This preserves the anatomy of the rudder, whose wood is otherwise completely degraded away.

Along the remains of both the port and starboard sides of the wreck, sections of hull planking attached to frames range from 14 x 3m to 4 x 1m (with planks on average 20cm wide and 4-5cm thick). Some strakes face upwards; on others the inside strake edges protrude upwards, indicating original impact damage and the ongoing process of the ship's gradual collapse during the wreck formation process. Many of these sections are still copper sheathed (Fig. 26).

Concentrations of cargo crates, some still intact, and others with their contents spilled, cluster along the break lines of the hull's sides. These include glass and ceramic religious artifacts (Fig. 19), ceramic tableware, white buttons, scissors, door locks, brown marbelized and white ceramic door knobs, horseshoes, metal files (Fig. 24), axes, coils of wire, various cosmetic and patent medicine glass bottles, organic bolts of cloth (Fig. 20), leather shoes, hats, flat irons and various other household goods and ironmongery.

Covering an area of 54,761m², the largely flat debris field (Area D) consists of random clusters of crates dispersed from the cargo holds. The majority are broken or eroded, exposing glass bottles of various types and colors. A few clusters close to the wreck site contain white ironstone table and toilet-wares, as well as blue-gray school children's writing slates. The largest concentration is situated at the southern end of the debris field, apparently the result of the main direction flow of the bottom currents.

While the site is coherent and displays articulated timbers and some cargo integrity, the ship is in a poor state of preservation compared to other excavated steamships. It would appear from the position of the starboard paddle wheel, which is canted over to starboard, that for a period of time the vessel lay over to starboard. Eventually the un-supported bow section collapsed and the stern twisted over to portside. Because of the weight of the engines and walking beam, the engine room area remains mostly upright.

The hostile environment of the Gulf Stream, its strong currents, galvanic effects and the abrasiveness of the mobile sediments are slowly wearing the wreck away. The site has been impacted by the topography of the seabed, the interplay of burial and exposure of its elements, and by accretion and scouring by the movement of sediments. The wood from the site is generally heavily abraded, damaged by marine life (mostly wood-burrowing worms), soft and lacks structural strength. Most of the iron structure and artifacts display extensive graphitic corrosion. Other components were observed to have experienced electrochemical corrosion. The site reveals that even 19th-century shipwrecks in deep water that have not been disturbed by fishing and other man-made destructive forces are still at risk from the elements.

A key objective of Phase 1 was to produce a pre-disturbance photomosaic of the wreck site and debris field. Each standard picture was 2048 x 1536 pixels. The location of each photo was correlated to the precise position of the camera using the LBL acoustic positioning system, which resulted in a geospatially correct representation of the site. The production of the photomosaic was a complex task that required development of new techniques to account for variations in lighting and other factors. The undulating topography of the wreck was also problematic, especially the walking beam engine and paddle wheels, which forced the ROV to fly at a higher elevation to ensure safe clearance in these areas.

The final photomosaic of the SS *Republic* contained about 2,500 high-resolution images (Fig. 4). The photomosaics of the wreck site, debris field and specific sections of the wreck proved an invaluable tool in understanding the archaeology of the site and formulating excavation strategies.

4. Excavation Results – Phase 2

The first artifact to be recovered during the Phase 2 excavation was the ship's bell (Fig. 3). Observed during the initial video survey of the port bow area, the bell was recorded *in situ* and measured at 46.5cm high and 47.5cm wide for the fabrication of a recovery container. Inspection revealed the letters 'SSEE', the end of the word *Tennessee*, which was the vessel's original name when launched. The bell was very badly corroded and was stored in a container filled with a solution of sodium sesquicarbonate until it was handed over to Odyssey's shore-based conservation facility.

Using the photomosaic as a planning tool, excavation commenced in Area E from the stern of the shipwreck's keel and sternpost, lying on their port sides, to the aft engine room bulkhead (Fig. 29). This area was chosen as the most suitable location to clear a sterile path to the keel and sternpost and for the ROV to operate into the current, so that disturbed sediment could be dispersed downstream. The area of seabed adjacent to the rudder and keel was relatively flat and devoid of artifacts and ship's structure. A 4m-wide path was excavated towards the sternpost and keel. The upper 5-20cm of mobile sediments were then removed by the ROV's Sediment Removal and Filtration System (SeRF) to expose a hard substrate composed of particles of terrigenous origin, the remains of calcareous and siliceous shells of protozoans (single-celled animals) and pteropod pelagic molluscs. Glass bottles of various types and sizes, and unidentified sections of ship timbers, were recorded and lifted in recovery baskets.

A shell-rich sandy slope leads up from the keel to the aft engine room bulkhead from the northeast to northwest at an angle of 20°. The 2m-high slope was excavated to expose the keel and allow access for the ROV to proceed towards the stern hold. While excavating the upper area of the slope, gold and silver coins were uncovered ($20 and $10 gold coins, as well as silver half dollars; cf. Bowers, 2009). These coins had spilled out of decomposed wooden storage barrels and become scattered near a cargo of glass bottles and disarticulated ship's structure. The coins were recorded *in situ* and recovered one at a time over a period of three months.

Excavation of the stern area revealed that the keel was intact from the sternpost to the aft engine room (Fig. 31), a distance of 15m, and visibly continued intact beneath the engine room. During the wreck formation process the stern had collapsed over to the unsupported port side, exposing the keel and a large section of hull. As the ship deteriorated, the starboard side was pushed outward and downwards, causing the cargo to spill onto the seabed. A wide variety of artifacts, including dominoes and personal items, such as ceramic figurines, horseman's spurs and even a child's tea service, provide a unique window into the daily life and culture of a mid-1860s American merchant venture.

Fig. 26. Copper hull sheathing attached to outer wooden strakes (Area E).

Fig. 27. Section of keelson and floor timbers in situ (Area E).

Fig. 28. Coal pile from the bunker in Area B.

Fig. 29. Composite photomosaic of the stern slope in Area E.

Fig. 30. Wooden ceiling planking and frames in Area E.

Fig. 31. Photomosaic of the stern complex (Area E) depicting at top the rudder (far left), keel and ceiling planking and strakes of portside. The starboard hull (at bottom) has collapsed outwards and is entirely dislocated from the keel.

Representative samples of each type of glass bottle were recovered from the stern cargo, and the remainder moved to an off-site storage area in a sterile zone. Similar storage areas were excavated off-site to receive broken timbers, coal and other items that needed to be cleared to expose underlying stratigraphy, but were deemed unsuitable for recovery. Detailed pre- and post-excavation photomosaics were produced of this excavated area (Fig. 31).

Area B contains the coal pile forward of the ship's boilers. The engine room (Area C) was not excavated because few cultural artifacts were visibly associated with it and because the ROV could not work easily in the area without the risk of its umbilical becoming snagged. The boilers and walking beam were recorded on video and separate close-up photomosaics created. A specially fabricated scoop and bucket was fabricated to remove the coal to a storage area in a sterile area adjacent to the debris field. Recording and recovering the hundreds of glass bottles, small ceramic containers and ink bottles located above and beneath the coal took six weeks. Removal of the sediment below this stratum exposed the badly broken up lower hull of the ship, validating the theory that the bow struck the seabed first and then broke up, spilling the cargo.

A unique discovery in Area B was a consignment of religious artifacts, which had spilled out of broken crates on the starboard side of the inner hull, just forward of the paddlewheel (Fig. 19). These included green and white glass crucifix candlesticks, ceramic candlesticks sets in the form of the Madonna and Child and St. Joseph, holy water fonts in three styles featuring angel figures, the crucified Christ, and a small ceramic 'grotto' figurine of the Blessed Virgin (Tolson and Gerth, 2009). Further along the starboard side of the vessel, partly buried in the seabed, was a large assemblage of white ironstone cargo pottery. Both paddlewheels were recorded and panoramic photomosaics produced.

Excavation in the bow area of the wreck (Area A) was limited to the forward hold because the bow was badly broken and scattered. Lower hull timbers and remains of the keel again indicated that the vessel struck the seabed bow first and slightly over to starboard. (By contrast, the sternpost, keel and rudder are all intact in the stern, suggesting that most of the force of the impact was absorbed by the bow section when the *Republic* struck the seabed.)

The final area to be selectively excavated (Area D) was the debris field. Due to its enormous surface area, it was never an objective to excavate this zone in its entirety. A Tracking Sub-Sea System (TSS) metal detector configured onto the ROV documented all metallic anomalies within the wreck, the debris field and large areas to the north of the site. The majority of the anomalies proved to be iron concretions. In addition to glass bottles, glass wares and ceramics recovered from the debris field, this zone also contained a collection of glass lenses, corroded brass telescopes and a corroded brass barometer from a shipment of nautical instruments, perhaps destined for a chandler serving the extensive maritime traffic of New Orleans. Spare lenses, and the equipment's location where the cargo crates spilled into the debris field, favors their identification as cargo rather than domestic assemblage.

All artifacts were recorded on Artifact Record Sheets, labelled and, where applicable, given first-aid conservation treatment. A total of 65,818 artifacts were recovered from the wreck of the SS *Republic*, ranging from ship's fittings to glass bottles, ceramics, slates, organics (cloth, leather) and coins. One of the most important archaeological assemblages is the glass bottles (Gerth, 2006), which may prove to be the largest and most diverse collection recovered from any American shipwreck. These bottles provide tangible evidence of the importance of various products in daily American life in the mid-19th century.

5. Conclusion

In conclusion, a combination of historical sources and the results of the underwater survey and excavation suggest the following site formation processes for the loss of the SS *Republic* (with historical data derived from the *Charleston Daily Courier*, 30 October 1865, 7 November 1865; the *Daily Courier*, 31 October 1865, 7 November 1865; the *New York Times*, 3 November 1865; and Vesilind, 2005: 117-32).

1. On the morning of 23 October 1865 the SS *Republic* encountered a gale off Savannah, which turned into a "perfect hurricane" before night, when the steamer was possibly off Carolina.
2. About 6am on 24 October, the engine could not be turned over manually. Almost two hours later the steam pump failed, the triangular sail was blown to ribbons and the paddle boxes and part of the paddle house were destroyed. Everything loose on deck was washed overboard and lost.
3. By around 9am the vessel was leaking badly. Four additional pumps from the forward deck were fired up. Rising water swiftly inundated the pumps and by noon had extinguished the boiler fires. All hands were set to work bailing with buckets.
4. At 11.00am the *Republic's* crew and passengers jettisoned as much cargo as possible in a last-ditch attempt to save the ship. Passengers spent at least 12 hours bailing out the hull, with one later testifying that he passed buckets of water at the extraordinary rate of 25-50 pails per minute.

5. At 9.00am on 25 October all the pumps gave out. The crew set to work building a raft because the ship's four lifeboats were insufficient to accommodate all passengers (who were otherwise still bailing water). Around 1.30pm the water level rose above the engine room. With at least 80 people, the captain abandoned ship.

6. At 4pm on 25 October 1865 the SS *Republic* "broke amidships and sank" in two sections as her deckhouse separated from the main deck and floated away. Captain Edward Young reported seeing the floating deck of the *Republic*, with her steam pipe intact, while rowing toward a rescue ship.

7. The hull impacted with the sea bottom on her starboard bow (Area A) at a depth of 500m.

8. On impact, the engine room forward bulkhead in Area C smashed open, discharging coal from the bunker northwest into the aft cargo hold (Area B). Coal and cargo became intermixed. The boilers and engine machinery broke loose.

9. The keel possibly snapped forward of the mast step. The ship then gradually settled midships to the stern and rudder, listing to starboard.

10. The uncushioned paddlewheels canted outwards until they stabilized at an angle of 10-15°. The unsupported portside at the bows collapsed over time.

11. Within a few years the strong 3-5 knot current 10m above the sea bottom rapidly eroded the ship's superstructure, scattering wooden hull remains.

12. An extensive part of the exposed cargo in the stern hold was washed more than 6m offsite by the 1-5 knot bottom current and accumulated in an unstratified debris field (Area D).

The cargo and the historical and archaeological conclusions from the wreck of the SS *Republic* are published in further detail in Part 2 of this report (Cunningham Dobson *et al.*, 2009), while the coins receive their own specialist publication (Bowers, 2009).

Acknowledgements

The authors of this report are enormously grateful to the entire Odyssey team whose steadfast commitment and breadth of expertise ensured that the *Republic* project succeeded. The authors extend huge thanks to the following:

Odyssey co-founders, Greg Stemm and John Morris, for their vision, endurance and unyielding determination to find the *Republic*; Marine Operations Manager Roy Truman whose soaring expectations guaranteed success; Project Manager Ernie Tapanes and his team of side-scan technicians, whose meticulous search operations and ex-traordinary patience ultimately led to the amazing discovery; Project Managers Tom Detweiller, Andrew Craig and Mark Martin for their rare gift in directing and managing shipboard operations and for their undying support of the entire operational team; ROV Supervisors Gary Peterson, Eric Peterson and Jim Starr and all the ROV technicians whose competence and adroit skills ensured that the artifacts would be recovered from the site with the utmost care and in tandem with the highest archaeological standards; Data Manager Gerhard Steiffert and his team of dataloggers, who painstakingly recorded every minute of every dive and managed the enormous mountain of data, photographs and underwater footage that was recorded; and the Master's officers and the crew of the *Odyssey Explorer*, without whom the time spent on the ship months away from home in sometimes terrible seas would have been unbearable.

To our good friend, colleague and archaeologist, Hawk Tolson, whose professionalism, encouragement and support have never wavered and whose adept research skills during those rare off-hours have provided a wealth of information. A mighty thank you is offered to John Oppermann and his entire research team who have supported this project with great energy and enthusiasm, in particular Kathy Evans and John Griffith. We are indebted to Adam and Eric Tate whose patience and Excel wizardry accessed the artifact data so relevant to the report. Gerri Graca, Odyssey's archivist extraordinaire, demonstrated exceptional resourcefulness locating essential and often obscure sources and other critical references. Fred Van De Walle, Chief Conservator and his dedicated team, Alan Bosel and Chad Morris, responded to our numerous queries and have set a standard of unparalleled conservation, recording, documentation and photography. To Laura Barton and her entire team for all the media support and wonderful graphics generated. A special thank you is extended to the designer Melissa Kronewitter.

To Dr. Sean Kingsley, Director of Wreck Watch International, we are profoundly grateful for providing his firm guidance, keen insight and editorial wisdom. A final acknowledgement is in special memory of the former Conservator Herbert Bump, who established precedents in the early stages of the *Republic* project that Odyssey has continued to foster and emulate.

Notes

1. *Official Records of the Union and Confederate Navies in the War of the Rebellion. Series I - Volume 17: Gulf Blockading Squadron (December 16, 1861 - February 21, 1862); East Gulf Blockading Squadron (December 22, 1862 - July 17, 1865), 159; Official Records of the Union and Confederate Navies in the War of the Rebellion. Series*

I - Volume 18 (1904), 124; *Official Records of the Union and Confederate Navies in the War of the Rebellion. Series II - Volume I* (1921), 683, 687.

2. For the *Tennessee* unable to escape the river and penetrate the Federal Blockade, see *Official Records of the Union and Confederate Navies in the War of the Rebellion. Series II - Volume I* (1921), 683, 687; *Official Records of the Union and Confederate Navies in the War of the Rebellion. Series I - Volume 18* (1904), 124. For the *Tennessee's* conversion into a troop transport vessel, see entry for 30 April 1862 in *The War of the Rebellion: a Compilation of the Official Records of the Union and Confederate Armies. Series 1 - Volume 6* (Washington, 1882). For the *Tennessee's* use as a supply vessel see entry for 13 May 1863 in *Official Records of the Union and Confederate Navies in the War of the Rebellion. Series I - Volume 20: West Gulf Blockading Squadron (March 15, 1863 - December 31, 1863)* (Washington, 1905), 184. For the renaming of the ship the *Mobile,* see entry for 1 September 1864 in *Official Records of the Union and Confederate Navies in the War of the Rebellion. Series I - Volume 21: West Gulf Blockading Squadron* (January 1, 1864 - December 31, 1864), 621. For the ship's sale at public auction, see entry for 30 March 30 1864 in *Official Records of the Union and Confederate Navies in the War of the Rebellion. Series II - Volume 1: Statistical Data of Union and Confederate Ships; Muster Roles of Confederate Government Vessels; Letters of Marque and Reprisals; Confederate Department Investigations* (Washington, 1921), 221.

Bibliography

Ballard, R.D., McCann, A.M, Yoerger, D., Whitcomb, L., Mandell, D., Oleson, J., Singh, H., Foley, B., Adams, J. and Picheota, D., 'The Discovery of Ancient History in the Deep Sea using Advanced Deep Submergence Technology', *Deep Sea Research I* 47.9 (2000), 1591-1620.

Bascom, W., *Deep Water Ancient Ships* (London, 1976).

Bowers, Q.D., *The SS Republic Shipwreck Excavation Project: the Coin Cargo* (OME Papers 7, 2009).

Brantz, M., *Baltimore: Past and Present with Biographical Sketches of its Representative Men* (Baltimore, 1871).

Capers, G.M., *Occupied City. New Orleans Under the Federals 1862-1865* (University of Kentucky Press, 1965).

Corbin, A., *The Life and Times of the Steamboat Red Cloud* (Texas A & M University Press, 2006).

Cunningham Dobson, N., Tolson, H., Martin, A., Lavery, B., Bates, R., Tempera, F. and Pearce, J., *The HMS Sussex Shipwreck Project (Site E-82): Preliminary Report* (OME Papers 1, 2009).

Cunningham Dobson, N., Gerth, E. and Winckler, J.L., *The Shipwreck of the SS Republic (1865). Experimental Deep-Sea Archaeology. Part 2: Cargo* (OME Papers 6, 2009).

Delaporta, K., Søreide, F., and Jasinki, M.E., 'The Greek-Norwegian Deep-Water Archaeological Survey', *IJNA* 35.1 (2006), 79-87.

Ford, B., Borgens, A., Bryant, W., Marshall, D., Hitchcock, P., Arias, C. and Hamilton D., *Archaeological Excavation of the Mardi Gras Shipwreck (16GM01), Gulf of Mexico Continental Shelf* (New Orleans, 2008).

Gerth, E., *Patent Medicines, Bitters, & Other Bottles from the Wreck of the Steamship Republic* (Shipwreck Heritage Press, 2006).

Heyl, E., *Early American Steamers, Volume I* (New York, 1953).

Kane, A.I., *The Western River Steamboat* (Texas A & M University Press, 2004).

Kelly, W.J., *Shipbuilding at Federal Hill Baltimore (c. 1662 1961)* (unpublished manuscript, 1961).

Kingsley, S., 'Odyssey Marine Exploration and Deep-Sea Shipwreck Archaeology: the State of the Art', *Minerva* 14.3 (2003), 33-37.

McCann, A.M., 'An Early Imperial Shipwreck in the Deep Sea off Skerki Bank', *Rei Cretariae Romane Favtorvm Acta* 37 (2001), 257-64.

Ridgely-Nevitt, C., *American Steamships on the Atlantic* (University of Delaware Press, Newark, 1981).

Scharf, J.T., *History of Baltimore City and County* (Philadelphia, 1881).

Søreide, F. and Jasinki, M.E., 1998, 'The Unicorn Wreck, Central Norway – Underwater Archaeological Investigations of an 18th-century Russian Pink, Using Remotely-controlled Equipment', *IJNA* 27.2 (1998), 95-112.

Tolson, H. and Gerth, E., *Faith of Our Fathers: Religious Artifacts from the SS Republic (1865)* (OME Papers 9, forthcoming).

Vesilind, P.J., *Lost Gold of the Republic* (Shipwreck Heritage Press, 2005).

2

The Shipwreck of the SS *Republic* (1865).
Experimental Deep-Sea Archaeology.
Part 2: Cargo.

Neil Cunningham Dobson & Ellen Gerth
Odyssey Marine Exploration, Tampa, USA

Between October 2003 and February 2005 Odyssey Marine Exploration surveyed and conducted an extensive excavation on the shipwreck of the 19th-century sidewheel steamer the SS *Republic* at a depth of approximately 500m in the Atlantic Ocean, over 150km off the southeastern coast of the United States. The *Republic* was en route from New York to New Orleans with passengers and a composite commercial and monetary cargo when she foundered during a hurricane on 25 October 1865.

Some 262 ROV dives took place on the *Republic*, accumulating approximately 3,500 hours of bottom time on the seabed. 16,000 digital still photographs were taken and over 3,000 hours of video footage recorded. During the archaeological excavation 14,414 artifacts and 51,404 coins were recovered, recorded and conserved. These assemblages have produced a unique image of daily life in post-Civil War America, unparalleled in scale and diversity on any wreck of a steamship.

1. Economic Background

The shipwreck of the steamship *Republic* was laden with an extensive and diverse collection of cultural assemblages, which, beyond the coin cargo (Bowers, 2009), were not documented in historical records of the vessel's final voyage. The gold and silver coins, minted in Philadelphia, New Orleans and San Francisco, and dating from the late 1830s to 1865, are believed to represent the largest collection of Civil War-era coins discovered on a shipwreck, including pristine and uncirculated examples (Figs. 4-5). Of greater archaeological importance is the plethora of trade goods, essential to daily life and commerce in mid-Victorian America (Fig. 1). The arrival in New Orleans of an assortment of bottled goods (patent medicines, inks, pickled foods, hair tonics and tooth powders), accompanied by leather footwear, hardware, and ironstone china, would have been vital to help kick-start the city's depressed economy.

Without a cargo manifest or related documentary evidence, the intended recipients of the *Republic*'s cargo will never be known. Yet the historical context in which these goods circulated can be partly reconstructed by an examination of New Orleans' *post-bellum* economic climate in tandem with other socio-cultural, health and demographic factors.

In the decades preceding the American Civil War the growing world demand for cotton led to the development of vast slave plantations in the lower Mississippi Valley.

New Orleans served as the central hub from where cotton was largely shipped either directly to Liverpool and other British ports or was trans-shipped through New York. During the 1850s the annual shipment of cotton to England rose from 582,723 bales to 1,426,966 bales, representing well over one-half of New Orleans' total exports. In the same period, French consumption also more than doubled from 125,067 to 303,157 bales. In addition to Liverpool and Le Havre, there was also a significant increase in cotton shipments to Bremen, Genoa and Trieste to serve the growing textile industries of the German states and northern Italy (Reinders, 1998: 37).

The cogs in this trade spine explain the preponderance of British products amongst the *Republic*'s ceramic and stoneware and glass bottle cargo: no outgoing merchant vessel would return from Britain via other ports without a profitable consignment. By 1860-61, cotton exports from New Orleans had peaked at a total of over 2.2 million bales per annum, valued at $110 million. Sugar and tobacco shipments followed as distant secondary commodities, while foodstuffs comprised the remaining bulk exports (McNabb and Madère, 2003; Reinders, 1998: 40-1). New Orleans was now the second largest commercial center in the United States behind New York and the most important cotton market in the world (Reinders, 1998: 37; Vandal, 2000: 18).

Because of its specialization in marketing agricultural

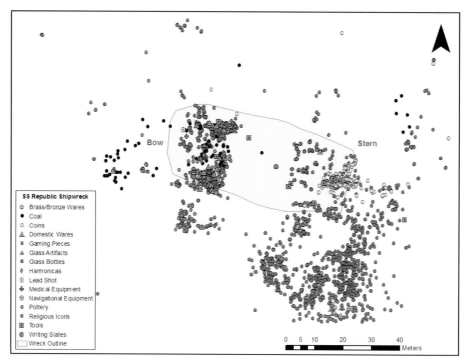

Fig. 1. Distribution of recovered cargo wares from the wreck of the Republic.

commodities, New Orleans in effect never developed into a major manufacturing center. In 1860, the city was ranked sixth in the nation in terms of population size, yet only seventeenth in value of its manufacturing productivity. While some light manufacturing had emerged by the 1850s, it was largely small-scale private enterprise, assorted industry and crafts of minor importance. The average New Orleans industry operated with limited capital and only employed a few workers (Reinders, 1998: 45-46). Most of these businesses did not survive the Civil War. Imported goods were abundant, inexpensive and readily available to large-scale retail merchants in New Orleans (McNabb and Madère, 2003; Stout, 2007: 4). Wholesale and import merchants also supplied smaller urban retailers, country shopkeepers, planters and individual peddlers. Many vendors were African American women who conducted trade in the streets, a traditional practice introduced from the African homeland.[1]

New Orleans' reliance on highly specialized cotton exports and imported goods, propelled by a competitive and prosperous mercantile class, was its Achilles heel. The importance of the city's port, and Louisiana's strategic position on the Mississippi, made it an early Union target during the Civil War and blockades seriously disrupted the city's trade, the welfare of her merchants and her blue-collar workers. Without the constant flow of goods, New Orleans could not function (McNabb and Madère, 2003; Stout, 2007: 4). The city's resources were further diminished with the imminent approach of the Union fleet in April 1862. With the enemy in sight, the Confederate army

Fig. 2. Reconstruction of the sidewheel steamer Republic *based on a painting of the SS* Tennessee *in the Peabody Essex Museum, Salem, Massachusetts. Painting: by John Batchelor.*

seized control of New Orleans and systematically destroyed the city's material wealth. Stores of cotton and tobacco were burnt. Railroads and steamships spirited away Confederate troops, documents and military supplies. The city's banks dispatched $6 million in gold specie out of town for safety (Capers, 1965: 155; Stout, 2007: 8).

In the aftermath of the Civil War, New Orleans was demoralized and impoverished. Unemployment, endemic even during times of relative prosperity, reached new heights after the war as the city was struck by a crippling economic depression. The recovery problems common to the entire South were greatly exacerbated by the city's unusually large population of urban dwellers. The challenges of

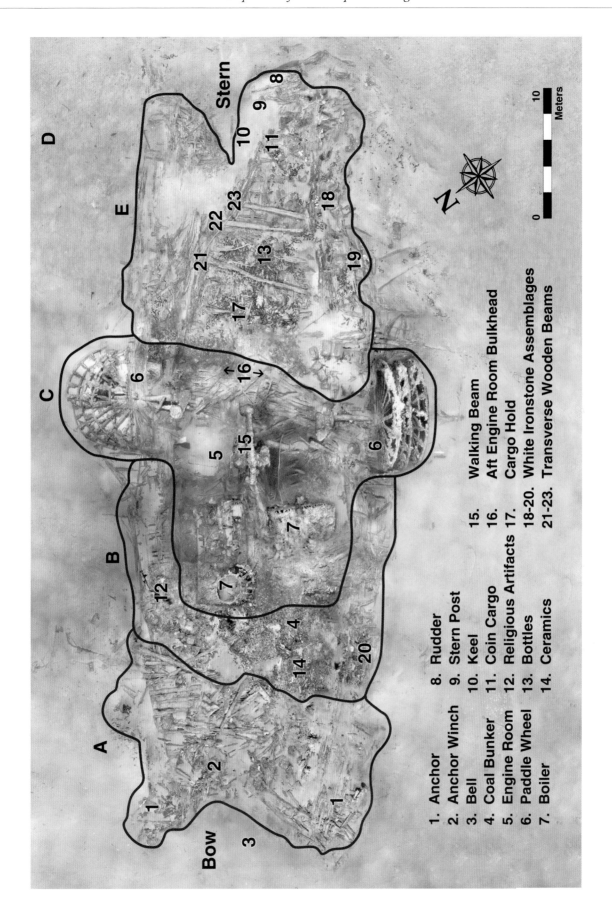

1. Anchor
2. Anchor Winch
3. Bell
4. Coal Bunker
5. Engine Room
6. Paddle Wheel
7. Boiler
8. Rudder
9. Stern Post
10. Keel
11. Coin Cargo
12. Religious Artifacts
13. Bottles
14. Ceramics
15. Walking Beam
16. Aft Engine Room Bulkhead
17. Cargo Hold
18-20. White Ironstone Assemblages
21-23. Transverse Wooden Beams

Fig. 3. Photomosaic displaying survey/excavation areas and the locations of prominent archaeological contexts.

Fig. 4. *Gold coins* in situ *in the stern area of the wreck of the* Republic.

Fig. 5. *Silver coins* in situ *inside a decomposed wooden shipping keg in the stern area of the wreck.*

Fig. 6. Bolts of cloth in situ *in the bows of the wreck (Area A) alongside scattered coal and glass bottles in the background.*

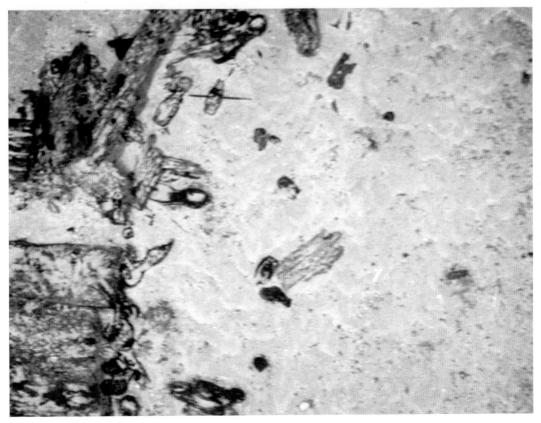

Fig. 7. Leather shoes in situ *in the debris field (Area D).*

Fig. 8. Glass champagne-style, whiskey and glass bitters bottles in situ *in Area E.*

Fig. 9. Glass whiskey and bitters bottles in situ *in Area E.*

Fig. 10. Glass champagne-style, mustard barrel, bitters and cathedral-patterned pickle bottles between frames and cargo hold bulkheads in Area E, some still stacked in their original rows after their packing crates had completely deteriorated.

Fig. 11. The coal pile in Area A intermixed with J.B. Thorn/John Tarrant ceramic medicine pots and lids, Holloway's Ointment pots, and glass patent medicine bottles.

Fig. 12. Assorted ironstone china in situ *in Area D.*

Fig. 13. Ironstone china footbaths, slop jars, tooth brush containers, and cups and saucers in situ *in Area D.*

Fig. 14. Ironstone china cargo in situ *in Area D, consisting of footbaths, slop jars, stacked wash basins and demitasse cups and saucers.*

Fig. 15. Detail of the ironstone china cargo in Area D, including footbaths, slop jars and demitasse cups and saucers in situ.

*Fig. 16. Welsh writing slates still stacked in the Area D debris field,
even though their original wooden shipping crates are entirely deteriorated.*

*Fig. 17. A cargo of porcelain and glass religious figural candlesticks
in situ in Area B; its packing crate is not preserved.*

Fig. 18. A copper-alloy telescope *in situ* in the debris field (Area D). Found near glass lenses and a brass barometer, it seems to have been part of a consignment of nautical instruments.

Fig. 19. Rectangular metal lining ingots *in situ* in the engine room (Area C). The ingots were intended to be melted down and poured into a bearing mold or tray to produce sheet metal for placement over the surface of the engine's moving parts to prevent wear and damage. Each is stamped S. Whites and J. W. Quincy of New York.

Fig. 20. A glass crucifix candlestick in Area B being transferred into a recovery basket by the ROV Zeus' limpet suction system.

Fig. 21. A glass bottle containing preserved gooseberries being recovered by the ROV Zeus' limpet suction system.

Fig. 22. A milk glass base of a ruby-colored glass oil lamp font being recovered by the ROV Zeus' limpet suction system.

Fig. 23. A J.B. Thorn of London's ceramic medicine pot being recovered by the ROV Zeus' limpet suction system.

Fig. 24. A glass bottle containing preserved peaches being transferred to a recovery
basket using the ROV Zeus' limpet suction system.

Fig. 25. An umbrella inkstand being recovered by the ROV Zeus' limpet suction system.

overpopulation were further intensified by the migration of thousands of former slaves who had abandoned the plantations and flocked to the city during the war and after emancipation in 1863. New Orleans' black population more than doubled from 24,500 in 1860 to 50,450 in 1870 (Stout, 2007: 2; Vandal, 2000: 18-19).

Nonetheless, New Orleans was virtually the only major city of the Confederacy to emerge from war without near-total destruction. It remained a gateway for economic traffic into the deprived South, as well as an established entrepôt for trade south of America's borders. It is within this socio-economic context of deprivation and yearning demand that the abundance of essentially utilitarian commodities onboard the *Republic* was shipped to market with great expectations.

2. Coins

When she foundered, the SS *Republic* was transporting an extensive consignment of coins (*Charleston Daily Courier*, 30 and 31 October, 11 November 1865). The excavation of her shipwreck yielded 51,404 coins in total: 4,135 gold and 47,263 silver issues, as well as four British florins and two silver 25 cents (Figs. 4-5). The specie consisted of 2,675 gold $20 double eagles and 1,460 $10 gold eagles, but mostly 47,263 silver half dollars. The latter included some coins of the Capped Bust design, but Liberty Seated coins predominated: an artistic innovation of engraver Christian Gobrecht that portrayed Lady Liberty seated on a rock, one hand holding a shield and the other a pole surmounted by a liberty cap, a symbol of freedom. The scene is surrounded by 13 stars, with the date below. The reverse displays a perched eagle, wings downward, holding an olive branch and three arrows (Bowers, 2005: 262).

A detailed presentation of the *Republic*'s coin mints and a functional interpretation is presented elsewhere (Bowers, 2009).

3. Glass & Stoneware Bottles

Some 58% of the artifacts recovered from the *Republic* comprised 8,429 glass and stoneware bottles, once stored in the ship's aft and forward cargo holds (Figs. 2-3, 8-11). These include an intriguing collection of medicinal 'cures' (2,672; 31.7% of the total), ink bottles and stands (2,447; 29.0%), food products (1,522; 18.0%), beauty products (958; 11.4%) and alcoholic beverages (830; 9.8%).

The combined volume and variety of bottled goods seems to represent the largest and possibly most diverse collection ever recovered from any shipwreck site. Their

subsequent study and analysis has provided a rare insight into prevailing social and economic conditions in New Orleans following the American Civil War. The assemblage simultaneously permits a broader interpretation of the country's socio-economic climate in an era when the North served as the major manufacturer and supplier of goods being shipped southwards and when the United States, as a whole, relied on an influx of British imports and, to some extent, products from Continental Europe. Significantly, the study of the *Republic* bottle assemblage has also divulged new information relating to the business histories of the companies that both used the containers and supplied their contents.

The collection reflects a transitional period in the development of glassmaking, the start of which had been underway for several decades (McKearin and Wilson, 1978: 13-14; Switzer, 1974: 5). The eclectic mix of technologies (such as the use of the pontil rod versus snap case) and other production features evidenced in the bottle collection represent a unique record documenting the variable pace at which improvements and innovations were taking hold in American glass factories. This new body of information contributes significantly to an important chapter in the commercial glass- and bottle-making industry in America.

A. Patent Medicines

A sample of 2,672 patent medicines and other medicinal bottles was recovered from the wreck of the *Republic* (31.7% of the total bottle assemblage). The dubious contents of the patent medicines and other medicinal bottles derived from recipes that often contained harmful narcotics laced with alcohol and other undisclosed ingredients (Gerth, 2006: 23-40). Proclaiming outrageous medical results, these dangerous compounds promised to treat everything from coughs and fevers to digestive ailments, constipation and nervous excitement. Even cancer and diabetes were within their advertised curative powers (Fike, 1987: 3; Gerth, 2006: 23).

Embossed names of remedies on bottles include Dr. McMunn's Elixir of Opium (Fig. 26), Mrs. Winslow's Soothing Syrup (Fig. 27) and H.T. Helmbold's Genuine Fluid Extracts. Most of these patent medicine proprietors lacked a valid medical license, yet could sell their proprietary products without prescription and without disclosing their contents (Fike, 1987: 3-4). While the medical profession and consumers had complained about the 'quack' medicine trade well before the turn of the century, it was not until the enactment of the Pure Food and Drug Act of 1906 that more stringent steps were taken to curtail the manufacture, false claims and sale of these often fatal nostrums (Davoli,

1998: 5; Fike, 1987: 3-4; Young, 1961: 239-40, 244; pers. comm. Byron Dille', June 2009).

Many of the ingredients used in patent medicines were grown in the South, yet there were very few southern patent medicine manufacturers. In fact, the year 1865 was not yet over before a Charleston druggist was shipping north the roots of Southern plants for use in J.C. Ayer's medicinal products (Young, 1961: 98). James Cook Ayer was a qualified doctor – a rarity among patent medicine manufacturers – who began to create his own line of patent medicines in the 1840s (Davoli, 1998: 3; Fadely, 1992). His Lowell Massachusetts patent medicine business produced 'remedies' such as Ayer's Cherry Pectoral and Ayer's Cathartic Pills, both of which were recovered from the shipwreck (Figs. 28-29). A few samples of the latter, packaged in small rectangular glass bottles, still contain their original pea-sized pills. By the time Ayer retired in the early 1870s, he had acquired a vast fortune from his patent medicine business. At his death in 1878, he was considered the wealthiest manufacturer of patent medicines in the country (Gerth, 2006: 30; *New York Times*, 4 July 1878).

While the preponderance of 19th-century patent medicines largely comprised bottled products, many of the 'remedies' were also sold in ceramic containers, including two types recovered from the *Republic*. The excavation yielded 71 small 'Holloway's Ointment' pots without lids (Figs. 11, 30), advertised at the time as being "for the Cure of Inveterate Ulcers, Bad Legs, Sore Breasts and Sore heads" as well as "Gout and Rheumatism". Thomas Holloway of England amassed a fortune selling his ointment and other medicinal products, later investing some of his wealth in establishing Royal Holloway College for Women, an architectural marvel that is today a part of the University of London. The 71 lidless Holloway specimens recovered may have been sealed with wax or wax paper, the remains of which have not survived.

Also recovered from the site in even larger quantities were ceramic medicine pots with accompanying lids, the bottom of each pot bearing the name of J.B. Thorn, London Chemist, and John A. Tarrant, New York, Sole Agent for the United States (Figs. 11, 23, 31). A number of such patent medicines used in the United States were thus British imports sold by US wholesale druggists such as Tarrant & Co., operative from 1859 to 1906 (Fike, 1987: 49-49). As noted in contemporary mid-19th century advertisements, Thorn's Compound Extract of Copaiba and Sarsaparilla was taken for the "cure of the afflicted… sanctioned by the faculty of medicine and recommended by the most eminent in the profession" (*Boston Directory*, 1 July 1856: 31). Later declared false and fraudulent under the 1906 Food and Drugs Act, the product was sold as a

remedy for venereal disease (gonorrhoea) and kidney infections (Cramps, 1921: 624).

Most American patent medicine manufacturers were located in Northern cities, including New York, Boston and Philadelphia. Before the Civil War, patent medicines had a total annual sale of $3.5 million. By the turn of the century, the total patent medicine business had escalated dramatically to $75 million (Fox, 1997: 16). As late as 1896, 10,000 people were engaged in the patent medicine manufactories of the United States, receiving collectively over $4 million a year in salaries and wages. New York City stood at the head of this industry with over 85 factories, employing a thousand people (Shrady, 1896: 939-40).

Throughout the Civil War, Northern patent medicine manufacturers remained enormously successful, supplying a sundry of remedies to the Union troops, preying on their fears of southern tropical afflictions and, in particular, water-borne dysenteric ailments. Official medical records of the time confirm that bowel complaints were most prevalent among the Union troops and caused the most deaths (Young, 1861: 95). To alleviate these digestive disorders troops took a variety of 'medicinal' bitters: herbal brews steeped in alcohol. One popular brand shipped on board the *Republic* was Dr. J. Hostetter's Stomach Bitters (93 green and amber bottles), first introduced to the market in 1853 (Fig. 32). Fortified by up to 47% alcohol, advertisements directed towards army consumption claimed that the bitters provided "a positive protection against the fatal maladies of the Southern swamps, and the poisonous tendency of the impure rivers and bayous". The Hostetter marketing campaign proved so successful that the War Department authorized the distribution of Hostetter's Stomach Bitters to the Union Army (Baxter, 1997: 1-2; Davoli, 1998: 4; Fike, 1987: 36; Young, 1961: 95, 129).

A major concern for the military was cholera, a lethal bacterial disease borne largely through contaminated water supplies and designated America's greatest scourge after its widespread ravages in 1849 in New York and New Orleans, spreading ultimately across the entire country into Canada. Cholera once again reached New Orleans in 1865 and broke out into an epidemic the following year. While contemporary eruptions in other cities were often mild and short-lived, New Orleans suffered greatly and repeatedly until 1868 (Dhiman *et al.*, 1997: 13).

Union soldiers especially feared yellow fever (Roberts, 2003: 139). While the fever's mosquito-bred, nautical origins and method of transmission remained a mystery at the time, the virus was known to flourish in southern sub-tropical and swampy environments. Throughout the 1860s, Western medicine had contended with its outbreaks. New Orleans, in particular, was no stranger to the disease. Between 1817 and 1905, the year of the city's last epidemic, more than 41,000 people died from yellow fever (Stout, 2007: 39-40; Young, 1961: 98).[2]

No doubt, Hostetter's and similar 'antidotes' provided bottled courage to frightened men in times of need (Baxter, 1997: 2). Veterans returned home addicted to bitters and other 'medicinals' that they believed had prevented these illnesses during the war, spurious remedies which they then passionately advocated to their families and friends (Davoli, 1998: 4; Young, 1961: 97). In fact, Hostetter's Bitters, known as the 'Soldier's Safeguard', was so successful that after the war shots of it were sold in local bars and saloons (Davoli, 1998: 4; Young, 1961: 95, 130).

Not surprisingly, a wave of medicinal bitters flooded the mid-19th century market, each competing for a share of this multi-million dollar business. Especially appealing was their tax-exempt status. Sold as a medicinal product with 'healing' roots and herbs, these high alcohol 'remedies' were not subject to the taxes levied on the sale of all liquors to help finance the Union War effort (Gerth, 2006: 44; pers. comm. Byron Dille', June 2009). Drake's Plantation Bitters was among the more successful brands (Fig. 33). Over 150 bottles were recovered from the *Republic* in varying shades of light and dark amber and a distinctive olive-yellow hue. The famous recipe, touting a potent 38% alcohol, was made from Caribbean St. Croix rum and sold in a unique log cabin-style bottle accompanied by claims that it cured virtually every disease known to mankind (Fike, 1987: 33; *Harpers*, 1 August, 1863; *P.H. Drake & Co's Gratuitous Medical Annual*, 1871-1872).

Unsanitary conditions in Army field hospitals, and the many deaths that resulted from dysentery and other diseases, contributed to a prevailing lack of confidence in doctors. Thousands of soldiers returned to civilian life inflicted with ruined digestions, malaria, wounds, emotional trauma and other psychological and physical ailments that troubled them for the rest of their lives. While wartime deprivations and crippling illnesses had undermined health on the home front, conditions at home were often equally harsh. Pervasive poverty and an inadequate diet contributed to the host of diseases that attacked weakened immune systems (Davoli, 1998: 4; Stout, 2007: 39-40; Young, 1961: 98). The post-war South thus offered a perfect market for patent medicines.

B. Ink Products

Close in quantity to the glass medicine bottles are inkstands and master ink bottles recovered from the wreck of the *Republic* (2,447 containers; 29.0% of the total), both of stoneware (96 bottles and 1,376 ink pots) and glass (171 bottles and 804 inkstands), some with their corks still intact

and retaining their original writing fluid. The majority of the differently shaped and shaded glass examples (Fig. 36) were produced in glassworks operating in New England, the Midwest and Middle Atlantic, the three glass-blowing regions of the United States (McKearin, 1978: 68, 269).

The glass inkstands from the *Republic* (Figs. 34-35) take the form of an assortment of conical and square 'schoolhouse' or 'cottage-style' bottles, but the majority are umbrella inkstands in varying shades of green and aquamarine (493 examples). While none of the glass specimens retain their paper labels, a handful still contain remains of their original writing fluid. A few of the square versions are embossed with company names, including a number bearing the name Guyot, an ink-making enterprise with its roots in 17th-century France (Fig. 34). Its founder, a French chemist, is often referred to as the 'father' of the modern ink industry (Carvalho, 2008: 86).

Some of the umbrella inkstands are embossed on the base with the letters NY. Research suggests that a New York ink maker may have custom-ordered these inkstands from a glassmaking firm and sold his own company product inside them (pers. comm. Bill Lindsey, March 2009). The *Republic's* cargo of umbrella inkstands, also known as pyramid ink bottles (Figs. 25, 35), were common throughout New Jersey glasshouses and were also produced by the Stoddard glasshouses of New Hampshire, as well as by most other glass manufacturers of the era (McKearin, 1978: 269; pers. comm. Byron Dille', June 2009).

The preponderance of ink containers on board the *Republic*, totalling 1,376, are plain and sturdy British-made stoneware pots (H. 22.0cm) mass-produced for the American market (Fig. 37). Added to the stoneware assortment are 96 brownish-orange salt-glazed master ink bottles in three distinct sizes (height variations: 17-18cm, 21-22cm and 25-26cm; Figs. 38-39), products of Britain's J. Bourne & Son's Denby and Codnor Park Potteries and identified by the company stamp near the base (Cambell, 2006: 137).[3] A further 16 unmarked large stoneware bottles are likely products of a separate British pottery and also probably contained ink, medicine or chemicals often stored in bulk quantity (Fig. 40).

The stoneware master ink bottles, designed for storing bulk ink to refill smaller inkstands and inkwells used in offices and schools, also carry the name of the London company P. & J. Arnold (Fig. 39). In its heyday, Pichard and John Arnold's early 19th-century firm manufactured over 30 varieties of ink (Carvalho, 2008: 180). By the middle of the century, their chemical writing fluid was widely imported into the United States in Bourne's stoneware bottles and had become a competitive threat to the domestic market (Odell, 2003).

The abundance of ink containers shipped aboard the *Republic* evokes both curiosity and speculation as to their purpose and use. Developments in New Orleans point to some plausible explanations. It has been suggested that the ink shipped to New Orleans, in tandem with the arrival of Yankee investors seeking economic opportunities, would have been essential for drawing up legal contracts conveying the purchase and transfer of cheap land and other commodities (pers. comm. Bill Lindsey, May, 2009).

More broadly, ink was the lifeblood of government, business, education and daily life. A very large military establishment that consumed paper and ink like a furnace was based in New Orleans. Conceivably, the writing containers were intended for use in New Orleans' schools: public, private and parochial alike. In 1863, General Nathanial Banks also authorized the establishment of black schools, which were partly supported by organizations such as the National Freedman's Relief Association that invested thousands of dollars on books, clothing and supplies from 1865-66 (Blassingame, 1973: 109-110). Finally, New Orleans was of course also a port from which commodities were trans-shipped to further destinations.

C. Food Products

Numbering 1,522 examples, bottles containing food products are the third largest category recovered from the shipwreck of the *Republic* (18.0% of the total), including a variety of pickled goods, sauces and preserved fruit. Most were retrieved empty, but a few examples still contained their original 19th-century contents: well-preserved chunks of pineapple and rhubarb, sliced peaches, blueberries and gooseberries (Figs. 21, 24, 41-43). Some 288 of the food bottles are of the ornately embossed Cathedral pickle and pepper sauce type (Figs. 44-45). Three of the latter still contain perfectly preserved red and yellow peppers. Cathedral-patterned bottles designed to emulate ornate church windows and arches were an American invention produced in hundreds of similar designs. Used by companies such as W.D. Smith, William Underwood and W.K. Lewis, the food products stored in these ornate bottles were intended to compete effectively with similar imported English products sold in plainer bottles.[4]

Of the many British food products competing with American goods, Lea & Perrins Worcestershire Sauce is best known (Fig. 46). Launched commercially in 1838, within a few years it was imported extensively into the United States by John Duncan's Sons, New York. By 1849 it was consumed west of the Mississippi as thousands of gold seekers made their way to the California gold fields. This popular condiment soon found a receptive market in

restaurants, hotel dining rooms and in the dining salons of passenger ships (Zumwalt, 1980: 269).

The large volume of Lea & Perrins Worcestershire Sauce bottles recovered from the wreck of the *Republic*, however, indicates that they were not all intended for passenger consumption, but were probably being shipped as cargo. Of the 285 bottles retrieved, 207 still retained their original glass-and-cork stoppers. All of the bottles are of British manufacture. Lea & Perrins Worcestershire Sauce was not actually bottled in the United States until 1877, when John Duncan had his company initials 'JDS' embossed on bases by Salem Glass Works. At this time, there was a marked changeover in the United States from British to American-produced Lea and Perrins bottles (pers. comm. Bill Lindsey, June 2009; Lunn, 1985: 1-2; Zumwalt, 1980: 269).

D. Beauty Products

The glass bottle assemblage also incorporates beauty products (958; 11.4%), many of which were associated with fashionable fragrances manufactured by American and European perfumers. Included in this category are approximately seven bottles that once contained Murray & Lanman's Florida Water (Fig. 47), the most popular product sold by Lanman & Kemp, a leading New York City wholesale druggist firm founded by Robert J. Murray in 1808. Touted as a multi-purpose toilet water with both cosmetic and restorative qualities, company advertising proclaimed the product was associated with the Spanish explorer Ponce de León and his legendary search for Florida's Fountain of Youth in 1513.

Of particular interest is the pervasive role of Lanman & Kemp in the 19th-century wholesale drug trade throughout the United States and worldwide, with major operations in Central and South America and in the Caribbean Islands, supported by travelling agents. Product orders were also sent through the maritime mail. Lanman & Kemp records document business correspondence addressed to the company dating to 1859 and 1861 that was shipped aboard the SS *Tennessee* from Vera Cruz in Mexico to New Orleans, when the steamship later renowned as the *Republic* was under the ownership of Charles Morgan.[5]

In addition to selling their own patent medicines, Lanman & Kemp's New York-based enterprise also sold other products. Records testify that these included those of James C. Ayer, Edward Phalon, J.A. Tarrant, Charles Osgood, Thomas Holloway, William B Moffat and B.L. Fahnestock, company names whose products are well represented in the *Republic*'s patent medicine cargo. The firm also dealt in opiates, medicinal and culinary herbs, spices, liquors, flavorings, perfume extracts and a sundry of other medical and non-medical items (cf. Lanman and Kemp Collection, Domestic Correspondence, and Company History, Hagley Museum Library). With its extensive business connections throughout the United States and abroad, it is plausible that Lanman & Kemp's drug firm was responsible for the shipment of at least some of the *Republic's* bottled goods other than just their own cosmetic line.

Also present among the beauty products are a host of hair potions bearing names such as Burnett's Cocoaine (Fig. 48). The invention of Massachusetts' Joseph Burnett may have been intended to exploit the public's fixation with the many cocaine-laced patent medicines flooding the market. Unlike his competitors, as a graduate of the Worcester College of Pharmacy Burnett stands out as one of the few fully qualified pharmacists in this field. Meanwhile, Phalon and Son's Chemical Hair Invigorator (Fig. 51), manufactured by a New York hairdresser and wigmaker, promised to preserve the hair and prevent it turning gray (Fadely, 1992). A handful of milk glass bottles contained Laird's Bloom of Youth Liquid Pearl, whose New York maker claimed it beautified and preserved the complexion and skin (Fig. 49). While seemingly benign, many of the beauty products of the era, particularly those for the hair, contained harmful ingredients such as lead acetate, which research today suggests is a carcinogen and likely contributed to the untimely death of many 19th-century consumers (pers. comm. Byron Dille', June 2009).

The beauty and cosmetic goods on the *Republic* were predominantly sold in glass containers and, with a few exceptions, were largely American products. Yet, approximately 50 stoneware cosmetic pots were recovered from the site in two distinct sizes (58cm and 79cm high), the product of the famous French Perfumer L.T. Piver, whose company name is transfer-printed on all of the pots (Fig. 50). By the 19th century, Piver's international business incorporated over one hundred branches around the world, including shops in Paris that catered to the wealthy, including the Bonaparte family. Over the years the Piver company launched an exhaustive range of health and beauty products, including a variety of perfumes, fragrant soaps and body creams.[6] The sturdy, unlidded stoneware pots retrieved from the *Republic* perhaps contained one of L.T. Piver's cosmetic creams or face powders.

E. Alcoholic Beverages

Closely paralleling the volume of the beauty products recovered from the *Republic* was a large consignment of beer (Fig. 53), whiskey, champagne and wine bottles (830; 9.8% of all bottles). Their thick dark glass reduced breakage and inhibited exposure to heat and light, preventing spoilage during transport and storage (Figs. 8-10). After the war,

as the population of the United States increased rapidly, more than 100,000 saloons were in operation throughout the country: by 1870, approximately one drinking institution for every 400 men, women and children (Gerth, 2006: 54). The large quantity of bottled wine, beer and other liquors shipped on the *Republic* just months following the war was intended to help restock the shelves of New Orleans' reinvigorated saloons.

4. Writing Slates

Some 61 rectangular writing slates were recovered in the Area D debris field from a larger consignment discovered on the shipwreck, including a deposit of uniform rows of slates standing upright on their sides as originally packed in their wooden shipping crates, which are otherwise completely decomposed (Fig. 16). An 1869 handbook for transoceanic shipments from the United Kingdom describes in detail the method for stowing both roofing and writing slates, which were typically shipped as ballast cargo. A packing arrangement comparable to the *Republic* is described, whereby "Slate is as brittle as earthenware and requires equal care; slate ought to be stowed on its edges and kept in that position; when flat it will be very liable to break" (Gerth and Tolson, 2008: 44; Stevens, 1869: 548).

The distinctive blue-gray coloring of the *Republic* slate shipment is a variety known as 'Old Vein', mined in the Blaenau Ffestiniog district of northwest Wales (pers. comm. Dafydd Roberts, National Slate Museum, August, 2008). While paper had become commonplace by the late 1800s, slates were used widely as writing tablets in schools when paper was scarce and expensive. This was very probably the case after the Civil War, particularly in the formerly Union-blockaded South.

The *Republic's* slates were probably intended for purchase and use in one of the many public, private or religious schools in New Orleans and perhaps even in the surrounding parishes (Gerth and Tolson, 2008: 45). A revealing letter written by the American Missionary Association teacher Edmonia Highgate in December 1866 described how her "French Creole" students from plantations in Lafayette Parish purchased their own slates and traveled between 3 and 8 miles to attend school. "So anxious are they to learn", she wrote, "that they walk these distances so early in the morning as never to be tardy. Every scholar buys his own book and slate."[7]

5. Pottery

The excavation of the *Republic* also yielded an abundance of sturdy white ironstone china pottery, largely utilitarian

Fig. 26. A Dr. McMunn's
Elixir of Opium glass bottle
with cork stopper inside
(H. 10.6cm).

Fig. 27. A Mrs. Winslow's
Soothing Syrup glass bottle,
a morphine-based formula
sold as a remedy for
teething infants (H. 12.1cm).

Fig. 28. A J.C. Ayer's
Cherry Pectoral glass
bottle (H. 18.5cm).

Fig. 29. A J.C. Ayer's
Cathartic Pills glass bottle,
which originally stored
pea-sized tablets to
treat countless ailments
including skin disease
(H. 5.3cm).

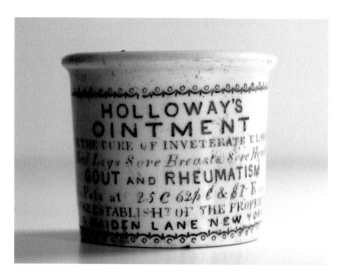

Fig. 30. A Holloway's Ointment pot for the cure of
various ailments, including sore breasts,
gout and rheumatism (H. 3.8cm).

Fig. 31. A J.B. Thorn of London's ceramic medicine pot
distributed by wholesale druggist John A. Tarrant of
New York (H. 4.6cm; Diam. 6.1cm).

Fig. 32. Dr. J. Hostetter's Stomach Bitters glass bottles once contained a potent herbal brew laced with alcohol (H. 22.0cm).

Fig. 33. Drake's Plantation Bitters glass bottles feature a distinctive log cabin design patented in 1862 (H. 25.0cm).

Fig. 34. A Guyot glass inkstand containing its original cork stopper (H. 6.6cm).

Fig. 35. Eight-paneled glass umbrella inkstands in assorted shades of green and aquamarine, and a rare amethyst example (H. 6.3cm).

Fig. 36. Master ink bottles with pouring spouts designed for refilling smaller ink containers (the form has H. variables of 19.5-30.3cm).

Fig. 37. A British-made stoneware
ink pot (H. 5.6cm).

Fig. 38. J. Bourne & Son stoneware ink
bottles once contained P. & J. Arnold's
writing fluid; both company names are
stamped on the bottles' bases
(H 14.4cm and 18.0cm).

Fig. 39. Detail of the company
stamp on a J. Bourne & Son
British stoneware bottle.
Also featured is the stamp
of the P. & J. Arnold London
ink-making firm.

Fig. 40. A large unmarked British
stoneware bottle for storing
bulk ink, chemicals and other fluids
(H. 25.5cm).

Fig. 41. An A. Kemp glass
preserve bottle containing remains
of pineapple (with modern plastic
protective cap) (H. 24.5cm).

Fig. 42. Sliced peaches, possibly
intended to be used as pie
filling, preserved in a glass bottle
(H. 30.0cm).

Fig. 43. Gooseberries preserved in a glass bottle (H. 30.0cm).

Fig. 44. Cathedral-patterned glass pepper sauce bottles featuring both the square and six-sided version (H. 22.5cm and 25.5cm).

Fig. 45. Cathedral-patterned glass pickle bottles were recovered from the wreck in four different sizes and once stored a variety of fruits and vegetables (H. 28.0cm and 22.5cm).

Fig. 46. A Lea & Perrins Worcestershire Sauce glass bottle with an intact glass-and-cork stopper (H. 17.8cm).

Fig. 47. A Murray & Lanman's Florida Water glass bottle (H. 22.8cm), advertized for both health and beauty purposes.

Fig. 48. A Burnett's Cocoaine hair potion glass bottle (H. 18.0cm).

Fig. 49. J. & G.W. Laird 'Bloom of Youth' milk glass bottles, its contents touted for "Beautifying & Preserving the Complexion and Skin" (H. 11.7cm).

Fig. 50. An L.T. Piver cosmetic cream or face powder stoneware pot (H. 7.9cm).

Fig. 51. A Phalon and Son's Chemical Hair Invigorator glass bottle (H. 17.5cm).

Fig. 52. A Van Buskirk's Fragrant Sozodont glass bottle (H. 14.1cm), its contents intended for cleaning and preserving teeth and gums.

Fig. 53. Black glass beer bottles. The dark color produced by iron oxide strengthened the glass and inhibited exposure to light, reducing spoilage (H. 24.5cm and 20.3cm).

ware mass-produced for the American market by England's Staffordshire potters (Figs. 12-15, 54-72). A number of pieces bear the maker's marks of prominent potteries, including T. & R. Boote, Joseph Goodwin, Jacob Furnival, and John Maddock & Son. Also known as English porcelain and stone china, ironstone china was first introduced by Staffordshire potters in the early 19th century as a substitute for porcelain. It was a modest ware that appealed to a less expensive market. In marketing terms, the name 'Ironstone China' was fitting because it was immediately identifiable, implied high quality and had hard durability. By the early 1840s, America received its first ironstone imports; English potters soon discovered that the inhabitants of the 'colonies' greatly preferred this unfussy, plain and durable china to more exotic wares. It was an immediate success and public demand soared.[8]

A sample of 2,775 pieces of white ironstone china was recovered from the wreck of the *Republic*. Some 1,186 saucers bear the maker's mark of John Maddock & Son; 266 of the saucers are 12cm-diameter demitasses; 17 are of 15cm diameter and 883 of 16cm diameter (plus 20 undefined). The saucers are accompanied by ironstone cups (1,067) of at least three different shapes and sizes (483 of 7.6cm height and 274 of 8cm height), including 365 of the smaller, more delicate demitasse (Figs. 54-58).

A sample of the eclectic ironstone table and toilet wares was also recovered in substantially smaller quantities. Table wares include 156 small dishes, 18 plates, eight drinking mugs, three soup bowls, a casserole serving dish and one coffee/tea pot. Utilitarian toilet wares essential to health and hygiene in an era lacking indoor plumbing include 27 water pitchers (Figs. 63-66), nine wash basins (Fig. 69), 19 assorted soap dishes/strainers/lids, 10 toothbrush holders and lids (or brush boxes with lids; Figs. 67-68), 10 chamber pots and 10 lids (Figs. 70-72), eight slop jars (Figs. 60-62), an additional seven lids, and eight footbaths (Fig. 59).

A few of the plain ironstone toilet wares were embellished with gold ornamental trim, the remains of which can be seen on a few individual vessels, including washbasins, chamber pots, pitchers, and toothbrush containers, the latter referred to as 'brush boxes' in 19th-century documents (pers comm. Robert Hunter, May 2009). Many of the ironstone examples feature decorative fruits, nuts, and grains, popular themes suggestive of the American prairies and presented as design elements formed on pot handles and as finials on lids.

Although clay was plentiful in areas of the United States, most dinner and toilet wares were imported until the late 19th century. American clay was reserved for making bricks, tiles and other practical utensils such as crocks and jugs.[9]

6. Religious Objects

In stark contrast to the mass of utilitarian cargo recovered from the wreck site was a distinctive concentration of about 96 religious objects shipped in a single wooden crate, still partly preserved on the seabed (Fig. 17). These included 34 pressed-glass candlesticks in the form of the crucified Christ (Fig. 20), produced in both white and green glass, as well additional porcelain candlestick pairs featuring the figurative form of St. Joseph and the Virgin Mary holding Jesus. The crate was also filled with porcelain figurines of the Virgin Mary, assorted angels, Virgin Mary holy water fonts, and angel and crucifix holy water fonts.

Crucifix-themed glass candlesticks were popular at the time of the *Republic*'s final voyage and were used in private homes, convents and churches. Between 1840 and the latter part of the century, several American glassworks produced such objects in a variety of colors, often opaque, to appear more like ceramic than glass. Typically sold in pairs, research suggests that the examples from the *Republic*, in both white and green glass, were manufactured by the Boston and Sandwich Glass Company of Massachusetts, founded in 1825 and credited with having produced the country's first pressed glass (pers. comm. Jane Spillman, April 2005; pers. comm. Dorothy Hogan-Schofield, July 2009; Barlow and Kaiser, 1983: 61).

The majority of religious artifacts recovered from the site are Continental hard paste porcelains, most of which are glazed, with a few unglazed pieces, the latter commonly referred to as bisque porcelain or biscuit ware. These include porcelain statuettes portraying 'Our Lady of Grace', presented as the 'Queen of Heaven and Earth', standing on a base, which appears to symbolize the globe with a depiction of the sun in the center. One version of the statue wears a veil; the other is adorned with a crown decorated with 12-stylized stars thought to represent the 12 Apostles (pers. comm. Father William Kurchinsky, April 2009).

Additional examples include small angel figurines, both standing and kneeling, one version kneeling on a square base with traces of its original black and red pigment; porcelain Holy Family candlestick pairs in three different sizes, one representing the Virgin Mary holding the infant Jesus, the other, St. Joseph with his characteristic lily; and three different forms of holy water fonts, one depicting the Virgin Mary standing inside a decorative shrine (representing 'Our Lady of Grace' or possibly, the 'Shrine of Our Lady of Lourdes), and another portraying Christ on the cross, designed for hanging on a wall; and lastly, a tiny angel with a small basin at its feet, whose diminutive size is suggestive of little tokens or gifts given to young children (pers. comm. Barbara Perry, April

Fig. 54. A British ironstone china demi saucer bearing the maker's mark of John Maddock & Son (Diam. 16.0cm).

Fig. 55. A British ironstone china demitasse cup recovered from amongst a large cargo of utilitarian wares intended for everyday domestic use (H. 6.4cm).

Fig. 56. A British ironstone china mug (H. 9.7cm).

Fig. 57. A British ironstone china cup (H. 7.6cm).

Fig. 58. A British ironstone china beveled cup (H. 7.7cm).

Fig. 59. A British ironstone china footbath with ornamental handles; decorative toilet wares were commonly sold as matching sets (H. 22.0cm).

  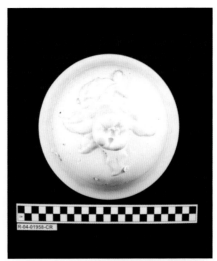

Figs. 60-61. A British ironstone china slop jar with decorative handles featuring fruit and harvest-related themes inspired by the American prairies (H. 31.5cm).

Fig. 62. A British ironstone china slop jar lid with ornamental finial (H. 10.5cm).

 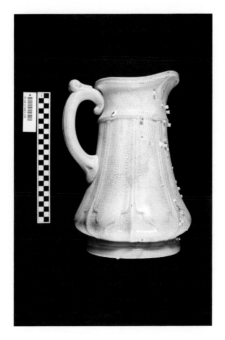 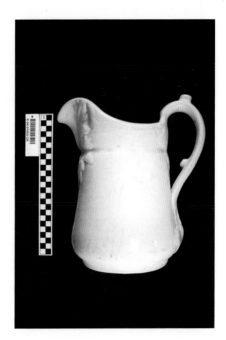

Fig. 63. An ironstone china water pitcher that would have accompanied a wash basin (H. 30.0cm).

Fig. 64. A British ironstone china water pitcher (H. 30.0 cm).

Fig. 65. A British ironstone china water pitcher (H. 24.0cm).

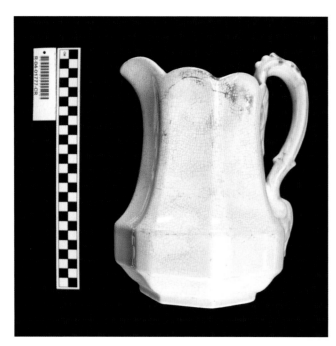

*Fig. 66. A British ironstone china
water pitcher (H. 19.5cm).*

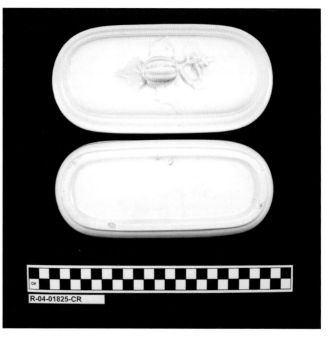

*Fig. 67. An ironstone china toothbrush holder with lid, known
as a 'brush box' in 19th-century documents (L. 21.9cm).*

*Fig. 68. An ironstone china toothbrush holder with lid
featuring a decorative finial similar to other pottery
wares recovered from the wreck (L. 21.9cm).*

Fig. 69. A British Ironstone china wash basin (H. 11.2cm).

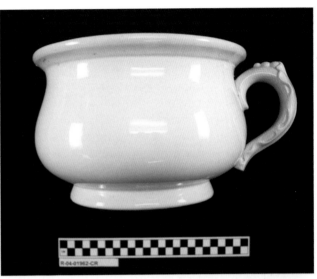

Fig. 70. A British ironstone china chamber pot (H. 14.3cm).

Fig. 71. A British ironstone china chamber pot (H. 14.3cm).

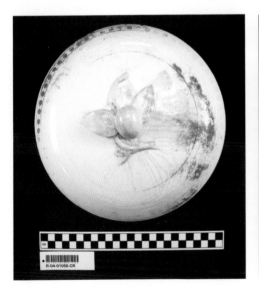

Fig. 72. A British ironstone china chamber pot or slop jar lid with remains of decorative gold trim (H. 10.5cm).

Fig. 73. A child's tea set adorned with black figures in classical garb reminiscent of ancient Greek vases (H. tea cups 4.6cm, L. saucers 8.5cm).

2005; pers. comm. Father William J. Kuchinsky, April and August 2009). Lacking maker's marks and factory records, the origins of these porcelain objects remain uncertain, but some appear to be similar to those bought and sold wholesale by the Swiss Benziger Brothers, whose New York City branch, founded in 1853, was in operation when the *Republic* sank.

The *Republic* figurines, however, most closely resemble hard paste porcelain wares produced in France, very probably Limoges, where dozens of 19th-century factories supplied New York City's import trade. Having launched the French porcelain import trade in the 1840s, the Haviland family, in particular, not only imported French wares to New York on a grand scale but also sold their imports wholesale to other American porcelain traders (pers comm. Robert Doares, July 2009; Wood and Doares, 2005: 24). This unique crate is published in detail elsewhere (Tolson and Gerth, 2009).

7. Miscellaneous

The other 3,080 artifacts recovered from the wreck of the *Republic* consist of an extraordinary diversity of goods, from four-holed white and brown porcelain buttons, bolts of cloth (Fig. 6), dominoes, harmonicas, horse spurs, clock parts, cane handles made of pewter, brass, wood and ivory, and 951 pieces of widely assorted hardware (ceramic doorknobs with metal shanks, spigots likely intended for use with barrels or kegs, door hinges, file rasps, keys, door locks and 278 spoons plus 13 further concretions containing multiple spoons; Figs. 79-82, 87-88). These goods were presumably intended for New Orleans hardware merchants hoping to rebuild a former trade or launch a new business.

Without the convenience of modern plumbing, Victorians washed their hair far less often than today, but combing and styling were essential to everyday hygiene and grooming. The excavation yielded a handful of combs, both straight and folding varieties, as well as individual stacks of concreted ladies' headbands (Figs. 83-85). Visibly similar to their modern-day plastic counterparts, the *Republic* shipment was made of vulcanite (vulcanized rubber), a typically black rubber-like substance first produced in 1843 by the American inventor Charles Goodyear (Wilson, 1917: 185).

A cargo of toiletries recovered from the *Republic* includes a dozen bone toothbrushes, their swine-hair bristles no longer intact (Fig. 86). 'Very Fine London' printed on the handle of a few examples reveal a British origin. Toothbrushes were first produced in England around 1780, but were not mass-produced in America

until after 1885. Accompanying this oral hygiene package were bottles of Van Buskirk's Fragrant Sozodont, created in 1859 by the New Jersey druggist Roswell Van Buskirk (Fig. 52). Advertisements claimed that this product would clean and preserve the teeth and harden the gums as well as "impart a delightfully refreshing taste and feeling to the mouth" (Fike, 1987: 187).[10] Retangular-shaped ironstone toothbrush holders with lids were also recovered from the *Republic* (Figs. 67-68).

The few one-off objects found on the wreck of the *Republic* site are suggestive of personal possessions stowed among the passengers' belongings or perhaps shipped in reduced quantities as limited consignments. Among these individual items is a seemingly rare and virtually intact child's tea set consisting of a teapot accompanied by four cups and saucers, a waste bowl, a sugar bowl and creamer (Fig. 73). Such sets of the era were intended not only as toys, but also to teach young girls how to serve tea properly. The assemblage features a neoclassical decorative theme bearing several complementary motifs. The use of black figures dressed in classical garb against a red background is reminiscent of Classical Greek vases. The decorations were applied to the plates and vessels with transfer prints and then the pieces were fired to make the decoration permanent (pers. comm. Barbara Perry, April 2005).

The excavation yielded four individual porcelain figurines, probably of French origin, the product of one or more of the many factories mass producing porcelain wares for the American market (pers comm. Robert Doares, July 2009). Each figurine represents a different character and theme. A man and his female counterpart, both without pigment or paint, were clearly intended to be a matching pair (Figs. 76-77). Their seemingly playful gestures and courtly attire are reminiscent of the 18th-century Rococo style, which placed an emphasis on portraying the carefree life of the aristocracy. Love and romance were common themes, marked by free and graceful movement. This elegant porcelain couple would have been admired by ladies of the era and presented in their homes on fireplace mantels or tea tables (pers. comm. Barbara Perry, April 2005). A third ceramic figurine depicts a country maiden with remains of red pigment, while a fourth 'neo-rococo' porcelain figurine represents a costumed female figure, a motif popular in the 19th century with its renewed interest in historical art styles.

A well-known class of artifact amongst the one-off finds on the site was an individual 'Rebekah-at-the-Well' teapot featuring the typical brown Rockingham glaze. In 1851 Edwin Bennet of Baltimore produced an earthenware teapot illustrating a scene from this biblical story, one of the most popular Bible stories of the time. From a practical utilitarian standpoint, the dark glaze was effective in hiding tea stains. However, the decoration itself was the more influential selling point and quite possibly offered the single greatest contribution to the huge popularity of Rockingham ware teapots (Perkins, 2004: 81). The best-known Rockingham products were made at Bennington, Vermont, yet almost every pottery in the eastern United States and Ohio also produced them (pers. comm. Barbara Perry, April 2005).

A unique porcelain figural inkstand cover portrays a woman sewing and accompanied by children reading at her side (Fig. 78). Hidden beneath this decorative piece is a tray with two small holders containing a removable ink and spill pot. Further detail depicts a small round face repeated on both of the pot holders. The inkstand is indicative of production in the Staffordshire Minton Pottery and Porcelain Factory founded in the 1790s to rapidly become the uncontested leader in the European ceramic market (Csenkey, 2002: 24; pers. comm. Barbara Perry, April 2005).

Additional one-of-a-kind artifacts recovered from the wreck of the *Republic* include an oversized porcelain cup and saucer with hand-painted leaves and flowers; a small transfer-printed tray probably manufactured in a British pottery (pers. comm. Barbara Perry, April 2005); a pressed glass bar bottle in the 'Ashburton' pattern with a ground and polished base, likely a product of the New England Glass Company; a pressed glass inkstand featuring the 'Argus' (thumbprint) pattern produced by Bakewell, Pears and Company or M'Kee and Brothers, both 19th-century Pittsburgh glass houses.

Of special interest are three distinctive glass oil lamp fonts, one of which was hand blown and features elaborate hand-decorated red glass threads, which were probably intended to conceal the yellowish oil (or more likely kerosene) that had recently been introduced as the lamp fuel of choice, both cheaper and less odorous than whale oil. The threaded decoration on the lamp was especially labor-intensive, thus making the object more expensive. The stem and foot of the *Republic*'s font are broken off, but the stem would originally have been about as long as the glass font and probably terminated in a colorless glass pressed foot or base (pers. comm. Jane Spillman, April 2005; Spillman, 2006: 15).

The second lamp is a clear glass font with a repeating cable and star patterned decoration, its stem and foot also broken away. The third lamp font, hand-blown with a ruby-colored overlay cut to clear glass, and an engraved, heavily faded vine decoration running along its shoulder, is accompanied by a pressed milk glass base (Figs. 22, 74-75). Produced by the Boston and Sandwich Glass Company of Massachusetts, this particular lamp would have been described as 'plated, cut and engraved' by the hardware and lighting companies that sold them (Barlow and Kaiser, 1989: 205-206). The overlay technique for producing the font involved encasing or plating the glass on the outside with a different color glass, and then cutting it back by hand to reveal the glass beneath. Such production began in the 1840s, when the Boston and Sandwich Glass Company set up a small furnace intended for the manufacture of colored glass for plated wares. The labor involved in the glassmaking and cutting made this piece considerably more expensive than most table lamps. Its use, like similar pieces of the era, was intended for city homes and large estates, where a staff of servants could maintain them in pristine condition (Barlow and Kaiser, 1989: 195).

The individual artifacts also include a lemonade or whiskey tumbler pressed in the 'Ribbed Ivy' pattern, possibly the product of M'Kee Brothers (pers. comm. Jane Spillman, April 2005; Spillman, 2006: 16); an ironstone relish dish with a popular shell pattern, probably from a British Staffordshire pottery (pers. comm. Barbara Perry, April 2005); a small porcelain vase with a budding flower motif and an underglaze cobalt blue decoration, typifying French production; two larger matching porcelain vases, also of probable French manufacture, referred to as 'wedding vases' or 'mantel vases' in light of a French custom whereby matched pairs were presented to young brides and grooms for display on their mantels (pers. comm. Robert Doares, July 2009) and a syringe-like device made of vulcanite (a hard rubber) believed to be for hygienic purposes (woman's douche), with the remains of a patent stamp suggestive of Nelson Goodyear's May 6th 1851 patent for processing hard vulcanite (Wilson, 1917: 185; Fig. 90).

After four years of relative economic isolation during the Civil War, the everyday goods from the wreck of the *Republic* – some sacred but most utilitarian – would have been both essential and welcome to alleviate years of hardship in everyday life in New Orleans. The ship's enormous shipment of largely everyday items, plus a small array of luxuries, would have helped rejuvenate the city's diminished stores. Unexpected and undocumented on most other 19th-century steamships of the era, the cargo of the *Republic* offers a unique window into the aspirations of Victorian New Orleans.

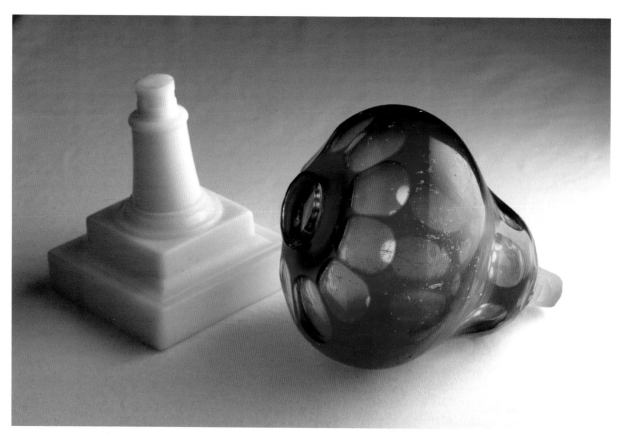

Fig. 74. A ruby-colored glass oil lamp font and milk glass base made
by the Boston and Sandwich Glass Company of Massachusetts.

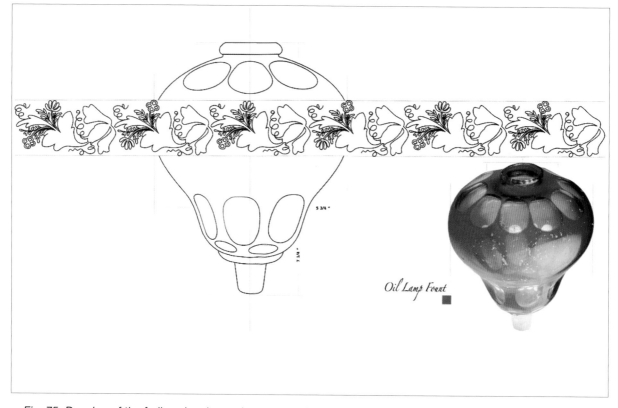

Oil Lamp Fount

Fig. 75. Drawing of the fading vine decoration engraved on the shoulder of the ruby-colored glass oil lamp font.

*Figs. 76-77. Porcelain figurines depicting a man and his female counterpart,
both without pigment or paint and of probable French production (H. 13.4cm and 12.5cm).*

*Fig. 78. A British Staffordshire figural porcelain inkstand cover portraying a woman sewing accompanied by children
reading at her side. The decorative tray at right, holding two removable ink and spill pots, would have been
hidden beneath the figures (H. inkstand cover 13.0cm; W. of base 15.4cm).*

Fig. 79. The ironmongery cargo includes doorknobs, locks, keys, rivits, spigots and files.

Fig. 80. The Republic's *varied cargo included consignments of dominos,
harmonicas, glass buttons and clock parts.*

Fig. 81. A concretion of pewter spoons before conservation.

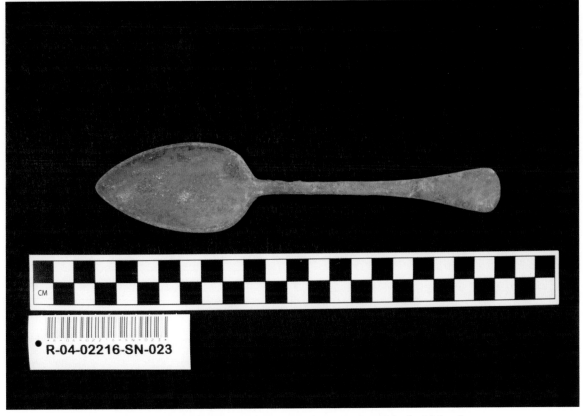

Fig. 82. A pewter spoon from the wreck of the Republic (L. 20.8cm).

Fig. 83. A straight-edged vulcanite comb (L. 17.8cm).

Fig. 84. A vulcanite folding comb (L. 8.9cm).

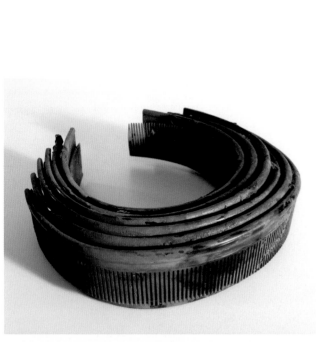

Fig. 85. Vulcanite ladies' headbands still in their original stacked shipping positions (Widths 12.3-14.9cm).

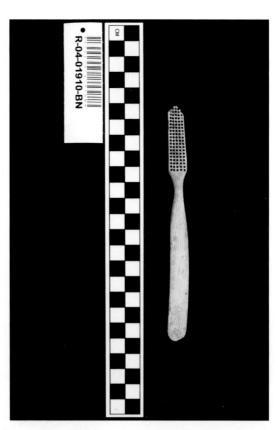

Fig. 86. A bone toothbrush (L. 17.0cm).

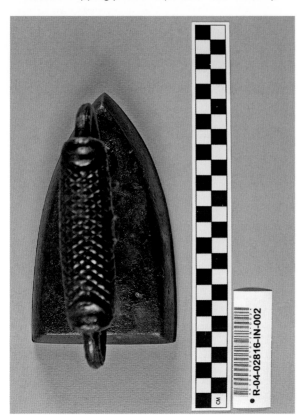

Fig. 87. A clothes iron (L. 13.4cm) with molded handle for extra grip.

Fig. 88. Iron scissors (L. 15.6cm).

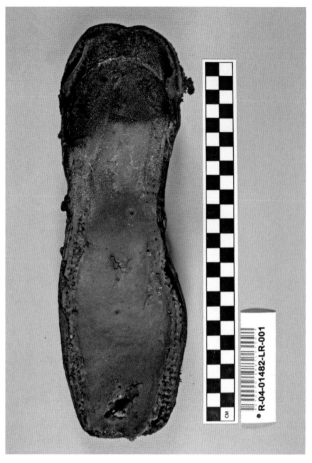

Fig. 89. The remains of a leather shoe from
the Area D debris field (L. 26.1cm).

Fig. 90. A vulcanite woman's douche used for
personal hygiene (L. 18.0cm).

Fig. 91. A rectangular metal engine lining ingot stamped with the names S. Whites and J. W. Quincy of
New York, the company that probably mixed the metals and cast the ingots (L. 21.4cm).

8. Conclusion: Comparative Analysis

New Orleans earned its economic status as the 'Queen of the South' by riding on a cloud of steam. Only after the introduction of the steamboat in Louisiana waters in 1811 could vessels comfortably counter the currents of the Mississippi to reach the city's wharves, over 150km from the river's mouth (Irion and Ball, 2001: 48). The SS *Republic* was a vital cog in revitalizing New Orleans after years of economic decline had stripped the city's shops of basic commodities and luxuries alike. Her cargo displays links with the US, France and notably Britain in the form of products transported in glass and stoneware bottles, Welsh writing slates, French porcelain wares and Staffordshire ironstone china. Valued at $340 million in 1860, US trade with the United Kingdom was triple the volume of the next country, France (Selcer, 2006: 90).

Due to rich historical sources, combined with key excavated sites, an abundance of data exists to examine the function and flaws of steam-powered vessels. The mid-19th century was a transitional time for steam-powered river, coastal and trans-oceanic ships. Much is known about the construction and capabilities of steamers through the comparative study of other 19th-century steam-powered vessels.

The shipwrecks of this type of craft are embedded in the field of marine archaeology today. Steamships were the largest and most complex machines of their era, unrivalled until the advent of the automobile and the construction of roads (VandenHazel, 1987: 331). They were largely classless and their passengers varied in economic and social status from wealthy vacationers to poor immigrants and everything in between (Lockhart, 2006: 4). The finds on such shipwrecks can reflect this diversity. Lockhart (2006: 89) has compellingly argued that using age as a measure of a wreck's importance should only be one of many criteria. Significance, more appropriately, should be based on the importance of the vessel's history, its influence on an area, country or culture, its relevance to the development of a country, its ability to provide information, its public interest and as an example of a specific technology.

The major archaeological significance of the SS *Republic* is its enormous collection of artifacts, which bridge the class divide. High-value gold and silver coins are intermixed with coal, humble glass bottles, modest everyday china, harmonicas and dominoes, a microcosm of the re-emerging vitality of contemporary New Orleans. Because of her great depth, much of the cargo that the *Republic*'s crew and passengers failed to jettison in a desperate attempt to save her survive on the sea bottom. By contrast, steamers lost in shallow waters were readily salvaged. As a consequence, the majority of such excavated steamship sites are largely defined by well-preserved hull remains and engines, many of which have been examined in detail. Numerous shipwrecks spanning the period 1838-93 – before and after the date of the *Republic*'s loss – provide comprehensive contexts for the evolution of steamers on lakes, rivers and seaways from northern Europe to the Americas.

Loaded with provisions for the US Army garrison at Fort Towson, Oklahoma, in March 1838 the sidewheel steamer *Heroine* snagged on the bed of the Red River. Her cargo was ruined, but the engine salvaged. Excavations have revealed that the hull and main deck are complete, stretching for 43m under the sand and with hatches still in place. Barrels of pickled pork and the intact rudder have been recovered. The *Heroine* is the only known historical shipwreck in the state of Oklahoma (Crisman, 2005: 220-21).

The hulls of two Morgan Line steamers have been recorded in detail. The *New York* left Galveston on 5 September 1846 with 30 passengers and a crew of 23 and hit a hurricane in the Gulf of Mexico. Located off the coast of Biloxi, Mississippi, the *Josephine* was an iron-hulled steamer built in 1867 and lost in 11.5m of water in the Chandeleur chain off Mississippi in February 1881 en route to New Orleans (Irion and Ball, 2001: 50-51, 54-55). Off the coast of Nova Scotia, the structure of the transatlantic steamer *Humboldt*, lost in December 1853 and at 2,181 tons one of the largest ships of her time, has been documented (Kenchington and Whitelock, 1996).

The 25.05m-long oak and pine *Eric Nordewall* was one of five paddle steamers built in the 1830s by the Ship Company for Steam Boat Trade to cater for the newly opened Gota Kanal, which crossed Sweden from the Baltic Sea to the west coast. She foundered on 4 June 1856 following 20 years of service after grounding on a shoal outside the town of Vadstena in Lake Vattern and plummeting to a depth of 45m. Her hull is in an outstanding level of preservation. Whereas the superstructure and interior fittings of the *Republic* have been completely stripped away by currents, the intact hull of the wreck of the *Eric Nordewall* is still "furnished with a pleasing decoration in the Empire style, very unlike the steel and glass fibre surroundings of the travel compartment of today. The wide benches along the walls of the saloons where the saloon passengers may have slept side by side with no partitions between them tell the same story" (Cederlund, 1987: 113).

The coastal paddle steamer blockade-runner *Denbigh*, one of the most successful and famous of the American Civil War, has been recorded near Galveston, where she was wrecked in May 1865 after being shelled whilst running the Union blockade (Arnold, 2005: 222-25; Arnold *et al.*,

2001). Very few artifacts survive but, lost in the same year as the *Republic,* her hull represents an important structural counterpoint to the *Republic's* cargo diversity. Further afield, the engine of the SS *Xantho,* a 32.3m-long iron-hulled paddle steamer built by Denny's of Dumbarton in 1848, and lengthened and refitted as a screw steamer in 1871 before being wrecked off Port Gregory, Western Australia, in shallow water in 1872, has been excavated, recovered and studied in detail (McCarthy, 1988: 342; McCarthy, 1995).

Unlike the *Republic,* many steamships foundered in waters that were sufficiently shallow to permit contemporary salvage. Thus, the cargo of the 2,000-ton capacity wreck of the stern-paddle-wheel steamer *Montana,* beached at St. Charles, Missouri, in 1884, was recovered immediately after her loss. Nevertheless, the site is of major importance because very few historical records chronicle the great service that river boats performed in America's western migration. 70% of her hull survives and displays frame-first technology, although a keel-plank and some of its bottom outer hull-planks were probably laid down before the floors. *Montana's* design does not easily fit into prevailing theories of bottom-, skeleton- or shell-first construction because only part of her structural strength derived from her hull. The rest came from her hogging-chain system, an external support (Corbin and Rodgers, 2007: 62, 64, 65, 67).

Finally, the side paddlewheel steamer *John Fraser,* lost in 1893 in 14m of water in Lake Nipissing, Ontario, was used to tow logs from assembly points such as the mouth of the Sturgeon River to sawmills, transported shantymen to the winter logging camps and towed flat-bottomed barges with supplies of hay, oats, barley, beans, salted meat, horses, sawmill parts, tools, cooking stoves, kitchen utensils, china and the personal belongings of settlers and forestry workers. She has been termed "a highly organized assemblage of people, machines and materials functioning together" (VandenHazel, 1987: 331). Detailed examination of the above hulls and their internal machinery – description of which is beyond the scope of this report – furnish a comprehensive reconstruction of the design and efficacy of steam power in the age of the *Republic.*

A similar deep-water site to the SS *Republic* is the side-wheel steamer SS *Central America.* Launched in October 1852 for the United States Mail Steamship Company, this three-mast, 82m-long vessel ran regular trips between New York and Panama. On the second day of battling a hurricane in September 1857 she sprang a leak and sank the next day, 256km off Cape Hatteras, North Carolina, in 3,000m of water and with the loss of 426 passengers and crew.

Using early remote technology, a high-value specie and gold ingot cargo was recovered along with many artifacts, including a diversity of glass and stoneware bottles, many

with distinctive shapes similar to those recovered from the *Republic,* yet found in substantially lower volumes. Examples include medicinal, wine and sauce bottles and a stoneware example with the J. Bourne & Son Denby and Codnor Park Potteries stamp (Thompson, 1998: 157), yet lacking the P. & J. Arnold London ink company mark that is distinctive to the stoneware master ink bottles shipped aboard the *Republic.* The SS *Central America* also carried white ironstone china, including a pitcher and blue-trimmed mugs, whose small size most suited a child (Thompson, 1998: 159). A breakdown of the specific quantities of glass bottles and ironstones wares on the *Central America* is currently unpublished.

Particularly unique to this wreck, however, were numerous intact passenger trunks, which unlike the multiple cargo items recovered from the *Republic,* provide a unique insight into the specific individuals who were travelling on board the *Central America.* The first trunk retrieved from the debris field belonged to two newlyweds and contained both men's and women's clothing, including custom-made linen dress shirts, a single-breasted waistcoat with patterned silk, a linen morning robe and a lace-trimmed dressing gown. Also stored in the trunk was a pair of Derringer pistols, a dog's head watch fob with garnet eyes and various toiletries, such as a hairbrush with hair still clinging to its bristles (Thompson, 1998: 140, 142-4, 148-9). No intact passenger cargo trunks were discovered on the *Republic,* which suggests that they were the first to be thrown overboard by the crew in a failed attempt to save the ship.

In terms of cargo content, a close parallel to the *Republic* is the *Arabia,* a wooden river steamboat built by John Snyder Pringle in Brownsville, Pennsylvania, in 1853. At 51.3m long, she was an average sized river steamboat. On 5 September 1856 the *Arabia* struck a submerged walnut tree in the Missouri River, which pierced her hull while she was heavily loaded with 222 tons of cargo destined for frontier merchants. Over the decades the river changed its course, so that when the wreck of the *Arabia* was discovered in 1988 by a team using a proton magnetometer she was located 13.5m under a Kansas farmer's cornfield.

Excavation of the ship uncovered a diverse cargo of trade goods still preserved in wooden barrels and crates, including Goodyear rubber shoes, boots, European ceramic dishes packed in straw, gold-rimmed eyeglasses, buttons, beads, doorknobs, shirts, glass-bottled food, medicine and spirit bottles, inkwells, clay smoking pipes, candles, textiles, spoons, bells, wrenches, guns and pocket knives. Many of these mid 19th-century wares are virtually identical to those recovered from the *Republic,* including brown marbelized and white ceramic doorknobs, keys, spoons, files and bottles with preserved fruit probably intended as pie filling, as well as the popular Dr. J. Hosttetter's Stomach Bitters (Hawley, 1995: 42, 58-9; Hawley, 1998: 77, 146, 208). Based on a concept of financial security in diversity rather than bulk, no two cases on the *Arabia* were alike. Aspects of this philosophy are shared in the *Republic*.

The loss of the *Arabia* was not a rare event. In the 44 years preceding 1897, 273 boats sank along the Missouri, 193 of them wrecked on snags similar to that which crippled the *Arabia* (Switzer, 1974: 2). So hazardous was river travel that the expected life of a Missouri river steamboat was less then five years (Hawley, 1995: 8).

Another of the Missouri's young victims was the steamer *Bertrand*, built in Wheeling, West Virginia, in 1864. The 48m-long, low draft vessel sank less than a year later on 1 April 1865 when the steamer struck a hidden snag at Portage La Force near De Soto Landing in Nebraska Territory. The *Bertrand* had departed from St. Louis bound for Fort Benton in Montana Territory two weeks earlier carrying at least 10 passengers and over 250 tons of agricultural and mining supplies, household paraphernalia, munitions, and clothing, as well as canned and bottled foodstuffs, wines and bitters. Also on board was an estimated 35,000 pounds of mercury, probably intended to help extract gold through the amalgamation process. Two contemporary attempts to salvage the cargo were largely unsuccessful, yet appear to have recovered most of the mercury (Switzer, 1974: 1).

As in the case of the *Arabia*, the *Bertrand* was discovered with its intact cargo well preserved in deep mud and silt. In 1968 and 1969 a recovery project supervized by archaeologists of the National Park Service and personnel of the Bureau of Sports Fisheries and Wildlife excavated the *Bertrand's* voluminous shipment of frontier-bound trade goods, yielding over two million artifacts. The hull was subsequently reburied (Corbin, 2002a: 14; 2002b: 201; Switzer, 1974: 1). Lost just six months prior to the *Republic*, the *Bertrand's* cargo of more than 6,000 glass and stoneware bottles bears striking similarities to the *Republic* (Switzer, 1974: vii), although the latter collection of over 8,000 bottles is larger in quantity and presents a broader diversity of bottle types.

Many of the finds had precise parallels to the *Republic*: keys, spoons, clock parts, buttons, doorknobs, door locks, axe heads and leather shoes, as well as combs made of hard rubber and ironstone china packed in wooden barrels (Petsche, 1974: 49, 60-61, 64-65, 69). The *Bertrand's* 6,000 glass and stoneware bottles include forms represented in the *Republic's* larger assemblage. In the bitters' category, 191 bottles of Dr. J. Hostetter's Stomach Bitters were found in 12-bottle cases on the *Bertrand* (Petsche, 1974: 50-51; Switzer, 1974: 33-4). Also represented in both assemblages are Drake's Plantation Bitters bottles (109 on the *Bertrand*), whiskey bottles produced in the Ellenville Glass Works,

beer, ale, wine and champagne bottles, and an assortment of foodstuff, including preserved fruit, condiments and sauces. Among the latter are the distinctive cathedral pickle and pepper sauces, Burnett's flavoring extract, and barrel-shaped mustard bottles with raised staves and bands distinctive to this bottle type (45 on the *Bertrand*) (Switzer, 1974: 16-20, 23-6, 29, 33-4, 36-7, 44-6, 48-50, 51-8, 78).

Additional bottled foodstuffs represented in the *Bertrand* collection include a probable competitor to the original Lea & Perrins Worcestershire Sauce bottles (33 on *Bertrand*). While the *Bertrand* examples feature glass stoppers embossed with the Lea & Perrins company name, the embossment on the shoulder of the bottles cunningly reads 'Worcester Sauce', not the traditional 'Worcestershire Sauce.' Unlike the *Republic's* authentic Lea & Perrins Worcestershire Sauce bottles, the *Bertrand* examples are vertically embossed with the E.F. Dixie company name, which research suggests was probably a Worcester, Massachusetts, firm competing in the 1860s with the more popular British brand and reusing original Lea & Perrins glass stoppers to promote its bottled sauce (Switzer, 1974: 59, 79; pers. comm. Bill Lindsey, June 2009). In the ink category, one case of the *Bertrand's* cargo contained 24 J. Bourne & Son's stoneware master ink bottles, also from the Denby and Codnor Park Potteries and similarly stamped with the mark of the P. & J. Arnold London ink company (Switzer, 1974: 67).

Buried for over a century in an anaerobic muddy environment, the *Bertrand's* bottles were largely well preserved with their contents intact, as were their corks, paper labels, wax and foil seals and stencilled wooden packing crates. A more detailed study of the *Bertrand* collection in tandem with that of the *Republic* will no doubt shed further light on how the *Republic* bottles may have been sealed, packed, stored and shipped.

In conclusion, starved of everyday commodities and luxuries, yet spared by early conquest and the subsequent importance to the Union war effort, New Orleans was once again a major port on the rise with great demands in 1865, when the *Republic* slipped beneath the waters of the Atlantic Ocean. Before the Civil War, arrivals at the Levee quay in New Orleans had averaged 300 steamboats a month, and about half that amount of oceangoing sailing ships (Van Zante, 2008: 65). Joseph Holt Ingraham reflected the prosperity of the time in *The Sunny South; Or, the Southerner at Home* (Philadelphia, 1860), where the Levee port was described as a "ceaseless maelstrom of motion... Imagine one broad field of such commercial life, four miles in unbroken extent, and you will have some idea of the 'Levee' at New Orleans."

However, virtually all trade ceased with the outbreak of war, with W.C. Corsan observing in *Two Months in* the Confederate States: an Englishman's Travels Through the South (London, 1863: 10-11) that in "time of peace, this immense area would have been piled up from end to end… [but] how different was the sight that met our eyes. Half a dozen paltry coasters, seeking a freight which was not to be found… while neither a bale of cotton, a hogshead of sugar, a bushel of corn, a packet of merchandise, or a man at work, could be seen from one end of that levee".

New Orleans resident Marion Southwood found oat-grass growing over the town's wharves during the war years and sadly reminisced that "where formerly all was life, bustle and animation, nothing is doing… The place looks as if it had been swept by a plague". The decay of the wharves made them so unstable that at the end of the war ships were compelled to land three and four deep on the few secure landing stages. In 1867, around $300,000 of the $3.1 million New Orleans city budget – the largest single item – was invested in the repair of the wharves and landings (Van Zante, 2008: 66).

The cargo of the SS *Republic*, in particular, is a unique archaeological witness to the origins and forms of imports circulating in New Orleans and the South in the immediate aftermath of the American Civil War. Although this shipwreck may be considered to be relatively recent chronologically, its rich archaeology helps considerably resurrect one of America's most important and intensively studied periods of history.

Acknowledgements

The authors of this report are enormously grateful to the entire Odyssey team whose steadfast commitment and breadth of expertise ensured that the *Republic* project succeeded. The authors extend huge thanks to the following:

Odyssey co-founders, Greg Stemm and John Morris, for their vision, endurance and unyielding determination to find the *Republic*; Marine Operations Manager Roy Truman whose soaring expectations guaranteed success; Project Manager Ernie Tapanes and his team of side-scan technicians, whose meticulous search operations and extraordinary patience ultimately led to the amazing discovery; Project Managers Tom Detweiller, Andrew Craig and Mark Martin for their rare gift in directing and managing shipboard operations and for their undying support of the entire operational team; ROV Supervisors Gary Peterson, Eric Peterson and Jim Starr and all the ROV technicians whose competence and adroit skills ensured that the artifacts were recovered from the site with the utmost care and in tandem with the highest archaeological standards; Data Manager Gerhard Steiffert and his team of dataloggers, who painstakingly recorded every minute of every dive and managed the enormous mountain of data, photographs and underwater footage that was recorded; and the Master's officers and the crew of the *Odyssey Explorer*, without whom the time spent on the ship months away from home in sometimes terrible seas would have been unbearable.

To our good friend, colleague and archaeologist, Hawk Tolson, whose professionalism, encouragement and support have never wavered and whose adept research skills during those rare off-hours have provided a wealth of information. A mighty thank you is offered to John Oppermann and his entire research team who have supported this project with great energy and enthusiasm, in particular Kathy Evans and John Griffith. We are indebted to Adam and Eric Tate whose patience and Excel wizardry accessed the artifact data so relevant to the report. Gerri Graca, Odyssey's archivist extraordinaire, demonstrated exceptional resourcefulness locating essential and often obscure sources and other critical references. Fred Van De Walle, Chief Conservator and his dedicated team, Alan Bosel and Chad Morris, responded to our numerous queries and have set high standards of conservation, recording, documentation and photography. To Laura Barton and her team for all the media support and wonderful graphics generated. A special thank you is extended to the designer Melissa Kronewitter and to George Salmon and Chad Morris for producing exquisite photography.

We are especially grateful to an elite group of professionals, who have so generously offered their invaluable time and vast knowledge to the SS *Republic* project: Jane Spillman, Curator of Glass, Corning Museum of Glass; Barbara Perry, Former Curator of Decorative Arts, the Mint Museum; Bill Lindsey, formerly Bureau of Land Management and author of the Society for Historical Archaeology/BLM Historic Glass Bottle Identification and Information Website; Robert Hunter, British and American ceramic scholar and editor of *Ceramics in America*; Dafydd Roberts, Keeper, National Slate Museum, Llanberis, North Wales; Reverend Father William Joseph Kuchinsky, Priest of the Catholic Diocese of Wheeling-Charleston, WV; Byron Dille', bottle collector and historian; Robert Doares, Porcelain Historian, Williamsburg, Virginia; and Dorothy G. Hogan-Schofield, Curator Of Collections, Sandwich Glass Museum.

To Dr. Sean Kingsley, Director of Wreck Watch International, we are profoundly grateful for providing his firm guidance, keen insight and editorial wisdom. A final acknowledgement is in special memory of the former Conservator Herbert Bump, who established precedents in the early stages of the *Republic* project that Odyssey has continued to foster and emulate.

Notes

1. See Louisiana State Museum, *Ante-bellum Louisiana: Urban Life*: http://lsm.crt.state.la.us/cabildo/cab9a.htm.
2. *Yellow Fever Deaths in New Orleans, 1817-1905* (Louisiana Division New Orleans Public Library): http://nutrias.org/facts/feverdeaths.htm.
3. *A Brief History of the Denby Pottery*: www.clariceware.com/The%20Denby%20Pottery%20story.htm; *A History of Denby*: www.denby.com.au/denby_history.html.
4. *Glenn Poch's Bottle Collecting Newsletter* 19 (1997): www.antiquebottles.com/poch/19.html.
5. See: http://dalessandris.net/lkpostalhistory.aspx.
6. For L.T. Piver's perfumes, see: http://www.piver.com/EN/historique.htm.
7. *Reconstruction: the Second Civil War. American Experience Mini Documentary*: www.pbs.org/wgbh/amex/reconstruction/schools/ps_highgate.html.
8. See: http://www.thepotteries.org/types/ironstone.htm.
9. See: http://www.thepotteries.org/a_z.htm.
10. *An American Time Capsule: Three Centuries of Broadsides and Other Printed Ephemera, Testimonials in Relation to the Merits of Van Buskirk's Fragrant Sozodont; for Cleansing and Preserving the Teeth, Hardening the Gums...* (Printed Ephemera Collection, Portfolio 122, Folder 35, New York, 1859).

Bibliography

Arnold, J.B., 'The *Denbigh*, a Civil War Blockade Runner'. In G.F. Bass (ed.), *Beneath the Seven Seas* (London, 2005), 222-25.

Arnold, J.B., Oertling, T.J. and Hall, A.W., 'The *Denbigh* Project: Excavation of a Civil War Blockade-Runner', *IJNA* 30.2 (2001), 231-49.

Barlow, R. and Kaiser, J., *The Glass Industry in Sandwich. Vol. 2* (Atglen, 1989).

Barlow, R. and Kaiser, J., *The Glass Industry in Sandwich. Vol. 4* (Windham, 1983).

Barua, D. and Greenough III, W.B. (eds.), *Cholera: Current Topics in Infectious Disease* (Springer-Verlag New York, 1992).

Baxter, F., 'A Century of Hostetter's Bitters or... It Pays to Advertise', *Bottles & Extras* 8.90 (1997), 1-5.

Blassingame, J.W., *Black New Orleans: 1860-1880* (University of Chicago Press, 1973).

Bowers, Q.D., 'Appendix B. Coins of the SS *Republic*'. In P.J. Vesilind, *Lost Gold of the Republic* (Shipwreck Heritage Press, 2005), 251-67.

Bowers, Q.D., *The SS Republic Shipwreck Excavation Project: the Coin Cargo* (OME Papers 7, forthcoming 2009).

Brantz, M., *Baltimore: Past and Present with Biographical Sketches of its Representative Men* (Baltimore, 1871).

Campbell, G. (ed.), *The Grove Encyclopedia of Decorative Arts* (Oxford University Press, 2006).

Capers, G.M., *Occupied City. New Orleans Under the Federals 1862-1865* (University of Kentucky Press, 1965).

Carvalho, D.N., *Forty Centuries of Ink* (New York, 2008).

Cederlund, C.O., 'The *Eric Nordewall* – An Early Swedish Paddle Steamer', *IJNA* 16.2 (1987), 109-33.

Corbin, A., *The Material Culture of Steamboat Passengers. Archaeological Evidence from the Missouri River* (New York, 2002a).

Corbin, A., 'Steamboat Archaeology on the Missouri River'. In C. Ruppé and J. Barstad (eds.), *International Handbook of Underwater Archaeology* (New York, 2002b), 193-206.

Corbin, A., *The Life and Times of the Steamboat Red Cloud* (Texas A & M University Press, 2006).

Corbin, A. and Rodgers, B.A., 'Steamboat *Montana* (1879–1884) – Leviathan of the American Plains', *IJNA* 36.1 (2007), 59-74.

Cramp, A.D., *Nostrums and Quackery, Volume II* (Chicago, 1921).

Crisman, K., 'The Sidewheel Steamer Heroine: Red River, Oklahoma'. In G.F. Bass (ed.), *Beneath the Seven Seas* (London, 2005), 220-21.

Csenkey, E., *Hungarian Ceramics from the Zsolnay Manufactory* (Yale University Press, 2002).

Cunningham Dobson, N., Tolson, H., Martin, A., Lavery, B., Bates, R., Tempera, F. and Pearce, J., *The HMS Sussex Shipwreck Project (Site E-82): Preliminary Report* (OME Papers 1, 2009).

Davoli, E.L., *Patent Medicines: Ethnic or Socioeconomic Indicators? Louisiana Department of Transportation and Development* (Presented at the First Annual South Central Historical Archaeology Conference, Jackson, Mississippi, 1998).

Fadely, D., *Hair Raising Stories* (Privately Published, 1992).

Fike, R.E., *The Bottle Book: A Comprehensive Guide to Historic, Embossed Medicine Bottles* (Salt Lake City, 1987).

Fox, S., *The Mirror Makers A History of American Advertising and its Creators* (University of Illinois Press, 1997).

Gerth, E., *Patent Medicines, Bitters, & Other Bottles from the Wreck of the Steamship Republic* (Shipwreck Heritage Press, 2006).

Gerth, E. and Tolson, H., 'Lost Cargo Writes History: Writing Slates from the Wreck of the Steamship *Republic*', *North South Trader's Civil War* 33.5 (2008), 38-50.

Gilman. J., *The SS Xantho Hull Reconstruction Project* (Western Australia, 2002).

Hawley. D., *Treasures of the Arabia* (Kansas, 1995).

Hawley. G., *Treasure in a Cornfield: The Discovery and Excavation of the Steamboat Arabia* (Paddlewheel Publishing, Kansas, 1998).

Heyl, E., *Early American Steamers, Volume I* (New York, 1953).

Irion, J.B. and Ball, D.A., 'The *New York* and the *Josephine*: Two Steamships of the Charles Morgan Line', *IJNA* 30.1 (2001), 48-56.

Kane, A.I., *The Western River Steamboat* (Texas A & M University Press, 2004).

Kelly, W.J., *Shipbuilding at Federal Hill Baltimore (c. 1662-1961)* (unpublished manuscript, 1961).

Kenchington, T. and Whitelock, C., 'The United States Mail Steamer *Humboldt*, 1851-53: Initial Report', *IJNA* 25.3 (1996), 207-223.

Lockhart, B., *Steamship Wrecks from the Late Nineteenth to Early Twentieth Centuries as Archaeological Sites* (MA Thesis, Flinders University, South Australia, 2006).

Lunn, K., 'Identification and Dating of Lea and Perrins' Worcestershire Sauce Bottles on Canadian Historic Sites: Interpretations Past and Present', *Canadian Journal of Archaeology* 5 (1981), 1-17.

McCarthy, M., 'SS *Xantho*: The Pre-disturbance, Assesment, Excavation and Management of an Iron Steam Shipwreck off the Coast of Western Australia', *IJNA* 17.4 (1988), 339-47.

McCarthy. M., *The SS Xantho Excavation 1983-1995* (Western Australia, 1995).

McKearin, H. and Wilson, K.M., *American Bottles and Flasks and their Ancestry* (New York, 1978).

McNabb, D. and Madère, L.E.L, *A History of New Orleans* (2003): www.madere.com/history.html.

New York Marine Register. A Standard of Classification of American Vessels, and of other such Vessels as Visit American Ports (New York, 1857).

Odell, J., *The Story of Butler's Inks. Oak Galls Beetles and J.J. Butler: The Early Years* (Digger Odell Publications, 2003).

Perkins, C.J., *Rockingham Ware in American Culture, 1830-1930* (University Press of New England, 2004).

Petsche, J.E., *The Steamboat Betrand. History, Excavation and Architecture* (National Park Service, US Department of the Interior, Washington, 1974).

Reinders, R.C., *The End of An Era. New Orleans 1850-1860* (Gretna, 1998).

Ridgely-Nevitt, C., *American Steamships on the Atlantic* (University of Delaware Press, Newark, 1981).

Roberts, G., *The Confederate Bell* (University of Missouri Press, 2003).

Scharf, J.T., *History of Baltimore City and County* (Philadelphia, 1881).

Shrady, G.F. (ed.), *Medical Record. A Weekly Journal of Medicine Vol. 50 July 4, 1896 – December 26, 1896* (New York, 1896).

Spillman, J.S., 'Sunken Treasure: The SS *Republic*.' In J.S. Spillman (ed.), *The Glass Club Bulletin of the National American Glass Club* 204 (2006), 13-17.

Stevens, R.W., *On the Stowage of Ships and their Cargoes with Information Regarding Freights, Charter-Parties, &c. &c.* (London, 1869).

Stout, W.A., *A Return to Civilian Leadership, New Orleans 1865-1866* (M.A Thesis, Louisiana State University and Agricultural and Mechanical College, 2007).

Switzer, R., *The Betrand Bottles: A Study of 19th Century Glass and Ceramic Containers* (National Park Service Department of the Interior, 1974).

Thompson, T., *America's Lost Treasure* (New York, 1998).

Tolson, H. and Gerth, E., *Faith of Our Fathers: Religious Artifacts from the SS Republic (1865)* (OME Papers 9, forthcoming).

Van Zante, G.A., *New Orleans 1867. Photographs by Theodore Lilienthal* (New York, 2008).

Vandal, G., *Rethinking Southern Violence: Homicides in Post-Civil War Louisiana, 1866-1884* (Ohio State University Press, 2000).

VandenHazel, B.J., 'The Wreck of the Side Paddlewheel Steamer *John Fraser*, Lake Nipissing, Ontario, Canada', *IJNA* 16.4 (1987), 331-41.

Vesilind, P.J., *Lost Gold of the Republic* (Shipwreck Heritage Press, 2005).

Wilson, G.H., *A Manual of Dental Prosthetics* (New York and Philadelphia, 1917).

Wood, B. and Doares, R., *Old Limoges: Haviland Porcelain Design and Décor, 1845-1865* (Atglen, 2005).

Young, J.H., *The Toadstool Millionaires: A Social History of Patent Medicines in America before Federal Regulation* (Princeton University Press, 1961).

Zumwalt, B., *Ketchup, Pickles, Sauces - 19th Century Food in Glass* (Fulton, 1980).

3

The SS *Republic* Shipwreck Excavation Project: the Coin Collection

Q. David Bowers
Stack's, Wolfeboro, New Hampshire.

A primary objective of the excavation of the shipwreck of the SS *Republic*, lost on 25 October 1865, 150km off Georgia on the southeastern coast of the United States, was to locate and study a historically-attested cargo of specie. Almost as soon as the intrusive phase of the project commenced, extensive coin deposits were uncovered in the stern hold. The excavation yielded 51,404 coins: 4,135 gold and 47,263 silver issues. These consisted of 2,675 gold $20 double eagles and 1,460 $10 eagles, with the rest silver half dollars, except for two silver 25-cents and four British silver florins. The coins were all recovered individually, one by one.

Cargoes of early American coinage from shipwrecks are relatively rare, with only three other major assemblages identified. The collection from the *Republic* is larger than all of these combined and offers a unique opportunity to examine coin production and distribution, mint operations and economic trends immediately at the conclusion of the American Civil War.[1]

1. Introduction

The majority of coins discovered by archaeologists and other modern explorers in or near American waters have consisted of issues from Mexico, Central or South America and other foreign lands. Important United States coins, whether gold or silver, have been remarkably inconspicuous. The plenitude of foreign coins and scarcity of US coins in shipwrecks is due partly to the timeframe involved. Into the 18th century losses of Spanish galleons at sea occurred in an era before the United States even existed as a political entity. Typically, these treasure-laden galleons were returning from lands of the New World conquered by the Spanish. Each year a harvest of silver and gold, much in the form of freshly minted coins and cast ingots, was gathered and sent back to Spain via a flotilla (Craig and Richards, 2003). On notable occasions, in particular in 1622 and 1715, the flotillas encountered the hurricanes of late summer and early autumn, which wreaked great destruction and sank many vessels, often close to the shore of present-day Florida (Fine, 2006; Mathewson, 1986).

The Mint Act of 2 April 1792 provided for the establishment of a federal mint in Philadelphia (Young, 1903: 7), the first foundation stone for which was laid on 31 July 1792, with Mint Director David Rittenhouse in attendance. The first significant production of US coins for circulation took place in 1793, with copper cents and half cents, followed by silver coins in 1794 and gold in 1795 (Evans, 1886: 81-5, 89; Schwarz, 1980: 76, 79-81, 83; *The United States Mint*, 1878: 3).

From the earliest times of settlement by Europeans in the New World, each year many ships were lost at sea, sometimes without a trace, in other instances documented by tales of woe – piracy, foundering in hurricane-whipped waves, or collisions with rocks or other vessels. With the foundation of the United States, just about every passenger vessel departing from a port such as New York City, Baltimore, New Orleans, Charleston and Boston carried some silver and gold coins, if not in bulk shipments then among the passengers' personal effects, since paper money was not desirable in distant ports of call.

Beginning in 1849, large quantities of gold from the California Gold Rush arrived in Eastern America (Bowers, 2002: 111-22). By 1864, $44 million-worth was mined and processed in California (Wells, 2005: 23). To facilitate the use of gold in coinage form, the Coinage Act of 3 March 1849 provided for two new denominations, the $1 coin (known as the gold dollar) and the $20 (the double eagle). These joined the $2.50, $5, and $10 values that had been produced since the 1790s. Gold dollars were first coined in 1849, double eagles not until 1850.

Production of the double eagle was quickly recognized as the most efficient way to convert bullion into coin form. The importance and significance of the double eagle is dramatized by the fact that from 1850 until 1933, the lifespan of this coin's issue, more than 75% of the value of all metal coined by the United States – copper, nickel, silver and gold – occurred in the form of double eagles.

As such, it was the denomination of choice for shipments by sea. With its popularity and intrinsic value, the double eagle naturally plays a key role in shipwreck losses from 1850 onwards.

United States silver coins, minted in quantity since 1794, also figure in accounts of losses in disasters at sea. However, this metal is usually badly corroded by salt water to the extent that the coins are often rendered unidentifiable. Many of the silver half dollars recovered from the SS *Republic* are a surprising and remarkable exception.

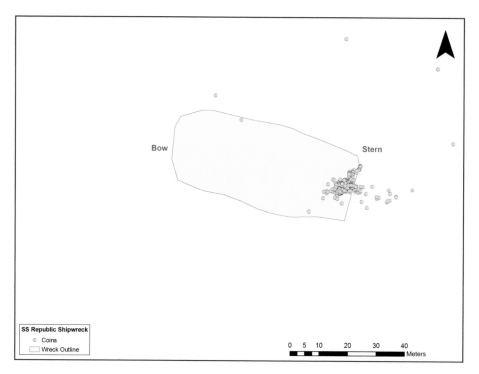

Fig. 1. Distribution map of gold coins on the shipwreck of the Republic.

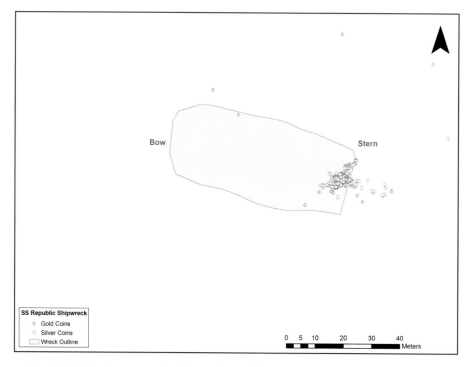

Fig. 2. Distribution map of gold and silver coins on the shipwreck of the Republic.

Fig. 3. Silver half dollar (top), gold $20 (bottom left) and $10 (right) coins from the wreck of the Republic.

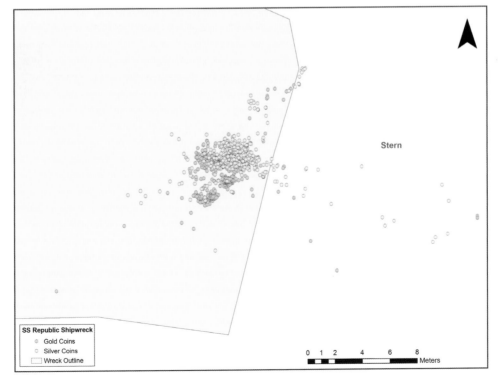

Fig. 4. Distribution of gold and silver coins on the Republic *site.*

2. American Shipwrecks & Coin Cargoes of the Age of Gold

The marvelous finds of the 'Forty-niners' in the streambeds of California inaugurated the Age of Gold, literally, with double eagles minted by the millions in the 1850s and 1860s, as well as a lesser amount of other denominations from the $1 coin to the $10 eagle. During these two decades a number of mints, in addition to the main Philadelphia Mint, were in operation, including branches at San Francisco (opened in 1854), New Orleans (1838), Charlotte (1838) and Dahlonega (1838). The last two mints, in North Carolina and Georgia respectively, produced gold coins of values from $1 to $5 but did not have presses able to make higher denominations.

In this era, gold coins, particularly in the form of double eagles, were staples in national and international currency. Paper money of state-chartered banks was not trusted, and even when federal Legal Tender bills were circulated beginning in 1862 they were of depreciated value in relation to silver and gold. Beginning in 1854, when the New York Assay Office and Sub-Treasury opened for business, New York City became the most important trading center for gold. Vast quantities of coins from California (Wells, 2005: 23), including double eagles in particular from the San Francisco Mint, arrived in the port on a regular basis. Usually the shipments traveled by steamships connecting from Panama, where the valuable cargo had been transferred overland from the Pacific side. From New York City, gold coins and rectangular ingots were sent by rail and other means to various cities in the United States, as well as by ship to foreign destinations, London in particular. To a lesser extent silver was also distributed from New York City, especially to Eastern destinations.

Of the thousands of American ships lost – over 8,000 in the Great Lakes alone (Bowers, 2008: 63) – relatively few are known to have carried large amounts of specie and, of these, only a handful have been found and valuable coins recovered. The SS *Republic* is the latest in this very exclusive roster. Indeed, there are just two other confirmed and documented major finds from the 'Age of Gold' (SS *Central America* and SS *Brother Jonathan*), the decades of the 1850s and 1860s, to which can be added a third possibility (SS *Yankee Blade*), information about which is vague. Two other relatively minor coin cargoes derive from the loss of the SS *New York* in 1846, yielding several hundred gold coins and over 2,000 silver ones, and from a small boat dispatched from the *William and Mary* in 1857.

The earliest documented major recovery comes from the wreck of the SS *Central America*, lost off North Carolina on 12 September 1857 (Thompson, 1998). The ship

carried to the ocean floor a vast cargo of gold coins and ingots headed from Aspinwall, on the Atlantic side of Panama, north to New York City. The wreck was found in 2,194m of water in the late 1980s by the Columbus-America Discovery Group. About 7,500 gold coins were recovered, dominated by more than 5,400 mint-fresh 1857-S double eagles, plus more than 500 gold ingots. (When cited after a date, letters stand for the mint name: O (New Orleans), S (San Francisco). The absence of any letter signifies Philadelphia.) Originating in San Francisco, the cargo had been shipped south to Panama City by the SS *Sonora*, from where it was transported 77km overland on the Panama Railroad to Aspinwall (Bowers, 2002: 887-1033). The gold coins and ingots, plus a small number of heavily corroded silver coins, were distributed mostly by the California Gold Marketing Group. The recovered treasure is reported to have yielded well over $100 million in sales. The documented coins and ingots have been carefully studied and comprehensively published (Bowers, 2002; Thompson, 1998).

Next in the short list of recovered shipwreck coin cargoes from the 'Age of Gold' is what is believed to be the SS *Yankee Blade*, a side-wheel steamer lost when it hit the rocky shore off Santa Barbara, California, on the foggy afternoon of 1 October 1854. About $152,000 in gold was reportedly lost when the ship sank. While researching *American Coin Treasures and Hoards* (1996), I was informed that in 1977 divers found several hundred 1854-S double eagles in the wreck of that vessel. However, the recovery, if there was one, was shrouded in secrecy. From about that time and continuing into the 1980s, 200 to 300 examples of 1854-S twenties have come on to the market through auction sales and private transactions. Each of these coins has 'saltwater Uncirculated' surfaces, as they were designated. In other words, the coins show signs of the action of sea and sand in relatively shallow water. The total market value of these double eagles was probably in the range of $1 million.

The third and final US shipwreck antecedent to the SS *Republic* is the cargo of the SS *Brother Jonathan*, lost in the Pacific off Crescent City, California, on 30 August 1865. The ship carried an unknown quantity of coins, but it yielded slightly more than a thousand pieces when the wreck was found in the 1990s. Most were double eagles of the 1865-S variety and a lesser number of 1864-S and 1863-S twenties, along with some other varieties (Bowers, 1999: 311-56). Most were sold at auction in 1999. The market value was in the $5 million range.

To the preceding shipwrecks – two confirmed, plus one unconfirmed – can be added another cargo of gold lost just off modern-day Fort Pierce, Florida, at the Indian River

Inlet. This consisted of a payroll of $23,000 in gold coins sent by sea in 1857 aboard the *William and Mary* from Charleston, South Carolina, south to the army post at Fort Capron in the custody of Major Jeremiah Yellot Dashielle. Upon arrival near the fort, Major Dashielle took the payroll with him in a small boat and headed toward the shore. The vessel capsized in the surf and the coins were scattered.

In the 1960s, an estimated 3,500 of the gold coins from the small capsized boat, from dollars to double eagles, were recovered. Most of the face value was in 1855-S and 1856-S twenties, each showing etched surfaces from the action of the sand, again classified as 'saltwater Uncirculated'. This find was incompletely reported, and today its exact contents are not known. In addition to the $20 issues, some were of lower denominations. Mainly distributed into the coin markets in the 1970s, the market value of this find may have been in the range of $500,000 to $1 million.

To this list may be added the relatively modest discovery of several hundred gold coins, plus over 2,000 silver coins, from the wreck of the SS *New York*, lost in the Gulf of Mexico on 7 September 1846 en route from Galveston to New Orleans (Bowers, 2008). The wreck was discovered at a depth of 15m, some 80km offshore (Irion and Ball, 2001).

These five instances constitute the significant US gold coin collections recovered from shipwrecks dating between 1846 and the 1860s and that were known by early 2003. To this list can now be added the dramatic find in the autumn of 2003 of the SS *Republic* coins, totaling over 50,000 coins – more pieces than all of the earlier-mentioned shipwrecked coins combined.

3. Money During the Civil War

On 17 October 1865 the SS *Republic* left New York City and headed toward the open sea en route to New Orleans. On board was a reported extensive coin cargo (*Charleston Daily Courier*, 30 and 31 October, 11 November 1865). At the time, such coins were especially precious because paper money was deeply depreciated (Bowers, 1999: 66). This situation dated back to the beginnings of the Civil War. In the second week of April 1861 Confederate forces in Charleston bombarded Fort Sumter in the harbor, reducing most of it to rubble and forcing the federal troops to surrender (Selcer, 2006: 60). President Abraham Lincoln declared war soon afterwards. The conflict was envisioned to be an easy win for the North, as Confederate troops were thought to be poorly equipped and trained. A call was issued for volunteer troops to enlist in the Union army for a period of three months, certainly enough time for an uncomplicated victory.

Parades and parties were held as soldiers marched off to war. The unexpected and overwhelming victory by

the Confederate troops at the Battle of Bull Run in July dispelled any lingering thoughts that the war would end soon. By that time the Treasury Department, largely depleted of readily available funds even before the war had begun, was in serious financial straits. By issuing Demand Notes – currency redeemable in gold – additional money was secured. Loans arranged through the help of bankers added to the revenue. As the year progressed, however, and the outcome of the conflict became increasingly uncertain, the public turned toward the hoarding of 'hard money'. In late December 1861, banks in New York and elsewhere stopped paying out gold coins in exchange for bank notes, the latter consisting of bills issued by more than a thousand state-chartered banks.

In early 1862 the Treasury Department issued Legal Tender bills; some $450 million 'Greenbacks' would be issued in the next three years alone (Selcer, 2006: 79). These were not redeemable in coins, but were exchangeable only for other such bills and, on a limited basis, in satisfaction of money owed to the government. Public distrust of paper money deepened, and silver coins soon disappeared from circulation. By the second week of July 1862, copper-nickel cents were gone as well. With no coins available for trade, business was conducted mostly in paper money and, for small transactions, in substitutes such as postage stamps, tokens and privately printed bills (Schwarz, 1980: 176-80).

In the meantime, gold and silver coins were still available, but only from banks and exchange brokers, who charged a premium for them in terms of Legal Tender bills. In January 1862, at the outset of hoarding, it took $1,010 in bank bills to buy $1,000 face value in gold coins. In December of that year, a dollar in note form was only worth 80 cents in money (Newcomb, 2005: 39). By October it took $1,235 in bank bills or the new Legal Tender bills to do the same. As the war progressed, the differential continued to rise. The apex was reached in July 1864, when $2,850 in bills was required to receive $1,000 in gold coins. By 1865, the year the *Republic* sank, economists observed that "while there is in existence in the country a certain amount of gold, $100 in bonds would have brought in the market only $50 in coin" (Newcomb, 1865: 42).

Over time, the situation for small coins eased and in 1863 copper-nickel Indian Head cents were again seen in commerce, together with an immense quantity of copper Civil War tokens bearing patriotic legends or the advertisements of merchants. Encased postage stamps, consisting of stamps mounted in a brass frame faced with mica, were encountered as well. To aid in small transactions, the Treasury Department issued Postage Currency bills of small size followed by Fractional Currency in values from 3 cents to 50 cents. In 1864, the bronze 2-cent piece first appeared, and these circulated widely, followed by nickel 3-cent coins in 1865 (Schwarz, 1980: 185-8).

In the meantime, in California and certain other West Coast areas, paper money was not used in commerce. The Constitution of California, adopted in 1850, expressly forbade the use of such bills, a measure intended to prevent losses from bank bills of failed institutions. Instead, commerce was conducted solely in coins, mostly gold, bolstered by a small supply of silver.

When the federal Legal Tender bills appeared in 1862, followed by National Bank notes in late 1863, this currency was exchangeable in California only at a discount, the amount being equal to the premium charged in the East. In San Francisco, gold double eagles were used at par to buy and sell goods. To settle a transaction in paper money, a higher price would be charged, equal to the exchange-rate difference. In New York City, paper bills were used to buy and sell goods at prices much higher than in San Francisco, and anyone wanting to pay in gold coins got a deep discount.

In early 1865, as the Civil War drew to a conclusion, it was widely anticipated that gold and silver coins would soon be seen again in commerce, exchangeable at par with paper money. However, because the financial condition of the federal government remained uncertain, with huge debts incurred in the conduct of the war, silver and gold were still hoarded and paper money remained the basis of commerce (Bowers, 1999: 72-77). Not until after 20 April 1876 were silver coins on a par with paper in terms of usage, and not until after 17 December 1878 would gold and paper be exchangeable.

4. Coins & Paper Money in Autumn 1865

In October 1865, the month that the SS *Republic* undertook its final voyage, the monetary situation in America remained in a confused state. In common circulation in the North were copper-nickel 1-cent pieces and, since spring 1864, the new bronze Indian cents along with bronze 2-cent pieces and, beginning in 1865, nickel 3-cent pieces. Civil War tokens were also still seen with frequency, although they had not been made in quantity since early 1864.

Fractional Currency bills flooded commerce and continued to be printed in large numbers. Legal Tender notes served for larger transactions, to which were added bills with the imprint of various National Banks. Bills of state-chartered banks were plentiful and were valued the same as federal paper money, but were in decline. On 1 July 1866, such bank bills became subject to a 10% tax in transac-

tions; in anticipation of this, few new bills were issued. Hundreds of state banks converted to National Banks. In any event, bills of state-chartered banks were usually rejected at places distant from where they were issued. Such currency issued by northern banks would not have been used in New Orleans.

In the South, the Confederate States of America had issued paper money since 1861, but it had depreciated greatly and was nearly worthless by early 1865. By the end of the war in April 1865, it had no value at all. In the North, gold and silver coins were plentiful in bank vaults and in the hands of exchange brokers, but not a single piece was to be found in everyday business. These coins could only be purchased by paying a premium in federal bills, but the differential had fallen sharply since its high point in July 1864.

In the West the situation remained the same: gold and silver coins were staples in commerce, while paper money was accepted only at a discount. Although New Orleans, the intended destination of the SS *Republic*, had been captured by the Confederates in 1861 and repatriated by Union troops in 1862, the monetary situation there was uncertain, even after war's end. Throughout the former territory of Confederate States of America, the South was being infused with Legal Tender and National Bank notes, but they were not widely trusted. The citizens of the Confederacy had held paper money during the war and subsequently experienced complete depreciation of their wealth; they were not inclined to trust the new paper being issued.

Accordingly, in October 1865, although federal bills could be spent to buy goods and services in New Orleans, gold and silver coins were much more desirable, even at a sharp premium. Anyone with such coins to spend had a distinct advantage in commercial transactions, and many of the passengers and businessmen aboard the SS *Republic* were intent on leveraging the value of their money in the beleaguered South.

5. Coins Aboard the SS *Republic*

Throughout this period, the gold $20 double eagle was the largest denomination of coin produced in the United States. The other gold coin in use for large transactions, but less common, was the $10 gold eagle. Gold $1 pieces were far less prevalent; although they had been minted for a long time, by 1865 they were not readily available in bulk.

For silver, the half dollar was the largest denomination in common use. Silver dollars existed, being minted in quantity from 1794 to 1803 and again beginning in 1840, but they were intended for use in international commerce and were not seen in everyday transactions. Accordingly,

Type	Metal Composition	Diam. (mm)	Weight (Grams)
British Florin, Gothic Type, 1851-87	Silver	30	11.3gr
25 Cent Sully-Gobrecht Liberty Seated, 'No Drapery', Arrows Omitted, 1856-66	Silver 90%, Copper 10%	24.3	6.22 (+/- 0.065 gr)
Reich's Silver Half Dollar Capped Busts, Lettered Edge, 1807-36	Silver 89.24%, Copper 10.76%	32.5	approx. 13.48
Gobrecht's Silver Half Dollar Capped Busts, Reeded Edge, 1836	Silver 89.24%, Copper 10.76%	30.5	approx. 13.48
Gobrecht's Silver Half Dollar Capped Busts, Reeded Edge, 1837-39	Silver 90%, Copper 10%	29.5-31.6	approx.13.36 (+/- 0.1)
Sully-Gobrecht Silver Half Dollar Liberty Seated Design, No Motto, 1839-52	Silver 90%, Copper 10%	31.6	13.36 (+/- 0.1)
Silver Half Dollars: Arrows and Rays, 1853; Arrows, No Motto, 1854-55; & Arrows Omitted, 1856-66	Silver 90%, Copper 10%	31.6	12.44 (+/- 0.097)
Gold $10 Gobrecht Coronet Design, No Motto, 1838-66	Gold 90%, Silver not over 5%, Copper 5%	26.8	16.718 (+/- 0.016): 15.0444gr or .4837 troy oz. pure gold
Gold $20 Longacre Liberty Head Design, No Motto, 1849-66	Gold 90%, Silver not over 5%, Copper 5%	34	33.436 (+/- 0.032gr): 30.0924gr or .9675 troy oz. pure gold

Table 1. Purities, dimensions and weights of all coin types excavated from the SS Republic.

on its final voyage in 1865 the SS *Republic* carried half dollars as the main component of its cargo of silver coins, while $20 double eagles were most common among the gold coins found, along with fewer $10 gold eagles.

No doubt the passengers carried a supply of other coins as personal possessions or perhaps stored them in the purser's safe. At the time these would have most commonly included bronze and copper-nickel cents, bronze 2-cent pieces, and nickel 3-cent pieces. Anyone carrying silver coins, from 3-cent pieces (called *trimes*) upward to half dollars or dollars, or gold coins of values from $1 to $20, would have bought these especially for the trip from an exchange office or bank in New York City. Collectively, in shipwreck parlance, such coins are known as 'passenger gold'.

An example of this smaller change perhaps includes two 25-cent silver coins (90% silver, 10% copper) found on the *Republic*. Both are of the Sully-Gobrecht Liberty Seated design, without drapery and with the arrows omitted, minted in Philadelphia in 1857 and New Orleans in 1859.

Their diameters are 24.3mm and each weighs 6.22gr. The four British florins recovered from the shipwreck (Gothic Type, 1859) are of silver, with diameters of 30mm and weigh 11.3gr (Table 1).

In bulk, gold and silver coins were usually stored in one of two ways. For transactions within cities, and also for many shipments sent by sea, coins were often transported in sturdy canvas bags. Gold coins shipped in quantity aboard the SS *Republic* were secured by lead seals imprinted 'BANK OF NEW YORK' and sealed by an authorized justice before being packed. This ensured the integrity of each bag's contents. Wooden kegs furnished a more practical alternative and were the containers used for the coin shipment aboard the SS *Republic*. Although kegs were more expensive, they had the distinct advantage of allowing large quantities of coins to be easily handled at the destination by being rolled along the ground. No special handling equipment was needed, as would have been the case if wooden crates had been used. Moreover, a sealed wooden keg offered

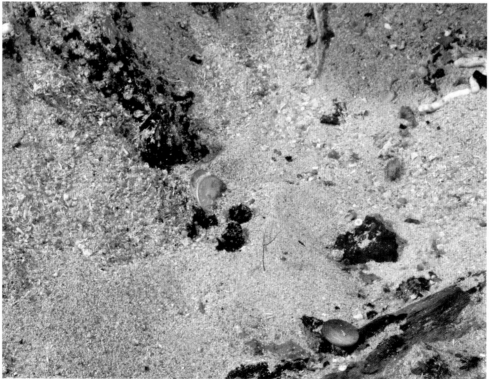

Figs. 5-6. Gold coins in situ, *starboard aft side of the wreck.*

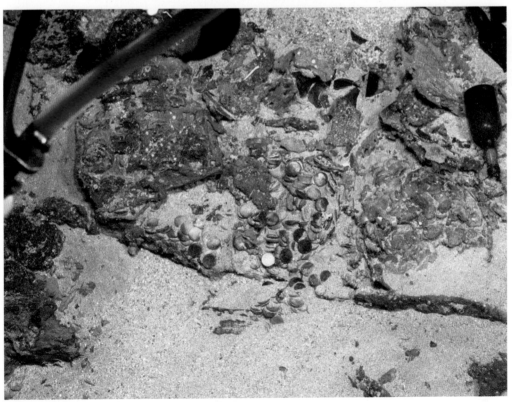

Figs. 7-8. Gold coins in situ, *starboard aft side of the wreck.*

Fig. 9. Remains of a wooden shipping keg for gold coins in situ.

Fig. 10. Gold coins stacked in situ in remains of a wooden keg.

Figs. 11-12. Gold coins (detail below) in situ *in remains of a wooden keg.*

Fig. 13. Silver coins in situ *within decomposed wooden kegs.*

Fig. 14. A concreted wooden coin keg in situ *next to the copper-sheathed rudder of the* Republic.

Figs. 15-16. Silver coins in situ (detail below) alongside glass beer bottles and glass umbrella inkstands.

Fig. 17. Silver coins in situ *in remains of a wooden keg alongside glass champagne-style bottles.*

Fig. 18. Silver coins in situ *within remains of a wooden keg.*

Fig. 19. Silver coins in situ *within a wooden keg being excavated one by one using the ROV's limpet suction device.*

Fig. 20. Silver coins in situ *within a wooden keg being excavated.*

Figs. 21-22. Concreted silver coins in a decomposed wooden keg prior to conservation.

Figs. 23-24. Concreted silver coins (and detail) prior to conservation.

better security than just a canvas bag. Surely those in charge of the *Republic* shipment had heard the many tales in circulation of small quantities of coins or other precious items on board a ship being switched or pilfered in transit, and knew that to steal and hide something as large and heavy as a keg was much more difficult. Alternatively, rectangular wooden boxes were used for some shipments of coins, but apparently not in this particular SS *Republic* voyage.

Some 90 silver coins excavated from the wreck of the *Republic* retain canvas imprints (Fig. 29), revealing that at least some of the coins were transported within bags stowed inside kegs. The relevant silver half-dollar issues identified with this feature are: 5 x 1856-O; 23 x 1858-O; 1 x 1859; 8 x 1859-O; 1 x 1860; 6 x 1860-O; 1 x 1861; 44 x 1861-O; 1 x 1862. Some 11 lead seals stamped 'BANK OF NEW YORK', used to secure and guarantee the contents of the silver coins stored inside canvas bags, were also recovered from the site. No similar canvas imprints are visible on the surfaces of the gold coins. However, they were similarly found within kegs and it is logical to presume a comparable form of transport combining canvas bags stowed inside wooden kegs.

When Odyssey Marine Exploration located the wreck of the long-lost SS *Republic*, it was hoped that significant quantities of gold coins would be found, based on newspaper reports of the loss. There was little expectation of recovering any significant quantity of silver coins. The few known collections from sunken ships carrying US coins had included gold, but hardly anything in the way of silver coins, and almost nothing in minor issues. It was thus a welcome surprise and a numismatic sensation when tens of thousands of silver half dollars were found on the *Republic* site.

The recovery of the SS *Republic* coins commenced in late 2003, at which time careful archaeological procedures were put in place to map and document the contexts of recovered items. This was done photographically, as well as using an electronic site grid. By February 2004 about 31,000 silver coins and 3,425 gold pieces had been brought up from the depths, amounting in face value to slightly less than 18% of the estimated coins lost. By late 2004 the count had reached 51,404, mostly augmented by a silver cascade of half dollars.

Analyses revealed that the gold coins consisted primarily of $20 double eagles (2,675, 5.2% of the total coins). A lesser number of $10 eagles were found (1,460, 2.8%), but no smaller denominations. The silver coins were almost exclusively in the form of half dollars (47,263, 92%). The find equated perfectly with the types of coins that would have been shipped in bulk for important transactions at New Orleans, the intended destination.

Many of the gold coins recovered were covered with grime and were discolored. Careful attention by the Numismatic Conservation Service (NCS) restored many of the pieces to their 1865 appearance, or reasonably close to it. As gold is the most inert and impervious of coinage metals, these issues were preserved to their pre-deposition condition. If anything, the surface grime served to protect the original finish, including a frosty mint luster on some of the pieces.

6. Silver Coins

The excavation of the wreck of the *Republic* yielded 42,498 legible and 4,765 illegible silver half dollars (Table 2; Figs. 27-31), easily the largest such assemblage discovered to date on any American shipwreck. In terms of chronology, this consignment breaks down into three clusters. Just 489 coins range between 1831-52 (1%), with the majority of 41,671 spanning the years 1853-61 (88.2%), with the greatest peaks in volume evident for the years 1858 (9,587) and 1861 (14,158). A sharp decline is witnessed for the period 1862-65, which is represented by just 338 issues (0.7%), of course reflecting disruptions in production and circulation during the American Civil War (1861-65). The dates of 4,765 issues (10%) are undecipherable.

The vast majority of the *Republic*'s silver coins, 39,601 (accounting for 93.2% of the total) derived from the New Orleans Mint. A further 6.4% of this consignment (2,716 coins) was minted in Philadelphia, and just 0.4% (181 issues) originated in San Francisco (Figs. 25-26).

The diameters of the silver half dollars vary from 29.5mm for John Reich's Capped Busts, Reeded Edge, 1837-39 type to 32.55mm for Reich's Half Dollar Capped Busts, Lettered Edge, 1807-36. Weights range from 12.44gr +/- 0.097gr for Arrows and Rays, 1853, Arrows, No Motto, 1854-55, and Arrows Omitted, 1856-66 to 13.48gr for Reich's Silver Half Dollar Capped Busts, Lettered Edge, 1807-36 and Gobrecht's Silver Half Dollar Capped Busts, Reeded Edge, 1836. Metal content varies from 89.24% silver and 10.76% copper between 1807-36 to 90% silver and 10% copper for the larger majority of the remaining coins (Table 1).

Although the earlier Capped Bust design coins dating back to 1832 are represented amongst the shipwreck's silver coinage (Fig. 27), the lion's share consists of Liberty Seated pieces (Figs. 28-31). This design, by talented engraver Christian Gobrecht, features Miss Liberty seated on a rock, one hand holding a shield and the other a pole surmounted by a liberty cap, a symbol of freedom. The motivation for the head of Lady Liberty derived from the enormously influential Roman Neoclassicicm of the Napoleonic era and the popular reproduction in art of the female portrait form based on Queen Agrippina in Rome's Capitoline Museum

Date	Mint	Total
1831	Philadelphia (1)	1
1833	Philadelphia (1)	1
1837	Philadelphia (3)	3
1838	Philadelphia (5)	5
1839	New Orleans (2); Philadelphia (3)	5
1840	New Orleans (5); Philadelphia (2)	7
1841	New Orleans (6)	6
1842	New Orleans (17); Philadelphia (10)	27
1843	New Orleans (34); Philadelphia (11)	45
1844	New Orleans (32); Philadelphia (1)	33
1845	New Orleans (33); Philadelphia (2)	35
1846	New Orleans (56); Philadelphia (7)	63
1847	New Orleans (64); Philadelphia (3)	67
1848	New Orleans (68); Philadelphia (1)	69
1849	New Orleans (55); Philadelphia (1)	56
1850	New Orleans (59)	59
1851	New Orleans (3)	3
1852	New Orleans (4)	4
1853	New Orleans (829); Philadelphia (403)	1,232
1854	New Orleans (3,434); Philadelphia (338)	3,772
1854/55	Philadelphia (20)	20
1855	New Orleans (1,864); Philadelphia (67) San Francisco (7)	1,938
1856	New Orleans (1,424); Philadelphia (102) San Francisco (7)	1,533
1857	New Orleans (747); Philadelphia (257) San Francisco (5)	1,009
1858	New Orleans (9,085); Philadelphia (481) San Francisco (21)	9,587
1859	New Orleans (4,502); Philadelphia (101) San Francisco (30)	4,633
1860	New Orleans (3,746); Philadelphia (31) San Francisco (12)	3,789
1861	New Orleans (13,532); Philadelphia (599) San Francisco (27)	14,158
1862	Philadelphia (137); San Francisco (48)	185
1863	Philadelphia (82); San Francisco (9)	91
1864	Philadelphia (8); San Francisco (9)	17
1865	Philadelphia (39); San Francisco (6)	45
18--	(Mint Unknown)	4,765

Table 2. Silver half dollars from the SS Republic by date and mint.

(Vermeule, 1971: 45). Thirteen stars surround her, with the date below. On certain issues of 1853 to 1855, small arrowheads are found on each side of the date (Figs. 28-29). The reverse displays a perched eagle, wings downward, holding an olive branch and three arrows, with UNITED STATES OF AMERICA around the border and the denomination noted as HALF DOL. below.

Liberty Seated half dollars, minted continuously from 1839 onward, were the design in use at the time of the ship's demise. Most were produced at the Philadelphia

Mint, but many had been produced at the branch in New Orleans and a lesser number at a facility in distant San Francisco. The branch mint coins are distinguished by a mintmark – O (for New Orleans) or S (for San Francisco) – on the reverse below the eagle. Issues from Philadelphia carry no capital letter.

The New Orleans Mint, which had opened for business in 1838, continued in operation under federal auspices until January 1861, at which time it was taken over by troops of the State of Louisiana, and later by Confederate

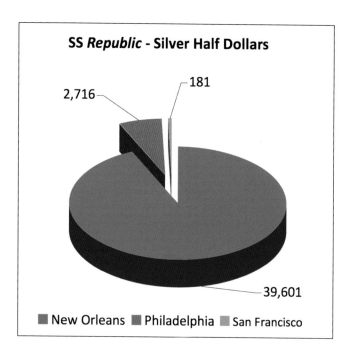

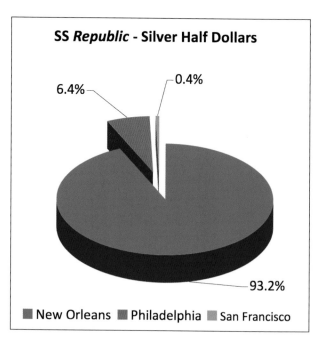

Figs. 25-26. Relative quantities and percentages of silver half dollar coins on the wreck of the Republic *according to mint locations.*

Fig. 27. Obverse and reverse of a Gobrecht Capped Bust silver half dollar of 1839, New Orleans mint.

Fig. 28. Obverse and reverse of a Liberty Seated/Arrows and Rays silver half dollar of 1853, New Orleans mint.

Fig. 29. Obverse and reverse of a Liberty Seated/Arrows and Rays silver half dollar of 1853, Philadelphia mint. Note the canvas bag imprints on the obverse.

Fig. 30. A unique silver half dollar of 1858, New Orleans mint, from the wreck of the Republic bears graffiti on the obverse announcing 'WAR' '1861', with the 'artist's' initials, EC, on the reverse.

Fig. 31. Obverse and reverse of a Liberty Seated silver half dollar of 1861, New Orleans mint. The tiny 'nose to rim' die crack on the obverse identifies this coin as struck under the Confederacy.

forces. Half dollars continued to be produced there after the mint was seized, using regular 1861-O Liberty Seated dies and the silver bullion on hand.

Early in the war, the Confederacy contemplated making its own half dollars. A.H.M. Patterson, a local engraver, was commissioned to create a distinctive reverse die, with the inscription CONFEDERATE STATES OF AMERICA. This design was to be mated with the regular Liberty Seated obverse, the latter considered still appropriate because it bore no identification to either the federal or Union government. Four of these patterns were struck.

By chance, the Liberty Seated obverse die selected to be used to create pattern strikings with the new reverse was one that had a tiny crack extending from the bridge of Miss Liberty's nose to the border at the left. This die had been used under Confederate authority to produce 1861-O half dollars with a regular UNITED STATES OF AMERICA reverse. A number of ordinary 1861-O half dollars recovered from the SS *Republic*, in exceptional Mint State condition, depict precisely such a tiny die crack at Miss Liberty's nose (Fig. 31). Here, certainly, are 1861-O half dollars that can be positively attributed to the Confederacy, silver coins minted after control was taken from the United States government.

For the 1861-O half dollars manufactured at the New Orleans mint, 330,000 were struck, first by the federal government early that year, followed by 1.24 million for the State of Louisiana, then 962,633 for the Confederacy. Many pairs of dies were used. However, as the die with the crack was used thereafter to make the distinctive Confederate A.H.M. Patterson patterns, it is believed that this die was still used by the Confederacy towards the end of the 962,633 run of the regular 1861-O.

Significantly, the silver coins from the *Republic* include over 100 examples of the first Liberty Seated half dollar struck in San Francisco – the 1855-S – considered to be a key variety in any grade. To these can be added other San Francisco coins, thousands of New Orleans issues and many Philadelphia coins. Until now, no shipwreck of the 1850s or 1860s has yielded quantities of silver coins; in comparison, only a few dozen half dollars, all extensively etched by seawater, were found on the SS *Central America* and on the SS *New York*.

7. $10 Gold Eagles from the SS *Republic*

The gold coins from the wreck of the SS *Republic* are extraordinarily significant. Virtually all the specimens proved to be in excellent condition after their conservation (Figs. 35-38), with many identified either as rarities or among the finest quality of their variety, or both.

Some 1,460 eagles ($10 gold coins) were found of all dates from 1838 onward (Table 3), from the date of the inception of the Liberty Head design, with dies created by Christian Gobrecht (cf. Vermeule, 1971: 43-7). (No $10 gold coins were made between 1804 and 1838.) The chronological spread is relatively uniform, with peaks evident for the years 1847 (345 coins; 23.6%), 1849 (175; 12%) and 1851 (132; 9%). Like the half dollars, most eagles were coined at the Philadelphia Mint (Figs. 32-33), with additional pieces struck at New Orleans (bearing an O mintmark) and San Francisco (S). A total of 934 of the issues were minted in Philadelphia (64%), 431 in New Orleans (29.5%) and 95 in San Francisco (6.5%). The issues are all 90% gold, not more than 5% silver and 5% copper, with 26.8mm diameters and weights of 16.718gr +/- 0.016gr or .4837 troy oz. pure gold (Table 1).

On the obverse of the *Republic*'s $10 gold eagles, the head of Miss Liberty faces to the right, with LIBERTY inscribed on a diadem. Surrounding are 13 stars and the date. On the reverse is seen a perched eagle, wings upward (an orientation opposite to that of the wings on half dollars), with UNITED STATES OF AMERICA around and TEN D. below.

By 1865 the largest quantity of any date of the $10 gold coin was the 1847, of which 862,258 were struck. Not surprisingly, coins of this year were the most numerous of those recovered from the SS *Republic*, with 345 conserved by NCS and graded by the Numismatic Guaranty Corporation (NGC). By contrast, just one 1841-O eagle was found, a logical reflection of its rarity, as just 2,500 were made. The roster of other remarkably rare issues for which fewer than five coins were recovered from the *Republic* site includes 1838 (4 found), 1852-O (3), 1857-O (3), 1858 (1), 1858-O (4), 1858-S (4), 1859-O (2), 1860-O (4), 1860-S (4), 1861-S (2), 1862-S (1), 1863 (1), 1863-S (3), 1864 (2), 1865 (1), and 1865-S (1).

Certain of these individual coins combine great rarity with remarkable condition. One of the most legendary rarities in the eagle series is the 1858, of which just 2,521 were struck. The single SS *Republic* specimen is one of the finest known, with most of its original mint frost still remaining. As another example, the solitary 1865-S is of the curious variety with this regular date over an inverted date. In other words, the date was first erroneously punched into the die upside down and then corrected.

Date	Mint	Total
1838	Philadelphia (4)	4
1839	Philadelphia (9)	9
1840	Philadelphia (11)	11
1841	New Orleans (1); Philadelphia (20)	21
1842	New Orleans (17); Philadelphia (17)	34
1843	New Orleans (35); Philadelphia (20)	55
1844	New Orleans (32)	32
1845	New Orleans (19); Philadelphia (2)	21
1845/46	New Orleans (13)	13
1846	New Orleans (1); Philadelphia (6)	7
1847	New Orleans (123); Philadelphia (221) San Francisco (1)	345
1848	New Orleans (9); Philadelphia (39)	48
1849	New Orleans (8); Philadelphia (167)	175
1850	New Orleans (16); Philadelphia (72)	88
1851	New Orleans (99); Philadelphia (33)	132
1852	New Orleans (3); Philadelphia (59)	62
1852/53	Philadelphia (6)	6
1853	New Orleans (13); Philadelphia (59)	72
1854	New Orleans (17); Philadelphia (22) San Francisco (41)	80
1855	New Orleans (7); Philadelphia (44)	51
1856	New Orleans (5); Philadelphia (22) San Francisco (27)	54
1857	New Orleans (3); Philadelphia (9) San Francisco (11)	23
1858	New Orleans (4); Philadelphia (1) San Francisco (4)	9
1859	New Orleans (2); Philadelphia (9)	11
1860	New Orleans (4); Philadelphia (9) San Francisco (4)	17
1861	Philadelphia (60); San Francisco (2)	62
1862	Philadelphia (9); San Francisco (1)	10
1863	Philadelphia (1); San Francisco (3)	4
1864	Philadelphia (2)	2
1865	Philadelphia (1); San Francisco (1)	2

Table 3. Gold $10 from the SS Republic by date and mint.

8. $20 Gold Double Eagles from the SS *Republic*

The $20 double eagles, first minted for circulation in 1850, of which 2,675 examples were excavated from the wreck of the *Republic* (Table 4; Figs. 41-45), were firmly established as the gold coins of dominance in banking and commercial circles. The wreck's consignment reveals a relatively even spread between 1850 and 1859, followed by a spike in volume from 1860-1865, which comprise 69.5% of the total (1,859 coins). The year 1861 accounts for 558 issues and 1865 for 573 coins – 42.3% of all double eagles recorded on the wreck. The geographic origins are very different to the ship's $10 gold coins, with 1,355 (50.6%) minted in Philadelphia, 1,248 in San Francisco (46.7%) and just 72 (2.7%) in New Orleans (Figs. 39-40). The issues are 90% gold, not more than 5% silver and 5% copper, with diameters of 34mm and weights of 33.436gr +/- 0.032gr, which equates to .9074 troy oz. pure gold (Table 1).

The $20 double eagles and other gold coins did not circulate in the East or Midwest in 1865, the year the SS *Republic* was lost, nor would they be seen in trade until

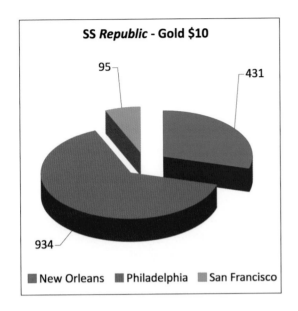

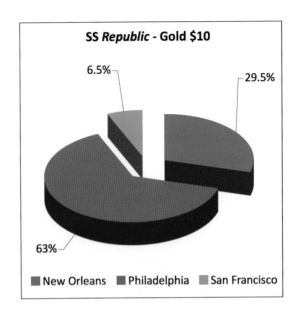

Figs. 32-33. Relative quantities and percentages of gold $10 Eagle dollar coins on the wreck of the Republic *according to mint locations.*

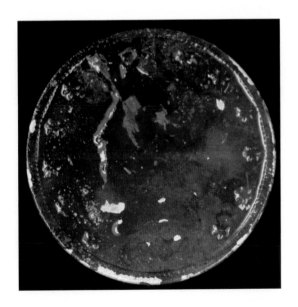

Fig. 34. Obverse and reverse of a Liberty Head gold $10 Eagle coin of 1854, New Orleans mint, before conservation.

Fig. 35. Obverse and reverse of a Liberty Head gold $10 Eagle coin of 1838, Philadelphia mint.

Fig. 36. Obverse and reverse of a Liberty Head gold $10 Eagle coin of 1846, New Orleans mint.

Fig. 37. Obverse and reverse of a Liberty Head gold $10 Eagle coin of 1859, New Orleans mint.

Fig. 38. Obverse and reverse of a Liberty Head gold $10 Eagle coin of 1865, San Francisco mint.

Date	Mint	Total
1850	New Orleans (10); Philadelphia (55)	65
1851	New Orleans (15); Philadelphia (53)	68
1852	New Orleans (20); Philadelphia (104)	124
1852/53	Philadelphia (9)	9
1853	New Orleans (7); Philadelphia (58)	65
1854	New Orleans (1); Philadelphia (42) San Francisco (9)	52
1855	New Orleans (3); Philadelphia (18) San Francisco (57)	78
1856	Philadelphia (17); San Francisco (65)	82
1857	New Orleans (4); Philadelphia (26) San Francisco (86)	116
1858	New Orleans (8); Philadelphia (9) San Francisco (68)	85
1859	New Orleans (2); Philadelphia (3) San Francisco (67)	72
1860	New Orleans (1); Philadelphia (96) San Francisco (70)	167
1861	New Orleans (1); Philadelphia (459) San Francisco (98)	558
1862	Philadelphia (9); San Francisco (127)	136
1863	Philadelphia (35); San Francisco (180)	215
1864	Philadelphia (42); San Francisco (168)	210
1865	Philadelphia (320); San Francisco (253)	573

Table 4. *Gold $20 from the SS* Republic *by date and mint.*

late December 1878. However, banks, exchange offices and the federal Sub-Treasury in New York City, as well as many companies and individuals, held such pieces as a store of value. As mentioned above, such coins were worth a premium in terms of Legal Tender notes and other paper money. No doubt most of the reported $400,000 in coins carried on board the SS *Republic* were in the form of double eagles. Destined for New Orleans, the $20 coins were expected to command attention and serve to purchase anything offered.

Similar to the situation for the $10 coins, the double eagles found on the *Republic* site, and conserved and graded by September 2004, were most numerous in those dates and mintmark varieties for which the greatest quantities had been coined. By 1865, the laurels in that category went to the 1861 Philadelphia issue, of which 2,976,519 had been struck. Reflecting this, most numerous among the treasure coins of the *Republic* were some 459 examples of the 1861.

In contrast, low-mintage varieties proved elusive, as

would be expected. Of the legendary 1854-O double eagle, of which only 3,250 were struck, just a single coin was found (Fig. 41). It is a remarkable example, however, with nearly full mint luster and quite close to Uncirculated condition. Of the many date and mintmark possibilities from 1850 to 1865, only one variety was not found, the 1856-O, of which 2,250 were made. The other New Orleans double eagles of the era range from scarce to rare and were found in lesser numbers than those of the Philadelphia and San Francisco mints.

Careful study by John Albanese and the experts at NGC revealed many interesting curiosities among double eagles (and some among eagles, as well). In the $20 series, some of the 1854 Philadelphia issues have the date in large numerals, these being scarcer than those with the date in slightly smaller digits. Of the 1855-S coins, some have a large S mintmark, while others have a small S letter, the latter being more numerous. Among those of 1860-S, 68 were found to have a small S mintmark, but just one has a large S. Mintmark differences were also found with the

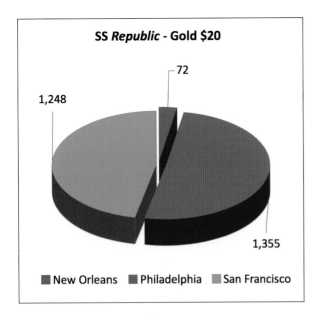
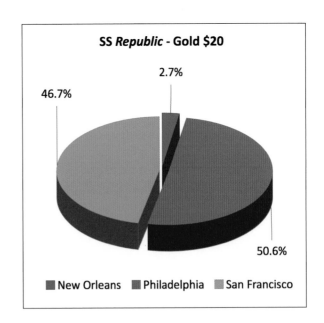

Figs. 39-40. Relative quantities and percentages of gold $20 Double Eagle coins on the wreck of the Republic *according to mint locations.*

Fig. 41. Obverse and reverse of a Liberty Head gold $20 Double Eagle coin of 1854, New Orleans mint.

*Fig. 42. Obverse and reverse of a Liberty Head
gold $20 Double Eagle coin of 1854, Philadelphia mint.*

*Fig. 43. Obverse and reverse of a Liberty Head
gold $20 Double Eagle coin of 1861, San Francisco mint.*

*Fig. 44. Obverse and reverse of a Liberty Head
gold $20 Double Eagle coin of 1865, Philadelphia mint.*

*Fig. 45. Obverse and reverse of a Liberty Head
gold $20 Double Eagle coin of 1865, San Francisco mint.*

1865-S double eagles, with slightly more than 200 having a small S, while fewer than three dozen bear a large S.

For a short time in 1861, the San Francisco Mint used a special reverse die made by engraver Anthony C. Paquet, with the words around the reverse in tall, heavy letters. Soon after, the director of the mint decreed that this style be discontinued, but not before 19,250 were struck. One of these was found on the *Republic,* in sharp contrast to 97 examples with the regular reverse style. Many of the double eagles are in Mint State (Uncirculated) grade.

9. Conclusion

The excavation of the *Republic* has yielded the largest collection of American coins, numbering 51,404, ever discovered on a shipwreck. The assemblage consists of 2,675 gold $20 double eagles, 1,460 $10 eagles and 47,263 silver issues.

En route from New York to New Orleans within four months of the end of the Civil War, the *Republic* was shipping an eclectic utilitarian cargo of glass and stoneware bottles (containing medicines, ink, foodstuffs and alcoholic beverages), writing slates, pottery wares, hardware and religious artifacts (Cunningham Dobson *et al.*, 2009; Gerth, 2006; Tolson and Gerth, 2009), all intended to re-stock the city's depleted shelves and possibly to be trans-shipped to other ports up the Mississippi River.

The coins were destined to help stimulate trade in New Orleans' re-emerging monetary economy. Prior to the war, nowhere in the nation was the banking system stronger than in the Deep South, home to the country's five cotton states: South Carolina, Georgia, Alabama, Mississippi and Louisiana. New Orleans, in particular, dubbed 'King Cotton', was America's wealthiest city by 1861 and had become a thriving banking and financial center providing credit for the city's business community and for the planters of the lower Mississippi Valley (Carter, 1985: 99). Yet by the summer of 1865 commercial banking had almost ceased to exist, the Bank of New Orleans alone representing one of the few financial institutions in the city that had managed to stave off complete collapse.

Without a cargo manifest or related historical evidence, the intended recipients of the *Republic*'s coin cargo are unlikely ever to be known. It can only be assumed that its loss 150km off the coast of Georgia, one in a series of tragedies that beset the South in the brutal war years, was a major setback for a city plagued by a scarcity of much needed capital.

Notes

1. This report is an expanded, updated and re-edited version of Q. David Bowers, 'Appendix B. Coins of the SS *Republic*' published in P.J. Vesilind, *Lost Gold of the Republic* (Shipwreck Heritage Press, 2005), 251-67.

Bibliography

Bowers, Q.D., *The Treasure Ship S.S. Brother Jonathan. Her Life and Loss* 1850-1865 (Wolfeboro, 1999).

Bowers, Q.D., *A California Gold Rush History Featuring the Treasure from the S.S. Central America* (California Gold Marketing Group, 2002).

Bowers, Q.D., *The Treasure Ship SS New York. Her Story, 1837-1846* (Wolfeboro, 2008).

Carter, D.T., *When the War Was Over. The Failure of Self-Reconstruction in the South 1865-1867* (Louisiana State University Press, 1985).

Craig, A.K. and Richards, E.J., *Spanish Treasure Bars From New World Shipwrecks, Volume One* (En Rada Publications, 2003).

Cunningham Dobson, N., Gerth, E. and Winckler, J.L., *The Shipwreck of the SS Republic (1865). Experimental Deep-Sea Archaeology. Part 1: Fieldwork & Site History* (OME Papers 5, 2009).

Evans, G.G., *Illustrated History of the United States Mint* (Philadelphia, 1886).

Fine, J.C., *Treasures of the Spanish Main: Shipwrecked Galleons in the New World* (Lyons Press, 2006).

Gerth, E., *Patent Medicines, Bitters, & Other Bottles from the Wreck of the Steamship Republic* (Shipwreck Heritage Press, 2006).

Irion, J.B. and Ball, D.A., 'The *New York* and the *Josephine*: Two Steamships of the Charles Morgan Line', *International Journal of Nautical Archaeology* 30.1 (2001), 48-56.

Mathewson, R.D., *Treasure of the Atocha* (Key Largo, 1986).

Newcomb, S., 'Were the Legal Tender Notes Necessary?' In W.J. Barber (ed.), *The Development of the National Economy. The United States from the Civil War through the 1890s* (London, 2005), 33-76.

Schwarz, T., *A History of United States Coinage* (London, 1980).

Selcer, R.F., *Civil War in America 1850 to 1875* (New York, 2006).

The United States Mint (Philadelphia, 1878).

Thompson, T., *America's Lost Treasure* (New York, 1998).

Tolson, H. and Gerth, E., *Faith of Our Fathers: Religious Artifacts from the SS Republic (1865)* (OME Papers 9, 2009).

Vermeule, C., *Numismatic Art in America. Aesthetics of the United States Coinage* (Cambridge, Massachusetts, 1971).

Wells, D.A., 'Our Burden and Our Strength'. In W.J. Barber (ed.), *The Development of the National Economy. The United States from the Civil War through the 1890s* (London, 2005), 3-32.

Young, J.R., *The United States Mint at Philadelphia* (Philadelphia, 1903).

4

Microbiological & Chemical Analysis of Bottles from the SS *Republic*

David L. Balkwill & April C. Smith
Department of Biomedical Sciences, Florida State University,
College of Medicine, Tallahassee, Florida.

Between October 2003 and November 2004, Odyssey Marine Exploration surveyed and excavated the shipwreck of the sidewheel steamer SS *Republic*, lost at a depth of approximately 500m in the Atlantic Ocean and over 150km off the southeastern coast of the United States. The *Republic* was traveling from New York to New Orleans with passengers and a composite commercial and monetary cargo when she foundered during a hurricane on 25 October 1865.

Particularly conspicuous within the diverse cargo were 8,429 glass and stoneware bottles once stored in the ship's aft and forward cargo holds (59% of all artifacts recovered from the *Republic*). These included the largest collection of medicinal 'cures', ink bottles and inkstands, food products, beauty products and alcoholic beverages found on an American shipwreck. The majority of bottles no longer contain their original contents, yet scientific analyses of a sample of bottles with intact contents has revealed bacterial and archaeal structural genes. Previously unknown phylogenies within the bacterial branch of the tree of life found in one bottle containing probable currants.

1. Introduction

In late 2005, Odyssey Marine Exploration submitted a series of organic samples to the Department of Biomedical Sciences at Florida State University's College of Medicine, Tallahassee, Florida, for scientific evaluation. The samples consisted of organic remains preserved in six bottles recovered from the wreck of the sidewheel steamship *Republic*, lost during a hurricane in 1865 at a depth of about 500m, approximately 150km off the coast of Georgia. Each glass bottle still featured its original seal and stoppers intact and/ or held residue suggestive of its original content.

The objective of the analysis of the bottles was to attempt to identify the contents and characterize the effects of low temperature, high pressure, and low light on those contents during 140 years of submersion in a deep-ocean environment. One simple question in the analysis was whether the original contents, both chemical formulations as well as preserved fruits, might have survived substantially in unchanged form from the time the ship sank.

The current report describes in scientific terms the types of bacteria found in sample bottles, indications of original contents, and an approximation of the physical processes affecting the samples within the various bottles. None of the original contents proved to be preserved intact, either due to seawater intrusion in at least two of the samples or consequent to microbial activity in the better-sealed samples.

However, the research found that in several samples, unfamiliar microbes (both bacteria and archaea) had developed. In one well-sealed container, apparently holding preserved currants (Sample E, R-03-00357-BE), most of the microorganisms present proved to be of an unknown, unidentified species, most likely even constituting new genera, families, or orders within the bacterial branch of the tree of life. Further study must confirm these results, but if they are sustained, a new group of previously undiscovered bacteria has been identified with the lost artifacts of the SS *Republic*.

2. Scientific Summary

All cells on earth are divided into two categories: prokaryotic cells and eukaryotic cells. Higher organisms are composed of eukaryotic cell types. Microorganisms, like bacteria and archaea, are prokaryotes. Hence, the tree of life as currently presented by science has three main domains: eukaryotes, bacteria, and archaea. Eukaryotes include plants, animals, fungi and protists.

This research focuses on the prokaryotes – the bacterial and archaeal domains. The eukaryotic domain in the samples presented here (mostly food items) is primarily responsible for providing a source of carbon to the bacteria and archaea present. For the purposes of following this report sample by sample, it is important to note that archaea are subdivided into three main lineages: *Crenarchaeota, Euryarchaeota* and the more newly defined *Koryarchaeota*, for which little information is currently available.

The following data were obtained using a 16S rRNA method for analysis of bacterial and archaeal structural genes (Wiesburg *et al.*, 1991). Phylogenetic trees were constructed to present a clear visual relationship between the clone sequences identified in these samples and known prokaryotic groups. Some chemical analyses were also performed for each bottle in an attempt to better characterize the prokaryotic communities in these samples, and whenever possible, their sources.

All six bottles were analyzed for the presence of both bacteria and archaea. Only two bottles were positively identified as containing archaea, while all six bottles were found to contain various types of bacterial cells. Bacteria are fairly ubiquitous and very adaptable to their surroundings. Therefore, it was expected that all samples would contain several different types of bacteria.

While some mesophilic archaea do exist, archaea are typically thought of as existing and thriving primarily in extreme environments. Cold temperatures like those surrounding the *Republic* shipwreck are considered extreme, so it was believed that archaea would be present, but not known. Although the contents of the bottles have not been scientifically confirmed, it is likely that the chemical composition of the food items (or other) present has been providing resident microorganisms with a continued energy supply for the past 140 years at the bottom of the ocean.

3. Scientific Results

1. Sample A (R-04-00245-BE; Fig. 1).

Deep brown glass bottle used for beer, lager or ale; its dark and dense glass, often referred to as 'black glass', served to strengthen the container and reduce breakage. H. 20.3cm, base diam 7.1cm, outer mouth diam. 2.7cm.[1]

Both bacteria and archaea were found in sample A. Many bacteria found in sample A were most closely related to a common marine bacterium, *Halomonas*, that is an extreme halophile (salt-loving) and often psychrophilic (cold-loving). Chemical analysis concluded that sample A contains extremely high concentrations of chloride (salinity ~87 ppt; seawater ~35 ppt), making this the perfect environment for a metabolically-versatile halophilic bacterium like *Halomonas*. A few clone sequences were found to be closely related to *Rhodospirillaceae,* which is also known to be metabolically versatile. Typically, members of this group are capable of growing photosynthetically in light and aerobically in the dark (by oxidative phosphorylation). However, other methods of growth are known, and increasing knowledge of mutants broadly expands their metabolic capabilities as well.

There were two other less well-defined bacterial groups from sample A, an unknown *Bacteroidetes* and an unknown member of the Gamma *Proteobacteria*. There are three primary *Bacteroidetes* classes, some that are known to be psychrophilic, and *Bacteroidetes* in marine waters are only second in abundance to *Proteobacteria*. During the past decade, members of *Bacteroidetes* have also been found in hypersaline environments, such as the media found in sample A. Both *Bacteroidetes* and Gamma *Proteobacteria* groups contain numerous enteric bacteria; so it was difficult to determine whether these clone sequences derive from human contamination or seawater intrusion. Because of the results from chemical analyses, it is unlikely that a great deal of seawater has intruded on sample A, although it is possible that enough seawater seeped in to allow certain adaptable bacteria to grow in this rather harsh environment.

Archaea from sample A were an extremely interesting group in that they all derived from the kingdom *Crenarchaeota* and clustered tightly together with no known close relatives. Previously, *Crenarchaeota* were known only as thermophilic microbes, meaning they are able to grow in extremely hot environments. Recently, psychrophilic *Crenarchaeota* have been identified using 16S rRNA methods, as in this study (Karr *et al.*, 2006; Murray and Grzymski, 2007; Perrault *et al.*, 2007). However, none of these microbes have been cultured to date.

2. Sample B (R-03-00432-BE; Figs. 3-4).

An aqua colored glass bottle embossed with the product name 'Phalon and Son's Chemical Hair Invigorator manufactured by New York City's Phalon & Son's Perfumery, a 19th-century firm that produced a line of toilet goods, including perfumes, hair restoratives and hair dyes. H. 17.3cm, base diam. 7.0cm, outer mouth diam. 2.8cm.

The clear liquid inside had an extremely potent smell reminiscent of a petroleum byproduct and may contain methanol, as many species from the bacterial genus *Paracoccus* are capable of using methanol as a carbon source. The only other group of bacteria in this sample was *Clostridium*, a gram-positive bacterium with versatile metabolic capabilities. This poses some confusion over the chemistry of the sample in the bottle, being that *Paracoccus* is obligatorily aerobic, while *Clostridium* is obligatorily anaerobic. Part of this sample is very oily, while the remaining liquid is more hydrophilic in nature, so it is possible that aerobic and anaerobic zones exist within the same sample. There were no archaea in sample B.

Fig. 1. A deep brown glass bottle (R-0400245-BE) intended for beer, lager or ale. H. 20.3cm.

Fig. 2. A small, barrel-shaped clear glass 'mustard barrel' jar (R-04-01417-BE). H. 12.5cm.

Fig. 3. An aqua-colored glass bottle (R-03-00432-BE) embossed with the product name Phalon & Son's Chemical Hair Invigorator. H. 17.3cm.

Fig. 4. A Phalon and Son's Chemical Hair Invigorator bottle being recovered from the wreck of the Republic using a limpet suction device.

3. Sample C (R-04-01417-BE; Fig. 2).

A squat and round, barrel-shaped clear glass jar, referred to as a mustard barrel, its distinctive shape used to store both dry and prepared mustard. H. 12.5cm, base diam. 5.1cm, outer mouth diam. 5.0cm.

When the analyses were initiated the cork was found to have fallen in on the sample. The preservative state of the jar at the time of recovery is unknown, so it is difficult to determine whether the contents of this jar are little more than marine sediment and seawater. The latter is very likely the case since the clone sequences present were primarily from the same group of common marine bacteria, *Halomonas* (as in Sample A). The only other bacterial genus present was *Idiomarina*.

Both genera are known for being halophilic, and chemical analysis determined that sample C had the second highest salinity of all six bottles (approximately 47 ppt). There were archaea present in this sample, but it should be noted that archaea can be easily found in cold marine sediments. Archaea from sample C are found primarily (all but one) in the *Euryarchaeota* kingdom, which is known for it members being extreme halophiles. If this sample once contained either dry or prepared mustard, its high salt content could account for the presence of extreme halophiles in this sample.

The three groups of archaea present included organisms distantly related to the *Picrophilus* genus, the *Methanoculleus* genus, and the same unknown group of archaea as seen in Sample A. *Picrophilus* is known for growing at extremely low pHs, while *Methanocelleus* is a methanogen known for producing methane as a byproduct while using carbon dioxide and hydrogen gas for growth. Because sample C had a pH of approximately 8.0 (near seawater), it is not likely that the clones from this sample have much in common with *Picrophilus*. However, it would not be surprising to find methanogens in this sample if the cork remained intact and all of the oxygen in the bottle had been used during the 140-year period post-dating the act of wreckage (because methanogens are strictly anaerobic microorganisms).

4. Sample D (R-03-00241-BE; Fig. 5).

A tall, aqua colored glass preserve bottle with a distinctive long cylindrical neck and rounded shoulders. Its cork is fairly intact and the bottle appears to contain a foodstuff resembling chunks of rhubarb, possibly intended as pie filling. There is a dark black precipitate in the bottle and a smell that indicates the presence of sulfide. H. 29.9cm, base diam. 7.5cm, outer mouth diam. 5.0cm.

The bacterial classes represented in this bottle include *Bacteroidetes, Spirochaetes, Clostridia,* and Delta *Proteobacteria* that are most likely of the *Desulfuromusa* genus. This grouping of microbes is very interesting because it indicates that this sample is most likely anaerobic (little to no oxygen present in the bottle). While only a few *Bacteroidetes* are known to function anaerobically, *Clostridia* obligatorily rely on anaerobic energy metabolism, and have been known to enter into co-cultures with anaerobic *Spirochaetes* during the degradation of cellulose to cellobiose (Pohlschroeder *et al.*, 1994).

It has even been reported that the presence of the *Spriochaetes* increases the depolymerization rate of cellulose by some species of *Clostridia*. Some *Spirochaetes* are also known to reduce thiosulfate and elemental sulfur to sulfide (H_2S), which may account for the dark black precipitate in this bottle. *Desulfuromusa* is also an obligate anaerobe, requiring conditions with little to no oxygen leading to a low redox potential (highly reducing environment), with the ability to reduce elemental sulfur to sulfide.

Within the class *Clostridia*, a genus with similar characteristics to the genus *Clostridia* exists – *Acetobacterium*. The difference between these two genera for the most part is their ability to form spores. Several clone sequences were closely related to *Acetobacterium bakii* with high similarity ranks, a psychrophilic acetogenic bacterium with the ability to produce acetate from H_2 and CO_2, which are often produced during respiratory reactions of other bacterial groups.

5. Sample E (R-03-00357-BE; Figs. 6, 8).

A tall, aqua colored glass bottle with a distinctive long-neck and rounded shoulders known today as a preserve bottle, containing a fruit resembling currants, possibly intended as pie filling. The cork is intact and appears fairly stable. H. 30.2cm, base diam. 7.5cm, outer mouth diam. 4.8cm.

Chemical analysis identified the liquid inside as having a pH of 4.0, which is extremely low, making the contents of the bottle highly acidic. It seems most likely that little or no seawater has infiltrated this bottle, as the pH of seawater is approximately 8.0. Salinity in this sample was approximately 30 ppt, just slightly lower than seawater. Low similarity ranks for nearly all clone sequences from this sample indicate that most of the microorganisms present are unknown, unidentified species, most likely even constituting new genera, families, or orders within the bacterial branch of the tree of life.

The majority of the clone sequences had some distant relationship to *Sulfospirillum*, which is known to be pH-tolerant, and reduces elemental sulfur to H_2S, while incompletely oxidizing an organic substrate (some form of carbon from the currants) to acetate. There was no black precipitate in the bottle and very little smell of sulfide, but this may be due to the low pH. Five clone

Fig. 5. An aqua-colored glass preserve bottle (R-0300241-BE) containing chunks of rhubarb; cork partly intact (and covered with a modern plastic cap for preservation). H. 29.9cm.

Fig. 6. An aqua-colored glass preserve bottle (R-03-00357-BE) containing fruit resembling currants, with its original cork intact (and secured with a modern plastic cap). H. 30.2cm.

Fig. 7. An aqua-colored glass preserve bottle with intact cork (R-03-00066-BE) and contents that appear to be gooseberries. H. 29.8cm.

Fig. 8. Currant bottle R-03-00357-BE being recovered from the wreck of the Republic *using a limpet suction device. A curious marine growth is attached to the mouth.*

Fig. 9. Gooseberry bottle R-03-00066-BE being recovered from the wreck of the Republic *using a limpet suction device.*

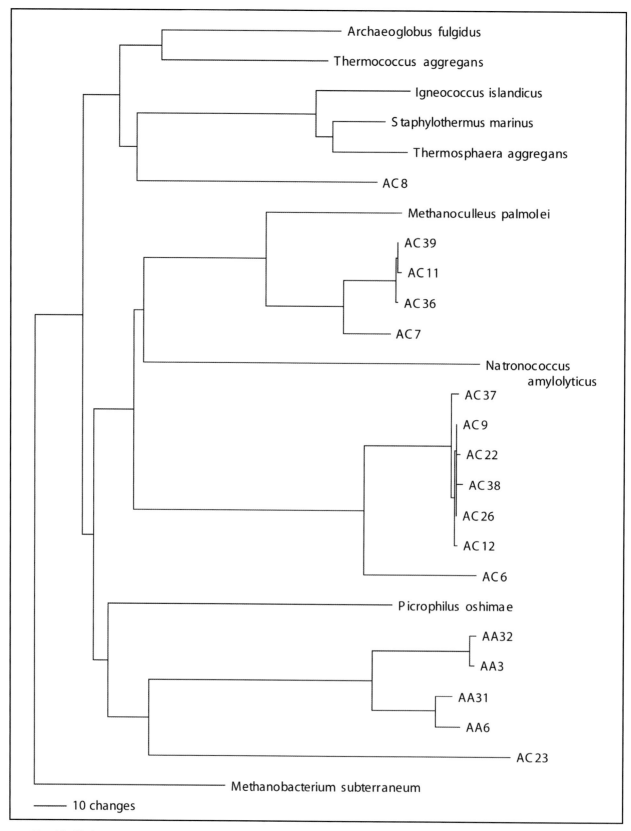

Fig. 10. Phylogenetic tree showing the relationships between archaeal clone sequences found in the six bottles described and known archaeal strains. Clone sequences are designated with two letters: A for Archaea, while the second letter is the sample bottle identification number used in this report. Letters are followed by a number representing the clone sequence for identification purposes.

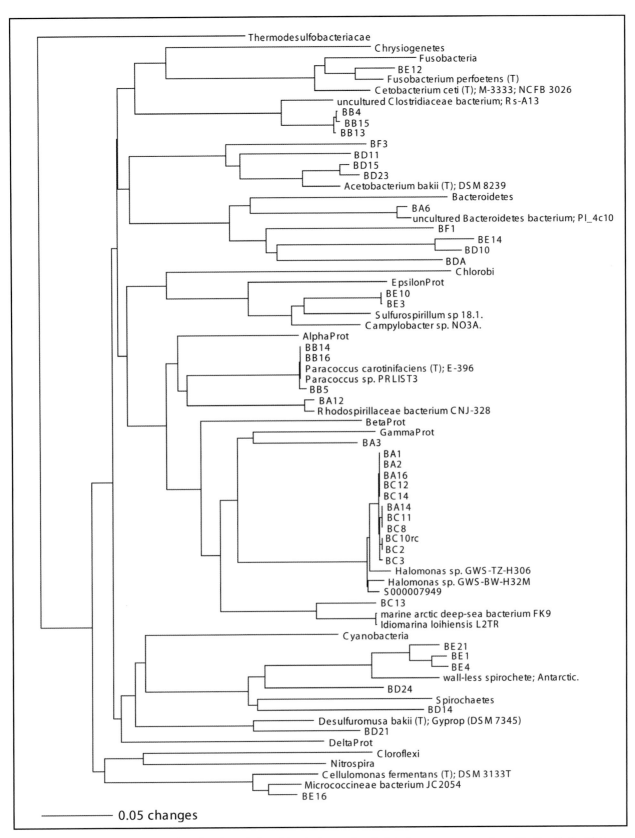

Fig. 11. Phylogenetic tree showing the relationships between bacterial clone sequences found in the six bottles and known bacterial strains. Clone sequences are designated with two letters: B for Bacteria, while the second letter is the sample bottle identification number used in this report. Letters are followed by a number representing the clone sequence for identification purposes.

sequences were located within the *Spirochaete* group, as previously discussed, and these organisms are likely reducing elemental sulfur as well at this low pH.

Two clone sequences were related to *Fusobacterium perfoetens*, which is known for being particularly sensitive to the presence of oxygen. The low pH in this sample could indicate that some fermentation of glucose has occurred by *Fusobacterium* species. All *Fusobacterium* species are parasites of humans and animals, so it is difficult to determine from where these microbes have derived. In any case, the microbial community composition within this bottle was indicative of an anaerobic environment with a moderately low redox potential.

6. Sample F (R-03-00066-BE; Figs. 7, 9).
A tall, aqua colored glass preserve bottle with a long cylindrical neck and rounded shoulders. The cork was well-secured and the bottle contained what appeared to be gooseberries, possibly intended as pie filling. H. 29.8cm, base diam. 7.4cm, outer mouth diam. 4.3cm.[2]

Clone sequences from this sample were only distantly related to currently known classifications. The highest similarity rank found was 0.6 for *Acetobacterium* (with 0 being the lowest, and 1.0 being the highest rank) indicating the possibility again for some acetogenesis to be occurring (H_2 +CO_2→acetate). There were also Spirochaete-like organisms in this sample, but the similarity ranks were so low they could not be included in this tree.

The final group identified from this sample derived from the *Bacteroidetes* group, as previously seen in samples A, D and E. Chemistry in this sample showed a slightly higher chloride content that seawater, but there is no sulfate present. Seawater is usually high in sulfate content, so it is likely that little or no seawater intrusion occurred in Sample F either.

4. Conclusion
In conclusion, at least four out of the six bottles analyzed were surprisingly well-sealed after 140 years at the bottom of the ocean, with little to no seawater intrusion. Growth temperatures of 4°C allowed for the growth of some interesting bacteria and archaea, many of which are adapted to living in extreme environments.

It is possible that some of the clone sequences retrieved from these samples are true psychrophiles (preferring cold temperatures), while others are mesophilic (preferring warmer temperatures, but not hot), yet capable of growing at colder temperatures. There was a variety of metabolic capabilities observed from these samples, but, as expected, the microbial diversity was limited due to temperature and the presence of limited electron donors/acceptors within these bottles.

Acknowledgements
We would like to thank William Landing, Professor of Chemical Oceanography in the Department of Oceanography at Florida State University, for his assistance with the chemical analysis of these samples.

Notes
1. Bottle descriptions in this report are by Ellen Gerth, and dimensions and photographs of the bottles taken on land are by Chad Morris, both of Odyssey Marine Exploration.
2. The dimensions of Sample F (R-03-00066-BE) and photographs of this gooseberry bottle are actually derived from a different, though typologically identical, bottle, R-04-02918-BE-001.

Bibliography
Karr, E.A., Ng, J.M., Belchik, S.M., Sattley, W.M., Madigan, M.T. and Achenbach, L.A., 'Biodiversity of Methanogenic and Other *Archaea* in the Permanently Frozen Lake Fryxell, Antarctica', *Applied and Environmental Microbiology* 72.2 (2006), 1663-66.

Murray, A.E. and Grzymski, J.J., 'Diversity and Genomics of Antarctic Marine Micro-Organisms', *Philosophical Transactions of the Royal Society B* 362 (2007), 2259-71.

Perreault, N.N, Andersen, D.T., Pollard, W.H., Greer, C.W. and Whyte, L.G., 'Characterization of the Prokaryotic Diversity in Cold Saline Perennial Springs of the Canadian High Arctic', *Applied and Environmental Microbiology* 73.5 (2007), 1532-43.

Pohlschroeder, M., Leschine, S. and Canale-Parola, E., 'Spirochaeta caldaria sp. nov., a Thermophilic Bacterium that Enhances Cellulose Degradation by Clostridium thermocellum', *Archives of Microbiology* 161 (1994), 17-24.

Weisburg, W.G., Barns, S.M., Pelletier, D.A. and Lane, D.J., '16S Ribosomal DNA Amplification for Phylogenetic Study', *Journal of Bacteriology* 173.2, (1991), 697-703.

Faith of Our Fathers: Religious Artifacts from the SS *Republic* (1865)

Hawk Tolson & Ellen Gerth

Odyssey Marine Exploration, Tampa, USA

Odyssey Marine Exploration's survey and excavation of the shipwreck of the steamer SS *Republic* between October 2003 and February 2005 identified the remains of a single crate transporting a consignment of approximately 96 religious objects. The contents included porcelain and glass candlesticks, and porcelain holy water fonts and figurines decorated with New Testament motifs of the crucified Jesus, the Virgin Mary and St. Joseph.

These wares are most closely comparable to products manufactured in provincial porcelain centers in France, such as Limoges and Vierzon, and by the Boston and Sandwich Glass Company in America. Of various merchants dealing in American and imported Gallic wares in the mid-1860s, the Benziger Brothers and most notably the Haviland Brothers of New York emerge as strong candidates for the objects' distribution to the South. Now in Odyssey's permanent collection, and being exhibited in traveling exhibitions, these sacred objects represent an interesting contrast to the mass utilitarian cargo stowed in the *Republic*'s hull, and speak volumes about the rise of Catholicism and piety at a time when the realities of the American Civil War were hitting home.

1. The Religious Artifacts' Wreck Context

The SS *Republic* was a sidewheel steamer traveling from New York to New Orleans with a composite commercial and monetary cargo when she foundered during a hurricane on 25 October 1865. Her wreck was discovered in 2003 by Odyssey Marine Exploration at a depth of around 500m in the Atlantic Ocean, approximately 150km off Georgia on the southeastern coast of the United States. Surveys and excavations recorded, recovered and conserved 65,818 artifacts, 51,404 of which were gold and largely silver coins (Bowers, 2009). These assemblages have produced a unique picture of daily life in post-Civil War America, unparalleled in scale and diversity from any other known wreck of a steamship (Cunningham Dobson *et al.* 2009; Cunningham Dobson and Gerth, 2009), at a time when New Orleans was still in the throes of economic depression.

During the production of a high-resolution photomosaic of the *Republic* wreck site, one discrete area defined by the presence of green and white glass and figural ceramics stood out in terms of archaeological uniqueness. The context consisted of a cluster of Christian-themed religious artifacts, completely exposed (except for a light coating of sediment) on the upper surface of the wreckage, forward of the starboard paddle wheel on an athwartships line with the remains of the base of the smoke stack (midships in the north of Area B). By its position within the geometry of the

wreck, it must originally have been stowed not far below deck against the starboard side of the hull on a line near the forward end of the engine room.

The deterioration of the wreck caused the hull to break open along the line of the keel on the starboard side, resulting in half of the hull detaching and falling outward to the north. As a consequence, the overhead vertical view of the crate context displayed in the photomosaic reveals the inboard sides of surviving cargo crates. Despite the disintegration of the original shipping container, the religious artifacts were located in a well-defined rectangular area measuring approximately 75 x 50cm. The artifact cluster was bounded on each side by intact wooden crates and a large unidentified mass of concreted iron aft. The forward end was flanked by a cluster of stoneware bottles and small wooden boxes, beyond which lay stacks of rectangular glass panes. The intact ceiling planking beneath the religious artifacts would have actually been outboard of the crate in the original orientation. Finally, the outboard edge of the artifact cluster was defined by the decayed remnants of the uppermost edge of the starboard hull consisting of degraded ceiling planking, frames, and exterior hull planking.

No trace of packing materials was visible amongst the religious artifacts, and the uppermost sides of the crate were completely disintegrated. Badly preserved wooden remnants of the lower shipping container verified that all of the artifacts had been stowed in a single crate. It is highly

Fig. 1. A consignment of glass and porcelain religious figurines and candlesticks forward of the starboard paddle wheel, and towards the bows, on the wreck of the SS Republic. Its wooden shipping crate is completely decomposed other than the edges of the base.

Fig. 2. The religious objects were stacked horizontally with alternating bases and tops/sockets to maximize space and tight packing. The context is adjoined by glass window panes set on their edges.

Fig. 3. The 75 x 50cm crate of religious objects before excavation; total depth of deposit 50cm.

Fig. 4. The religious objects in situ *alongside an unidentified iron concretion in the background.*

Artifact Type	Medium	Final Nos.
Crucifix Candlesticks	Green glass	18 Intact/ 7 Fragments – 22 Total
Crucifix Candlesticks	White glass	8 Intact/ 6 Fragments – 12 Total
St. Joseph Candlesticks	Porcelain	14
Virgin Mary & Child Candlesticks	Porcelain	13
Virgin Mary Figurines	Porcelain	4
Virgin Mary in Alcove Holy Water Fonts	Porcelain	3
Standing Angel Figurines	Porcelain	17
Kneeling Angel Figurines	Porcelain	
Standing Angel Holy Water Fonts	Porcelain	
Crucifix Holy Water Fonts	Porcelain	11

Table 1. The different forms and numbers of religious artifacts on the SS Republic.

improbable that glass and porcelain objects would have been packaged without some form of padding; the original material was almost certainly organic in nature and has disintegrated or simply been swept away by powerful bottom currents. The religious artifacts would probably have been packed in straw, similar to the stowage system utilized on the *Arabia*, a wooden river steamboat wrecked along the Missouri River on 5 September 1856 and heavily loaded with 222 tons of cargo destined for frontier merchants (Hawley, 1995: 22).

The *in situ* configuration of the religious artifacts visible on the surface of the wreck site before excavation consisted of at least three principal sub-clusters:

1. Candlesticks in the form of molded crucifixes, produced in both green and white glass.
2. Candlesticks in the form of standing human figures made of porcelain.
3. Small porcelain holy water fonts intended for hanging on a flat surface such as a wall.

Excavation revealed an even greater variety of artifacts in a total of four storage layers.

2. Recovery

Recovery of the religious artifacts was undertaken using an advanced Remotely-Operated Vehicle (ROV) nicknamed Zeus. The left manipulator arm was fitted with a rubber bellows-type device called a 'limpet', which applies suction through a connection to the ROV venturi system. This tool facilitates the delicate lifting of objects without any risk of crushing or scratching (Figs. 7-8, 10-11). The limpet can also blow a jet of water with varying force, which is useful for dusting marine sediments away from partially buried objects prior to photography or recovery without disturbing their contexts.

The religious artifacts were found in a relatively tight concentration, suggesting little post-depositional disturbance. Some 96 finds were picked up by the ROV and placed in plastic buckets for transport to a 'fourplex', a large metal lifting basket with multiple divisions for the separation of archaeological materials according to context, which was then recovered to the surface work platform (Table 1). The 96 individual religious objects recovered from the wreck of the *Republic* must be considered a minimum number. Additional objects from this context may potentially have been washed away during the natural deterioration of the wreck.[1]

3. Packing Structure

Although the religious artifacts' cluster had been subjected to natural disturbance, resulting in the disintegration of the unsupported shipping crate and causing the contents to spill downward and outward, it was still possible to discern aspects of the original packing arrangement in four layers. The depth of the context measured approximately 50cm in total.

In the upper level the figural porcelain candlesticks were stacked in rows on their sides, with their bases and candle sockets alternating in order to ensure tight packing. Adjacent to the figural candlesticks, but clearly placed separately from them, the white and green glass crucifix candlesticks were similarly set on their sides, with bases and candle sockets alternating (Figs. 2-3). At the aft end of the cluster to the east lay an extensive intrusive iron concretion (Fig. 1). Its relocation exposed additional white glass crucifix candlesticks beneath it, confirming that these artifacts were packed the length of the inboard (southern) half of the crate.

With the removal of the uppermost crucifix and figural candlesticks, a second layer of artifacts was identified. The crucifix candlesticks continued, perceivably packed in a single row running from east to west along the length of the inboard (southern) half of the crate, with the green examples to the west end and the white ones to the east. Excavations proved that the inboard half of the crate had been completely packed with crucifix candlesticks. The west quadrant of the outboard half of the crate contained flat-backed holy water fonts intended for hanging. These bear a crucifix design molded onto the surface and a basin at the bottom to serve as a reservoir. Again, they were packed in an alternating orientation with bases alternately inboard and outboard.

A third layer of religious icons – Virgin Mary figurines – commenced below the figural candlesticks. They are distinguishable from the bases of the figural candlesticks by being hollow instead of solid and by displaying a tiny hole in the centers.

With the removal of the Virgin Mary figurines and the remaining figural candlesticks, a fourth and final layer of artifacts was identified (Fig. 9). This deposit consisted of typologically mixed religious artifacts: holy water fonts in the shape of an alcove containing a standing figure of the Virgin Mary; very small fonts in the shape of a standing angel with a basin at its feet; figurines of kneeling angels on rectangular bases; kneeling angels on circular bases; and standing angels on circular bases. The angels appeared to have become intermixed with the lower figural candlesticks, mainly in the easternmost end of the crate.

After all of these artifacts were recovered, the almost completely deteriorated outer edges of the shipping crate

were exposed, alongside a scatter of white and brown porcelain buttons that had migrated downward during the excavation (Fig. 12). This juxtaposition suggests that these may also have been transported inside the crate, perhaps in a sealed envelope or carton. Further excavation at this point revealed the ceiling planking of the *Republic*'s hull. No wood from the shipping crate's base was present.

Of all of the religious artifacts encountered, only the angels and the crucifix candlesticks (and of the latter, only those from the lowest layers) displayed any damage. This took the form of candlestick sockets that had snapped along seams where separate pieces had been joined together during manufacture and at the hexagonal bases, both natural stress points. In several cases amongst the angels, the wings – another natural weak point – had broken off.

4. Catalogue & Description

The *Republic* religious objects collection can be sub-divided into three functional divisions: candlesticks, figurines, and holy water fonts. While the cruciform candlesticks are glass products, all of the other candlesticks and figurines are hard paste porcelain. Of these examples, all are glazed with the exception of two types, the standing angel and kneeling angel on a rectangular base, which are both unglazed 'bisque' wares. The latter angel type represents the only objects among the group that bear traces of paint or gilt. The others are all undecorated white wares. Within the above three divisions, the artifacts can be further catalogued into ten distinct classes, as follows:

i. Green Glass Crucifix Candlestick (Fig. 13)

22 examples, H. 24.8cm to 25.0cm. For the latter, H. of base 2.9cm, W. of base 10.3cm, H. of candle socket 4.4cm, W. of candle holder 2.2cm, W. of candle holder and rim 5.4cm.

The candlesticks were produced in two sections, a top and bottom piece inter-connected by a joining wafer. The height variation only results from the globule of molten glass used to join the upper and lower sections of the candlestick during the manufacturing process. In addition, the vertices of the hexagonal candle socket bases are not always lined up with those of the hexagonal bases. Within this product line it is recognized that "variations in height were produced by the thickness of the wafer of glass joining the parts" (McKearin and McKearin, 1948: 386).

In both the green and white glass crucifix candlesticks (see catalogue entry 2 below), the body of the object takes the form of a three-dimensional crucified and emaciated

Fig. 5. ROV Zeus excavating figural porcelain candlesticks and green and white glass crucifix candlesticks in the top layer of the crate.

Fig. 6. Alternating bases and sockets of the porcelain figural candlesticks.

Fig. 7. ROV Zeus prepares to recover a glass crucifix candlestick using its limpet suction pad.

Fig. 8. Recovering a white glass crucifix candlestick to an excavation basket using Zeus' limpet suction pad. The candlestick's reddish stain may have been caused by contact with iron materials on the seabed.

Fig. 9. Excavation of the fourth and lowest layer of the religious artifacts revealed mixed religious artifacts, including porcelain holy water fonts in the shape of an alcove containing a figure of the Virgin Mary.

Fig. 10. Recovering a porcelain Virgin Mary figurine using Zeus' limpet suction pad.

Fig. 11. A glazed porcelain kneeling angel figurine from the lowest level of the crate
being delicately recovered on Zeus' limpet suction pad.

Fig. 12. White and brown porcelain buttons in the base of the crate.

Christ, with a slanted Latin inscription reading 'INRI' set on a banner affixed to a Latin-style cross above his head, which is inclined onto the right shoulder. The Gospel According to John (19:19-20) describes Pontius Pilate writing an inscription, which read "Jesus of Nazereth, King of the Jews" in Greek, Latin and Hebrew. In Western art only the Latin version is generally depicted, abbreviated to 'INRI' (*Iesus Nazarenus Rex Iudaeorum*). The figure also wears the crown of thorns, an act of mockery inflicted by Roman soldiers on the 'king of the Jews' in a malicious and deliberately humiliating imitation of their own emperor's festive crown of roses (Ferguson, 1961: 38).

The crown of thorns became a widely venerated item after King Louis IX brought what was believed to be this relic to France in the mid-13th century. The king received the relic from Baldwin II, the Latin Emperor of Constantinople, in 1238. It was then revered in a chapel that King Louis had built. The appearance of the crown of thorns in art post-dates this historical episode (pers. comm. Father William Kuchinsky, September 2009; Hall, 2008: 85).

Jesus is modestly clad in a twisted wrap of cloth about the hips. Four nail heads are visible, one through each wrist and one through each foot.[2] The feet are laid side by side on a crude footrest attached to the cross. No wound is visible on either the left or right side of the figure. Such iconography has prevailed in Western art since this emaciated Christ form, head fallen on the shoulder, and later wearing the crown of thorns, evolved in the 11th century (Hall, 2008: 84). During the Renaissance and beyond, artists depicted the crucified Christ with his head usually tilted toward the right shoulder in keeping with John 19:30, where the Apostle explained that at the moment of death Christ bowed down his head (Ferguson, 1961: 150; Webber, 1992: 97).

ii. White Glass Crucifix Candlestick (Fig. 14)

12 examples, H. approximately 25.1cm; H. of base 2.9cm, W. of base 10.3cm, H. of candle socket 4.3cm, W. of candle holder 2.2cm, W. of candle holder and rim 5.3cm.

These objects, typologically identical to the translucent green glass crucifix candlesticks above, were crafted in an opaque white glass with a hollow, hexagonal base and top, which serves as the socket for securing the candle. The figural body of the candlestick assumes the form of the crucified Christ, with the inscription 'INRI' above the head. The body of the candlestick appears to display lines from a two-piece mold, and is joined to the candle socket (which bears no obvious mold marks) by an assymetrical globule of glass applied by hand.

iii. Porcelain St. Joseph Candlestick (Fig. 15)

Six examples of a large-sized male figure, H. 20.5cm, W. of base 7.4cm, inner diameter of handle apertures 1.2cm, H. of candle holder 4.4cm, inside W. of candle socket 2.8cm, W. of candle socket plus exterior rim 5.3cm.

Six examples of a medium-sized male figure, H. 17.4cm, W. of base 6.2cm, inner diameter of handle apertures 1.1cm, H. of candle holder 4.2cm, inside W. of candle socket 2.2cm, W. of candle socket plus exterior rim 4.5cm.

Two examples of a small-sized male figure, H. 15.4cm, W. of base 5.3cm, inner diameter of handle apertures 0.9cm, H. of candle holder 3.5cm, inside W. of candle socket 2.0cm, W. of candle socket plus exterior rim 4.1cm.

These objects made of hard paste porcelain (pers. comm. Pat Halfpenny, July 2009) are often referred to in contemporary mid-19th century literature as 'bisque' or 'biscuit ware', hollow, with a glaze, and white in color. They bear no traces of gilt or paint. The majority of the *Republic* examples display chips and cracks. The main body consists of the figure of a standing male, identified as St. Joseph, holding in the left hand what appears to be a hammer or mallet and a lily flower in the right, a symbol of chastity and one of St. Joseph's sacred attributes. The object in the left hand may alternatively represent a book, which in religious art symbolizes both learning and authorship (Ferguson, 1961: 33-4, 127; Hall, 2008: 183, 198-9). Unfortunately, the detail on these candlesticks is unclear, perhaps the result of the plaster molds in which they were cast losing definition with repeated use. Porcelain factories producing less expensive wares possibly used worn molds longer than higher-end operations (pers. comm. Robert Doares, September 2009).

The figure very probably represents 'St. Joseph the Worker', who is commonly depicted with a hammer or mallet or some other instrument of work, notably a squaring tool, saw or plane. The devotion to St. Joseph under this title apparently grew in the 19th century with the advent of the Industrial Revolution (pers. comm. Father William Kuchinsky, September 2009).

The St. Joseph figure has a moustache, a short beard and wears a long undergarment belted at the waist with a long cord. Over this he is clad in a long robe, open at the front. The feet appear to be bare. These candlesticks exhibit what seem to be join marks from a two-piece mold, although the candle socket appears to have been attached separately.

Initially depicted in paintings as an elderly man with a white beard, the devotion to St. Joseph grew stronger around the 13th century. Following the support of St.

Teresa of Avila (amongst other), the cult of St. Joseph began to blossom in the 15th and 16th centuries when he appeared in art as a younger man, though still mature (Ferguson, 1961: 33-4, 127; Hall, 2008: 183, 198-9; pers. comm. Father William Kuchinsky, September 2009).

iv. Porcelain Virgin Mary with Child Candlestick (Fig. 16)

Six examples of large-sized figure, H. 20.8cm, H. of base 1.1cm, W. of base 7.5cm, interior Diam. of handles 1.1cm, H. of candle holder 4.9cm, inside W. of candle socket 2.8cm, W. of candle socket plus exterior rim 5.4cm.

Four examples medium-sized, H. 17.6cm, H. of base 1.0cm, W. of base 6.2cm, interior Diam. of handles 1.0cm, H. of candle holder 3.9cm, inside W. of candle socket 2.2cm, W. of candle socket plus exterior rim 4.4cm.

Three examples of small size, H. 15.6cm, H. of base 1.0cm, W. of base 5.4cm, interior Diam. of handles 0.8cm, H. of candle holder 3.6cm, inside W. of candle socket 2.0cm, W. of candle socket plus exterior rim 3.9cm.

These objects, typologically identical to the St. Joseph figurines other than in the main subject matter, are of hard paste porcelain, hollow, with a glaze, and white in color. No traces of gilt or paint. Cracks are common across the body. The main body consists of the figure of a standing Virgin Mary holding the infant Christ in the crook of her left arm, the right hand apparently supporting one of the baby's feet. She is dressed in a long flowing robe that covers her head over a second garment belted at the waist. She stands on what may be a half-sphere. Possible join lines from a two-piece mold are present on the main section, and the candle socket appears to have been attached separately.

The iconography of the 'Madonna', the Virgin Mary as the mother of Jesus Christ, dates back as early as AD 431, when the Council of Ephesus encouraged the diffusion of this image as demonstrative of Mary's status as the mother figure of the Christian Church in official doctrine (Hall, 2008: 333-4). Following apparitions of the Madonna in France between the mid-late 1830s and late 1850s, her popularity in art intensified enormously (see under catalogue entry 6 below).

v. Porcelain Figurine of the Virgin Mary (Fig. 17)

Four examples, H. 20.2cm, W. 8.2 x 3.8cm, H. of base 5.0cm, W. of base 7.5cm.

These objects are of hard paste porcelain, hollow, with a glaze, and white in color. They bear no traces of gilt or paint. The figurine takes the form of the Virgin Mary standing, arms outstretched, in three examples with a crown of 12 stars or flowers, which probably represent both the Twelve Tribes of Israel and the Twelve Apostles (pers comm. Father William Kuchinksy, April 2009). The Virgin Mary wears a long, flowing robe that covers her head beneath the floral circle over another long garment belted at the waist. She stands on a half-sphere composed of a five-footed pedestal base with a depiction of the sun in the center, which was probably inspired by Sister Catherine Labouré's visions of Our Lady in Paris in 1830 in which the Virgin wore a white silk robe with arms outstretched in a stance that typcially symbolized the Immaculate Conception. Mary apparently informed Sister Labouré that the globe on which she stood "represents the whole world, and France in particular, and eveyone in it" (Perry and Echeverría, 1989: 93). Mary's face and eyes are slightly downcast and her head gently tilted to the left. There are no obvious mold lines and the base was probably attached separately.

The figure of the Virgin Mary standing alone 'in glory' symbolizes her unique status as the personification of the Mother Church. Mystical documents of the 12th and 13th centuries often referred to her as the Queen of Heaven, *Regina Coeli*. She is also the maiden of the Immaculate Conception, a popular theme from the 17th century onwards through Jesuit inspiration (Hall, 2008: 334). The term refers to Mary's conception by divine intervention and reflects a doctrine that states that in order to serve as a suitable vehicle for Christ's arrival on Earth, it was necessary for her to be sinless. Thus, she was conceived of as free of Original Sin and was predestined to beget the redemption of man from the sin of Eve. The Immaculate Conception became an article of faith in 1854 under the authority of Pope Pius IX (Ferguson, 1961: 72; Hall, 2008: 335-3).

The dozen stars above Mary's head may represent both the Twelve Tribes of Israel and the Twelve Apostles. In the *Art of Painting* of 1649, the Spanish painter and author Francisco Pacheco formalized the rules for this stylistic form, writing that the Virgin of the Immaculate Conception should be depicted "as a young woman of twelve or thirteen years, dressed in a white robe and blue cloak, her hands folded on her breast or a meeting in prayer; the moon to be a crescent (the antique symbol of chastity), horns downward; round her waist the Franciscan girdle with its three knots." This representation, occasionally with some changes, is the most recognizable artistic rendition of the subject. For the inspiration behind the popularity of the Virgin Mary in mainstream religious art, see catalogue entry 6 below.

vi. Porcelain Holy Water Font in Form of Virgin Mary in Flowered Alcove (Fig. 18)

Three examples, H. 14.7cm, H. of water font 2.4cm, W. of base 6.1cm, W. of base plus water font 5.0cm, H. of recessed alcove 10.4cm, W. of recessed alcove 6.0cm, H. of Mary figure 5.3cm, Diam. of flowers 1.7cm.

This is a holy water font, with the standing figure of the Virgin Mary in the guise of our Lady of Grace, adorned in a head scarf and with open arms. The figure stands in a flower-framed alcove surmounted by a cross. The base is hollow and there are no apparent mold join lines. The clay may have been pressed into an open mold and the base, figure and flowers attached separately.

The Virgin Mary's head is covered by a scarf or hood and she wears a flowing garment belted at the waist and what appears to be a cloak fastened at a single point on the central upper chest. She stands in a flower-framed alcove topped with a cross; four five-petalled blossoms flank the alcove, two on each side, with a single, larger four-petalled flower centered at the top of the alcove. Interestingly, the flower centers are the same for both the four- and five-petal versions, and resemble the flowers/stars that form the crown of the standing Virgin statue depicted on the Virgin Mary figurines above, suggesting manufacture by the same artist or in the same workshop. The base of the sculpture appears to be a reservoir for holy water.

From the end of the medieval period and into the early Renaissance, the Mother and Child were sometimes represented in art in a rose arbor or in front of a trellis-fence of roses forming an enclosed area. Since the earliest years of Christianity, the rose has been steeped in symbolic meaning. The red blossom represents the blood of the martyr, while the white blossom symbolizes purity, particularly that of the Virgin Mary, who is sometimes referred to as the 'rose without thorns', a result of the tradition that she was untouched by the effects of original sin. The representation of the garden finds its origin in the Song of Solomon (4:12), with the 'enclosed garden' now symbolizing Mary's virginity or Immaculate Conception (Ferguson, 1961: 37, 42; Hall, 2008: 340).

The four five-petalled blossoms on the *Republic* religious artifacts also resemble the flower of the strawberry, an emblem of perfect righteousness. When depicted in the company of other flowers and fruits, it can stand for "the good works of the righteous or the fruits of the spirit" (Ferguson, 1961: 38, 40). In keeping with this concept, the Virgin Mary has been depicted in a gown emblazoned with bunches of strawberries.

Representative of humility, violets are yet another flower associated with the Virgin Mary, who St. Bernard described as the "violet of humility". These flowers are sometimes illustrated in parallel with the strawberry to symbolize that humility is a characteristic of the truly spiritual (Ferguson, 1961: 38, 40). The most common depiction of the rose as a symbol of the Virgin is the heraldic or mystic rose (Webber, 1992: 177, 179), however, which the examples on the *Republic* artifacts most strongly resemble.

Of greater symbolic importance, however, for the interpretation of the *Republic*'s Virgin Mary holy water fonts and her form on candlesticks and as figurines is the iconographic association of the Blessed Virgin as our Our Lady of Grace and Our Lady of the Miraculous Medal. This image derived from the Marian apparitions, which took place in Paris between July and December 1830, when 24 year-old Sister Catherine Labouré, a young novice of the Daughters of Charity, perceived visions of the Blessed Mary (pers. comm. Father William Kuchinsky, August and September 2009; Lindsey, 2000: 78, 81; Perry and Echeverría, 1988: 92-3). Our Lady is said to have appeared before Catherine between these months, and on 27 November charged her with the task of striking a medal in her honor. All who wore the medal would receive grace in abundance (Lindsey, 2000: 82; Perry and Echeverría, 1988: 93).

The wearing of the medal, minted in 1832, became immensely popular and soon became known as the Miraculous Medal by virtue of the large number of cures associated with it (pers. comm. Father Kuchinsky, August 2009; Carrol, 1992: 168; Lindsey, 2000: 82; Perry and Echeverría, 1988: 94). The original title of the medal as the 'Medal of the Immaculate Conception', and its widespread popularity, are said to have paved the way for the belief in the proclamation of the Immacutate Conception, which became official Catholic dogma in 1854 (McDannell, 1995: 135).

The shrine or grotto in which the figure of the Virgin Mary stands, and its association with holy water, however, is also indicative of a symbolic connection with the Shrine of our Lady of Lourdes, which developed around the visions of the Virgin Mary that occurred in 1858 in the grotto of Massabielle near Lourdes in southern France. On 11 February of that year, a woman in white appeared before Bernadette Soubirous, a young and illiterate peasant girl who had been gathering firewood near her home in the Pyrenees mountains. At this time, and in subsequent apparitions, the lady asked for prayers, penance and the conversion of sinners. She also requested that a chapel be built on the site of the vision and that the girl wash and drink from a fountain in the grotto. No fountain existed at the time, but on 25 February when Bernadette dug at the ground designated by the apparition, a spring began to flow. The following day the first healing miracle occurred when a quarryman with an injured right eye regained his sight after bathing in the muddy spring water. Following her initial vision in February until 16 July 1858, the young girl had 17 spiritual visitations (McDannell, 1995: 133-4).

Only on 25 March, during the sixteenth apparition, did the Blessed Virgin reveal herself as the Virgin of the Immaculate Conception (McDannell, 1995: 134; pers. comm. Father William Kuchinsky, August 2009). Mary appeared standing with her hands held out and palms open towards the ground, in a pose captured in the image depicted on the Miraculous Medal and also consistent with the portrayal of the small figurine housed in the shrine of Lourdes (Carroll, 1992: 163). The image of Mary on the Miraculous Medal pre-dated and perhaps – as has been argued in some instances – inspired Bernadette Soubirous' apparitions at Lourdes (Carroll, 1992: 168). The generic flowers adorning the *Republic* religious artifacts' small porcelain shrine or grotto may be symbolic of the rose bush above which Our Lady stood when she presented herself as the Immaculate Conception.

While Bernadette's visions stopped as quickly as they had begun, an increasing number of pilgrims traveled to Lourdes to visit the young girl and the site of her apparitions. By 1862, Church authorities deemed the visions worthy of the concern of the faithul and sanctioned the cult of the Immaculate Conception at the Lourdes grotto (McDannell, 1995: 134-5). Further, while the purity of the Virgin had a long tradition in Western Christianity, the 'official' Catholic dogma that Mary was conceived without stain of original sin, was still relatively new, having been promulgated in the modern era just four years prior in 1854. Hence, the vision of our Lady of Lourdes in 1858 helped to popularize this new Catholic doctrine (McDannell, 1998: 135). In fact, as early as October 1858, less than two months after news of the apparition had widely circulated throughout France, Catholic papers in both New Orleans and New York published accounts of the events at Lourdes, which became the most important apparition site of the 19th century (McGreevy, 2003: 27-28).

Significantly, Our Lady of Lourdes is typically depicted in art with her hands before her in prayer at chest level, most probably portraying the moment she revealed herself to Bernadette. With her arms down she is recorded as having raised her eyes to heaven, folding her hands over her breast and saying "I am the Immaculate Conception" (pers. comm. Father William Kuchinsky, September 2009). Yet in the *Republic* holy water fonts her arms are held wide open, possibly signifying that this artistic style represents

an early form of expressing the apparitions at Lourdes. More probably, however, the *Republic* style portrays the earlier apparition of Our Lady of Grace experienced by St. Catherine Labouré in 1830. Yet, in this context the Virgin Mary is depicted in a decorative grotto associated with holy water, a setting which is suggestive of the famous events that occurred decades later at Lourdes.

vii. Unglazed Porcelain Standing Adoring Angel Figurine (Fig. 19)

Two examples examined, H. 10.7cm, H. of base 1.6cm, W. of base 4.1cm.

The angel, of indeterminate sex, stands on a circular base, left foot bent and hands clasped at the level of the chin and with wings outstretched. It wears a short tunic with a sash around the waist and is barefoot. In artifact R-04-01737-CR one hand is broken off, a wing is chipped and the ceramic body cracked.

The eroded base of standing angel R-04-01737-CR is decorated with what appears to be a person lying on his or her right side, knees slightly drawn up. Alongside is what seems to be a fish. If correct, the fish has obvious meaning as a major symbol of the Christian Church.

An amorphous mass of material extends from the top of the base behind the legs of the angel and up to the lower hem of the tunic: its main purpose was evidently to reinforce the figurine at a weak cast point. The method of manufacture is unclear, although it was probably cast in several pieces. Molding in pieces, whether tableware (i.e. handles of cups) or figural objects, is a normal part of porcelain production. The separate pieces are then adhered together with liquid porcelain slip, after which any evidence of the connection is brushed away. Today, even Royal Doulton figurines, while appearing smooth and crafted of a single, continuous piece, are made by molding heads and arms separately and then attaching them to the main body – a process that is not apparent visually in the end product.

There are several practical reasons for manufacturing in separate pieces, not least the ability to stack together more efficiently in a single kiln heads, arms and wings of similar size and shape. These thinner, more fragile figurine parts are more liable to slump or crack in the kiln, so it would have been far less costly and time consuming if an unattached wing cracked during firing than if a complete figurine cracked, which have would have entailed discarding the entire piece (pers. comm. Robert Doares, September 2009). As in the case of the small kneeling angels and angel font described below, these standing angel figurines were quite possibly designed as tokens or prizes for young Catholic students who performed their lessons well. This practice was customary in 19th-century Catholic schools and plausibly evolved from an earlier tradition (pers. comm. Barbara Perry, September 2009).

viii. Unglazed Porcelain Kneeling Adoring Angel Figurine (Fig. 20)

Five examples examined, H. 6.2cm, H. of base 1.1cm, W. of base 3.2cm.

On four examples an angel of indeterminate sex kneels on a rectangular base that stylistically appears to represent a pillow or cushion. The angel's hands are clasped together next to the lips, with wings outstretched, but to a lesser extent than the standing angels. The angel rests on both knees, wearing a long robe that covers the feet. The base bears traces of what appear to be bright red and black pigment – black at the four corners and the remainder colored red on the base and overlap on bottom edge of R-04-01738-CR-001. R-04-01738-CR-003 also displays a brown spot on the top back of the wing and another on the bottom back of the drapery. R-04-01739-CR features two spots of brown/black pigment on the back of the hair. This may be the sole remnant of widespread paint, which has otherwise entirely been eroded away by the marine environment. The method of manufacture is unknown, although it was probably cast in several pieces that were later joined. Broken and chipped wings and cracked bodies are common.

One example of a second sub-type of kneeling angel, in this instance glazed, was recovered from the wreck site, reposing on an oval base. This angel has shoulder-length hair, perceptibly longer than on the other angel figurines, and so assumes a more feminine appearance. The angel is seated on both knees, wearing a long robe that leaves the soles of the feet exposed. The hands are clasped out in front of the body at chest level and the wings are tightly folded back. There are no traces of gilt or pigment.

ix. Porcelain Standing Adoring Angel in the Form of a Holy Water Font (Fig. 21)

Five examples examined, H 7.1cm, W. 2.5cm, H. of figure base 0.9cm, W. of figure base 2.4cm, H. of water font base 1.1cm, W. of water font base 1.8cm, W. of water font mouth 3.6cm.

This angel, of indeterminate sex, stands on a small, irregularly-shaped rectangular base to the front of which is attached a small water font, possibly in the shape of a shell. The hands are clasped together against the chest, with wings outstretched vertically. The angel wears a short, unbelted tunic, covered by a long robe that is open at the front. The feet are bare. No traces of gilt or pigment. The method of manufacture is unknown, although the wings and font were probably cast separately from the main body, to which they were later joined.

x. Porcelain Crucifix Holy Water Font (Fig. 22)

Six large examples examined, H. 20.9cm, H. of button base 1.1cm, H. of water font 5.3cm, W. of water font 9.0cm, exterior Diam. of suspension hole 4.5cm.

Four small examples examined, H. 18.4cm, H. of button base 1.0cm, H. of water font 4.7cm, W. of water font 7.5cm, exterior Diam. of suspension hole 3.8cm. Cracks and chips on bodies and bases of both sizes common.

These artifacts were probably intended for hanging on a wall. Each features a crucified Christ on a Cross of Lorraine with an obliquely slanted banner above the head reading 'INRI' (see above). The figure, head reclining toward the right shoulder and with a piece of cloth wrapped around the hips, is flanked by two schematic kneeling angels, each down on one knee on opposite sides of the base of the cross, with hands clasped before the face. The wings are outstretched and the figures appear to be wearing long, flowing robes. A 3.3cm (inner) diameter ring is present at the top of the piece for suspension. The back of the object is flat, with visible brush/smoothing marks on the reverse. It was probably made by pressing a sheet of clay into an open mold, then attaching the font at the bottom and the Christ figure as separate pieces.

In the above categories 7-10, the *Republic's* religious artifacts illustrate the theme of angels. The Old and New Testament 'angel' was a messenger or bringer of tidings. The 5th-century treatise *De Hierarchia Celesti* classified the various ranks of angels into nine categories or choirs. These, in turn, were grouped into three hierarchies:

A. First Hierarchy or Counsellors: Seraphim, Cherubim, Thrones. The members of this group encircle God in everlasting adoration; the Seraphim are representatives of Divine Love, the Cherubim of Divine Wisdom, and the Thrones of Divine Justice.

B. Second Hierarchy or Governors: Dominations, Virtues, Powers. These have authority over the elements and stars.

C. Third Hierarchy or Messengers: Princedoms/Principalities, Archangels, Angels. The Princedoms are the guardians of earth kingdoms, the Archangels are

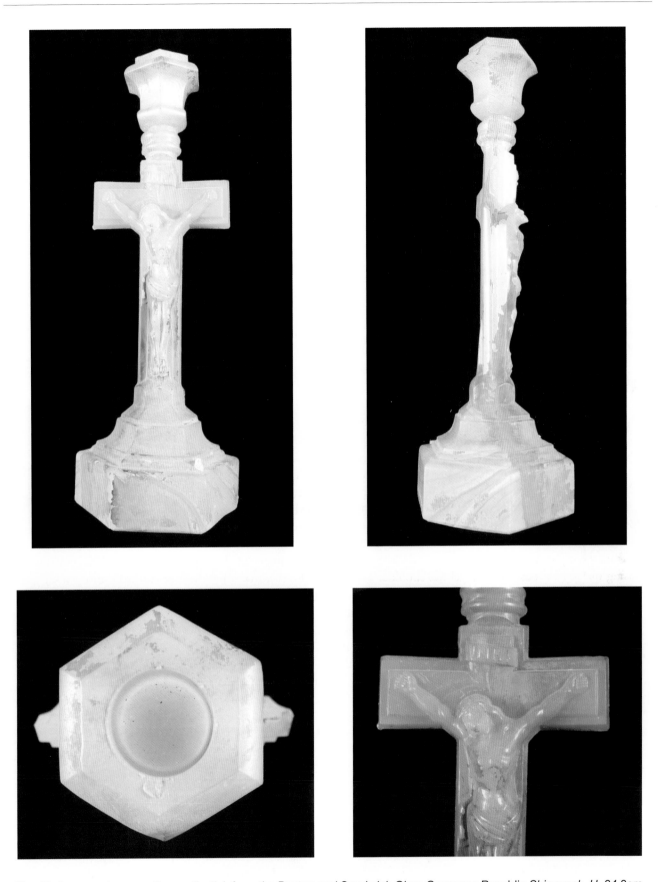

Fig. 13. A green glass crucifix candlestick from the Boston and Sandwich Glass Company; Republic Shipwreck, H. 24.8cm.

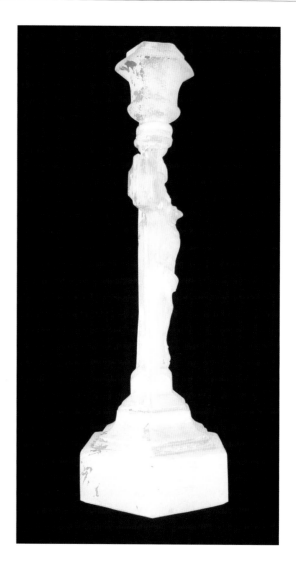

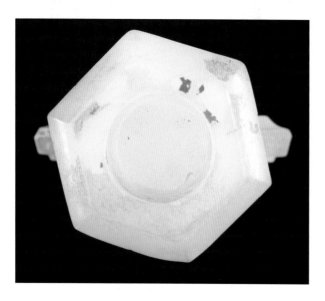

Fig. 14. A white glass crucifix candlestick from the Boston and Sandwich Glass Company; Republic Shipwreck, H. 25.1cm.

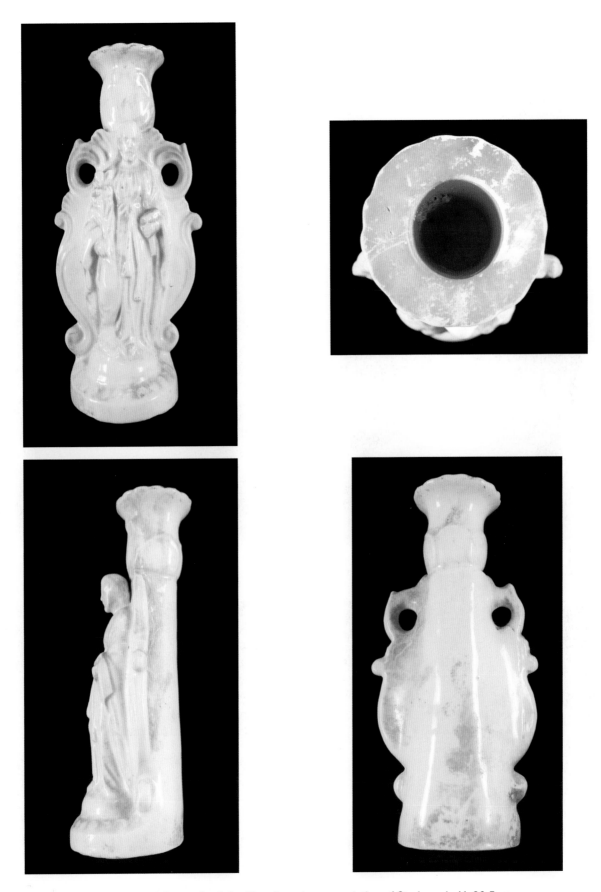

Fig. 15. A porcelain candlestick with a figural representation of St. Joseph; H. 20.5cm.

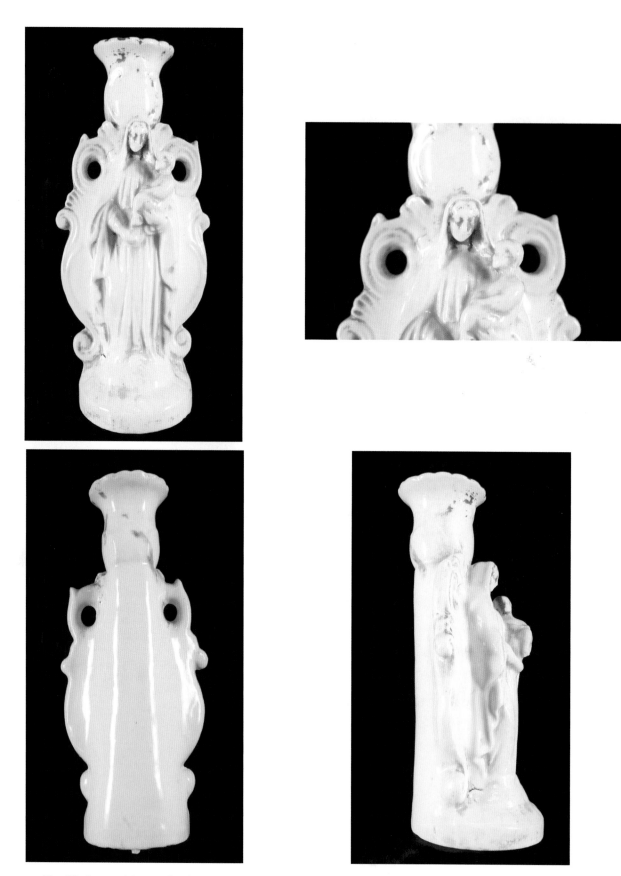

Fig. 16. A porcelain candlestick with a figural representation of the Virgin Mary with child; H. 20.8cm.

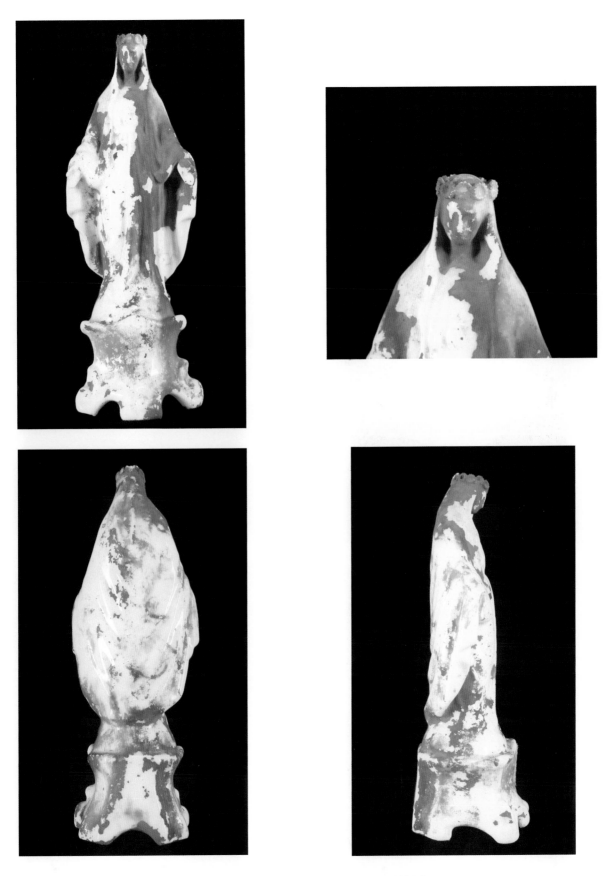

Fig. 17. A porcelain figurine of the Virgin Mary; H.20.2cm.

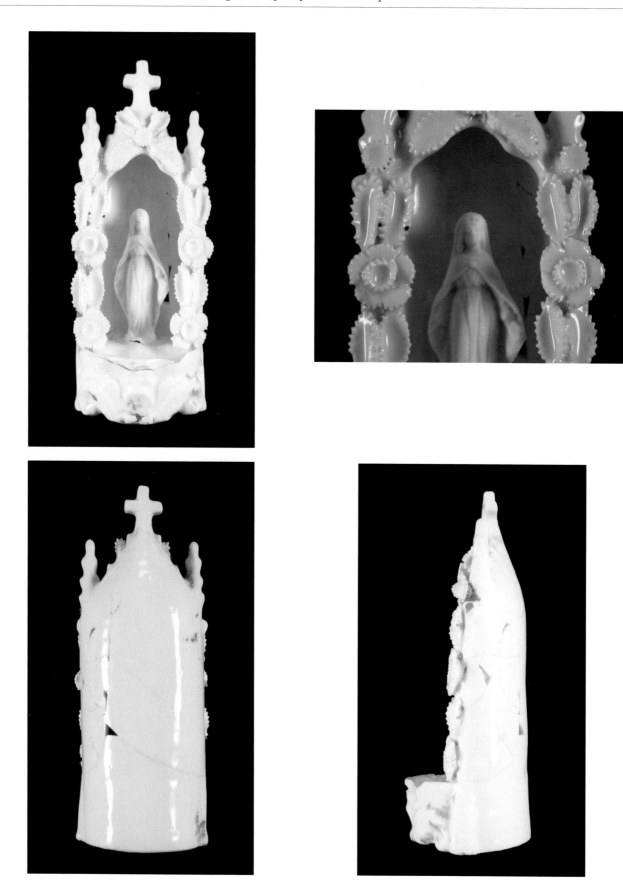

Fig. 18. A porcelain holy water font in the form of the Virgin Mary in a flowered alcove; H. 14.7cm.

Fig. 19. An unglazed porcelain standing angel figurine; H. 10.7cm.

Fig. 20. An unglazed porcelain kneeling angel figurine; H. 6.2cm.

Fig. 21. A porcelain standing angel in the form of a holy water font; H. 7.1cm.

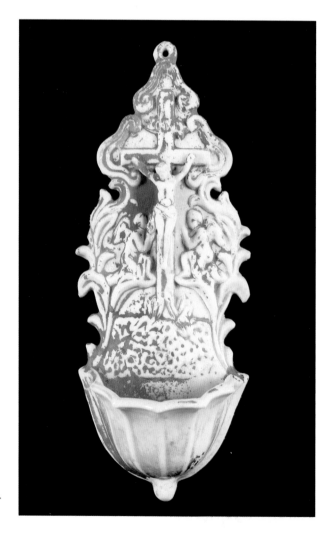

Fig. 22. A porcelain crucifix holy water font; H. 20.9cm.

heaven's warriors, and the angels are protectors of the innocent and just. Both angels and archangels are messengers of God to humans.

The angel and archangel as messengers are of greatest interest to the interpretation of the *Republic* religious artifacts. Usually shown with wings (representative of a divine mission), they are sexless, though generally appear in feminine form. In terms of age, they are adolescent or younger, usually wearing loosely draped garments (Ferguson, 1961: 46; Hall, 2008:18).

5. The *Republic* Religious Wares: Origins

Relatively modest and cheap religious goods such as those transported in the *Republic*'s crate of religious artifacts are rarely discussed in works of minor ecclesiastical art. As a consequence, determining their place of manufacture is far from simple. Opinions about the origins differ relatively widely. Consultant Jill-Karen Yakubik identified the white ceramic candlestick figurines as mass-manufactured porcelain of German or French manufacture, possibly products made by David Haviland in Limoges, France (pers. comm., January 2007). However, Christine L. Krosel, Director of Archival Research for the Catholic Diocese of Cleveland (pers. comm., January 2007), has observed that the artifacts resemble low-cost commodities sold by the Benziger Brothers, a major supplier of such objects during the 19th century who had a branch in New York City when the *Republic* took on cargo prior to its final voyage. From early on in the research, Barbara Perry, former Curator of Decorative Arts for the Mint Museum of Art, Charlotte, also suggested that the porcelains were possibly of French origin.

While a definitive origin can be proposed for the glass crucifix candlesticks, the issue of the place of manufacture and subsequent sphere of distribution of the porcelain figurines and candlesticks is far more complicated. The production of such religious objects was extremely competitive, and comparable examples were sold in America by various 19th-century dealers, many of whom were Catholic publishers and booksellers, as well as manufacturers and importers of religious articles. Among the earliest were notably P.J. Kenedy & Sons, whose Baltimore company relocated to New York City in 1838, Benziger Brothers, and Fr. Pustet and Company. Others probably also included the Haviland family, Charles Ahrenfeldt and John Vogt, all of whom focused largely on the manufacture and import of French porcelain.

Competition was fierce. In 1874, for instance, the popularity of Benziger's products resulted in the compa-

ny issuing a notice to advise customers that another firm was closely imitating its catalogue (Zalesch, 1999: 1, 25), presumably a caution against the inadvertent purchase of less impressive copies. Advertisements placed in *Sadlier's Catholic Almanac* for 1865 further reflect the widespread force of market currents in these products.

The suggestion by some ceramic scholars that these wares may actually be of Bohemian origin is unlikely. The product lines of Czechoslovakia included figurines that are patently far livelier and impressive works of art and which lacked religious themes until the early 1850s (cf. *Porcelánová Manufaktura Royal Dux Bohemia, A.S. 150 Let Ve Sluzbách Krehkosti a Krasy*, R-Studio, 2003: 6, 8, 10, 12, 18). Bohemian biscuit figurines of the Madonna with Christ and John the Baptist (from Slavkov, *c.* 1850), allegorical-themed colored biscuit statuettes of 'Fire', 'Water', 'Wind' and 'Soil' from the 'Four Elements' cycle (from Klasterec, *c.* 1856), and white glazed porcelain 'statues' of the Apostle Philip and John the Evangelist (from Loket, *c.* 1850), are all far more natural and expressive than the *Republic* figurines (Poche, 1955: pls. 30, 46-7, 92-3). Even though more commercially conscious products were designed following the cold reception of Loket's wares at the German Industrial Exhibition in Berlin in 1844, Bohemian figurines never lost their vitality inspired by early 18th-century Meissen models and life-size marble statues by Rusconi, Legros and others crafted for the Roman Basilica in the Lateran, Rome (Poche, 1955: 50-1).

The identification of the probable place of manufacture, subsequent distributors and the context of demand for the figurines on the wreck of the *Republic* reveal a specific set of religious, economic and social conditions linking Europe with the New World.

6. Glass Crucifix Candlesticks & the Boston & Sandwich Glass Company

Crucifix candlesticks such as those conspicuous in the crate on the *Republic* probably represent the single largest category of sacred-themed figural candlesticks produced in the 19th century. Just about every major American glass company offered at least one form from *c.* 1840 until the latter part of the century. Research has identified approximately 31 different varieties, very probably an incomplete sampling of the total number of manufactured forms that were produced in a variety of colors, heights and decorations (Felt, 1999: 66; pers. comm. Jane Spillman, April 2005).

The problem of attributing a given pattern to a particular manufacturer is complex. The pressed glass industry was constantly in flux, with companies opening, closing, changing locations and being absorbed. Such conglomerations frequently transferred current mold styles between member factories. In addition, blank pieces were sold to other companies for surface decoration and marketed as the decorators' own products (Edwards and Carwile, 2005: 5). Moreover, it appears that no single manufacturing concern owned exclusive rights to any given design, so imitation was rife to the degree that even plant workers were incapable of distinguishing between sources (McKearin and McKearin, 1948: 385).

Developed since the late 1820s, the pressing machine had introduced a revolution in glassware manufacture that facilitated the production of less expensive tableware to cater to an expanding market. In a brief span of time, vast quantities of pressed glass were accessible in sparkling new forms. Mass production lowered manufacturing costs and consequently retail prices, vastly expanding the market for products, especially for lamps and candlesticks (Edwards and Carwile, 2005: 4; McKearin and McKearin, 1948: 332, 377-8). During the period 1820-40, around 100 glass factories were in operation across America (Watkins, 1950: 52, 83).

The glass crucifix candlesticks from the *Republic* are clear examples of the post-1821 pressed glass manufacturing process. In essence, to produce such wares molten glass was poured into a multi-part metal mold (brass was preferred, but iron was also suitable), after which a metal piston or plunger was driven into its opening, pushing the glass into all the crevices and spaces in the mold (McKearin and McKearin, 1948: 336).

The majority of pressed glass candlesticks produced in the period spanning 1827-35, known as the 'first design group', are attributable to the Boston and Sandwich Glass Company. Candlesticks made during this period evidently required "as much hand labor as finer wares" owing to their use of "free-blown, pattern-molded, and manipulated parts" (McKearin and McKearin, 1948: 381).

During the so-called 'second period' of design (1835-60), candlestick styles became heavy and rather simple by comparison. They relied on basic patterns, but with a more widespread selection of colors. In addition, variety in design was achieved by the technique of molding the top and bottom pieces individually, then connecting them with a wafer of glass (McKearin and McKearin, 1948: 381-2). The Boston and Sandwich Glass Company was known to have pressed hexagonal candlesticks in two or three parts, which were united by such molten glass wafers (Watkins, 1950: 80, 83). Two types of pattern for the candle sockets were common, the 'petal' and the 'hexagonal', both of which had extensions forming the upper part of the candlestick shaft. Illustrations of these forms display a clear resemblance to

the sockets on the *Republic* crucifix candlesticks (McKearin and McKearin, 1948: 9, 20, 30, 37, pls. 197, 199, 200).

It is not known with certainty when molds for making pressed glass candlesticks in a single piece first developed – both the 1850s and 1860s are possible, as exemplified by New England candlesticks, whose mold marks run uninterrupted from the socket to the base (pers. comm. Dorothy Hogan-Schofield, July 2009). Whatever the truth, the *Republic* examples did not exploit this technology. Crucifix candlesticks molded in two parts, such as the *Republic* examples, have been conclusively attributed to the Boston and Sandwich Glass Company based on multicolored fragments found in excavations conducted at Sandwich, but which are undated. These candlesticks featured a fluted hexagonal socket, a hexagonal base and occurred in two sizes and a range of colors. Crucially, the smaller Crucifix candlesticks bore a narrow relief band bearing the letters 'INRI' at the top of the cross. These attributes are considered to be "exclusively Sandwich" (McKearin and McKearin, 1948: 384, 385).

The earliest American examples of crucifix candlesticks are believed to have been produced by two Massachusetts firms, the Boston and Sandwich Glass Company and its competitor, the New England Glass Company, both of which manufactured at least three similar styles between them, a fact that complicates accurate attributions. Two of the styles were widely copied by additional glass companies with only slight differences (Felt, 1999: 66-7).

However, all of the crucifix candlesticks excavated from the site of the Boston and Sandwich Glass Company exhibit a unique manufacturing feature (Barlow and Kaiser, 1983: 61): the pieces were all cast in separate two-piece iron molds, the socket and base then fused together by a glass wafer or merese at the top of the standard while the glass was still hot (pers. comm. Jane Spillman, April 2005). While the New England Glass Company pressed similar crucifixes, their candlesticks were molded in one piece as opposed to two, and the first rise of the base of the candlestick was often set higher (1.5-2.5in compared with 1.25-1.5in) than that of the Boston and Sandwich candlestick base (Barlow and Kaiser, 1983: 61).

The crucifix candlesticks recovered from the *Republic*, in both white and green glass, clearly incorporate the distinctive wafer nestled between the standard and socket, thus attributing their production definitively to the Boston and Sandwich Glass Company, which produced these candlesticks in great numbers from 1840 to 1880, typically selling them in pairs of 8-12in height (pers. comm. Jane Spillman, April 2005; pers. comm. Dorothy Hogan-Schofield, July 2009; pers. comm. Kirk Nelson, July 2009; Barlow and Kaiser, 1983: 61). Founded in 1825, the company was one of the first glass firms to utilize the press for the mass production of glass and was one of the leading manufacturers of pressed glass prior to the American Civil War (pers. comm. Dorothy Hogan-Schofield, July 2009).

It is apparent from the number of crucifix candlestick fragments excavated at the site of the former glassworks that their manufacture ranked among the top of the production line, where the many Catholics employed by the company exercised influence on the firm's products, including the manufacture of figural crucifix candlesticks (Barlow and Kaiser, 1983: 61). A strong commercial connection also existed between the Boston and Sandwich Glass Company and New York City, where since 1859 the company had a showroom and agent, Jacob J. Nichols. By at least 1877, and perhaps earlier, the showroom floor was located on Barclay Street, the center of the city's trade in religious articles and from where goods were sold to the public, as well as to glass and crockery dealers (pers. comm. Dorothy Hogan- Schofield, July 2009).

7. The Benziger Brothers

Due to the unparalleled availability of catalogues of religious objects sold by the Benizger Brothers in America, these merchants serve as a useful point of embarkation for assessing the history of the *Republic*'s religious figurines. Benziger Brothers was founded in the village of Einsiedeln, Switzerland, in 1792, when the founder, Joseph Charles Benziger, opened a small concern dealing in religious objects. The Napoleonic invasion, however, drove him from his Swiss home and wrecked his business. Upon his return in 1800 from sheltering in Feldkirch, Austria, he started business anew as a bookseller.

In 1833, Joseph was succeeded by his sons, Charles and Nicholas, in a firm christened Charles and Nicholas Benziger Brothers. Two years later they added the lithographic reproduction (including hand coloring) of religious pictures to the publishing concern. Both brothers retired in 1860, leaving the firm in the hands of their six sons, the third generation to run the company. Further initiatives under their leadership included the addition of more progressive printing techniques. The line of publications expanded to include *Alte und Neue Welt*, an illustrated German Catholic magazine, several illustrated family books of devout reading, school and prayer books, and a *Bible History* printed in an impressive 12 languages. During the period 1880 to 1895 a fourth generation of Benziger's rose to man the helm, at which point the firm's name was changed to Benziger and Company (*Benziger Brothers*, 1912: 6-7).

The year 1853 witnessed a stark expansion with a branch of the company established in New York. A second branch

Fig. 23. Daily life in the Benziger Company's 19th-century factory in New York, as represented in a contemporary brochure.

opened in Cincinnati in 1860, a third in St. Louis in 1875 and a fourth in Chicago in 1887 (*Benziger Brothers*, 1912: 7; Zalesch, 1999: 2). By 1894 the Benzigers monopolized the manufacture of most church goods sold in America at its new Brooklyn factory, where they expanded to produce large gas and electric fixtures, altar rails and pulpits. Paintings and sculptures continued to be imported, however.

In 1999, Saul Zalesch published the results of a content analysis of Benziger's American trade catalogues, seven of which have been archived at the Library of Congress. They cover the years 1873 to 1888, unfortunately post-dating the artifacts on the *Republic*. Nevertheless, they serve as an intriguing point of possible product comparison. In 1873, Benzigers produced a complete descriptive and illustrated catalogue of church goods available in America. Extensive lines of both paintings and sculpture were available; the company was evidently already well established in both markets. Zalesch (1999: 3) noted that over the period covered by the catalogues, the artistic products offered by Benziger "changed steadily, though not radically". This conservatism suggests that even though the first catalogues were printed some eight years after the *Republic* sank, they might still reflect stock available *c.* 1865.

One significant socio-cultural pattern promoted by the Benziger Company was a serious effort to provide inexpensive religious paintings by maintaining fixed low prices for the smallest sizes. This meant that even the poorest Catholics could afford to hang these images in their homes. Where figurines were concerned, a similar pricing trend is more difficult to verify. Such items were more expensive and product lines changed often (Zalesch, 1999: 4-5). In addition, the cheapest examples – the bisque or biscuit ware – were only offered in the 1874 catalogue, where they were priced in just a single general catalogue entry. Still, the prices charged for the smallest sacred figurines in the 1874 *Catalogue of Religious Articles* were nevertheless relatively low and reflect the company's desire to make them widely available even to the lowest-income homes.

The 'biscuit statues', as they are called in the catalogue (or 'bisque'), were the least expensive figurines carried by Benziger. This term is given to a clay body fired without glaze. Most potters bisque-fire at low temperature to facilitate handling and glaze at a considerably higher temperature to make the body more durable. Some artists fire the body high and low to extract brighter-colored glazes (Peterson, 2002: 141).

Three subjects dominated the Benziger product line: the Virgin Mary with the Christ child; the Immaculate Conception; and St. Joseph, each of which was available in an impressive 14 sizes (Zalesch, 1999: 5). The smallest, at 2.5in high, was priced at only 4 cents, making these sacred figures accessible to even the poorest Catholics. According to Zalesch (1999: 5), the prices of the smaller figures were "artificially inexpensive" in comparison to the larger versions, whose price increased four-fold for the 5-inch version. Another example was a 7-inch Our Lady of Lourdes figurine that sold for 46 cents, while the 8-inch version cost 84 cents.

Interestingly, the sculptural wares occupied more pages in the Benziger catalogues than any other class of goods because 'statuary' was the most common type of decoration in both churches of the Roman Catholic faith and the home chapels of more prosperous worshippers. According to Zalesch (1999: 15), "Only within the Roman Catholic community do we find less affluent people in the 1870s and 1880s with a genuine affection, even reverence, for what was essentially 'high art' statuary."

A. Sale Items from the 1874 Benziger Inventory

An examination of the 1874 Benziger catalogue, the closest in date to the *Republic*'s final voyage, reveals categories and items that possibly correspond to the religious artifacts recovered from the *Republic*, although comparisons are distinctly hampered by a lack of illustrations.

i. Holy Water Fonts

This category includes a number of listings that may correspond to the four types of holy water fonts among the *Republic*'s religious artifacts. These include the adoring angel, the 'alcove Virgin' and the two sizes of the flat, wall-hung font representing the crucifixion. The catalogue lists examples of "plain china," "pewter", "china, gilt and ornamented", "biscuit, white", "glass" and "real bronze". The *Republic* examples would most likely conform to the plain china, white biscuit or gilt and ornamented china categories (although some surface treatments may have worn off or deteriorated during prolonged immersion underwater).

The comparative examples from the catalogue include No. 31: plain china, crucifixion, large, $2.25; No. 32: plain china, crucifixion, small, $1.50. No dimensions are given in the catalogue, but two different sizes employing this motif were recovered from the wreck of the *Republic* and may explain the difference in the above pricing; No. 54: gilt and ornamented china, Blessed Virgin in Chapel, $5.70. The catalogue does not specify whether these are to be hung or are free standing, but three entries at the end of this category are described as "To stand, china, gilt, and ornamented", one of which, No. 56, is described as "Chapel" and priced at $5.70. No listing corresponds to the adoring standing angel font.

ii. "Biscuit Statues"

Zalesch (1999: 17) emphasizes that "only a few subjects were available in biscuit", which was evidently relatively rare. Interestingly, the biscuit/bisque figurine subjects presented in the Benziger catalogues include "Immaculate Conception, Virgin with child, or St. Joseph" in 14 different sizes and ranging in price from $0.04 for the smallest to $4.95 for the largest. However, the only example directly corresponding to those recovered from the *Republic* is the Virgin Mary style (possibly catalogued by the Benzigers as Immaculate Conception), which, at 8in in height, corresponds to item No. 407, priced $0.57. Four of these figurine types were recovered from the *Republic*, three with a crown of flowers or stars and one without, all of the same approximate height.

It is tempting to place the candlesticks of St. Joseph holding a lily and the Virgin Mary holding the Christ child in this category in keeping with the Benziger theme of "Immaculate Conception, Virgin with child, or St. Joseph" as its most popular biscuit offerings. However, the

Benziger 'statues' cited in its catalogue are not designed to hold candles; candlesticks are listed under a separate heading. Thus, it must be inferred that they regarded 'statues' and 'candlesticks' as two distinctly different items with different functions. And in their sizes of 6in, 7in and 8in, only item No. 407 is a direct typological match at a height of 8in. The closest parallels for the 6in and 7in figures are items No. 405 and 406 at 5.25in and 7.25in respectively, selling for $0.24 and $0.50.

B. Glass Crucifix Pattern Candlesticks

The Benziger Brothers almost certainly bought and sold glass candlesticks manufactured by the Boston and Sandwich Glass Company and their competitors. In the Benziger listings for candlesticks, there are no figural examples. Only one style, No. 104, "Glass Candlesticks, Crucifix Pattern", was available in "Plain or White Glass" at 10in or 11.5in in height and priced at $4.90 and $6.90 per dozen, respectively.

The *Republic* religious artifacts do include examples in both green and white glass of 25cm height (9¾in), which are close to the dimensions of the Benziger entry. This is the only entry in the categories corresponding to the *Republic* religious artifacts that is accompanied by an illustration. However, with their four-tiered base and molded 'INRI' inscription above the head of the Christ figure, the *Republic* examples do not match the Benziger illustration with its six-tiered base and absence of the 'INRI' placard.

C. Small Colored Benziger 'Munich Statues'

The class of goods known as 'Munich statues' in the sale items from the 1874 Benziger catalogue are believed to have undoubtedly been the original line of 'sculpture' carried by the Benziger company because they are highly visible in the pre-1879 catalogues (Zalesch, 1999: 16). The catalogues describe Munich stations of the Cross as "figures painted in natural colors", which suggests that these products were painted with flesh tones and rich colors for clothing.

This category is listed in the 1874 Benziger catalogue and includes No. 516, "Adoring Angel, kneeling", at 6in high and priced at $3.35. No. 517, "Adoring Angel, standing" is 8in and priced at $3.10. Aside from apparent iron oxide staining, the kneeling angels on rectangular bases recovered from the *Republic* appear to bear traces of red and black pigmentation on their bases. At 10.7cm (4in) and 6.2cm (2½in) in height, both the standing and kneeling angels from the wreck were much smaller than those

listed in the Benziger catalogue. This smaller category has no listing.

Since the *Republic* departed from New York, where the Benzigers had established their first American branch in 1853, it is logical to propose that the crate of religious artifacts on the ship originated in this city. While there are indeed general similarities between the *Republic* collection and the Benziger products, the evidence is far from conclusive in confirming these merchants as distributors. Nevertheless, the Benziger catalogue examined dates from 1874, nine years after the *Republic* sank, and thus may represent a change in product lines available since the time when the New Orleans order was placed.

The earliest catalogue examined by Zalesch (1999) is labeled Number 21. If accessible, a catalogue dated closer to 1865 might reveal more merchandise with closer similarities to the *Republic*. When the ship sank, Benziger's New York operation had been active for 12 years. Even if the Benzigers had a hand in the *Republic*'s shipment, however, they were merely the end cog in a far more geographically wide wheel of import and distribution. Further research points to a European source and separate probable importer and wholesaler for the *Republic*'s porcelain figurines and porcelain candlesticks.

8. The Haviland Companies & the French Porcelain Trade

The subject matter of the Virgin Mary amongst the *Republic*'s porcelain figurines and candlesticks is very probably associated with apparitions of the Virgin Mary in Paris between July and December 1830 and at Lourdes in 1858. On the back of these revelations, a vibrant trade in religious goods, known as 'L'Art Saint-Sulpice', sprung up in France, where a small neighborhood in Paris had become famous for producing and marketing some of the material culture of mid-19th century Catholicism: holy water fonts, medals, statues, crucifixes and other objects essential to the many Catholic devotees across Europe and the United States (Laderman and Léon, 2003: 427; McDannell, 1995: 168).

By 1862 over 120 Parisian firms marketed mass-produced religious goods manufactured on site or in factories outside the city for the rapid spread of religious orders promoting new devotions. These varied 'objects of religion' were largely used in church decoration and domestic worship (McDannell, 1995: 168, 170). In tandem with these events, many 19th-century provincial porcelain manufacturers maintained decorating studios, sales offices and showrooms in Paris, from where merchants could readily acquire porcelain wares for further retail (pers. comm. Robert Doares, September 2009).

Throughout the early 19th century, merchants of New York and Philadelphia had supplied French porcelain to a relatively small and select American clientele, while the bulk of their trade consisted of reasonably priced English earthenware. All this changed in the early 1840s when New York's David Haviland, an importer of British Staffordshire china, traveled to Limoges in France and started to focus on the import of French porcelain into the United States on a huge scale (Wood and Doares, 2005: 24; pers. comm. Robert Doares, July 2009). Until recently, the story of Haviland's immigration to France and his transformation of the French porcelain industry has remained largely unexplored by ceramic scholars (pers. comm. Robert Doares, September 2009).

Haviland launched his business by purchasing French wares from Charles Pillivuyt of Vierzon and various factories around Limoges, but subsequently monopolized the market by becoming a licensed manufacturer of porcelain. The foundations of his factory were built in Limoges between 1853 and 1865. After 1870 his company evolved into the largest porcelain manufactory in France (Wood and Doares, 2005: 24-25).

Pre-Civil War porcelain imports into New York clearly reflect the transformative role played by the Haviland family in the French porcelain trade as David Haviland supplied his merchant brothers in New York and their customers in the American South with Limoges porcelains, ultimately becoming the leading purveyors of these wares (Wood and Doares, 2005: 24). Customs records document that in 1841 1,400 packages of French porcelain abruptly appeared in New York, for the first time outstripping the approximately 1,250 packages of imported English china. Several members of the New York Haviland family swiftly joined this French commercial revolution over the next years. By 1853, 8,594 packages of French china were reaching New York each year, compared to an ever-declining 374 packages of English wares. Two years later the Havilands were responsible for more than 50% of French porcelain exports to New York (Doares and Wood, 2007: 8).

The center of their commercial empire was near (and after 1865 located on) Barclay Street, fittingly home to St. Peter's, the first Catholic Church in New York (pers. comm. Robert Doares, July 2009; *New York Times*, 20 August 1916). Barclay Street developed into the heart of the city's trade in religious goods (McDannel, 1995: 170; Williams, 1991: 191). From the establishment of William Higgins' Catholic publishing and religious goods business there in 1817 and the arrival of Sadliers in 1860, followed by others such as the German firm Fr. Pustat & Co in 1865, and P.J. Kenedy and Sons in 1873, Barclay Street was a nest of bustling merchants and a ready-made wholesale market

(Healey, 1951: 34-5; Laderman and Léon, 2003: 427; Mc-Dannell, 1995: 170).

In 1852, D.G. and D. Haviland were based at 47 John Street, New York. From 1854, Haviland, Petini & Co started trading French imports in Manhattan. In 1857, Underhill, Haviland & Co. operated from 22 Vesey Street, while Haviland, Merritt & Co. were at 500 Broadway in 1863, and Haviland, Merritt & Co at 30 Barclay Street by 1868 (pers. comm. Robert Doares, July 2009).

Downtown Manhattan's Barclay Street district in effect became a Catholic cultural icon through establishments' sales of mass-produced Catholic-inspired goods that would later be known as 'Barclay Street Art', a derogatory term for books, statuary and other religious objects that were considered cheap and pretentiously pious (Laderman and Léon, 2003: 247; McDannell, 1995: 170). Yet, its booming presence symbolized American Catholicism's thriving culture.

In addition to supplying numerous downtown Manhattan-based china dealerships, the Haviland family also sold wholesale to other American porcelain traders. Advertisements from the pre-war period publicized auctions of French china imported by Haviland, which was purchased by other companies and then retailed further (pers. comm. Robert Doares, July 2009; Wood and Doares, 2005: 24;). This is an extremely plausible route by which the Benziger Brothers obtained their products.

The American South, in particular, was a notable major market for the Havilands' porcelain trade prior to the Civil War. The brothers of David Haviland, who had been engaged in the importation of pharmaceuticals and chemicals before he went to France, helped him exploit their well-established business connections in Charleston, South Carolina, Augusta, Georgia and Mobile, Alabama, in the two decades before the Civil War. In fact, the Southern trade was so important to the Haviland porcelain enterprise that it went bust in 1863 after the region's vital clientele was no longer accessible during the Civil War. That year the New York offices of Haviland Brothers and Company declared bankruptcy. In 1864, however, the French concern restructured under David Haviland's son Charles Edward as Haviland and Company, which flourished into the 20th century (pers. comm. Robert Doares, July 2009; Wood and Doares, 2005: 25).

Without comprehensive records, we are unlikely to determine with certainty what porcelains the various Haviland companies were buying or manufacturing in France and from which manufacturers in the 1845-65 period, before they were in full porcelain production themselves. Yet the deeply embedded role played by the Haviland companies in the French porcelain import trade during the 1860s strongly suggests they could have certainly had a hand in the import, wholesale and/or distribution of the *Republic*'s religious porcelains (pers. comm. Robert Doares, July 2009).

Documentary sources at Limoges are devoid of references to the production of religious objects before the sale of a crucifix by Baignol at la Seynie around 1790. Only after 1832, however, did biscuit-ware 'statues' of the Virgin Mary emerge following the inspiration of her appearance at Paris and later at Lourdes. After events at Lourdes, veneration of the Virgin Mary crossed to the United States through the import and distribution of Lourdes water and the dissemination of replica grottos, which not only served as material reminders of the power and influence of Mary but became an important element in Catholic devotional life in America (McDannell, 1998: 133).

The French revolution of 1848 served a *coup de grâce* that put many porcelain factories in Limoges out of business. In this sense the Limoges imports found on the wreck of the *Republic* may relate to a school of production dating between 1849 and 1865. In this period, and up to *c.* 1900, church sculpture was manufactured in myriad small factories across Limoges, including, as a random minor sample (D'Albis and Romanet, 1980: 100, 104, 112, 117, 122, 198):

• A factory of Michel Nivet, founded April 1826 at 15 rue de Paris. Two kilns and 116 workers. Wares were unstamped.
• A Factory of Ruaad, 1829-69. In 1844 the company had two kilns and 200 workers. Wares were unstamped.
• Henri Ardant & Cie., 1858-78. 6 de la rue Cruveihier. Specialized in biscuit ware and wares marked 'HA & C'.
• The House of François Pouyat, 1837-1912. Jean Pouyat established a modest factory at La place des Carmes in 1837. By 1844, his company operated two kilns and employed 128 people. Products were marked 'JP' with an 'L' below, 'L France' or 'J. Pouyat'.

While precise attribution to regions and factories is impeded by the absence of identifying factory marks on most mid-century French porcelain, the Virgin Mary figurines from the wreck of the Republic, however, display identical stylistic traits to examples that have been attributed to Limoges, including the same five-footed base drapery and belted form (D'Albis and Romanet, 1980: 197). The sole difference is in the treatment of the heads of the Republic examples, which are tilted to the left, while those on the Limoges 'statues' look modestly downward.

While the Havilands maintained an overwhelming presence in the Limoges porcelain trade, market competition thrived, in particular with Charles Ahrenfeldt, who exploited the chaos which his competitors experienced during the Civil War years. Ahrenfeldt had established himself at Limoges as an exporter in 1859, and his operations were geared almost exclusively towards US customers. His company exported all kinds of merchandise from wine to 'bimbeloterie' and retained an extensive web of agents and correspondents in Berlin, Zurich, London, New York, San Francisco, Melbourne and Paris (D'Albis and Romanet, 1980: 164).

The commercial competition of Ahrenfeldt was apparently acute. In a letter of December 1866, Charles Edward Haviland complained of "des énormes bêtises que nous avons commises et des advantages que les autres prennent sur nous. Vogt, Charles Field [Haviland] et Ahrenfeldt prenent plus de commissions que jamais et chacun d'eux plus que nous… ils achetent tous ce qu'ils peuvent dans les fabriques" (D'Albis and Romanet, 1980: 164).[3] Haviland did not appreciate being beaten to freshly fired goods by his competitors, particularly his cousin, Charles Field Haviland, who had acquired through marriage one of the largest porcelain factories in Limoges, and by the upstart Charles Ahrenfeldt. The year the *Republic* sank was a transitional one for Charles Edward Haviland, who continued to import other factories' products while struggling to launch into full whiteware production himself.

9. Conclusion: Religion & the Great Babylon of the South

The origin of the SS *Republic*'s religious artifacts and the mechanism of their distribution to New Orleans can be reconstructed with a fair degree of probability. The figurines and candlesticks of porcelain were imported from Limoges on the back of France's status as the heartland of apparitions of the Virgin Mary. Long-distance trade enabled American customers to feel closer to the Madonna and thus ultimately to God. Very possibly shipped by members of the Haviland family, they would have been stored alongside Bibles, holy water from Lourdes and glass crucifix candlesticks manufactured by the Boston and Sandwich Glass Factory on warehouse shelves in or near Barclay Street in New York. But what was the religious and social context behind their final voyage to New Orleans?

At the simplest level, the increased demand for religious goods was stimulated by the growth in personal piety endorsed by the Catholic institutional hierarchy in conjunction with the Victorian protocol of filling the American home with material objects that nurtured Christian beliefs and doctrine. These practices evolved out of the centuries-old European Catholic tradition of the 'holy corner' set aside in private homes for personal prayer. The small size of the *Republic* religious artifacts, exemplified by the highly limited capacity of the holy water font basins, suited domestic rather than church use. Another relevant factor was the expansion of the Catholic parochial school system and its growing need for books and objects to support catechism lessons for American Catholic immigrant children (Primiano, 1991: 191).

Yet if the demand for the *Republic*'s humble crate of objects represents a microcosm of mainstream religious trends, then more profound currents of demand may be proposed, including the rise of Catholicism through Irish immigration and the impact of war. New Orleans offered a perfect market of oppressed, down-trodden and god-fearing people. Between 1820 and 1860 over 550,000 immigrants arrived in the Crescent City, the second leading port of entry in the United States during the antebellum period following New York (Niehaus, 1965: 25).[4]

By 1850 the majority of New Orleans' white population was foreign-born. Irish Catholics, in particular, comprised more than half the city's population (Miller, 1999: 29, 36). While nearly 54,000 Germans had entered the port between 1820 and 1850, with a further 126,000 arriving in the next five years, most did not linger long in the city but continued on to the Midwest cities of Ohio, Illinois, Indiana, Wisconsin and further west to California. The German immigrants that remained in New Orleans in 1860 comprised about one-tenth of the city's population. New Orleans was also home to over 10,000 largely Catholic, French-born residents who mainly left France between 1840 and 1860 during the political disturbances preceding the Second *Republic* in 1848 and the dictatorship of Louis Napoleon in 1852 (Parrillo, 2008: 87). The appetite of the French for religious wares from their homeland is obvious.

By contrast, Irish immigrants who sailed with the cotton trade via Liverpool typically remained in New Orleans primarily because their funds afforded no passage further. The majority came after 1830 and consisted mainly of peasant Catholics who arrived in the pre-famine years or escaped Ireland's devastating potato blights of the 1840s. The city retained proud links with home: two years after the Irish famine of summer 1845, the Irish Relief Committee in New Orleans solicited $50,000 for the starving back home (Niehaus, 1965: 35-6, 132).

Living conditions for new migrants were often deplorable, typified by open sewers in the streets and poor sanitation systems that contaminated drinking wells (Niehaus, 1965: 33; Parrillo, 2008: 86). The Irish were forced to compete for work with slaves and free blacks at the bottom of the food chain. Many ended up in dangerous, low-paying manual jobs such as the building of roads, levees and railroads, laboring on the docks and in the warehouses, and digging ditches and canals (Miller, 1999: 30).

Disease and death among the Irish population was rampant in a city periodically swept by malaria, cholera, and yellow fever epidemics. The mortality rate was especially high for Irish canal workers.[5] According to an 1833 report, 600 laborers died annually of 'the fever'. Other accounts estimated that seven out of 10 Irish working men succumbed to tropical disease. As the wave of immigration crested mid-century, the poor Irish arrivals were held responsible as both the importers of the scourge and as the source of the city's extended epidemics.

The spread of cholera was equally threatening to the Irish worker, peaking with 6,000 deaths during a three-week span in autumn 1832, followed by subsequent outbreaks in the succeeding antebellum decades. Nearly every Irish 'ditcher' was also exposed to malaria, easily spread by infective anopheles mosquitoes breeding in New Orleans' low-lying, swampy terrain. The virus frequently left its victim debilitated for years and in no condition to support his family (Niehaus, 1965: 31-2).

Despite the myriad difficulties encountered, as a whole the Irish survived this turbulent period and started to ascend the social and economic ladder (Niehaus, 1965: 58). By 1850, the Irish in New Orleans numbered around 25,000 people amidst an overall population of about 50,000 Catholics, and had become a dominant element in the city's Catholic Church, its most important institution. The Irish exerted a powerful voice in Church affairs and, significantly, in the Church's institutional expansion across the city (Miller, 1999: 37; Niehaus, 1965: 98, 110).

Around 1833 the Irish community obtained a city charter to buy land for the development of a profound new religious urban infrastructure, including orphanages, free parochial schools, hospitals, parish missions and confraternities ministering to a growing and diverse Catholic population. Devotional activities were encouraged through the dissemination of religious books, catechisms and devotional tools and aids, including holy cards, beads, statuary and other objects much like the *Republic*'s cargo of religious-themed porcelain figurines and candlesticks (Miller, 1999: 32, 37; Niehaus, 1965: 98, 110-11). As the largest and most visible Catholic group, Irish Catholics increasingly defined American Catholicism by the mid-1850s.

Juxtaposed with the sacred Catholicism was the profoundly profane. The New Orleans of 1865 was a city that the faithful considered to be in desperate need of salvation. On reaching New Orleans in 1836, James Davidson, a young Virginian lawyer touring the Deep South, observed that "I am now in this great Southern Babylon – the mighty receptacle of wealth, depravity and misery." Unlike any other city in America, New Orleans tolerated prostitution as a bastion of commercial sexuality, which crossed the color line. Three months after Civil War ended in July 1865, the city leaders passed ordnance 6302 OS to establish behavioural requirements for "public prostitutes and women notoriously abandoned in lewdness" (Long, 2004: 2-4). It is not impossible that the *Republic's* crate of religious objects was intended to serve as an aid to missionary work combating the great Southern Babylon.

Even without these varied contexts, each of which could explain the demand for the *Republic's* religious objects, the widespread spiritual stirrings caused by war and death were without doubt the most significant catalyst for the growth in faith during the American Civil War. At the basest level religion provided comfort for the families of the 620,000 dead and led to changes in ideas of heaven from a rather distant and strange place to a home to which the boys would return. In the ten years following the war, 94 books on heaven were published, compared to fewer than one book a year before the war (Paludan, 1998: 30-1).

When it became clear that the hostilities would not be brief, the army was fed a steady print diet of evangelical sermons as explanations of the Confederate cause. In 1863 the Church published five new papers: *The Soldier's Friend; Army and Navy Messenger; The Soldiers' Visitor; The Soldier's Paper*; and *the Army and Navy Herald*. As the Reverend Stiles wrote in 'Fruits of the Revival in the Army' in *The Soldier's Visitor* of September 1863:

> "The simplest way to convert a nation is to convert its army. Fire all the young men of great people with the spirit of Christianity, and now disband them and send them home to make all the laws, fill all the offices, control all the families, and inspirit all the churches of the land – and what… could prevent that whole nation from being carried over bodily to the Lord's side."

It has been argued that the Church took advantage of the psychological trauma of soldiers' daily encounters with death to proclaim the gospel of peace, happiness and hope. By December 1864 an estimated 140,000 soldiers in the Confederate army had converted to Christ (Berends, 1998: 132, 135, 137, 146). With the Catholic population in the war numbering 200,000 men, of which 145,000 were Irish, this increasingly vocal group of Americans also saw the war as a way to advance Irish nationalism by linking it with the defence of the American republic (Miller, 1998: 265, 273).

The same trauma of reality and uncertainty hit home hard, where Confederate women too found justification and consolation in God. They organized regular prayer groups in towns and villages across the South because, as a young New Orleans mother recorded, "If it was not for religion that keep me up, I would kill myself" (Faust, 1998: 251, 253).

In the absence of specific documentary evidence, the psychology underlying the commercial demand for the modest crate of religious objects shipped and lost on the SS *Republic* eludes us. However, of all cities of all ages across America, the great Southern Babylon of New Orleans perhaps needed all the divine inspiration and help it could get in the dark days at the very end of the American Civil War. Limoges in France, the Boston and Sandwich Glass Company and the Haviland brothers emerge as the most likely protagonists to have profited from this new market.

Acknowledgements

To John Oppermann and his entire research team we extend huge thanks for supporting this project with great energy and enthusiasm. We are especially indebted to Gerri Graca, Odyssey's archivist, whose exceptional resourcefulness locating essential and often obscure sources and other important references was critical to the project. A mighty thank you to Fred Van De Walle, Chief Conservator and his dedicated team, Alan Bosel and Chad Morris, who responded to our frequent queries and have set strong standards of conservation, recording, documentation and photography. The laboratory photographs and artifact dimensions in this report were produced by Chad Morris. J. Lange Winckler helped interpret the scene on the base of a standing angel figurine as a human and fish. Much appreciation to Laura Barton and her team for media support and the wonderful graphics generated. A special thank you is offered to Odyssey's designer Melissa Kronewitter.

We are privileged to have had the opportunity to correspond with an expert group of professionals who have generously contributed their invaluable time and immense knowledge to the SS *Republic* project, in particular about the glass and porcelain religious artifacts. We are grateful to the following: Jane Spillman, Curator of Glass, Corning Museum of Glass; Barbara Perry, Former Curator of Decorative Arts, the Mint Museum of Art; Reverend Father William Joseph Kuchinsky, Priest of the Catholic Diocese of Wheeling-Charleston, WV; Robert Doares, Porcelain Historian, Williamsburg, Virginia; Dorothy G. Hogan-Schofield, Curator of Collections, Sandwich Glass Museum; Pat Halfpenny, Director of Museum Collections, Winterthur Museum and Country Estate; and Kirk Nelson, Director of the New Bedford Museum of Glass.

And last, we extend a mighty thank you to Dr. Sean

Kingsley, Director of Wreck Watch International, to whom we are profoundly grateful for providing his steadfast guidance, keen insight and editorial wisdom.

Notes

1. Discrepancy exists between the number of objects recorded as recovered during the excavation of the *Republic* and catalogued post-conservation. The authors prefer to use the original numbers as viewed *in situ* and during recovery through DVD-based research.
2. Excavations in Jerusalem in 1968 discovered the bones of a crucified 24-28 year-old male in a 1st century AD burial cave, including a right heel-bone with an 11.5cm-long iron nail hammered through it (Gibson, 2009: 110). This evidence suggests that in some cases Roman soldiers seem to have used the heel bone to secure the crucified person in place and to prevent premature falling out of position.
3. Tr.: "the great mistakes which we have committed and the advantages that the others make over us. Vogt, Charles Field [Haviland] and Ahrenfeldt take more commissions than ever and each of them more than us … they buy everything that they can in the factories."
4. See: *The Cabildo, Antebellum Louisiana: Immigration* (Louisiana State Museum): http://lsm.crt.state.la.us/cabildo/cab1.htm).
5. Supra Note 4.

Bibliography

Barlow, R.E. and Kaiser, J.E., *The Glass Industry in Sandwich, Vol. 4* (Barlow-Kaiser Publishing Co., 1983).

Benziger Brothers. Catalogue of Religious Articles, Lithographs & Engravings (New York, 1874).

Benziger Brothers. Church Raiments of Our Own Manufacture, 1910 Catalogue (Reprint, St. Athanasius Press, 1910).

Benziger Brothers. Catalogue of All Catholic Books in English. "One Hundred and Twenty Years" (New York, 1912).

Berends, K.O., '"Wholesome Reading Purifies and Elevates the Man". The Religious Military Press in the Confederacy'. In R.M. Miller, H.S. Stout and C.R. Wilson (eds.), *Religion and the American Civil War* (Oxford University Press, 1998), 131-66.

Bowers, Q.D., *The SS Republic Shipwreck Excavation Project: the Coin Collection* (OME Papers 7, forthcoming 2009).

Carroll, M.P., *The Cult of the Virgin Mary: Psychological Origins* (Princeton University Press, 1992).

Cunningham Dobson, N., Gerth, E. and Winckler, J.L., *The Shipwreck of the SS Republic (1865). Experimental Deep-Sea Archaeology. Part 1: Fieldwork and Site History* (OME Papers 5, 2009).

Cunningham Dobson, N. and Gerth, E., *The Shipwreck of the SS Republic (1865). Experimental Deep-Sea Archaeology. Part 2: Cargo* (OME Papers 6, 2009).

D'Albis, J. and Romanet, C., *La Porcelaine de Limoges* (Paris, 1980).

Doares, R. and Wood, B., 'Archival Diversity and the Pursuit of Haviland Porcelain History', *American Ceramic Circle Journal* 14 (2007), 4-24.

Edwards, B. and Carwile, M., *Standard Encyclopedia of Pressed Glass 1860-1930* (Paducah, KY, 2005).

Faust, D.G., '"Without Pilot or Compass". Elite Women and Religion in the Civil War South'. In R.M. Miller, H.S. Stout and C.R. Wilson (eds.), *Religion and the American Civil War* (Oxford University Press, 1998), 250-60.

Felt, T., 'Figural Candlesticks Part 1 – Crucifixes', *Glass Collectors Digest* 12.5 (1999), 65-71.

Ferguson, G., *Signs and Symbols in Christian Art* (Oxford University Press, New York, 1961).

Gibson, S., *The Final Days of Jesus. The Archaeological Evidence* (New York, 2009).

Hall, J., *Dictionary of Subjects and Symbols in Art* (Boulder, 2008).

Hawley. D., *Treasures of the Arabia* (Kansas, 1995).

Healey, R.C., *A Catholic Book Chronicle. The Story of P.J. Kenedy & Sons 1826-1951* (New York, 1951).

Israel, F.L., *1897 Sears Roebuck Catalogue, No. 104* (New York, 1968).

Laderman, G. and Léon, L.D., *Religion and American Cultures. An Encyclopedia of Traditions, Diversity and Popular Expressions. Vol 1* (Santa Barbara, 2003).

Lindsey, D.M., *The Woman and The Dragon. Apparitions of Mary* (Louisiana, 2000).

Long, A.P., *The Great Southern Babylon. Sex, Race and Respectability in New Orleans 1865-1920* (Louisiana State University, 2004).

McDannell, C., *Material Christianity* (Yale University Press, 1995).

McGreevy, J.T., *Catholicism and American Freedom* (New York, 2003).

McKearin, G.S. and McKearin, H., *American Glass* (New York, 1948).

Miller, R.M., 'Catholic Religion, Irish Ethnicity, and the Civil War'. In R.M. Miller, H.S. Stout and C.R. Wilson (eds.), *Religion and the American Civil War* (Oxford University Press, 1998), 261-96.

Miller, R.M., 'A Church in Cultural Captivity: Some Speculations on Catholic Identity in the South'. In R. Miller and J.L. Wakelyn (eds.), *Catholics in the Old South: Essays on Church and Culture* (Mercer University Press, 1999).

Montgomery Ward & Co., *1895 Catalogue and Buyers Guide, No. 57, Spring and Summer* (New York, 1969).

Niehaus, E., *The Irish in New Orleans 1800-1860* (Louisiana State University Press, 1965).

Paludan, P.S., '*Religion and the American Civil War*'. In R.M. Miller, H.S. Stout and C.R. Wilson (eds.), *Religion and the American Civil War* (Oxford University Press, 1998), 21-40.

Parrillo, V.N., *Diversity in America* (New York, 2008).

Perry, N. and Echeverría, L., *Under the Heel of Mary* (London, 1988).

Peterson, S., *Working With Clay* (London, 2002).

Poche, E., *Bohemian Porcelain* (London, 1955).

Primiano, L.N., 'Post Modern Sites of Catholic Sacred Materiality'. In P.W. Williams (ed.), *Perspectives on American Religion and Culture: A Reader* (Massachusetts, 1991).

Selcer, R.F., *Civil War in America 1850 to 1875* (New York, 2006).

Watkins, L.W., *American Glass and Glassmaking* (London, 1950).

Webber, F.R., *Church Symbolism: An Explanation of the More Important Symbols of the Old and New Testament, the Primitive, the Mediaeval and the Modern Church* (Detroit, 1992).

Wood, B. and Doares, R., *Old Limoges: Haviland Porcelain Design and Decor, 1845-1865* (Schiffer Publishing Ltd, 2005).

Zalesch, S., 'The Religious Art of Benziger Brothers', *American Art* 13.2 (1999), 59-79.

6

The Jacksonville 'Blue China' Shipwreck & the Myth of Deep-Sea Preservation

Hawk Tolson
Odyssey Marine Exploration, Tampa, USA

A major argument in favor of preserving shipwrecks *in situ* – a modern ideal of cultural resource management promoted by some archaeologists – is the invariable conviction that deep-ocean sites located beyond 75m of water will achieve a state of relative equilibrium in the depths unaffected by wave action and other forces of nature. However, new primary data demonstrate that shipwrecks within the ecosystem of the Atlantic Ocean's Gulf Stream and other areas not only face a level of biological activity much higher than comparable depths in more nutrient-deprived waters, but are also subjected to severe damage from deep-sea trawling.

One example is a shipwreck examined by Odyssey Marine Exploration (OME) at a depth of 370m, the Jacksonville 'Blue China' wreck, which has been badly damaged by trawls, with over 75% of the ship structure and its contents destroyed and inadvertently removed from the site in recent years, with the remainder displaying strong patterns of drag disturbance. What was originally intended to serve as a preliminary survey in 2003 developed into a rescue mission in 2005. Despite the poor state of preservation, sufficient material culture was examined to identify and reconstruct elements of this mid-19th century ship. This wreck is an example of an emerging global pattern for shipwreck destabilization and destruction in deep water.

1. Introduction

In his classic work of the 1970s, Keith Muckleroy (1978: 157) defined a shipwreck as "the event by which a highly organized and dynamic assemblage of artifacts are transformed into a static and disorganized state with long-term stability." Furthermore, his model for transformation processes – both cultural and non-cultural (human and natural) – that affect a submerged shipwreck envisaged a result whereby a wreck would eventually reach a state of equilibrium and stability within the confines of its new environment, following burial beneath bottom sediments.

With no criticism intended for Muckelroy's pioneering genius, it can nonetheless be argued that his legacy has been both misunderstood and misused to justify '*in situ* preservation' as a model for underwater cultural heritage management by some. Today the term carries heavy political connotations and refers less to an environmental condition than to modern archaeologists' and cultural resource managers' ideal that everything in this abyssal 'Eden of Preservation' should be left alone because deepwater sites are 'frozen' in a secure state of equilibrium.

This belief is, according to some, set in political concrete in Article 2.5 of the UNESCO Convention on the Protection of the Underwater Cultural Heritage, which stipulates that "The preservation *in situ* of underwater cultural heritage shall be considered as the first option

before allowing or engaging in any activities directed at this heritage." Along identical lines, Article 6 of the ICOMOS Charter for the Protection and Management of the Cultural Heritage declares that "The overall objective of archaeological heritage management should be the preservation of monuments and sites *in situ*." Excavation is to be avoided in favor of non-destructive, non-intrusive survey methods (Godfrey *et al.*, 2004: 344).

The negotiations leading to the adoption of this Convention made it clear that the 'first option' consideration was originally meant to be the marine archaeological equivalent of the medical maxim to 'first do no harm'. Unfortunately, the tenet of the 'first option' has now been embraced by some resource managers and archaeologists as a preference and excuse to justify an absence of protective or preservative measures on many shipwreck sites.

The re-burial of shipwreck materials can decelerate rates of decay and, in a small number of pioneering cases, has seen short-term success in shallow water. Lacking funds and/or facilities for hull conservation, several projects have relied on this preservative option for long-term wood storage *in situ* following excavation and documentation. Thus, the hull of the 16th-century Basque whaler in Red Bay, Labrador, was excavated, dismantled, recorded and then reburied at a depth of 8-12m (Grenier, 1998: 269). Only time will tell whether this is a practical long-term solution.

Fig. 1. A beer can and plastic bag next to a heavily concreted iron anchor at 821m depth on site E-82 in the Straits of Gibraltar.

Fig. 2. Trawler fishing cable snagged on iron cannon on site E-82 in the Straits of Gibraltar.

Fig. 3. A mid to late 19th-century shipwreck in around 100m in the English Channel (site 2T3a6a-2) with fishing net rope caught on its structure. Snagging by trawler nets, scallop dredge heads, foot rope and steel cable is prevalent in the Channel and breaks off and displaces any ship's structure or cargo in its way.

This process often involves sandbagging or covering a wreck with a synthetic mesh designed to trap and hold sediment and foster the re-growth of natural flora and fauna, which theoretically helps seal and protect archaeological remains, as initiated in about 13m during stabilization trials on HMS *Colossus*, lost off the Scilly Isles in 1798 (Camidge, 2003: 12). A similar strategy of *in situ* preservation through reburial was adopted for the *Avondster*, a 4m-deep Dutch East Indiaman wrecked in 1659 on the shores of Galle Harbour, southern Sri Lanka (Manders, 2006), to deter looters and stop biological and chemical deterioration. Part of the site was covered with polypropylene nets in the hope of promoting the deposition and retention of the sediment cover, thus facilitating a return to the anaerobic environment that originally preserved the archaeological remains. Strips of artificial sea grass matting placed around the *William Salthouse*, a wooden sailing vessel lost in 1841 in 13m of water off Port Phillip Heads in Victoria, Australia, eliminated scour and increased the deposition of sediment across the site (Staniforth, 2006: 54). PVC ports are sometimes installed in such reconstructed seabeds to measure chemical activity and deterioration.

Expanding on Muckleroy's research into site-formation processes, Tilmant (1993: 59) observed that wrecks and newly submerged artifacts are quickly colonized by organisms that require a hard substrate for life and growth. In addition, Murphy and Johnsson (1993: 108) have emphasized that the depth and environmental conditions surrounding a shipwreck site determine the level of additional disturbance resulting from wave action. Environmental factors dictating site stabilization include:

A. The nature of initial site deposition (cause of wreck event and breakup, if any).
B. Weather-related disturbance prior to stabilization.
C. Composition and slope of seabed.
D. Growth rates of organisms that colonize the hard substrate of a site.
E. The chemical and electrochemical environment of the wreck site affecting the rate of concretion growth.

Again, the creation of anaerobic conditions through burial beneath bottom sediments is currently judged to be a critical aspect of stabilization (Ward *et al.*, 1999: 565-6).

Fig. 4. A mid to late 19th-century shipwreck in the English Channel (site 2T11w24b-1) at a depth of 124m, where a cargo of probable white ironstone bowls and plates has been partly smashed and dragged out of context by beam trawlers or dredges.

Destructive cultural impacts on shallow water wrecks are, of course, reasonably well known. In addition to large-scale looting, these sites can be impacted by piers and jetty construction, for instance, as well as harborworks, pipelines and dredging (Stewart, 1999: 576-77). More recently, Quinn (2006: 1420) has rejected the widespread theory that considers wrecks to exist in a state of equilibrium with the surrounding environment and acknowledges that "wreck sites act as open systems, with the exchange of material (sediment, water, organics and inorganics) and energy (wave, tidal, storm) across system boundaries. Wrecks are therefore generally in a state of dynamic (not steady-state) equilibrium with respect to the natural environment, characterized by negative disequilibrium, ultimately leading to wreck disintegration."

2. Deep-Sea Preservation
When the shipwreck of the side-wheel steamer *Central America* (Herdendorf, 1995: 95) was discovered in 1987 at a depth of 2,200m, little information was available about the preservation of wrecks located deep on the ocean floor. Deep-sea shipwrecks theoretically have a fundamental preservation advantage by sinking more or less intact, rather than by the grounding and stranding that leads to the loss and breakup of wrecks in coastal shallows. Research on ancient wreckage dating between 100 BC and AD 400, lost in over

750m off Skerki Bank, northeast of Tunis, led the research team to suggest that ancient wooden ships, unlike modern steel vessels, founder and sink at a relatively slow speed and so come to rest upright on the seabed. "They most likely have a higher probability of sinking intact in deep water", proposed Ballard *et al.* (2000: 1616-17), "since they fill with water instead of breaking up on rock outcrops or coral reefs. Their subsequent burial in the bottom appears to be a function of initial impact, bottom type, sedimentation rates, and eventual benthic processes acting over long periods of time."

Deep-water wreck sites are defined here as those located in depths of 75m or greater, just beyond the range of recreational scuba divers and only accessible by manned or unmanned vehicles and saturation, rebreather or mixed gas divers. This predominantly restricts access to these sites to professional or military divers with large budgets and advanced equipment. Such deep-sea sites formed below the normal wave base have been considered traditionally to have been spared from the destructive scrambling processes caused by waves, currents and mobile sediment.

Recent investigations of deep-water wrecks, however, have proven that the basic principles of this body of theory are in many cases unjustified. The natural processes of deterioration may slow, but they certainly do not cease. Both shallow and deep sites are subjected to both human intervention and natural transformation processes.

Fig. 5. At a depth of around 100m in the English Channel, Odyssey's site 35F is an extremely rare c. mid-17th century merchant vessel. The hull has been almost completely ground down by trawlers. Wooden planking and a small part of the cargo of elephant tusks and 'manilla' bracelets (used as currency) only survive where they have been sealed in place by the cargo/ ballast of heavy iron cannon. Trawler cable (at left) is snagged next to ivory and is the probable cause of its snapped ends.

The diverse species known to inhabit the deep depend for their food on the detritus and biological matter that falls from above, given a lack of photosynthetic processes in the abyss. Ongoing research suggests that the voracious natures of deep-sea organisms may result in rapid consumption of the organic components of deep-water wrecks (Stewart, 1999: 581). In addition, the effects of scouring on both shallow and deep-sea wreck sites, especially during the early stages of their formation when physical processes dominate, can be equally damaging. Scour is particularly destructive because it not only results in physical deterioration, but also triggers chemical and biological reactions by exposing previously buried surfaces and stripping away protective concretion/corrosion layers (Quinn, 2006: 429).

The challenge of decelerating wreck destruction in deep water is aptly exemplified by the case of the wreck of the American Civil War ironclad *Monitor* (1862), resting at a depth of 71m off North Carolina's Cape Hatteras. Upon discovery, the US government rapidly enacted protective legislation to prevent looting and unwanted salvage. A comprehensive management plan drew on *in situ* preservation as its main objective, although provision was made for some artifacts to be recovered for museum display "out of concern that they would be lost to strong currents or looters" (Broadwater, 2006: 79).

However, experts later determined that adherence to the *in situ* preservation policy would have resulted in the destruction of *Monitor* by natural forces because the processes of deterioration were visibly accelerating. The ironclad suffered severe structural stresses and was exposed to strong currents, trawl nets and even illegal salvage. John Broadwater (2006: 79-80) has stated that "There was a growing realization that even under an *in situ* preservation policy, it was time to consider alternative plans for more rigorous research and recovery at the wreck site." The recovery of significant items from the site, including the engine, propeller and turret, has enabled millions of visitors to enjoy the history of *Monitor*.

Emerging evidence makes it clear that the deep ocean is, in fact, not immune from either natural or human impacts. Odyssey Marine Exploration's deep-sea investigations have revealed unexpected levels of deterioration, as in the case of the wreck of the side-wheel steamer *Republic*. Despite its depth of more than 500m, the site was still influenced by the Gulf Stream, whose rapidly flowing warm and nutrient-rich waters wore down the wreck physically, chemically and biologically. Other examples, distinct from Odyssey's research, include the *Central America* site where, even at a depth of 2,200m, wood, iron and cupreous metals were all subjected to various levels of degradation.

The *Lusitania* (1915) and *Andrea Doria* (1956) have also been found to be corroding at an alarming rate, and when the *Titanic* (1912) was discovered and examined in 4,000m of water, the majority of exposed hull remains had lost nearly all of their organic components, while the metal itself was discovered to be swiftly deteriorating. Rusticles, tiny microbes that feed off the ship's iron before falling off with the metal in five- to ten-year cycles, are rapidly destroying one of the world's most famous ships.[1]

In his model, Keith Muckleroy (1978) did address the issue of shipwreck sites being affected by post-depositional cultural processes, such as salvage and looting. Admittedly, so far casual looting of deep-ocean sites has been less problematic than in diver-accessible locations for logistical reasons alone. What he could not account for were technological developments post-dating his research, including inadvertent impacts such as trawling and 'wreck fishing' that directly target deep shipwreck sites. Until now, the effects of these forces have been a matter of speculation and theory, but Odyssey's recent projects have qualified their damage as a scientific fact.

Ocean floor trawlers skim the seabed with 1-8 ton nets that stretch over 12m high and 60m wide. Large, heavy rubber rollers called rock hoppers, intended to prevent the nets from snagging on rocks, have already been shown to destroy cold-water coral and other fish habitats, with an impact that has been compared to "racing several monster trucks across the sea floor".[2]

The fishing that is practiced in the Western Approaches to the English Channel has been demonstrated to have significant adverse impacts on wrecks as well. In these over-exploited waters, fish populations concentrate in the vicinity of hard substrates that project above the seabed, including shipwrecks, which function as artificial reefs. Trawlers target these locations and gill nets are deliberately set over and around such sites; when fishing nets are hauled in, if they do not break or become irretrievably snagged they catch on, drag and disarticulate the site's structure (Figs. 3-5). Odyssey has observed sites choked with entangled nets. In the western English Channel some of the cannon visible on the surface of HMS *Victory* (1744) have been dragged out of position by trawl nets and a lobster trap verifies the conscious targeting of this rich biological oasis by fishermen (Cunningham Dobson and Kingsley, 2009:

5-6). While the damage to this and other sites observed in the English Channel has not been revisited on multiple occasions over a period of years, enabling comparative analysis from year to year, the destruction caused by this kind of trawling is typified by the vivid example of a site discovered and documented by Odyssey, the Jacksonville 'Blue China' wreck (Site BA02).

3. Site Description – 2003

Approximately 370m beneath the Atlantic Ocean, and within the body of the Gulf Stream current off the Florida/Georgia coast, the Jacksonville 'Blue China' wreck was first investigated by Odyssey in early 2003. The site was brought to the company's attention by a trawl fisherman who had retrieved cultural material from the location in his nets. Bottom currents across the site were observed to range from 0.5-1 knot, with water temperature and salinity varying seasonally and according to local weather conditions. The seabed environment is sparsely populated by flora and fauna.[3] In 2003, the site consisted of a large, low-lying mound of coherent wreckage measuring about 30 x 10m in extent.

A large quantity of hull remains were identified partly buried under the sand bottom, indicating the presence of a wood-planked and framed vessel. The long axis of the site runs generally north-south, with two encrusted anchors at the southern end denoting the bows. Numerous iron concretions were scattered around the site, but the nucleus of the mound consisted primarily of an extensive cargo of ceramics and glass bottles.

Based on a preliminary survey, the wreck appeared to consist of the lower section of a medium-sized mid-19th century wooden merchant vessel, possibly a coastal trader, with highly visible stacks of blue shell-edged ware. The wreck contained an estimated 2,500 artifacts distributed across what appeared to be frames or floors and the lowest section of the hull, which protruded above the seabed. A considerable quantity of the cargo had survived intact, including ceramics and dark green glass bottles (Tolson *et al.*, 2008).

Many of these wares survived in their original stacked positions following the disintegration of their surrounding packing materials (Figs. 7-8). The stacked pottery, however, had fallen over and apparently been spread across the site relatively recently by trawls, which had severely disturbed its integrity. Initial examination of the cargo identified glass bottles, stacks and individual pieces of pottery and porcelain of at least two different types, several boxlike objects that might have been small wooden crates, a ship's pulley, two anchors, wooden hull remains and various concretions.

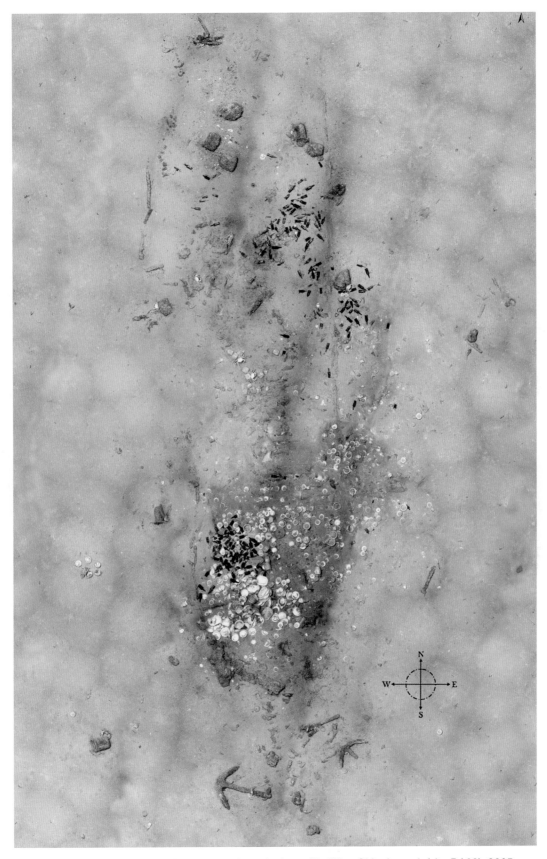

Fig. 6. Photomosaic of the 370m-deep Jacksonville 'Blue China' wreck (site BA02), 2005.

Fig. 7. The cargo of English blue shell-edged ceramic plates, bowls and serving platters at the southern end (bow) of the Jacksonville 'Blue China' wreck site, with a consignment of glass bottles in the background.

Fig. 8. Detail of English blue shell-edged ceramic plates, serving platters and slipware bowls from the Jacksonville 'Blue China' wreck.

More specifically, the stacked cargo included blue shell-edged octagonal platters in three sizes, large shallow soup bowls of similar design, and plates of the same style. Also present were thick glass bottles, dark green in color, possibly used to store alcoholic beverages; scattered Chinese porcelain 'ginger jars' bearing a blue decoration; paneled clear drinking glasses; stoneware pottery that may have been domestic assemblage rather than cargo; large pitchers with sharp-edged pouring spouts and banded patterns of decoration; and possible elements of ship's tackle. The site was videotaped in detail during this preliminary survey, but footage provided no indication of the vessel's origins or specific cause of sinking. Following the recovery of three items from the site, Odyssey filed an arrest on the wreck to protect it from looters.

4. Site Description – 2005

In early 2005, Odyssey returned to the Jacksonville 'Blue China' wreck (Fig. 9). On reaching the site, the cameras on the Remotely-Operated Vehicle (ROV) Zeus revealed direct and indirect evidence of fresh trawl damage. The former consisted of actual trawl scars visibly crossing the site and drag displacement of artifacts. Indirect evidence consisted of smashed artifacts and ship's structure and a lack of benthic organisms (which are typically slow to develop

and spread) in the vicinity of the wreck. Sites such as this in untrawled areas are typically veritable oases for marine life, but in this case the wreck was deserted by biological activity (pers. comm. Tom Dettweiler, February 2005).

In stark contrast to the previous visit, little undisturbed stratigraphy now survived. The ship's structure had been largely flattened, with only a few relatively deep crevices in the hull preserving some stratigraphy below the trawl disturbance zone. The cargo was also more dispersed, with a greater percentage of artifacts chipped and broken.

As a result, a pre-disturbance survey of the wreck was conducted, with some of the endangered artifacts recovered for their own protection. A high-resolution photomosaic was produced in combination with close-up underwater still photography of the remains (Fig. 6).

During this survey, formerly unrecorded material was identified: small kegs of what appeared to be white lead, whose staves and hoops had completely deteriorated; yellow slip-decorated earthenware chamber pots and undecorated whiteware consisting of plates, bowls, chamber pots, wash basins and salve jars; hand-painted ceramic teaware, including tea bowls, saucers, cream jugs and sugar bowls decorated with floral and berry motifs; two individual printed plates, one bearing a Blue Willow pattern, the other a brown Asiatic Pheasants pattern; two different types of clay smoking pipes; transparent green, aqua and clear

Fig. 9. Broken pottery vessels on the Jacksonville 'Blue China' wreck, 2005.

glass bottles of a variety of shapes and functions; small lead spheres (possibly shot), approximately 1cm in diameter; green and clear glass tumblers; and small ingots of lead or solder (Figs. 10-14). Ship's domestic assemblage included the remains of a telescope and a sextant, the glass globe or font of an oil lamp, a ceramic gravy boat, a millstone and two possible wooden hatch rollers. The pottery is largely diagnostic of British (Staffordshire and Cardiff) markets, with a limited quantity of Oriental imports from Canton. This material culture will be described in a comprehensive manner in a subsequent report.

Using a delicate 'hover and recover' strategy, rather than sitting directly on and disturbing the seabed, Odyssey's 8-ton ROV was flown above the wreck, while its manipulator arms recovered a cross-section of artifacts. Limited trial-trench excavation confirmed the near-total absence of stratigraphy at the site, which had been flattened into a single layer of artifacts overlying the hull remains. Analysis of the recovered artifacts has confidently revealed a date of 1840-60 for the wreck, but so far has not produced a candidate for the identity of this lost ship. This collection of artifacts has been conserved, document-

Fig. 12. English mugs, cat's-eye slip decoration framed by double narrow brown bands. H. of larger jug 11.4cm. Jacksonville 'Blue China' wreck.

Fig. 13. Ginger jars, Canton, China, c. 1840-60. Porcelain, H. 15.3cm. Two of four examples found on the Jacksonville 'Blue China' wreck.

Fig. 10. An intact English tea saucer with a floral pattern. England, c. 1845-55, H. 14.6cm. Jacksonville 'Blue China' wreck, 2005.

Fig. 11. English slipware jugs, tan and blue-grey bands flanked by two brighter blue bands. Larger jug H. 19.6cm. Eight jugs were recovered in four different sizes. Glass tumblers had been packed inside them to maximize storage space. Jacksonville 'Blue China' wreck.

Fig. 14. Glass tumbler and bottles. Mold-made American paneled tumbler, 1845-75. Patent medicine bottle, tapered, narrow neck, designed for limited evaporation around the cork. Turn-mold, utilitarian bottle with indented base. Jacksonville 'Blue China' wreck.

ed and recorded and now resides in Odyssey's permanent collection, where it is available for study and educational purposes.

5. Conclusion

In general, deep-sea wrecks have been regarded as a resource that can and should be preserved *in situ* because they were believed to be largely stable. Odyssey's work continues to show that such sites are not immune from natural and cultural impacts, and that these impacts are potentially much more widespread and destructive than initially believed. Microorganisms and chemical processes continue to break down wreck materials and deep-ocean currents scour them. Stewart's (1999: 585) conclusions remain as valid for deep-water sites as they do for shallow wrecks: "Too often, underwater sites, especially shipwrecks, are treated simply as 'time capsules'. In reality, underwater sites, like those on land, are the result of complex formation processes that can result in the mixing of strata, destruction of artifacts, and deposition of new material. For this reason, understanding the formation processes present must become a primary goal of archaeologists studying submerged sites."

Odyssey's experience on the Jacksonville 'Blue China' wreck demonstrates that even shipwrecks lying in hundreds of meters of water are in reality not beyond the reach of destructive human influences. Such sites provide habitats for fish and so become targets for trawl nets in the Atlantic Ocean, as well as wreck fishing in the Western Approaches to the English Channel. For multiple reasons, the philosophy of benign neglect – the current prevailing model of *in situ* preservation – is neither a practical nor a responsible solution in many cases.

The pattern of modern damage on the Jacksonville 'Blue China' wreck is just one small example of an emerging problematic pattern. As more research is conducted at depth, the scale of the problem and absence of wrecks 'frozen in time' is becoming increasingly obvious (Soreide, 2000). Odyssey's late 17th-century site E-82 (the *Sussex* Shipwreck Project) lies in 821m in the Straits of Gibraltar and was found to be contaminated by fishing nets and modern debris (Figs. 1-2), including beer cans and socks concreted to iron cannon and even plastic bags containing asbestos labeled 'DANGER' (Cunningham Dobson *et al.*, 2009). Odyssey's site 35F, a 17th-century merchant vessel discovered in the western English Channel, features trawler marks to such an extent that it resembles a deeply-ploughed field, and the wooden hull has been very heavily eroded and disarticulated. Only frames and strakes immediately adjacent to the keel survive well below the turn-of-the-bilge. Compared to the ubiquitous presence on shallow-water sites of large quantities of intact pottery vessels, a mere handful of heavily abraded sherds survived on both this wreck and site E-82 discovered off Gibraltar.

Other marine archaeologists are arriving at the same conclusions about this phenomenon. The Woods Hole Oceanographic Institution (WHOI) has detected at least two trawl nets and one gill net wrapped around the windlass of the wreck of the schooner *Paul Palmer*, lost in 1913.[4] In the Mediterranean Sea, Brendan Foley of WHOI has recalled how "we optically surveyed the sea floor off the island of Malta, for centuries a center of maritime commerce. At depths of 500+ meters, we expected to encounter marine life and hoped to discover ancient shipwrecks. Instead, we found only furrows in the sediments, indicating intensive trawling… occasionally we have seen evidence of dragging at depths approaching 1000 meters. It is unlikely that many ancient archaeologically significant sites will survive in areas subjected to trawl fishing."[5]

Ballard (2008: 136) has also observed trawl marks in deep waters off Malta, the Gulf of Naples, Egypt and in the Black Sea. During the survey of Skerki Bank, he and his team reported that "In many of the areas searched, intense bottom fishing activities made search efforts impossible. In some cases, the presence of nets prohibited towing ARGO [an ROV] through the area, while in other places, the bottom had been so intensely scoured that surface artifacts had more than likely been removed years before" (Ballard *et al.*, 2000: 1594).

The site of the early 19th-century Ormen Lange shipwreck excavated in 170m off Bud, Norway, by the Norwegian University of Science and Technology, is covered with modern rubbish: tangles of wire, fishing equipment, steel frames, more than 50 kitchen appliances, a complete kitchen, oil drums and even a 1950s car (Bryn *et al.*, 2007: 100-101). As offshore oil production expands from an anticipated one-sixth to one-fourth of total world production and fiber optic cables are being laid throughout the oceans of the world, drilling and production platforms, pipelines and even trans-oceanic cables are increasingly threatening ancient and historic shipwrecks (Stewart, 1999: 576-77). Throughout the world, offshore wind farms and their attendant network of anchors, cables and power lines are proliferating.

The expansion of oil drilling activities in deep water has already resulted in an increase in the number of deepwater wrecks discovered, especially in the Gulf of Mexico. In recognition of this reality, the United States Minerals Management Service, in fulfillment of its legislative mandate to protect cultural heritage, requires the petroleum industry to mitigate offshore oilfield activities by conducting high-resolution remote sensing surveys. These must be undertaken in areas with a significant probability of historic shipwreck presence (Irion *et al.*, 2008: 79).

The example of the Jacksonville 'Blue China' wreck is far from an isolated case, but it is a wake-up call to scientists to record a sample of this unique maritime cultural heritage before it is irretrievably destroyed. The ideal of preservation *in situ* is a myth that does not always respect or safeguard the past.

Acknowledgements

This paper had its modest beginnings as a brief conference presentation in 2005. Subsequent iterations have benefitted mightily from the contributions of Sean Kingsley, Neil Cunningham Dobson and Ellen Gerth, and has reached its current incarnation thanks to the editorial talents of Greg Stemm, Laura Barton and John Oppermann. I'd also like to acknowledge the contributions of British and American ceramic scholar Robert Hunter and the exquisite photography produced by Gavin Ashworth. My personal thanks to all of them.

Notes

1. See Johnston, L., *Life at the Bottom of the Ocean*: http://www.deepimage.co.uk/wrecks/titanic titanic%20pages/titanic-science-mainpage.htm and Cullimore, R. and Johnston, L., *Rusticles Thrive on the Titanic*: http://oceanexplorer.noaa.gov/explorations/03titanic/rusticles/rusticles.html.
2. Schulte, G., 'Trawling Blamed for Loss of Corals', *The Washington Times*, 13 May 2005: http://www dets.com/News/trawling_damage.htm.
3. Internal Odyssey report by J. Lange Winkler (Odyssey Marine Exploration, 2003).
4. http://www.whoi.edu/sbl/image.do?id=10977& litesiteid=2740&articleId=4958 and http://stellwagen .noaa.gov/maritime/paulpalmer.html.
5. Foley, B., *Impact of Fishing on Shipwrecks*: http:/www. whoi.edu/sbl/liteSite.do?litesiteid=2740&articleId =4965.

Bibliography

Ballard, R., 'Searching for Ancient Shipwrecks in the Deep Sea'. In R.D. Ballard (ed.), *Archaeological Oceanography* (Princeton University Press, 2008), 132-47.

Ballard, R.D., McCann, A.M., Yoerger, D., Whitcomb, L., Mindell, D., Oleson, J., Singh, H., Foley, B., Adams, J., Piechota, D. and Giangrande., C., 'The Discovery of Ancient History in the Deep Sea Using Advanced Deep Submergence Technology', *Deep-Sea Research* I 47 (2000), 1591-1620.

Broadwater, J., 'The USS Monitor: In Situ Preservation and Recovery'. In R. Grenier, D. Nutley and I. Cochran (eds.), *Underwater Cultural Heritage at Risk: Managing Natural and Human Impacts* (Heritage at Risk Special Edition, ICOMOS, Paris, 2006), 79-81.

Bryn, P., Jasinski, M.E. and Soreide, F. *Ormen Lange. Pipelines and Shipwrecks* (Oslo, 2007).

Camidge, K. *HMS Colossus Progress Report 2003*.

Cunningham Dobson, N. and Kingsley, S., *HMS Victory, a First-Rate Royal Navy Warship Lost in the English Channel, 1744. Preliminary Survey and Identification* (OME Papers 2, 2009).

Cunningham Dobson, N., Tolson, H., Martin, A., Lavery, B., Bates, R., Tempera, F. and Pearce, J., *The HMS Sussex Shipwreck Project (Site E-82): Preliminary Report* (OME Papers 1, 2009).

Godfrey, I.M., Gregory, D., Nyström, I. and Richards, V., 'In Situ Preservation of Archaeological Materials and Sites Underwater'. In F. Maniscalco (ed.), *Tutela, conservazione e valorizzazione del patrimonio vulturale subacqueo. Mediterraneum, volume 4* (Naples, 2004).

Grenier, R., 'The Basque Whaling Ship from Red Bay, Labrador: a Treasure Trove of Data on Iberian Atlantic Shipbuilding Design and Techniques in the mid-16th Century'. In F. Alves (ed.), *Proceedings International Symposium on Archaeology of Medieval and Modern Ships of Iberian-Atlantic Tradition. Hull Remains, Manuscripts and Ethnographic Sources: A Comparative Approach* (Centro Nacional de Arqueologia Nautica e Subaquatica/Academia de Marinha, Lisbon, 7-9 September, 1998), 269-93.

Herdendorf, C.E., Thompson, T.G. and Evans, R.D., 'Science on a Deep-Ocean Shipwreck', *Ohio Journal of Science* 95.4 (1995), 4-224.

Irion, J.B., Ball, D. and Horrell, C.E., 'The US Government's Role in Deepwater Archaeology: the Deep Gulf Wrecks Project', *Journal of Historical Archaeology* 12 (2008), 75-81.

Manders, M.R., 'The In Situ Protection of a Dutch Colonial Vessel in Sri Lankan Waters.' In R. Grenier, D. Nutley and I. Cochran (eds.), *Underwater Cultural Heritage at Risk: Managing Natural and Human Impacts* (Heritage at Risk Special Edition, ICOMOS, Paris, 2006), 58-60.

Muckleroy, K., *Maritime Archaeology* (Cambridge University Press, 1978).

Murphy, L.E. and Johnsson, R.W., 'Environmental Factors Affecting Vessel Casualties and Site Preservation'. In *Dry Tortugas National Park Submerged Cultural Resources Assessment* (National

Park Service Submerged Cultural Resources Unit, Santa Fe, 1993).

Quinn, R., 'The Role of Scour in Shipwreck Site Formation Processes and the Preservation of Wreck-associated Scour Signatures in the Sedimentary Record – Evidence from Seabed and Sub-surface Data', *Journal of Archaeological Science* 33 (2006), 1419-32.

Soreide, F., 'Cost-effective Deep Water Archaeology: Preliminary Investigations in Trondheim Harbour ', *IJNA* 29.2 (2000), 284-93.

Staniforth, M., 'In Situ Site Stabilization: the William Salthouse Case Study'. In R. Grenier, D. Nutley and I. Cochran (eds.), *Underwater Cultural Heritage at Risk: Managing Natural and Human Impacts* (Heritage at Risk Special Edition, ICOMOS, Paris, 2006), 52-54.

Stewart, D.J., 'Formation Processes Affecting Submerged Archaeological Sites: an Overview', *Geoarchaeology* 14.6 (1999), 565-87.

Tilmant, J.T., 'Relationship of Dry Tortugas Natural Resources to Submerged Archaeological Sites.' In *Dry Tortugas National Park Submerged Cultural Resources Assessment* (National Park Service Submerged Cultural Resources Unit, Santa Fe, 1993).

Tolson, H., Gerth, E. and Cunningham Dobson, N., 'Ceramics from the "Blue China" Wreck'. In R. Hunter (ed.), *Ceramics in America 2008* (The Chipstone Foundation, Milwaukee, 2008), 162-83.

Ward, I.A.K., Larcombe, P. and Veth, P., 'A New Process-based Model for Wreck Site Formation', *Journal of Archaeological Science* 26 (1999), 561-70.

7

The HMS *Sussex* Shipwreck Project (Site E-82): Preliminary Report

Neil Cunningham Dobson
Hawk Tolson
Odyssey Marine Exploration, Tampa, USA

Anthony Martin
Gifford Ltd, Chester, United Kingdom

Brian Lavery
Curator Emeritus, National Maritime Museum, Greenwich, United Kingdom

Richard Bates
Fernando Tempera
Topaz Environmental & Marine Ltd, School of Geography & Geosciences, University of St. Andrews, Scotland

Jacqui Pearce
Museum of London Archaeology, United Kingdom

In December 2005 and January 2006, Odyssey Marine Exploration conducted a comprehensive pre-disturbance survey and limited trial-trench excavation on a shipwreck near the Straits of Gibraltar as part of the HMS *Sussex* Shipwreck Project. The site, designated E-82, lies in international waters in the Mediterranean Sea at a depth of 821m in the Straits of Gibraltar.[1] The research was undertaken within the framework of an agreement between the project sponsor, Odyssey Marine Exploration (OME), and the Her Majesty's Government of the United Kingdom (HMG), which has exercized its sovereign right to claim ownership of the wreck of HMS *Sussex*. This report introduces the technology utilized and the environmental and archaeological results obtained during the first deep-sea shipwreck excavation in the Mediterranean Sea.[2]

1. Introduction

An archaeological investigation of site E-82, possibly the wreck of the third-rate 80-gun British warship HMS *Sussex,* lost off Gibraltar during a severe storm on 19 February 1694, commenced in December 2005 after the discovery of the wreck site in 2001 using side-scan sonar (Fig. 1). This followed a decade of documentary research, archaeological survey and site identification, and adhered to an unparalleled, stringent Project Plan submitted to, and accepted by, the *Sussex* Archaeological Executive (SAE), a team of archaeological consultants approved by the Government of the United Kingdom.[3] This preliminary report introduces the technology and field methodology developed for the project and presents the primary environmental, biological and archaeological data obtained in order to help clarify how shipwrecks form in deep water, to

assess the level of artefact and structural remains preserved and to determine whether site E-82 is a valid candidate for HMS *Sussex*.

The archaeological investigation of deep-water shipwreck sites is a relatively new discipline that demands specialized diving equipment and expertise. On site E-82, the main archaeological tool was a 7-ton Remotely-Operated Vehicle nicknamed Zeus, which functioned as the archaeologists' eyes and hands. Zeus was custom-equipped with specialized illumination and recording systems, including high definition, multi-camera stations using still and digital photography, video supported by powerful lighting platforms, and highly sensitive excavation, sifting and artifact recovery tools.

All of the archaeological techniques and recording methods were designed to dovetail with international standards for archaeological investigation practices currently utilized on land. No best-practice guides have been formulated to date for deep-sea shipwreck survey and excavation, but OME's experienced personnel conducted the world's first deep-sea shipwreck excavation from 1989-1991, scientifical-ly recording and recovering 16,480 artifacts from a Spanish colonial shipwreck wrecked off the Tortugas Islands in 1622. Based in part on this experience, OME self-imposed professional standards recommended for terrestrial field-work on the *Sussex* project, such as those formulated by the UK Institute of Field Archaeologists.

Pursuant to the project plan approved by the SAE (the *Sussex* Archaeological Executive), the investigation of site E-82 was sub-divided into three main phases of activity:

• Phase 1, Stage 1A: site survey (non-intrusive).
• Phase 1, Stage 1B: site evaluation (including limited trial excavation of a maximum 10% of the wreck site).
• Phase 2: intensive excavation of target areas.

This report concentrates on the results of Phase 1, Stages 1A-1B. Phase 2 awaits the resolution of political de-velopments (see Section 10 below). The Phase 1, Stage 1A non-disturbance methodology designed for the investiga-tion of site E-82 demanded an inter-disciplinary approach incorporating the following diverse components:

1. A 1000 x 1000m bathymetric survey centered on the wreck, with line spacing of 20m beyond the confines of the wreck and 10m over it.
2. A 300 x 300m bathymetric survey centered on the wreck, with 2m line spacings.
3. Environmental study of the site and seabed.
4. Marine biological characterization.

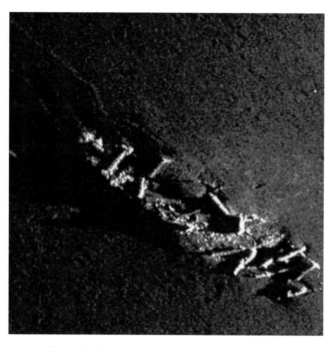

Fig. 1. Side-scan sonar of shipwreck site E-82.

Fig. 2. Odyssey's research platform during the Sussex shipwreck project, the 76m-long, 1431-ton Odyssey Explorer.

5. Video survey: coverage of the 300 x 300m square area centered on the wreck.

6. Pre-disturbance photomosaic (60 x 30m area).

7. Production of a pre-disturbance master site plan based on the photomosaic.

8. Imposition of an electronic grid over the wreck site for the contextual recording of artifacts, trench locations and modern intrusions (Fig. 13).

9. Measurement of all surface archaeological features. The heavily concreted iron cannon and anchors were surveyed as individual elements. Measurements were taken from the ROV while it maintained a constant altitude over the wreck. Metric data were acquired from target points, such as the cascabel and muzzle ends of cannon. The ROV laser pointer was centered on each target point and a total of 10 fixes in the x and y planes were taken for each one in reference to the site grid. The measured data were then processed and the averages of the 10 values plotted on the site grid.

10. Designation of sterile lanes for ROV movement to ensure non-disturbance of the wreck's integrity.

11. Recording of modern contamination on the wreck site.

12. The removal of 4-10cm of sterile sediment overlying the cultural remains on the site to 'dust off' the surface archaeological features.

13. Production of a second photomosaic and a related master site plan following the exposure described in Item 12.

By agreement with HMG, the Phase 1, Stage 1B trial excavation permitted one 3m-wide evaluation trench to be excavated at the south-western end of the wreck, tentatively interpreted as the stern. Its precise location and dimensions would be determined by the results of Phase 1, Stage 1A, but would be limited to 10% of the total wreck area. Due to the dense nature of concretions on the surface of site E-82, a judgemental methodology was finally adopted, whereby five small trial trenches were opened with the objective of assessing the level of site preservation and determining the ship's orientation on the seabed.

2. Field Methodology

Odyssey's research platform during the *Sussex* shipwreck project was the 76m-long, 1431-gross-ton *Odyssey Explorer* (Fig. 2). This ship is fully-equipped to support deep-sea exploration and is classed to Ice Class 3 for operations in extreme latitudes. It has accommodation for a crew and staff of 41 people and contains deck-mounted deployment capability, umbilical cable and recovery equipment suitable for the operation of a work-class ROV system. The *Odyssey Explorer* has the ability to work offshore without re-supply for 60 days.

An ROV formerly used in the heavy-duty cable industry for trenching and cable-burying operations was adopted for the project, with the capacity to operate in strong currents with requisite powerful precision-controlled thrusters and state-of-the-art manipulator arms. The ROV system was also required to be well-balanced for operations in proximity to delicate artifacts and shipwreck structure. The ROV used on site E-82 was the Soil Machine Dynamics Ltd. 'Nereus', now renamed Zeus (Fig. 3). At 7.26 tons and measuring 3.7 x 3.1 x 2.38m, Zeus has the capacity to conduct all aspects of seabed survey, excavation and recovery with sustained duration at depths down to 2,500m. Zeus has been rendered safe for use in delicate archaeological environments through buoyancy compensation and a precision control system. When configured for field operations after a series of sea trials, the ROV operates at neutral buoyancy, overcome for descent to the sea floor by using its thrusters in a powered dive.

There are three main electronic navigation aids that work together to enable Odyssey to conduct accurate positioning and measurement: GPS, Ultra Short Baseline (USBL), and Long Base Line (LBL). This hardware works in conjunction with a navigation software program called 'Winfrog'. Integration of these positioning and acoustic systems, along with custom proprietary computer software, enables tracking of the work platform to a position above the site, the ROV to the seabed and then provides for precise measurement across the wreck site.

During sub-sea operations, a transducer/receiver head is mounted on a pole that can be deployed and retracted through the work platform hull. This device triangulates the position of the ROV as it descends toward the seabed, sends acoustic signals back and forth to the ROV and, later on in the process, to sub-sea acoustic beacons secured on the seabed. The Winfrog program then decodes and displays this data, which is also correlated with Odyssey's own proprietary data-logging software. For survey, the ROV is also fitted with a Kongsberg Simrad Mesotech 6000m Digital Sonar.

Zeus is powered by a pair of 75kW electro-hydraulic power packs, combining for a total vehicle power of 150kW from a 50Hz supply. The propulsion system consists of eight reversible hydraulic thrusters: four 43cm-diameter units aligned on the horizontal plane, and four 30cm-diameter units operating on the vertical plane. Each thruster's speed is controlled via electro-hydraulic valves.

For manipulation, Zeus is fitted with two Schilling

The fieldwork staff on site E-82 comprised:

Role	Name	Organization
Company Director	Greg Stemm	OME
Project Manager	Tom Dettweiler	OME
Project Manager	Andrew Craig	OME
Principal Investigator	Anthony Martin	Gifford Ltd
Director of Field Archaeology	Neil Cunningham Dobson	OME
Director of Field Archaeology	Hawk Tolson	OME
Director of Field Archaeology (Substitute)	Christopher Preece	OME
Geoscientist	Richard Bates	TEAM, Fife *
Marine Biologist	Fernando Tempera	TEAM, Fife *
Historian	Lange Winckler	OME
Consulting Project Conservator	Herb Bump	OME
Conservator	Wyatt Yeager	OME
Data Manager	Gerhard Seiffert	OME
Data Logger	Alexandre Soenen	OME
Data Logger	John Vorus	OME

The project post-excavation specialists comprised:

Role	Name	Organization
Geo-Environmental Assessment	Richard Bates	TEAM, Fife *
Petrological Analysis	Peter Kokelaar	Department of Ocean & Earth Sciences, University of Liverpool
Naval Historian	Brian Lavery	Curator Emeritus, National Maritime Museum, Greenwich
Wood Species Analysis	Jill McVee	Histology Unit, University of St Andrews
Pottery Specialist	Jacqui Pearce	Museum of London Archaeology
Brick Analysis	Terence Paul Smith	Museum of London Archaeology
Marine Biology	Fernando Tempera	TEAM, Fife *
Wood Species Analysis	Alyson Tobin	School of Biology, University of St Andrews

* *Topaz Environmental and Marine Ltd.*

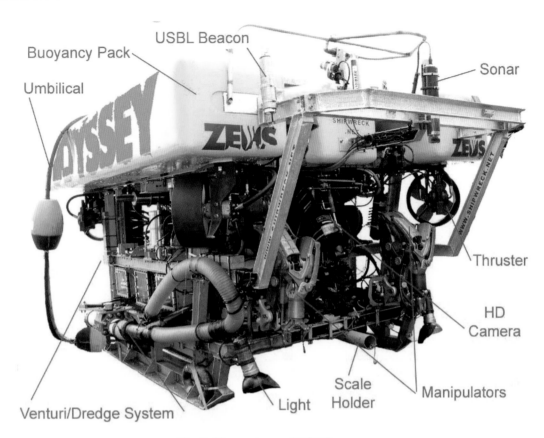

Fig. 3. The anatomy of ROV Zeus.

Conan seven-function 'master/slave' manipulator arms at either side of the front of the vehicle with a reach of 1.79m, a working arc of 120° and a lifting capacity of 170kg at full extension. A master/slave feature causes the manipulator arms to duplicate in seabed operations the movements of the operator on the research ship above. The rest of the ROV system consists of Odyssey's unique, proprietary sediment collection and filtration system (SeRF™), a shipboard deck crane acting as a launch and recovery system, an umbilical winch on the aft deck, a surface control cabin from which the ROV is directed, an acoustic vehicle location and navigation system and an electrical power distribution system.[4]

Conducted at considerable distances from the surface, the collection of sediments or their displacement by dredging presents unusual technical complexities. To meet this challenge, Odyssey has developed techniques and proprietary equipment for controlled excavation and sediment removal. For excavation and artifact recovery, a specialized sediment sifting and collection pump and a limpet suction device are utilized.

From a turbine water pump located at the rear of the ROV, water is drawn in through the intake and diverted through a hose to a venturi fitted on the starboard side of the vehicle. This creates suction without the use of any moving parts, which can be adjusted for sufficient strength to lift or move large, heavy objects. The flow can also be reversed through a valve to enable the hose to discharge rather than suck, a capability that is sometimes useful for gently dusting overburden during archaeological operations under controlled conditions, as well as for clearing blockages in the hose.

In addition to providing dredging functions for site clearance, the venturi pump is the central component for operating both Odyssey's proprietary Sediment Removal and Filtration System (SeRF™) and the suction limpet. This system meets the challenge of collecting and sifting sediments at great depth. Standard shallow-water marine archaeology practice generally employs large suction dredges to remove sand and sediment, which is sometimes sieved for small finds and ecofacts.

SeRF™ incorporates a dredge head/nozzle with separate collection and filtration elements housed in a box-like structure mounted on the stern of the ROV. When the system is engaged, collected sediments and small finds are channeled into a collection and filtration chamber, instead of being exhausted. This chamber captures very small artifacts, such as buttons or seeds (amongst a far wider variety of assemblage forms), while sediments are discharged through an opening to the rear of the container. The SeRF™ unit is also configured to retain the sediments within which smaller artifacts are embedded. The container for excavated spoil contains a wire mesh shelf that can be removed following recovery of the ROV and used to transport collected artifacts and sediment directly to the ship's artifact processing and conservation facility for study and recording.

Delicate artifacts are retrieved from the seabed using a silicone rubber limpet suction device. Known simply as the 'limpet', it consists of a soft bellows-shaped tube with a small suction pad at the distal end. These are available in different sizes, with suction pads ranging from diameters of 2-10cm (Fig. 9).

The limpet assembly is fitted to the port manipulator and powered by the venturi pump. It can be used to pick up delicate items, such as small buttons weighing a few grams or less, or even tiny glass ampoules. When fitted with a large suction pad, the limpet can lift objects comparable to a 60-liter Roman amphora weighing 45kg or more. On previous projects, this device has been used to recover glass inkwells, panes of window glass, thin sheets of slate, ballast stones and coins without any physical or cosmetic damage to the artifacts.

Photography and lighting are a vital component of any ROV archaeological survey or excavation in deep water. Zeus serves as the eyes as well as the hands of the archaeologist, so a complex suite of cameras was added to her on-board equipment. These high-resolution cameras, combined with Halide Mercury Incandescent (HMI) lighting, supply the archaeologist and ROV operator with high-quality images, significantly surpassing the visibility that might be experienced by a diver. The main cameras also have pan and tilt controls.

Large HD Plasma monitors aboard the work platform allow the archaeologist, ROV pilots and project manager to view every aspect of seabed operations, including close-up images of items only a few millimeters in size. In addition, two desktop computer screens set side-by-side display the Winfrog results of navigation/survey activity. Data from the ROV is simultaneously transmitted to three separate on-board work areas: the 'ROV Shack', which houses the ROV pilots; the 'Online Room', which houses the surveyor, navigator, and datalogger; and the 'Offline Room', the work area for the archaeologists, project manager, and specialist observers.

A ship-wide intercom communication system links the archaeologist directly to the ROV pilot, the surveyor/navigator, the data loggers, the officers on watch and the ROV deck crew. During all operations involving excavation, documentation, or any other potential disturbance of the wreck or its environment, the archaeologist supervizes all ROV tasks and is in constant contact with all stations. The Offline Room also contains a high-speed Laser Jet printer, a large format plotter for producing site photomosaics, a dedicated graphics computer, a curator's computer where all the images, logs and other artifact records are stored and a large map table for producing site plans and illustrations.

Deep-water archaeology demands accurate sea bottom survey and navigation capabilities. For these purposes, Odyssey has adapted advanced sub-sea acoustic systems to establish accurate positioning information for the location of the ROV and its manipulator arms or other tools during exploration and excavation activities, with the objective of achieving accurate relative position recording at all times. Detailed positioning information creates an analog to the physical grid and hand-measurement recordings common in shallow-water wreck investigations.

In addition, Odyssey has developed a unique data logging system (compatible with Microsoft 'Access' software) to record all events and activities. Known as DataLog®, it receives and processes data from the ROV in real time. All activities, artifact manipulations and environmental and archaeological observations are recorded through the selection of choices from drop-down menus and accompanied by a typed comment from the datalogger. The system is manned 24 hours a day when the ROV is in the water and automatically logs all events, including time, date, dive number and X, Y, Z coordinates of any activities.

Every second of every dive is recorded in triplicate on high-capacity digital DVD. Archaeological and other interesting footage for which detailed examination is desirable is also recorded on High Definition tape. Detailed photo and video records are kept by the crew and these logs allow complete reconstructions and analysis of each dive. Data sheets, maps and reports for a variety of individual requests are created from this extensive digital archive.

Artifacts, wreck structure and other objects of interest collected using the limpet and manipulators can be placed in numbered plastic baskets and containers that are set in sterile areas within reach of the ROV. Artifact baskets/containers are placed into a 4-Plex, a large metal basket with 16 divisions for separation of archaeological materials by context. Each division is numbered and every bucket/basket numbered and photographed for recording in DataLogger®.

3. Site Description

Site E-82 is located to the south-east of Gibraltar at a depth of 821m. The seabed consists of clay and sand formed on the surface of a soft bluish sediment base (Table 1).

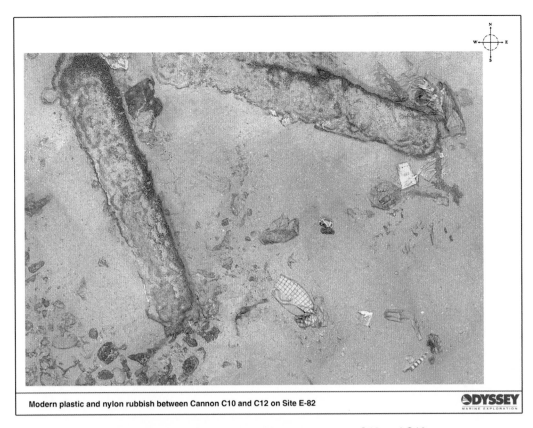

Modern plastic and nylon rubbish between Cannon C10 and C12 on Site E-82

Fig. 4. Modern plastic trapped between cannon C10 and C12.

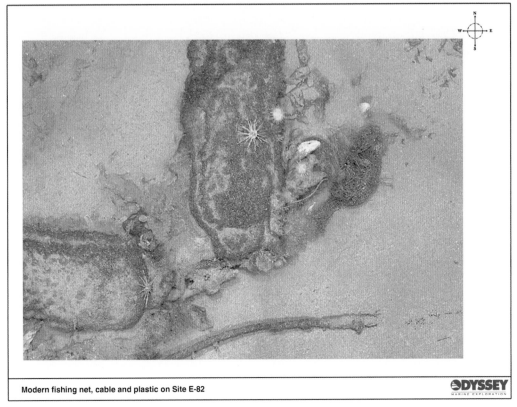

Modern fishing net, cable and plastic on Site E-82

Fig. 5. Modern plastic, fishing net and trawler cable near cannon C5 and C6.

Contrary to prevailing stereotypes of wreck formation, observation of this site, and many other deep-sea sites discovered by Odyssey, indicate that no correlation exists between increased depth and superior site preservation. In fact, site E-82 displays widespread evidence of accretion and scouring caused by the constant movement of sediments and currents across the site. Evidence of modern pollutants is especially extensive (Figs. 4-5). Rather than 'frozen in time' on the seabed, site E-82 lies in a highly dynamic and unstable environment of deterioration and decay.

The prevailing surface currents mostly derive from the north-east. Between the surface and depths of about 300m, rates vary from nearly slack to 5 knots. Beyond this depth, the lower stratum of water is a high-salinity layer, with flow rates varying from near slack to 3 knots at the seabed. The water temperature of approximately 13° centigrade is relatively consistent.

In addition to 92 hours of survey data recorded on high-definition video, a pre-disturbance photomosaic and a second 'post-dusting' photomosaic served as the primary visual tools to characterize site E-82 and select optimum areas for trial trench excavation (Fig. 11). To collect the primary data for the preparation of each photomosaic, ROV Zeus ran 81 parallel transit lines across an area of 60 x 30m, spaced 80cm apart, at a constant speed of 0.5 knots, creating a stable horizontal altitude platform of 2.5m above the seabed from which to photograph. A 75% overlap of flanking lines was maintained to ensure the highest level of coverage control, and three 1m-long scales were placed on the site to generate information on dimensions. Creation of the pre-disturbance macro-photomosaic required 2,902 individual digital still photographs to be taken and the 'post-dusting' close-up of the wreckage itself was assembled from 642 images.

The surface manifestations of the wreck, lying on a north-east/south-west axis, measure 26.5m long and 6.5m wide maximum. A total of 17 iron cannon, two anchors and large areas of concretions functioning as sealing layers were visible on the site's surface at the time of the survey. Towards the north-western flank is a dense rectangular concentration of stones, interpreted as possible ballast (Fig. 6). Each individual artifact and context was measured *in situ*, photographed, and videoed in Stage 1, Phase 1A (Figs. 7-9).

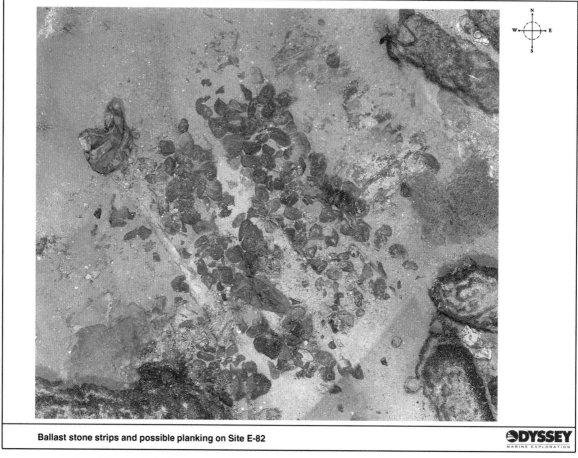

Ballast stone strips and possible planking on Site E-82

Fig. 6. Possible ballast stones and planking on the north-western side of the wreck.

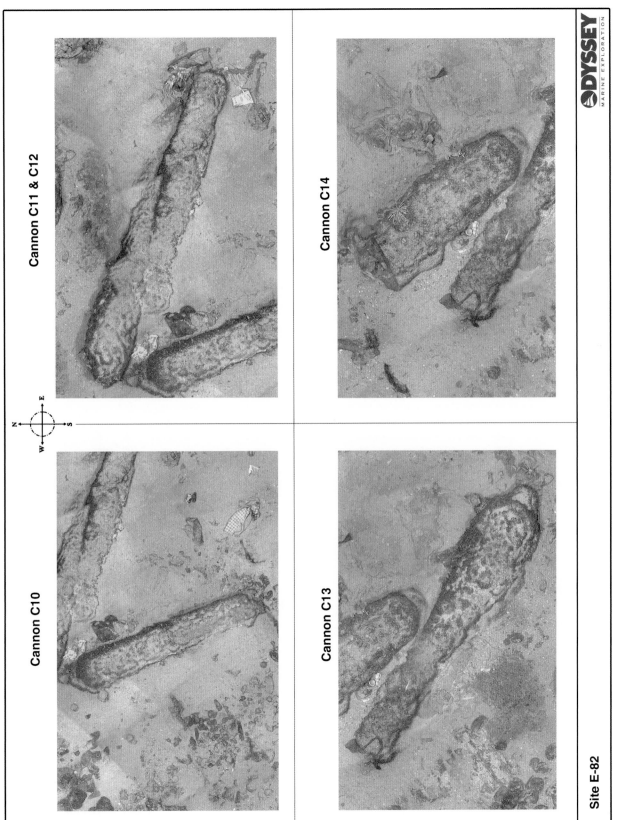

Site E-82

Fig. 7. Heavily concreted iron cannon from the shipwreck. Note the modern plastic pollutants around cannon C10, C11 and C12.

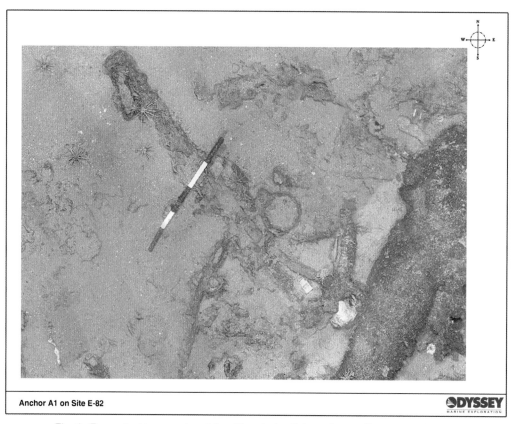

Fig. 8. Encrusted iron anchor A1, with substantial modern pollutants to the east.

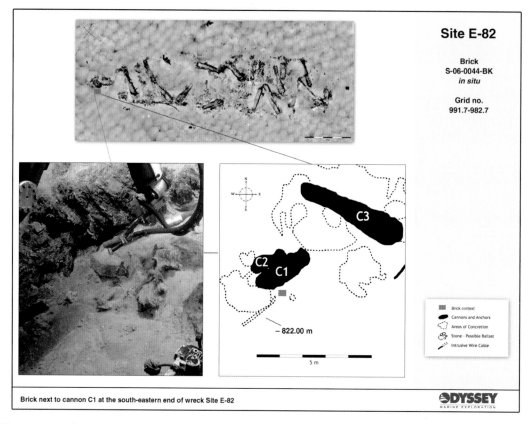

Fig. 9. The context of a brick fragment, probably from the galley, recovered from the south-eastern end of the wreck.

A disturbing volume of modern rubbish has polluted the wreck site and continues to accelerate its degeneration. Visibly snagged beneath cannon and scattered across the site are black plastic bags containing domestic waste, scrap wire, cable, rope and sections of fishing nets (Figs. 4-5). Plastic intrusion is especially notable north of cannon C9. Some of the plastic bags have ripped open, spilling their contents over the archaeological deposits and seabed sediments. Plastic food containers and tin cans penetrate at least 30cm beneath sediments around cannon C14, while a beer can is encrusted onto the surface of cannon C10. More hazardous material includes asbestos waste clearly labeled 'DANGER' (Cunningham Dobson, N., *Cambridge Expedition 2001. An Archaeological Investigation*: figs. 18, 19, 75). This rubbish probably derives from a combination of vessels sailing the busy shipping lanes around the Straits of Gibraltar, as well as washed offshore from land, and has mixed into the site matrix through vigorous current activity. Trapped fishing trawler gear is extensive on the south-western area of the wreck and extends over an area of 5m on a south-west to north-east axis.

To assess the seabed topography, two bathymetric sur-veys were conducted. A 1000 x 1000m bathymetric survey area centered on the wreck was based on 76 east-west tra-verses of the ROV, which maintained a minimal line spacing of 20m beyond the confines of the site and a 10m line spac-ing over the wreck itself. Over 36,375 depth measurements were assessed, corrected for tidal variation, to derive the final bathymetric profile. A more intensive bathymetric survey was conducted over a grid of 300 x 300m, with ROV Zeus operating in auto-depth mode to maintain a constant altitude above the seabed and running 151 east-west tra-verses at a line spacing of 2m. A total of 22,000 individual acoustic readings were accumulated by the altimeter and processed to develop the bathymetric profile (Fig. 10).

The bathymetric survey exposed a largely flat seabed gently sloping to the north-west by 3°, with a maximum amplitude of some 2.32m across a 60 x 30m core area centered on the wreck. The average depth of the site is -821.7m, with a maximum amplitude of 0.78m across the visible wreck. The shallowest area lies at -821.35m to the north-east in the vicinity of cannon C10. The deep-est area of the wreck is located on its western flank at -822.13m (Fig. 12).

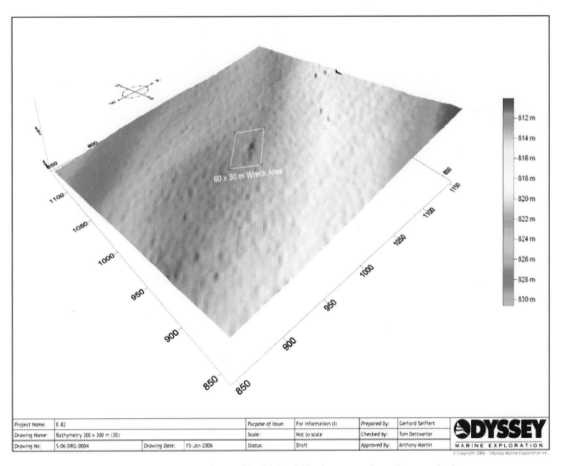

Fig. 10. 3D bathymetric profile (300 x 300m) centered on the wreck site.

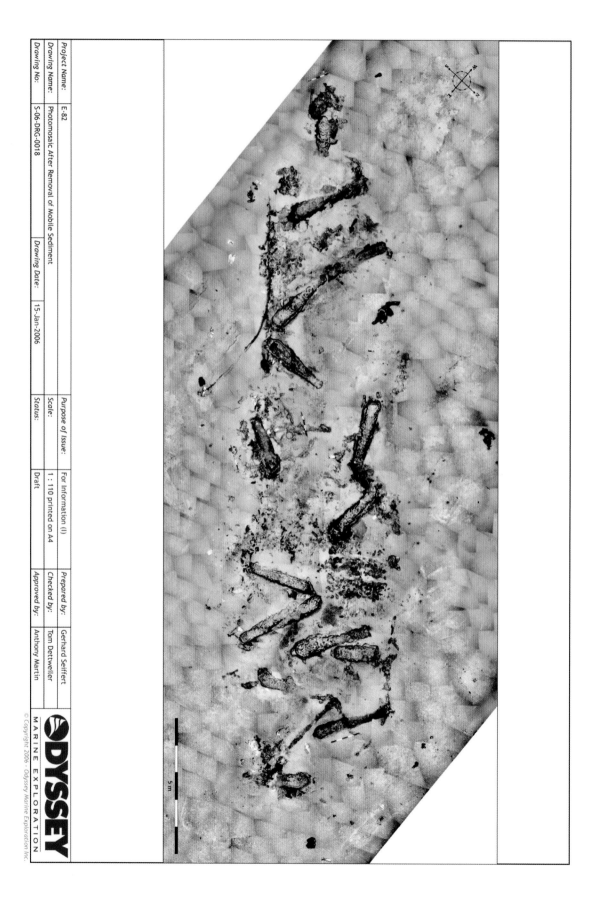

Project Name:	E-82			
Drawing Name:	Photomosaic After Removal of Mobile Sediment			
Drawing No:	S-06-DRG-0018	Drawing Date:	15-Jan-2006	

Purpose of Issue:	For Information (I)	Prepared by:	Gerhard Seifert
Scale:	1 : 110 printed on A4	Checked by:	Tom Dettweiler
Status:	Draft	Approved by:	Anthony Martin

Fig. 11. Photomosaic of the wreck after the removal of mobile sediment.

Site E-82

Fig. 12. Master plan of shipwreck site E-82.

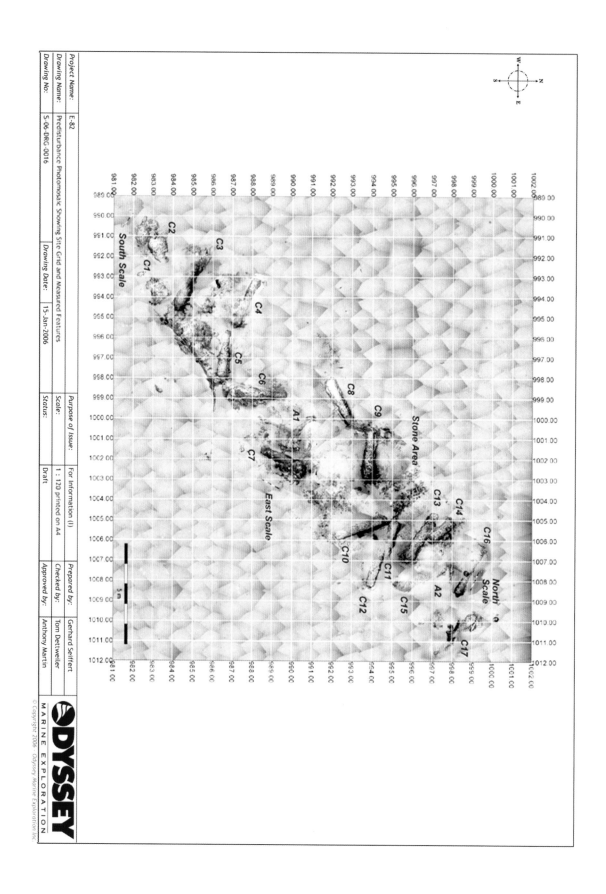

Fig. 13. Photomosaic of the wreck, with the superimposed electronic site grid used for contextual recording.

Layer	Thickness (mm)	Max Depth Below Seabed (mm)	Sedimentological Description	Context Equivalence
Surface	20-100	100	Light brown, soft unconsolidated mud. Occasional coarser material. Occasional concretions of yellow & orange (iron stained) concretions. Occasional to persistent bioturbation, 30-150mm long vertical burrows, 2-15mm diameter tubes; burrows sometimes horizontal.	1
	20-40	140	Discrete & diffuse boundary seen to layer below 20mm-40mm thick.	1
Gray clay	100-300	440	Light gray, soft semi-consolidated mud-clay. Occasional light brown discrete horizons & light gray, silt grain size horizons (5-15mm) Dislocation surfaces, sub-horizontal, 2-20mm wide. Dislocation surfaces often with silt grain size & complete shell (bivalve dominant)/shell fragments. Surfaces cross whole core & partially through core. Occasional organic flakes typically less than 2mm size.	2
	5-15	455	Usually discrete boundary, occasionally diffuse boundary seen to layer below 5-15mm thick.	2
Organic	20-150	605	Organic layer of mixed wood fragments up to 25mm long. Mixed complete (up to 25mm) shell & broken shell fragments. Red/yellow concretions (iron) up to 35mm long.	2
	2-20	625	Usually discrete (2-8mm), sometimes diffuse (10-20mm) boundary into stiff clay.	3
Stiff gray clay	>50	>675	Stiff gray clay, occasional partings of silt with shells. Uniform color. Uniform remoulded CP values.	3

Table 1. Summary of seabed stratigraphy across site E-82.

4. Environmental Analysis

On the advice of Dr. Richard Bates of Topaz Environmental and Marine (TEAM) of the Department of Geography and Geosciences at the University of St. Andrews, a block area of 300m per side around the site was selected to conduct a mini-core program and shear vane measurements. Coring focused on three lines spaced 150m apart in total, with the centerline passing through the middle of the wreck. Five core samples were taken along each line at intervals of 75m for a total of 15 cores. On the wreck site itself, samples were obtained using the same mini-coring techniques, but on an area measuring 60m long and 30m wide. Five lines of the grid were covered, spaced 6m apart, with core samples taken every 6m, thus producing 30 samples in total (Fig. 14).

The core tubes consisted of 45cm lengths of clear cylindrical PVC pipes fitted with a core deployment mechanism (Fig. 15-16). This enabled the tubes to be inserted vertically into the seafloor using the manipulator arms of the ROV, simultaneously permitting water to escape out of vents cut into the tubes' upper lengths (Fig. 17). Each tube was chamfered on the base to facilitate cutting into the sediments. Management of the ROV for position on the seafloor was achieved through a local transponder grid, allowing cores to be located with centimetric accuracy.

To characterize the geotechnical properties of the cores, upon recovery full descriptions and visual classifications were recorded using standard sediment descriptions (grain size, bedding) and color classification with a Munsell Soil Chart. This method also revealed significant structural features, such as delamination surfaces and fractures. Where present, macrofossils were recorded, together with the content of the organic horizons and, in particular, the type and size of organic components.

The results of the core samples taken from Environmental Sampling Area I focused on the visible wreckage and revealed the stratigraphic sequence of the upper levels of seabed to comprise a 2-10cm layer of light brown, unconsolidated mud with persistent bioturbation, succeeding a stiff gray clay with occasional partings of silt and shell (Table 1). The sediment recovered was consistently observed to have a shear vane value too low to register.

The 15 cores in the wider Environmental Sampling Area II produced three distinct core sequences. The first was similar to the sterile cores taken from Environmental Sampling Area I; the second possessed minor organic traces (fragments less than 2mm long); and the third sequence contained major organic traces of wood, fragments of broken shell and corroded iron. Some of the wood fragments were sufficiently well-preserved and of sufficient size to perceive growth rings. The distribution of these cores was plotted onto a site plan. Based on this information, it was decided to locate the remaining 15 cores at points that would refine the distribution and boundaries of the zones of nil organic presence, minor organic presence and major organic presence.

The complete environmental program took 54 cores, an increase of nine above the minimum performance spec-

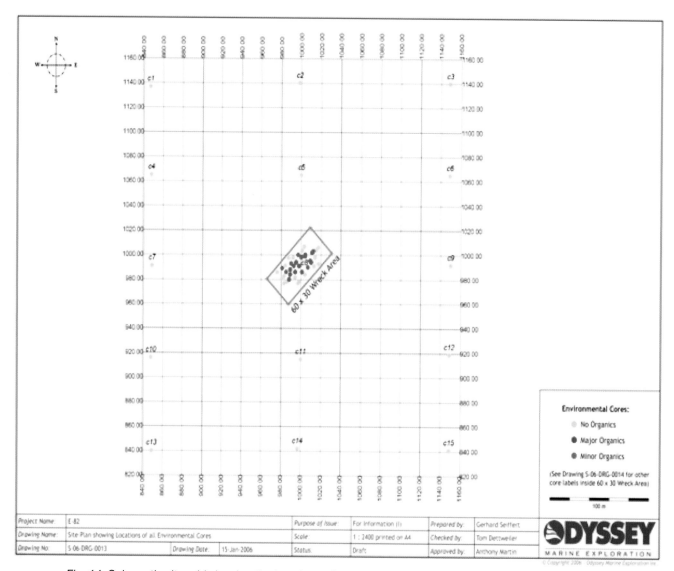

Fig. 14. Schematic site grid showing the locations of environmental cores taken during Phase 1, Stage 1A.

Fig. 15. Preparing environmental core tubes for descent onto the wreck.

Fig. 16. A 2m 'long core' installed on ROV Zeus for descent onto the wreck site.

ification. The sediment recovery within the cores varied from 30% to 100%. The environmental data redefined the boundaries of the wreck site by demonstrating that the zone containing significant major organic material should be taken into consideration. The visible wreck material covers an area of some 164m², while the newly projected wreck site covers 348m² – an increase of 112% (Fig. 18). This dimension assumes that the outermost cores containing wreck material constitute the furthest site boundaries. The wreck area, however, may expand out even further to the cores that did not exhibit wreck material, and it is also possible that wreck material may exist deeper than the cores were able to penetrate.

5. Site Biology

To assess the interactive effects between the wreck site and the marine biology, Fernando Tempera of Topaz Environmental and Marine (TEAM) of the Department of Geography and Geosciences at the University of St. Andrews initiated a suite of non-intrusive analytic measures to characterize the biological oasis effect formed on the shipwreck and on the flora and fauna residing on and around the vessel. The effects of the localized sea life and ecosystem on the

disintegration and decomposition of the shipwreck and its contents were also determined.

Analyses drew on a 993m² geo-referenced image mosaic, which was composed of 55m² hard bottom and 938m² of soft bottom, classed as bathyal hemipelagic fine muds and silts. The site is also characterized by extensive burrowing activity in the form of holes, burrows, mounds and trails, indicative of the presence of endofauna and bioturbation processes.

A total of 40 distinct epibenthic megafaunal life forms belonging to six different phyla were identified (from anemones to shrimp, hermit crabs, diamond back squid, white starfish, electric rays and blackbelly rosefish, amongst others). Of these forms, seven were sessile on the hard bottom artificially provided by the archaeological artifacts. Most extensively, gorgonians of a few tens of centimeters length protrude from the artifacts, but their density is not high. Accounting for 14 of the species, fish represent the highest diversity. A total of 16 species were observed in association with hard bottom, while 24 occur on soft bottoms. Four of these co-existed in both types of seafloor. Seventeen species are of commercial value.

The values of species richness (number of species per area of habitat) illustrate a concentration of conspicuous

Fig. 17. Environmental data being acquired using a core tube descending into the seabed.

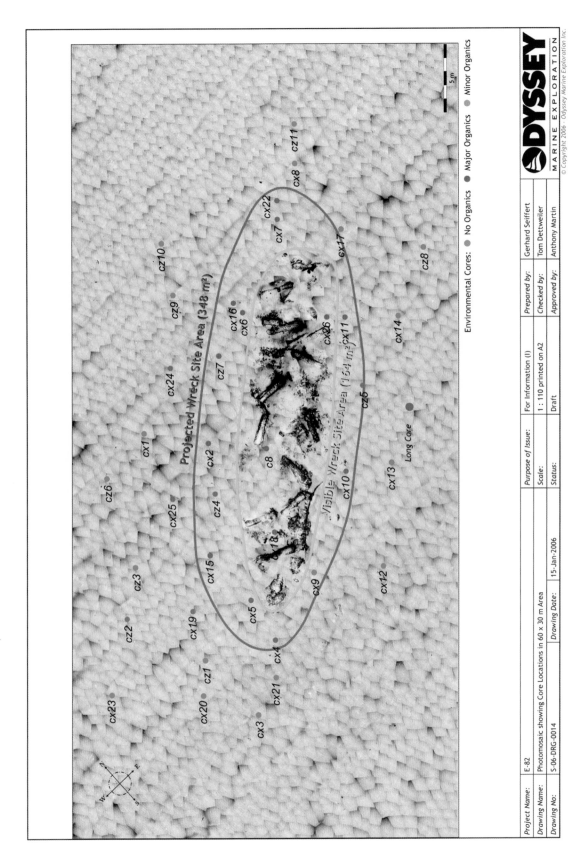

Fig. 18. Photomosaic showing core locations and expanded wreck site area based on coring results. The yellow outline delineates the extent of the visible wreck. The red outline defines the predicted minimum extended wreck site revealed by core testing and analysis, although the wreck area could continue further out to the cores that contained minor organics and beyond to areas whose depth was not penetrated by coring.

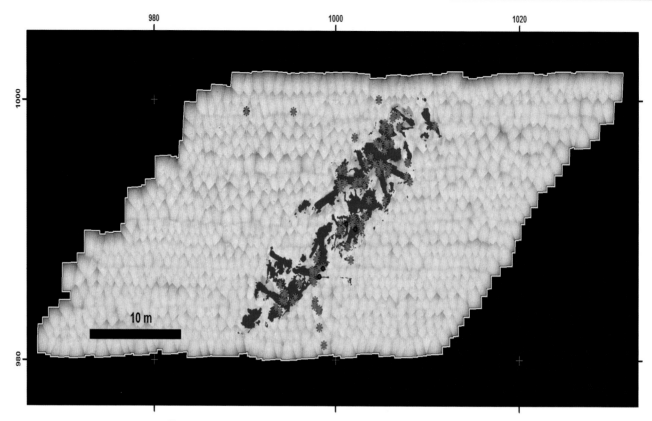

Fig. 19. Distribution of cidarid sea urchins across the wreck site.

megafaunal species on the hard bottom artifacts: 29.1 species/100m² over the artifacts, compared to 2.6 species/100m² on sediments. The difference is even larger if only the sessile epibenthic species are taken into account – 12.7 species/100m² over the wreck, compared to 0.4 species/100m² on sediments.

No flora (macroalgae or seagrasses) was observed because the site is located below the euphotic zone. Neither reefs of cold-water corals, nor massive sponges have been identified. The density of gorgonians was also insufficient to classify the habitat as a coral garden. These facts are significant because the presence of such deep-sea features would have had important implications on the nature conservation valuation of the artifacts.

The epibenthic sea urchin *Cidaridae sp.* was selected to investigate the ecological role of the artifacts as aggregators of marine life creating any oasis effect. This is a slow-moving epibenthic macroinvertebrate for which fully-grown individuals are easily recognizable on the video and stills imagery collected. The species was present both on hard and soft bottoms. Thus, a spatial analysis of the relationship of the individuals with the presence of hard bottom analysis was considered a suitable indicator of the extent to which the artifacts influence the surrounding marine life.

The analysis of the density of cidarid urchins provided values of 2.018 individuals/m² for hard bottoms and 0.013 individuals/m² for soft bottoms, amounting to a 158-fold difference in abundance between the two habitats (Fig. 19). Some 90% of the individuals are found within 15cm of hard structures. Despite the significant number of species attached to the artifacts, the total amount of biofouling can be considered trivial.

6. Pre-disturbance Recording of Surface Features

A. Cannon

Site E-82 contains 17 visible cannon (Figs. 7, 11, 12), while concretions identified 1m west of cannon C8 and between cannon C3 and C4 may represent additional buried guns. Several hard obstructions detected close to the visible wreck mound during the environmental coring program probably represent additional examples. These iron guns can be divided into three categories based on recorded lengths: cannon of less than 2m length, which are either partly buried or fractured; longer than 2m, but less than 2.5m long; in excess of 2.5m long (Table 2).

Cannon No.	Cannon Length (m)	Grid No.
C1	1.51	991.1-992.4/982.8-983.8
C2	1.04	991.0-991.8/983.2-983.7
C3	2.94	991.8-994.7/983.9-985.8
C4	2.68	993.2-995.5/986.8-988.4
C5	2.62	995.7-998.2/986.3-986.9
C6	2.80	998.4-999.2/986.8-989.7
C7	2.48	1001.4-1003.0/988.5-990.7
C8	2.63	997.9-1000.3/991.7-993.1
C9	2.86	1000.3-1002.9/993.5-994.2
C10	2.78	1004.8-1006.0/992.2-994.8
C11	2.70	1004.9-1006.9/994.6-995.3
C12	2.66	1005.8-1008.4/993.8-994.8
C13	2.87	1004.7-1007.1/995.6-997.3
C14	1.60	1004.9-1006.2/996.8-998.2
C15	2.15	1007.6-1008.5/995.2-996.9
C16	2.74	1006.3-1008.8/998.2-999.8
C17	2.22	1009.7-1010.4/998.5-999.2

▫ = < 2m incomplete/partly buried

▪ = > 2m but < 2.5m

▪ = > 2.50

Table 2. Site E-82 cannon measurements and grid contexts.

During the late 17th century, as previously in history and for some decades later, no precise proportional relationship existed between the length of a cannon and the weight of shot fired. The most accurate means of determining the classification of cannon is to determine the diameter of the bore. The bore of broken cannon C14 was positively measured at 8.5cm, which could correspond to a generously bored 3-pound cannon with significant wind-age. Cannon C3, at 2.94m (9'6") the longest example on site E-82, is a possible 24-pounder. The minimum expected length for a 24-pounder in the second half of the 17th century would be 9'6", corresponding to published surveys of similar guns (Caruana, A., 1994, *The History of English Sea Ordnance 1523-1875, Vol. I*. Rotherfield, 98-122).

Cannon C8 is most likely identifiable as a 6-pounder of the 'new' English design (Cunningham Dobson, N.,

Cambridge Expedition 2001. An Archaeological Investigation, 33) and is tentatively dated to the period of gun founding between approximately 1660 and 1719. Pursuant to a request from the UK Ministry of Defence, the remains of cannon C8 were handed over to the Spanish Institute of Underwater Archaeology in Cartagena, Spain, for conservation. Repeated requests for access to this and other artifacts from site E-82 for study and publication remain unanswered by the Institute.

B. Anchors

Two concreted iron anchors and a possible anchor fluke characterize the surface of site E-82 (Fig. 12). Anchor A1 lies midship on a north-west to south-east axis, with its arms to the east and ring preserved to the west. Its shank is 2.3m-long, the arms 1.4m-wide and the ring's diameter about 40cm. The arms are broadly bowed, with indistinct palms, while the anchor in general, especially the shank, is extremely delaminated and corroded. The seabed around

it is heavily covered with leached iron and encrustation. No stock is visible.

Anchor A2 lies to the north-eastern end of the wreck on an east-west orientation (Fig. 8). Its shank is 3.1m long and arms 1.3m wide. The gently bowed arms face due east and appear to incorporate a reinforced and thickened collar at the throat. As far as can be observed from the anchor's concretion, the southern fluke palm seems to be undeveloped (compared to the classic Admiralty anchor form). The northern fluke is trapped under cannon C16. The circular ring is visible with a hole at its center to the east, engulfed by white plastic bags. A 'knotted' linear concretion stain observable immediately below the ring, extending northeast to south-west, may be a stock.

C. Ballast

A cluster of roughly rounded stones, each measuring approximately 20 x 10cm maximum and extending across an area of about 2.10 x 1.55m, is a distinct feature on the

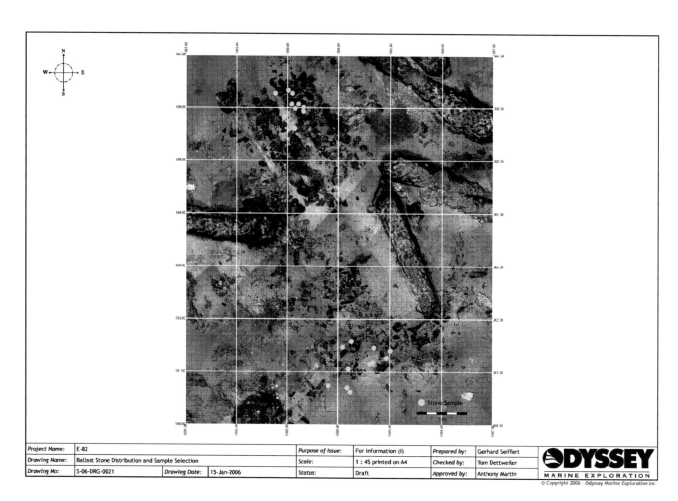

Project Name:	E-82			Purpose of Issue:	For Information (I)	Prepared by:	Gerhard Seiffert
Drawing Name:	Ballast Stone Distribution and Sample Selection			Scale:	1 : 45 printed on A4	Checked by:	Tom Dettweiler
Drawing No:	S-06-DRG-0021	Drawing Date:	15-Jan-2006	Status:	Draft	Approved by:	Anthony Martin

ODYSSEY
MARINE EXPLORATION
© Copyright 2006 - Odyssey Marine Exploration Inc.

Fig. 20. The locations of possible ballast stones recovered for petrological analysis (labelled in yellow).

north-western flank of the wreck site (Figs. 6, 12). A second scattered cluster of stones extends to the south-east.

The north-western zone consists of three discrete strips of stones, each 2.10m-long and running in a north-west to south-eastern orientation between cannon C9 to the south, C13 to the north and C10 to the east. Both the northern and central strips of stone are devoid of sediment, while the southern cluster is largely concealed. The northern strip is about 88cm-wide and contains some 73 visible stones, while the central one measures about 70cm-wide and consists of some 58 stones. Only about 22 stones are visible amongst the southernmost cluster. Immediately north-east of the northern stone strip seems to be a coherent area of wooden planking (see Section 9 below). While it is tempting to assume that these strips of stone are ballast, the amount visible is clearly insufficient to constitute a classic ballast pile. For the purposes of this report, and pending further investigation, however, it will be assumed that these stones are likely ballast.

A significant archaeological feature between these possible ballast strips, north-east and south-west of the central cluster, are clearly defined linear voids extending parallel to the main ballast orientation (north-west to south-east). In the case of the southern void, sharp edges define its length. These 'ghost' linear recesses may occupy the locations of decomposed wooden frames or riders, which, on the basis of the photomosaic, would have measured approximately 15cm in width (Fig. 6).

Towards the eastern flank of the center of the shipwreck is a second exposed section of possible ballast stones between cannon C7 to the south and C10 to the north. This scattered material is strewn amongst intrusive modern glass bottles across an area of some 2.2 x 1.9m. At least 55 stones define this feature.

A sample of 20 stones was recovered for geochemical and petrological analyses to identify their geological source (Fig. 20). Geochemical analysis was conducted on a subsample of ten stones by TEAM and petrological analysis performed on a sub-sample of a further 10 stones by Dr. Peter Kokelaar of the Department of Ocean and Earth Sciences at the University of Liverpool. The assemblage comprises rounded to well-rounded stones with a high density, indicative of deliberate selection to maximize weight displacement in relation to minimal spatial volume. Nine of the ten samples subjected to geochemical analysis derived from an igneous origin with a metamorphic imprint classified as altered ultramafic rocks.

The stone is unusual, but could have originated in a single field location because all the rock types are found in or around ophilite complexes. The TEAM analysis concluded that the three most likely coastal candidates where ophilites are found in the UK are the Lizard in Cornwall, Unst and Ballentrae in Scotland. Complementary petrological analysis similarly identified possible origins for the stones at coastal ophiolite exposures in the UK, such as the Lizard Ophiolite Complex of Cornwall and the Unst Ophiolite of Shetland. However, the Ballantrae Ophiolite of south-western Scotland has been discounted because its beaches lack this assemblage form. A wider potential for the origin of the stones in the coastal fringe of the Mediterranean was also acknowledged.

Further opinion about the results of the geochemical and petrological analysis was sought from Dr. Alan Bromley of PetroLab, Falmouth, a specialist in the geology of the Lizard peninsula. Bromley's examination concluded that some of the stones contain the relatively rare mineral glaucophane, which excludes the Lizard peninsula as the source of site E-82's possible ballast. However, outcrops exhibiting glaucophane are indigenous to the Shetland Islands and Anglesey. A source in the British Isles is therefore possible. Other European sources for ophiolitic stones include Brittany, the heel of Italy and the Greek shores of the Aegean.

7. Phase 1, Stage 1B. Trial Excavation

Following the dusting of the uppermost layer of 1-4cm of mobile sediment covering the archaeological surface features, a second master photomosaic was produced (Fig. 11) to serve as the primary tool for managing decisions about the positions of trenches during Stage 1, Phase 1B. In turn, this facilitated the production of a master site plan (Fig. 12). Archaeological features and apparent sterile zones on the photomosaic were examined to design a strategy for trench locations, distribution, size and orientation (Fig. 21). Excavation proceeded systematically in six trenches in horizontal stratigraphic units, with the objectives of assessing the wreck's level of preservation and orientation, without disturbing any of the concretions.

A. Trench 1

Trench 1 examined the area between cannon C14 and C16 for the presence or absence of wooden planking to define the form of preserved wooden structure and to assess site stratigraphy and the relationship between the visible wreck site and the visually sterile area beyond the confines of the site to the north-west. The position of Trench 1, which measured 1.0 x 0.6m, was chosen to shed light on the orientation of the wreck and, hence, to provide information about any surviving cargo (Fig. 21).

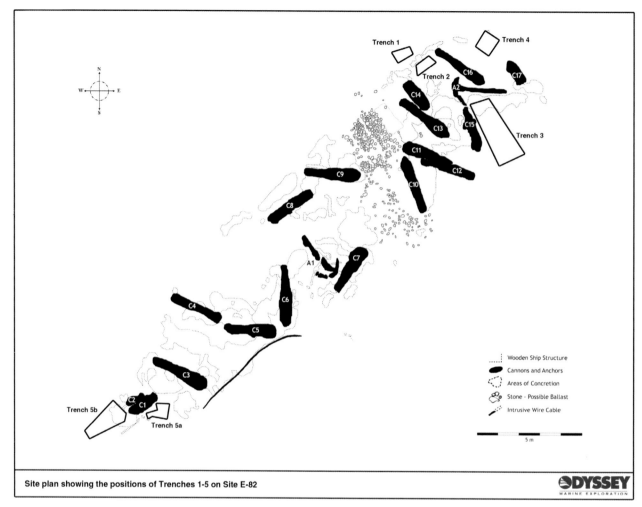

Site plan showing the positions of Trenches 1-5 on Site E-82

Fig. 21. Plan depicting the locations of trial Trenches 1-5b

The excavation of the upper layer of sediment (Context 2) exposed a layer characterized by a common distribution of concreted iron fragments (Context 4), which appeared to overlie what initially resembled wooden planking, but proved to be a concretion crust (Context 5). A deposit of sediment stained with dark patches, presumably from the leaching of organic residues into the clay silt, was observed (Context 6) beneath the concretion crust (Fig. 22; Table 1).

Excavation ceased in Trench 1 following the exposure of Context 6 to leave Context 5 undisturbed. No timber structure was exposed, although of course planking may survive beneath the concretion layer. Instead, the trench was extended to the north-east by strategically 'leap-froging' over a concreted iron feature lying north-east/south-west at an angle of 90° to the longitudinal axis of Trench 1. (This second sondage to the north-east was designated Trench 2.)

B. Trench 2

The objective of Trench 2, measuring 0.8 x 0.6m, was to investigate the stratigraphic relationship between the wreck site and the visually sterile area to the north-west. The excavation exposed a stratigraphic sequence about 15cm thick in the form of gray clay containing shell and organic smears (Context 2). This overlay more consolidated gray clay, about 54cm thick, with no visible inclusions (Context 3). Trench 2 was excavated to a total depth of 69cm.

This visually sterile area yielded various artifacts from Contexts 1 and 2 in the form of an iron cannon ball, three potsherds, two brick fragments, a copper table/jug leg and fragments of nail concretions and wood, but no evidence of coherent planking. During the exposure of the north-east facing trench section, a wooden plank featuring an iron nail stain was exposed in the section face. Further cleaning revealed what seems to be identifiable hull planking extending south-west to north-east across the face of the trench. The wood is 9cm thick and located at a depth of 15cm below the seabed. The presence of this timber confirmed that within Context 3 the environmental characteristics of the site have preserved significant sections of hull timber, not just small fragments. A complex stratigraphic relationship seems to exist between the wreck site and the visibly sterile seabed to the north-west of this location, including the presence of sub-surface timbers, whose precise character will only be determined by further exploratory excavation.

C. Trench 3

Trench 3 (Fig. 21), 2.4 x 1.0m and penetrating to a depth of 41cm, yielded evidence of substantial timbers embedded within Context 2. The wood remains are extensively gribbled and in a poor state of preservation, with extremely eroded surfaces inter-cut by worm holes. Fragments of sulphur leaching from iron concretions are visible to the east of the trench, while intrusive modern debris was present to the west.

Trench 3's hull planking is seemingly indicative of frames and planks preserved in their original configuration. The coherence of the structural remains is less intact in the south-eastern end of test trench: all that could be observed were large lumps of highly decomposed unidentifiable black material (Fig. 23), partly corroded iron apparently obscuring the underlying strakes. What appear to be eroded trunnel ends were observed on the surface of this timber.

Trench 3 seems to contain four frames, each sided 28cm wide, spaced 18cm part and extending in a north-west to south-east direction out of the northern face of the trench. Three-quarters of the way southwards, the trench is inter-cut by two extensive longitudinal timbers, most probably identifiable as stringers, over 40cm wide, which are positioned at an angle of about 65 degrees in relation to the frames and extend in a south-west to north-east direction. Artifacts recovered during the excavation of Trench 3 consisted of eight potsherds, six nail concretions, a fragment of rope and fired brick.

Fig. 22. Features exposed in Trench 1 after excavation.

Fig. 23. Frames and possible stringers (at right in foreground) exposed in Trench 3.

D. Trench 4

Trench 4, measuring 0.8 x 0.8m, was positioned at the north-eastern end of the wreck site, some 1.5m north-east of cannon C16. As soon as the excavation commenced, a compact concreted layer (Context 7) was encountered stratified below a very thin layer of Context 2. As the excavation proceeded cautiously, disarticulated fragments of wood were observed in Context 7. One of these appeared to feature trunnel holes. The concreted mass measures 38 x 22cm.

Excavation and recording of the concreted mass and three sections of straight-sided wood were undertaken. Two of these sections descend at an angle of 100-110 degrees from the top sides of the concretion. The third section runs horizontally beneath, from one side of the trench to the other. This feature, measuring 24 x 13cm and incorporated into the concreted mass, possibly represents the side of a wooden box located at a depth of 47cm below the seabed.

At this stage, the excavation ceased to leave Context 7 undisturbed *in situ* in order to concentrate on the primary objective of the trial excavation phase of Stage 1, Phase 1B: to locate wooden structure and diagnostic material culture without resorting to the removal of concretion layers.

E. Trenches 5a and 5b

To test for the presence of wooden ship structure and attempt to determine the vessel's orientation, Trench 5a, measuring 1.6 x 0.8m, was positioned at the south-western flank of the visible wreck site on the eastern flank of cannon C1 (Fig. 21). Excavation between cannon C1, C2 and C3 revealed an upper layer of semi-consolidated sediment (Context 2). Once removed, an iron concretion was exposed in the north-western corner of the trench. The semi-consolidated sediment superseded a darker gray clay (Context 3). Coherent ship structure extending diagonally across the western side of the trench along a north-east to south-west axis was recorded in Context 3 (Fig. 24).

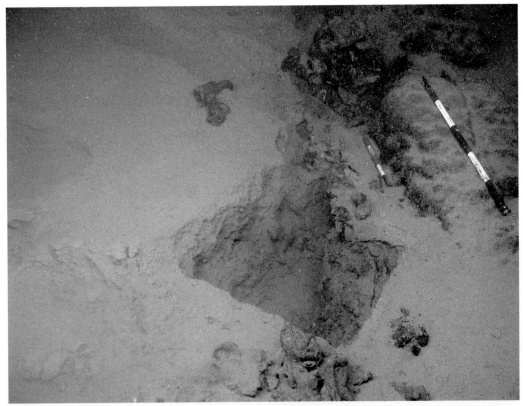

Fig. 24. A substantial timber extending across the western side of Trench 5a, with cannon C1 at right.

To examine its continuation without disturbing cannon C1 and C2, Trench 5b was excavated on the south-west side of cannon C1. What appeared to be heavily encrusted iron cannon balls were identified between the north-western edge of Trench 5a and cannon C1. The stratigraphic succession in Trench 5b, measuring 1.8 x 0.9m, proved identical to Trench 5a, with the same timber element tapering inwards towards the south-west (Fig. 25). To record whether the timber extended any further, excavation was continued in this direction, demonstrating discontinuity. In total, the Trench 5b wood complex measures 1.6m in length and tapers from 60cm-wide to the north-east to 20cm-wide at the south-west. The angled north-east side dovetails precisely with the axis of the timber exposed in Trench 5a and may be considered a 3.2m-long coherent element of the same structural unit.

At this preliminary stage of research, the structural timber in this trench can possibly be identified as located towards the eroded terminal of the ship's hull. The timber features a 90 degree rabbet on both sides. This feature, combined with the tapering of the wood, is not indicative of a keel, and must represent a structural component located at a higher elevation, possibly the keelson. The initial interpretation points towards this feature representing the end of a warship's hull towards the bow, where the lines of the ship assumed a fluted 'V' shape in plan. If correct, this interpretation would imply that the ship settled on the seabed in an upright formation and that the erosional surface lies on a relatively level plane. These assumptions need to be tested further, and it must be emphasized that this possibility remains tentative at this stage.

8. Pottery Assemblage

Surprisingly, ceramic remains of any form (kitchen, table and luxury wares) proved to be elusive on site E-82. The site formation pattern gives the impression that the ceramic domestic assemblage has been extensively scattered and relocated off-site or remains buried. The likelihood that this fragmentation and disturbance is solely the result of the wreck process is extremely low. The material's absence must be largely explained by post-depositional disturbance by trawler cables shattering ceramic vessels and causing low-density fragments to be washed off site by the prevailing north-eastern currents or to be covered completely by sediment.

The non-disturbance survey of the wreck revealed a total absence of ceramic material, and only 12 sherds were recovered during excavations in Trenches 1, 2 and 3. This material was submitted to Jacqui Pearce of Museum of

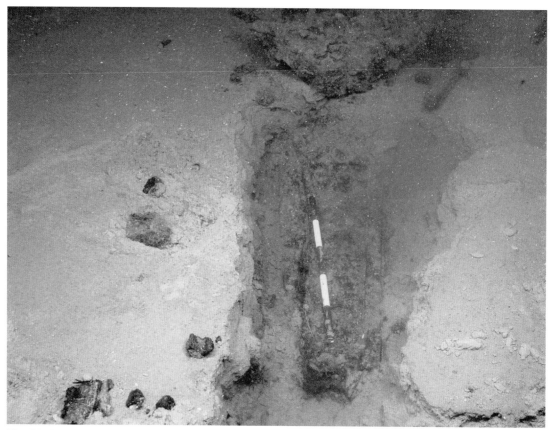

Fig. 25. A substantial timber in Trench 5b, possibly the keelson, tapering inwards towards the south-west.

London Archaeology for identification and assessment. All of the sherds are very small (2.0-5.0cm in length), none weigh more than 13g, and all are highly abraded, consistent with long-term submergence and exposure in a high-energy marine environment. In four instances the sherds are so badly burnt that the original fabric and glaze colors are impossible to recognize with certainty. Two or three sherds may be from a single vessel, but all others derive from different ceramic containers. Positive identification has proven difficult, a consequence of the condition of the pottery's few diagnostic attributes. Initial consultation with a ceramic petrologist was unable to confirm suspected sources.

The pottery does not appear to be cargo, given the evidence for use (sooting), but represents domestic assemblage: part of the everyday shipboard equipment. Two decorated sherds (S-06-0033-CS and S-06-0034-CS) are both probably from ceramic vessels produced in Italy in the 16th or 17th century. Even if the ship wrecked at site E-82 originated in England, this is consistent with the attested presence of imported pottery of this type in London in late 16th- to early 17th-century contexts. Such pottery is generally thought not to have been in circulation beyond the third quarter of the 17th century.

Coarse whiteware sherds with volcanic inclusions may have an origin in the Iberian peninsula. A fine, green-glazed red earthenware is more difficult to source without further scientific analysis. This fabric, however, is not local to the London area, although one sherd of redware is comparable with pottery produced in the London region during the 17th and 18th centuries.

On the balance of probability, a wreckage date in the 17th century seems most likely for this assemblage. The presence of Italian and Iberian wares does not suggest that the ship is not of English origin, as these wares were widely distributed across Europe. The sherd of possible London-area redware is unlikely to have been present on a ship without an English connection because this ware was not widely traded inter-regionally and certainly was not exported. There is no pottery in the examined sample that was definitely developed after the late 17th century.

9. Vessel Structure

Despite site E-82's overall poor level of preservation, the removal of mobile sediment during cleaning operations and the trial trench excavations identified coherent sections of ship's structure:

1. An area of apparent articulated planking was exposed

during light surface 'dusting' between the possible ballast stones and cannon C13 on the north-western side of the wreck (Fig. 6). Extending beneath the stones, this feature may represent either ceiling planking or strakes within the lower hull (see below). Horizontal and parallel plank edges seem to extend in a south-west to north-east direction parallel to the main longitudinal axis of the wreck site. At least 11 possible planks are visible, while an identical surface discoloration south west of the ballast stones may denote their continuation. An unusual feature observed between these possible ballast strips, to the north-east and south-west of the central cluster, are clearly defined linear voids running parallel to the main orientation. Both of these lines are not covered by stones and, in the case of the southern void, sharp edges define its length. These 15cm-wide 'ghost' recesses may occupy the locations of decomposed frame stations or riders.

2. Trench 3: substantial hull planking, poorly preserved, extending down to a depth of 41cm (Fig. 23). Four frames sided 28cm wide, spaced at 18cm intervals, run in a north-west to south-east direction out of the northern face of the trench. Three-quarters of the way southwards, the trench is intercut by two extensive longitudinal timbers – possibly stringers – over 40cm wide, which are positioned at an angle of about 65 degrees in relation to the frames. These latter timbers extend in a south-west to north-east direction.

3. Trench 5a: a coherent timber exposed between cannon C1, C2 and C3 extending diagonally across the western side of the entire 1.6m-long trench along a south-west to north-east axis (Fig. 24). Trench 5b: the continuation of the Trench 5a timber was exposed on the south-west side of cannon C1. In total, this wood complex measures 1.6m in length in Trench 5b and tapers from 60cm-wide at the north-eastern end of the trench to 20cm-wide to the south-west (Fig. 25). A rabbet cut at a 90 degree angle characterizes both sides of the timber. The angled north-eastern structure seems to dovetail precisely with the axis of the timber exposed in 5a and may be considered a coherent element of the same structure.

Several intact nail concretions recovered from site E-82 measure 7.0cm and 8.3cm long. Due to concretion growth, these artifacts are generally amorphous and featureless. Exceptions include S-06-0017-CN, which displays a clear square section profile, and two further nails with circular heads, of which S-06-0030-NA is 6cm-wide.

At this preliminary stage of limited trial excavation, the structural hull timbers offer little more than tentative interpretative possibilities. All wood surfaces are heavily

eroded, pitted, warped and covered with worm holes. The site E-82 timbers unanimously display cracks developed along the natural grain, creating uneven depressed and blistered planes. All of the timbers are charcoal gray in color (almost certainly the result of contact with the soft, semi-consolidated mud-clay in an anaerobic environment). This sedimentological matrix does not seem to favor good preservation, and the water-saturated clays 10-30cm beneath the surface of the seabed seem to have fully decomposed some sections of planking, such as the timbers in the south-eastern end of Trench 3.

At present, the recorded timbers seem to consist of lower sections of the ship's structure located around the turn-of-the-bilge. The hull displays some continuity and coherence, evident in the approximately 11 possible planks inter-connected between probable ballast stones and cannon C13 on the north-western side of the wreck. These planks underlie the stones and, as far as can be perceived visually on the photomosaic, are concentrated at a level lower than the frame station lines to the south-west. This configuration would suggest that the planks may be strakes and not ceiling planking, which would be expected to cover and conceal the frames. Alternatively, the transversal 'ghost' timbers inter-cutting the ballast could be riders, which would identify the underlying longitudinal wood as ceiling planking and not strakes.

The evidence from Trenches 5a and 5b at the south-western extremity of the wreck site may suggest the possibility that one end of the shipwreck has been identified. These trenches contain a single timber extending down the entire length of Trench 5a, which was 1.6m long, and for 1.6m in Trench 5b, providing a total length of 3.2m. It tapers from 60cm-wide at the north-eastern end of Trench 5b to 20cm-wide to the south-west, suggesting the presence of an eroded terminal component of the ship's hull. The timber features a 90 degree rabbet on both sides. The widening of the wood is not indicative of a keel and is a likely structural component located above this element. The initial interpretation points towards the possibility that this feature represents the terminal at the bow, where the lines of the ship assumed a fluted 'V' shape in plan. If correct, this would imply that the ship settled on the seabed in an upright formation and that the erosional surface lies on a relatively level plane. However, these assumptions will need to be tested further, and it must be emphasized that this possibility is just one of several tentative interpretations at this stage.

Eight fragments of wood recovered from Trenches 3 and 5 were submitted to Alyson Tobin and Jill McVee from the School of Biology and Histology Unit at the University of St. Andrews for thin-section preparation, species identification and possible provenance analysis. Samples from site E-82 were also examined at Kew Gardens. Two fragments were too carbonized for analysis, while the remaining six fragments were positively identified as white oak, pine, laurel and sycamore. Determining a tight geographical provenance for the trees has not been possible.

10. Conclusion

The pre-disturbance survey and trial trench excavation of site E-82 presented a unique opportunity to examine a deep-water shipwreck of probable 17th century date. This collaborative HMG/Odyssey project has contributed extensively to the current largely theoretical and developing paradigm of shipwreck site formation in the abyss. Despite the political complications that disrupted the recording of Phase 1, Stage 1B (see below), significant scientific data has been secured, which addressed the archaeological objectives agreed within the historical agreement devised by Her Majesty's Government and Odyssey Marine Exploration. The HMS *Sussex* Project has proved that both detailed non-disturbance archaeological survey and scientific excavation can be conducted at depths exceeding 800m to a high standard of data procurement.

The formation of site E-82 is intriguing. Contrary to mainstream perceptions of shipwreck preservation improving in relation to depth, articulated within public perception as 'time capsules', a major contribution of the current project has been the presentation of contradictory data. The site has clearly trapped significant quantities of modern rubbish – plastic bags, cartons, tin cans, glass bottles, trawler wire and fishing net, not to mention more hazardous material, such as asbestos. Much of this material is integrated into the matrix of concretions surrounding iron artifacts and has burrowed its way into the wreck, disturbing archaeological contexts.

The presence of these intrusive elements is actually relatively modest compared to many shipwreck sites surveyed by OME in deep water. The impact of modern contamination on the integrity of deep-water site formations must now be taken into consideration alongside the complex interplay of environmental and cultural factors now accepted as moulding wreck formations, from the pre-impact to recoil and post-depositional effects. With such shipwrecks being disturbed in this manner, compounded by destabilization by fishing trawlers and, in some areas, by sand and gravel dredging, the stereotypical ideal of preservation *in situ* is clearly not always workable and is sometimes an inappropriate utopia of maritime cultural heritage management.

In addition to the near-total absence of pottery visible on the site's surface and excavated in the trenches, the erosion of the hull is a second highly conspicuous feature of site E-82's formation. The ship, in fact, compares extremely poorly to the coherence of many hulls surveyed and excavated in shallow, often high-energy environments. The ceaseless strong current of 3-5 knots present beneath 300m of water seems to have been sufficiently powerful during the last three centuries to have eroded the shipwreck down to a flat plane, with archaeological remains sealed in place by overlying cannon, anchors, concretions and probable ballast.

The geographical position of site E-82 is consistent with the reported location of the sinking of the third-rate, 80-gun HMS *Sussex*. The wreck's visible surface features measure 26.5m long and 6.5m wide. When compared with the dimensions the *Sussex* – 47.90m on the gun deck, 40.36m on the keel and a beam of 12.60m – these figures come up short. Nevertheless, given the fact that the upper sediment of the seabed in the wreck environment comprises soft clay, a significant proportion of the vessel may remain buried. The extension of the site beneath the sediments to the north-east remains undetermined. It is potentially revealing that the environmental core analysis located major organic material at distances of up to some 10m beyond the confines of the visible wreck manifestations, which would extend the projected wreck area by 112% (from 164m² to 348m²) or more.[5]

Based on the authoritative British Library Additional Manuscripts 9289, Brian Lavery has demonstrated that the *Sussex*'s cannon comprised:
- 24 demi-cannon
- 30 culverins (18-pounders)
- 22 6-pounders
- 4 sakers (5 1/4-pounders)

The exclusively iron cannon form the main feature of the wreck and are consistent with a north European/English ship of the late 17th century, though probably not Mediterranean, because such ships had fewer guns and usually a proportion were cast in brass rather than iron. Research relating to the armament installed on the *Sussex* indicates that the guns were almost certainly all cast of iron. In the late 17th century, and for several decades earlier, the Royal Navy obtained its stocks of guns by commissioning cast ordnance from a few English iron foundries, by purchasing stock from Holland and Scandinavia, and especially by seizing guns from captured ships. The ships of France and Spain were typically armed with bronze guns, mainly as a consequence of long prior experience with their own problems manufacturing suitable iron weapons and largely due to the nature of ores available and foundry methods.

Guns C15 and C16 are the most easily identifiable and seem to match 6-pounders that could have been fitted on the half deck and coach towards the stern of the *Sussex*. The bore on C14 indicates that it is a 3-pounder, a relatively rare calibre, but recorded to have been on the poop deck of the *Sussex*. Since three guns that appear to be the same size as C14 were found near the north-eastern end of site E-82, this pattern is perhaps an indication that the stern lies in this direction. None of the evidence arising from this examination, or from the analyses of the artifactual and ecofactual data recovered, discounts the site from being the wreck of HMS *Sussex*. Therefore, the working assumption that this site can be considered an ongoing candidate for the *Sussex* remains valid.

The fieldwork designed to identify the wreck at site E-82 remains incomplete. Operations were suspended on 15 January 2006 when the *Odyssey Explorer* returned to port in Gibraltar to re-fuel and change crew. On the afternoon of 17 January, OME departed from Gibraltar to resume operations. In the face of direct hostility from the Spanish Guardia Civil, the ROV was not deployed. Instead, the ship was forced to return to Gibraltar and the project was temporarily suspended.

At the time of departure from site E-82, Odyssey's management had no reason to consider that access would be denied upon return, since the Spanish Government had indicated that Odyssey's operations would not be disturbed, pursuant to the company's invitation for Spanish archaeologists to join the expedition. The deterioration of relations was abrupt and the aggressive nature of the confrontation required immediate action to ensure the health, safety and security of all staff aboard the *Odyssey Explorer*. Given this immediate threat, Odyssey was compelled to take the extreme decision to vacate the shipwreck site.

This protocol, however unsatisfactory, is in line with various advisory guides. The ICOMOS Charter on the Protection and Management of the Underwater Cultural Heritage (1996), Article 11, states that 'The health and safety of the investigating team and third parties is paramount. All persons on the investigating team must work according to a safety policy that satisfies relevant statutory and professional requirements and is set out in the project design.'

Similarly, the Institute of Field Archaeology's *Standard and Guidance for Archaeological Field Evaluation* (2001, 3.3.9), advises that 'Health and Safety regulations and requirements cannot be ignored no matter how imperative the need to record archaeological information; hence Health and Safety will take priority over archaeological matters.' This priority is reiterated and repeated verbatim in the IFA's *Standard and Guidance for Archaeological Exca-*

vation (2001: 3.3.11) and *Guidance for Nautical Archaeological Recording and Reconstruction* (2007: 5.10).

At present, access to site E-82 remains denied to Odyssey by the Spanish government despite the wreck's location in international waters, as recognized by the UK Government. Consequently, the site cannot be reinstated and all six excavation trenches, in addition to the two reception pits, were left open. Thus, Odyssey was unable to complete the measurement of features exposed in the excavated trenches and to produce the intended photomosaics of each trench, which has complicated the interpretation of the wreck's archaeology.

Concern over the possible vulnerability of these deposits remains acute, but is hopefully alleviated by the constantly moving sediments, which are likely to seal exposed surfaces in a very short period of time. It should also be noted that Odyssey was forced to abandon expensive operational equipment on-site, including six transponders, two datum plates, a mini-plex container and four ranging rods.

Reinstatement of the site, including backfilling of the trenches (and preferably the replacement of the sediment dusted off the visible site), would be desirable to maintain the integrity and stability of the site and its archaeological deposits for the future. However, despite Spanish approval of proposals by Odyssey for these archaeological investigations, the requisite steps necessary to proceed have not been completed by Spanish authorities. Return to the site remains an unresolved intention.

Meanwhile, a final report on site E-82 is under preparation for publication and will include a comprehensive presentation of all archaeological data obtained to date, specialists' reports on the environmental program, marine biology, pottery and brick, geochemical and petrological studies of the ballast, the wood species, and site interpretation.

Acknowledgements

The authors wish to express their sincere thanks to John Simkins, Maddy Southey and John Crockford of the UK Ministry of Defence; Andrea Parsons of Gifford UK and the staff of Gifford Gibraltar, who provided Anthony Martin with material support; and to Frank Mallon, Stuart Webster and Graham Scott of Wessex Archaeology.

Notes

1. The precise co-ordinates of the wreck site are not disclosed in this paper because the shipwreck project remains ongoing and to protect the archaeological integrity of the wreck site from unauthorized interference.
2. The objective of this report is to introduce the primary archaeological data of site E-82, not to present an

historical and archaeological interpretation of the ship's identity or of HMS *Sussex*.

3. The SAE (*Sussex* Archaeological Executive) is a self-regulatory body appointed jointly by HMG and OME, comprising six British and American scholars, to approve archaeological standards employed by Odyssey on-site.

4. The full complexity of the technology on-board the *Odyssey Explorer* (including conservation and archaeological facilities) and custom-designed for ROV Zeus are beyond the limits of this report, and will be presented in the final publication.

5. Two reception pits were cut 10m beyond each end of the visible wreck site in which to deposit temporarily, and in a comparable marine environment, material culture and any timbers not destined for recovery. A discontinuous timber was exposed in the north-eastern pit, indicative of possible archaeological continuation beyond the visible site parameters.

8

Deep-Sea Fishing Impacts on the Shipwrecks of the English Channel & Western Approaches

Sean A. Kingsley

Wreck Watch Int., London, UK

Odyssey Marine Exploration's Atlas Shipwreck Survey Project in the western English Channel and Western Approaches has recorded 267 shipwrecks across 4,725 square nautical miles. A high density of the sites displays evidence of detrimental impacts from the deep-sea fishing industry, predominantly trawler, scallop dredge and gill net fishing activities.

This report summarizes the effects of deep-sea fishing on all shipwrecks in the Atlas zone. The wreck of HMS *Victory*, a first-rate Royal Navy warship lost in October 1744, is examined in particularly focused detail. Three main sources are utilized and compared: side-scan sonar analysis, visual site reconnaissance of all targets using a Remotely-Operated Vehicle, and a statistical analysis of fishing in relation to wreck locations based on 73,385 aerial sightings and 838,048 VMS (Vessel Monitoring System) satellite observations of fishing vessels operating inside Odyssey's shipwreck survey zone between 1985 and 2008.

This research leads to the conclusion that the shipwrecks in the study zone have been, and continue to be, targeted, inadvertently disturbed and/or systematically exploited for deep-sea fishing due to their nature as nutrient-rich biological oases and shelter for an abundance of fish populations. Whereas steel wrecks display a level of expected structural robustness in many cases, the majority of the archaeologically significant wooden sites are at high risk, some extremely so. Largely isolated beyond the parameters of national and international legislative protection, the small percentage of surviving sites that constitute unique cultural heritage requires attention and a plan for preserving the archaeological data that can still be secured from them.

This report is intended to assess methodically and statistically a problem that is unquantified and poorly recognized to date within marine archaeology. The intent is not to cast blame on fisheries. Rather, it is to present the factual data in order to develop plans for taking into account all different user groups of underwater cultural heritage, particularly the crucial role fishermen serve society and the economy. This report is rooted on the principle that the relationships between fishermen, ecologists, archaeologists, historians, salvors, sport divers, heritage managers and marine construction companies working legally in the study region are, and must remain, respectfully symbiotic.

These results reflect specifically the conditions in one geographical area, but bring to the fore an issue that should be studied worldwide to help develop a rational and effective approach for protecting and preserving deep-sea maritime heritage.

1. Introduction

Between May 2005 and October 2008, Odyssey Marine Exploration documented 267 shipwrecks in the western English Channel and Western Approaches as part of the ongoing Atlas Shipwreck Survey Project. These sites date between the mid-17th century and the modern day and lie in depths of up to 190m. All fieldwork was conducted beyond the territorial waters of the UK and France.

The research compiled to date demonstrates that the preservation of archaeologically significant deep-sea shipwrecks in the English Channel seems to be generally extremely poor. The levels of wreck deterioration identified during Odyssey's non-intrusive survey program exceed those recorded by other organizations on shallow sites within the same body of water. Five dominant interlocking factors explain the poor preservation reality:

1. Extreme storm waves within the relatively shallow English Channel.

2. Significant bottom currents and resulting sediment transport.

3. Post-depositional trawler/dredging impacts.

4. Post-depositional wreck fishing.

5. The depth charging of sites during and after World War II to prevent submarines hiding in wreck shadows.

Evidence suggests that the most detrimental of these impacts on wreck deterioration today seems to be the modern fishing industry (Figs. 1-3). Although the far-reaching effects of this economic activity on marine ecosystems has been examined qualitatively and quantitatively in great detail since 1970, when the International Council for the Exploration of the Sea (ICES) initiated an inquest into the effects of trawls and dredges on the world's seabeds (Council Resolution 1970/5/1), its effects on shipwrecks of historical importance remain almost completely undocumented and undefined.

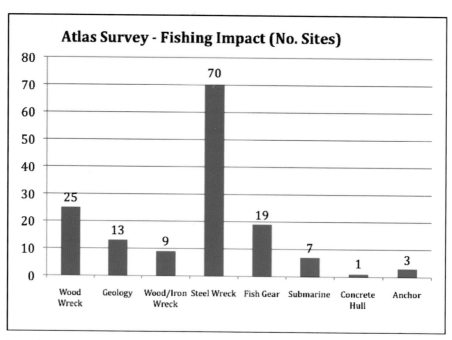

Fig 1. Wrecks and anomalies affected by all fishing impacts in the Atlas shipwreck survey zone (nos. of sites).

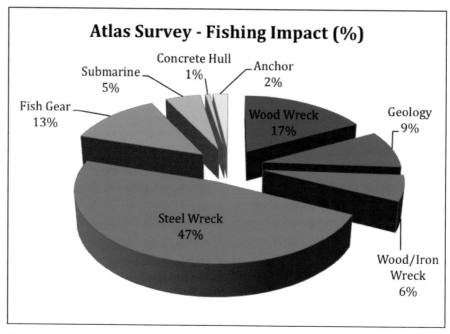

Fig 2. Wrecks and anomalies affected by all fishing impacts in the Atlas shipwreck survey zone (%).

Of the 267 shipwreck sites inspected by Odyssey to date in the Atlas survey zone, 112 shipwrecks (including 25 wooden wrecks, 70 steel wrecks and 7 submarines) display direct trawler and wreck fishing impacts and damage that definitively proves that shipwrecks of all ages are at high risk.

Wreck Watch Int., in consultation with Odyssey Marine Exploration, is currently undertaking a comprehensive analysis of the character, distribution and scale of these impacts. The destruction of wooden wreck sites is especially worrying because after the effects of currents and trawling they typically display little relief above the sea bottom. Consequently, they are not easily identified by fishermen or avoided by trawlers. Hull remains and small finds are generally only preserved in sections of wreck sites where a sealing layer of cargo (such as concreted wooden barrels), cargo concretions or iron cannon have pinned archaeological remains *in situ* (Figs. 43, 45). Of the total number of sites discovered by Odyssey in the English Channel and Western Approaches, it is notable that very few pre-date

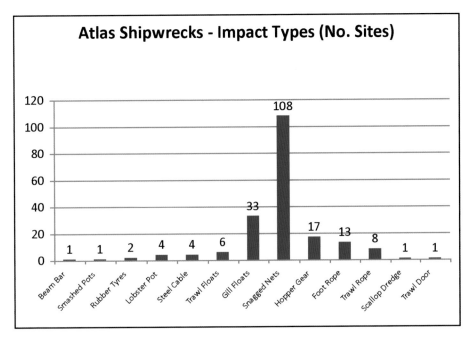

Fig 3. All fishing impact types on shipwrecks in the Atlas shipwreck survey zone.

1800, which is an inaccurate reflection of the maritime history of this area (see Section 6 below). This suggests that many important shipwrecks have already been lost, along with the knowledge embedded within them.

Where no heavy and durable cargo, ballast or ordnance has sealed sections of wreckage *in situ*, it is realistic to expect that sites of major archaeological significance have been – or are in the process of being – completely destroyed. The near-total absence of ceramic cargoes suggests that consignments of pottery wares are similarly insufficiently robust to survive trawler and dredging impacts.

2. Deep-Sea Fishing & Marine Ecology

A. History of Trawling

Environmental awareness of the potentially destructive power of fishing technologies on the marine environment is a centuries-old dilemma. As early as 1376 a Commons Petition to King Edward III of England complained about a newly introduced fishing gear, the 'wondyrechoun', a "three fathoms long and ten of men's feet wide" state-of-the-art device

> "made in the manner of an oyster dredge... upon which instrument is attached a net so close meshed that no fish be it ever so small which enters therein can escape... the great and long iron of the wondyrechoun runs so heavily and hardly over the ground when fishing that it destroys the flowers of the land

below water there... the fishermen take such quantity of small fish that they do not know what to do with them; and that they feed and fat their pigs with them, to the great damage of the commons of the realm and the destruction of the fisheries, and they pray for a remedy" (Alward, 1932: xx).

These proto-ecologists were already aware of the 'wondyrechoun's' negative impact on the marine environment; historically the invention of the beam trawler in the 14th century was greeted with hostility from the outset. In 1583 the Netherlands banned its use for shrimping in estuaries and the French made its use a capital offense the following year.

The large-scale, intensive 'ploughing' of the seabed, however, is a relatively modern phenomenon. In Britain the fisheries of the North Sea opened up to beam trawlers in the early 19th century, when 'West End Fish' were sold to the upper classes of London. Once the steam railway engine was developed in the late 1820s, seafood could be distributed and sold across great distances while fresh on an unprecedented basis. By the early 1860s, over 100,000 tons of fish were being transported by Britain's railways each year (Roberts, 2007: 141-2).

By 1820 a nucleus of Devonshire fishermen had settled in Dover and Ramsgate to fish the Channel and joined Belgian, French and Dutch fishermen in the North Sea and off the French and Belgian coasts (Alward, 1932: 11-12). By 1877, the principal ports for some 1700 deep-sea trawlers in the Atlas survey catchment area of the English Channel were Plymouth and Brixham (the birth places of the trawling industry in the UK), and

Dover and Ramsgate to the east (Young, 1877: 21. 46). Otter boards were introduced in 1880, enabling vessels to deploy larger nets (Jennings *et al.*, 2001: table 5.1). The introduction of the steam trawler in Britain in 1882 expanded the geographic scope of the fishing industry and the temporal capability of trawlers to operate offshore (Alward, 1932: 9). At this time steam trawlers were working up to 48km from land (Duke of Edinburgh, 1883: 36).

Immediately after World War II and the boom in human demography, fisheries development intensified dramatically, with production rising from 17.7 to 28.4 million tons globally. Between 1959 and 1972 rapid geographic fishing expansion led to annual world catches rising further from 30 to 60 million tons. The introduction of technological developments such as synthetic fibers, chain mats to protect the belly of nets and more powerful ship engines facilitated substantial increases in the size and weight of fishing gear and, in turn, fishing systems that could cover huge areas of ocean efficiently.

From 1972 to 1982 fisheries production rose again from 60 to 68 million tons worldwide as some coastal states extended the commercial parameters of fished waters. In the early 1980s the weight of many fishing boat beam trawls increased from 3.5 tons to 10 tons and formerly unexploited fishing grounds were penetrated for the first time. This period witnessed the final expansion of distant water fleets into the Indian Ocean, South Pacific and southwest Atlantic in search of high-value species such as tuna, shrimp and cephalopods. Between 1983 and 1992 annual catches increased from 68 to about 85 million tons globally, and issues of sustainability and the environmental implications of fisheries finally became a subject of widespread concern and environmental debate (Hall, 1999: 3, 4, 49).

The unsustainable scale of trawling on global fishing communities in the wake of the widespread overexploitation of resources has been acknowledged and examined scientifically for over 60 years. Severe overfishing in many developing countries resulted in a series of dramatic fishery collapses. Within 15 years of World War II the otter trawl fishery industry in the southeastern North Sea caused marked declines in elasmobranchs and larger-bodied invertebrate species. In the early 1950s the Hokkaido sardine, the North Sea and Atlanto-Scandinavian herring and the Californian pilchard decreased or collapsed. In Port Phillip Bay, southeastern Australia, the scallop fishery started in 1963 collapsed in 1968. The anchoveta of Peru dwindled from 12 million to 2 million tons in the early 1970s. In the Gulf of Thailand, the North Sea and West Africa, over-hunted long-lived species started to be replaced within the food chain by more adaptable short-lived ones (Hall, 1999: 4, 5, 59, 75). Research in the northern Irish Sea, where commercial scallop fishing has been active since the late 1930s, has concluded that this industry "may have already altered the community structure sufficiently that a return to its pre-dredging state is impossible, possibly

Fig 4. The wreck of a 1930s steel cargo vessel (site T34n43d-1; Target 366) with fishing nets across the bows and anchors. Atlas shipwreck survey zone, depth 156.5m.

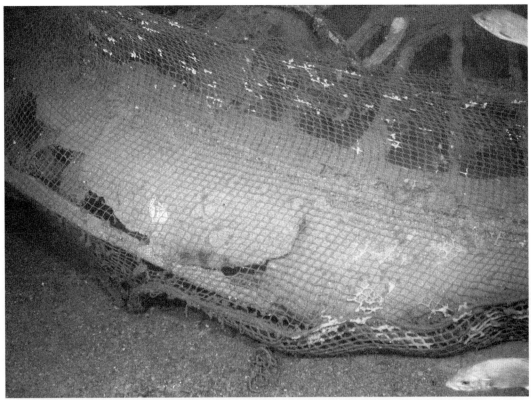

Fig. 5. Snagged fishing net on a 20th-century steel wreck (site T34n37d-1; Target 494). Atlas shipwreck survey zone, depth 144.8m.

Fig. 6. Dense fishing net snagged on the inside of a heavily impacted 20th-century steel wreck (site T3a61g-1; Target 183). Atlas shipwreck survey zone, depth 105.8m.

Fig. 7. Fishing nets snagged across the sides and deteriorated interior of German submarine U-326, sunk in 1945 (site T12n9e-1; Target 373). Note the abundance of conger eels resident within its hull. Atlas shipwreck survey zone, depth 164.4m.

owing to permanent changes in the substratum…" (Bradshaw *et al.*, 2000: 94, 101).

As a consequence of the threat of this uncontrolled expansion, the International Council for the Exploration of the Sea (ICES) initiated an inquest in 1970 into the effects of trawls and dredges on seabeds (Council Resolution 1970/5/1). This was followed in 1988 by the ICES Study Group on Effects of Bottom Trawling, convened in response to Council Resolution 1987/2/7 to collect information available since 1972 and to report on the development of bottom trawling gear, existing literature, national research and proposals for coordinated research (Fonteyne, 2000: 16). As a consequence of this ongoing monitoring, manifold issues of zoning, fish quotas and trawler decommission have been heavily debated and in some cases implemented.

B. Fishing Equipment & Channel Fishing Ports

Fishing within the English Channel is, of course, an extensive and significant economic pursuit. In 2006, 95,138 tons of fish were landed by UK vessels alone in England and Wales with a sale value of £137,623,000 (Walmsley and Pawson, 2007: 8, table 2.2). Within the territorial and

offshore waters of southern England, a variety of methods are employed by commercial fishermen. The four main types of trawl/dredge systems are defined according to methods adopted to keep the nets open (based on Gray, 1995: 7-13, 66):[1]

i. Otter Trawl

The mouth of the net is held open by weighted ground rope, floats on the headline and the lateral paravaning effect of the otter boards or 'doors'. The bridles, warps and otter boards help to drive the fish towards the net. Trawl gear is either dragged along the seabed when targeting demersal fish or through the water column to catch pelagic fish. 'Tickler' chains attached along the front of the demersal nets dig into the seabed, disturbing flatfish, which then swim up into the path of the net. The use of large rubber discs or steel bobbins on the ground rope enables the trawl to be towed over rocky ground (rock hopper gear).

More than one otter trawl net can be towed by a single boat (multi-rig trawl gear). Otter trawls are used to catch demersal roundfish (cod, whiting and haddock), flatfish (Dover sole, plaice and turbot), pelagic fish (herring, sprat and bass) and crustacea and molluscs (cuttlefish and squid).

ii. Pair Trawl

This configuration is towed by two boats, each attached to the trawl by a single warp. The degree to which it is held open varies with the distance between the two boats and there is no need for otter boards. This method is used for both demersal and pelagic fish, mainly by inshore trawlers.

iii. Beam Trawl

This net is designed to exploit demersal fish. Modern beam trawlers usually have two beams, one towed on either side to give stability. A chain matrix is often attached to the bottom of the net to prevent damage caused by boulders when used over rocky ground, and tickler chains are attached between the steel runners when targeting flatfish on sandy ground.

iv. Dredges

Dragged along the seabed, these are used for digging or scraping up molluscs such as scallops, oysters, mussels, clams and cockles. Scallop dredges are attached to a beam, and two beams are usually towed either side of a boat (the number of dredges depends on engine power). A dredge consists of a bar bearing metal teeth that rake up the molluscs and collects them in a reinforced net or bag (Fig. 38). Heavy dredges with longer teeth dig deeper into the seabed and are required to extract scallops (recessed in the seabed), whereas lighter dredge gear scrapes queen scallops from the surface of the seabed. There are various types of scallop dredges, the most common design being the 'Newhaven' dredge, which is between 0.5 and 1m wide with a spring-loaded tooth bar that helps prevent the dredge becoming snagged on rocky and stony areas. The 'French' dredge, up to 2m in width, is heavier than the Newhaven dredge and utilizes a diving plate to force the dredge into the seabed.

In addition to trawlers and dredges, offshore impacts include fishing with gill nets on wrecks and the laying of lobster/crab pots. In the case of wreck fishing with gill nets, single sheets of netting (either fixed or drift) are set vertically taut to enmesh demersal or pelagic roundfish. Gill nets set for demersal roundfish are fixed to the seabed by a weighted ground rope and anchors or other weights at intervals and kept taut by a series of floats attached to the head rope. Gill nets with mesh size of between 120 and 160mm are set over rough ground and wrecks for cod, pollack, ling, conger eels, rays and dogfish. Small-meshed (<120mm) tangle nets are set for sole and plaice on smooth grounds, whereas larger ones (>200mm) are set for rays, turbot and brill. Boats of 6-8m can set over 5,000m of net, although the average is in the region of 1,500-3,000m.

Lobster/crab potting is an extensive activity in the English Channel. A pot used to catch crustacea is generally comprised of a steel frame (sometimes plastic coated) covered in netting forming the trap, which is then anchored by a weighted base. The two main types are the 'inkwell' and 'parlor' pot. The inkwell pot is dome-shaped, commonly used for brown crabs and crawfish, which enter from the top of the pot. The parlor pot, used for lobsters, crabs and sometimes prawns, is rectangular-shaped, comprising two chambers. Crustacea enter a baited chamber and, when trying to escape, enter the second chamber where they remain trapped. The continual development of more powerful hydraulic capstans has given the fleets the ability to haul more pots. A two-man crew may work up to 600-700 pots. Boats nearing 10m in length and crewed by three fishermen can work in excess of 1,000 pots and are capable of hauling around 500 pots in one day.

Since the 1980s, large pot boats, some over 20m in length and capable of working in excess of 2,000 pots, have been constructed with live storage facilities on board to exploit offshore stocks of brown crab. Fresh bait is used to entice crabs into pots, whereas partly decomposed food is more successful for attracting lobsters. Fish offal (heads and back bones), non-commercial and low value species (dogfish, conger eel, gurnard, sprat, herring and mackerel) are favored bait. Potting activity is highest during the warmer months, with pots set out to 48km from shore for crabs, lobsters and crawfish.

Information pertaining to the coastal fisheries of England and Wales for 2005-2006 (Walmsley and Pawson, 2007: 45, 47-49, 51-54, 56, 58, 82, 83) demonstrates that within the catchment area of the Atlas shipwreck survey zone the majority of the offshore fleet is based in Devon and Cornwall. A major queen scallop fishery exists off southern Cornwall and south of the Western Approaches, while rich grounds for brown crab occur far offshore in southern Cornwall. South Devon's total landings in 2006 were 24,225 tons with a value of £33.7 million.

Major deep-sea fishing fleets are based in South Devon at Brixham, Kingswear, Salcombe and Plymouth. This area supports one of the largest brown crab potting fleets in the UK, comprising vivier-equipped offshore boats each setting up to 2,000 pots out to the middle of the Channel and often landing their catches into France. The fishery peaks during the warmer months. Devon SFC bylaws set a close season from July to September for scallops and also limit the type, size and number of dredges allowed (the use of French dredges is now prohibited).

At Brixham, one of the largest ports in southwest

England, 13 of the 25 beam trawlers are between 15-35m long. Kingswear is mainly a brown crab port with around 30 boats setting pots. Together with the potting fleet in Salcombe, this area is one of the main brown crab fisheries in the UK. Around seven boats of >10m set between 800 and 1,500 pots each in the mid-Channel area. Some of these boats are equipped with live storage facilities and often land directly to the Continent. In addition to brown crabs, spider and velvet crabs are also retained, and the smaller boats set pots for lobsters.

Salcombe supports a fleet of around 12 potting boats, six of which are more than 10m long. Some of the larger boats land in France, whilst the rest of the fleet lands to live storage facilities in the port. The numbers of pots fished vary greatly depending on the size and capability of each vessel, but the larger boats usually set over 1,200 each. The traditional inkwell pot is most commonly used offshore.

Plymouth's offshore fleet consists of up of 25 boats using otter trawls, beam trawls, scallop dredges and mid-water trawls, and includes two mid-water freezer trawlers. In winter and spring Scottish vessels target bass using pair trawls, and fishermen from other locales occasionally target

anchovy, pilchard and herring. In summer a number of the local trawlers change to scalloping and are joined by visiting scallopers from around the UK. Around 10-15 boats set pots for crabs and lobsters from April to the end of December.

Off Cornwall, beam trawlers fish for monkfish, megrim, lemon sole and sole. Otter trawlers exploit more seasonal fisheries, with cod and whiting landed in autumn and winter and flatfish and rays landed all year round. Some of the larger netting boats work as far as 112km offshore, fishing gill nets in the deep-water grounds to the southwest and south of Ireland for hake. Some fishing vessels based in Looe operate up to 64km offshore. Total landings in Cornwall accounted for 11,173 tons in 2006 valued at £28.3 million.

Newlyn is one of the largest fishing ports in England and Wales and where the majority of offshore boats are based in Cornwall. A regular fleet of around 40 trawlers and 50 static gear boats land their catches into the daily fish market, along with visiting boats from Brixham, Looe, Mevagissey, Ireland and the Channel Islands. Most of the 23 local beam trawlers are 25-29m in length and operate exclusively offshore for monkfish,

Fig. 8. Dense fishing net caught on the side of a post mid-20th century wooden shipwreck (site T3a19c-1; Target 152). Atlas shipwreck survey zone, depth 91.6m.

Fig. 9. Fishing net cable snagged on a mid to late 19th-century wooden shipwreck (site 2T3a6a-2; Target 648). Atlas shipwreck survey zone, depth 83.6m.

Fig. 10. Fishing net caught on a concreted iron cannon on a 19th-century wooden shipwreck (site 2T7a64f-2; Target 624). Atlas shipwreck survey zone, depth 108m.

Fig. 11. Fishing net snagged on an iron concretion on a mid to late 19th-century
wooden shipwreck (site 2T11a4a-1; Target 587). Copper hull spikes and heavily deteriorated
planking in the foreground. Atlas shipwreck survey zone, depth 96.2m.

megrim, lemon sole and sole. Up to 60 boats, between 5-25m, set enmeshing nets from this port, the larger boats fishing hake and setting gill nets and tangle nets for monkfish, turbot and rays well offshore and often taking an important bycatch of lobsters and crawfish. About 18 boats, six of which are over 12m, set pots for brown crabs both inshore and offshore.

Of 30 vessels operating from the important port of Padstow, the majority use static gear such as nets or pots. Some of these boats were originally built for trawling, but dwindling catches of sole, cod, hake and mackerel have resulted in fishermen switching to netting. The netters take turbot, monkfish, cod and pollack, and the larger boats fish offshore for hake. Between late December and the end of March, up to 20 non-local beam trawlers participate in the local sole fishery. Fourteen boats are involved in the pot fishery during the summer, the larger and faster vessels working anything up to 1,000 pots each as far away as Lundy Island. Nearly all the boats bring their pots ashore between late December and March to avoid the worst of the weather and also to prevent damage from the visiting beam-trawl fleet. Most of the shellfish are exported weekly by vivier truck to Europe direct from the quay.

Due to strong tides within the Severn Estuary and the lack of sheltered bays, fishing within south and north Wales is largely restricted to within 9.6km of shore.

C. Quantifying Trawler Disturbance on Marine Ecosystems

Marine ecologists have no illusions about the destructive nature of bottom trawling. In a seminal paper, Watling and Norse (1998) drew an analogy between the effects of mobile fishing gear on the seabed and the clearcutting of a forest on land (Table 1). They identified one major difference, however, in the scale of the relative disturbance. Whereas forest clearcutting is estimated to fell a vast 100,000km² of woodlands per year worldwide, the area trawled annually is about 150 times greater. Each year trawling disturbs an area of seabed as large as Brazil, the Congo and India combined and results in local and global impacts on the structure, species composition and biogeochemistry of benthic communities (Watling and Norse, 1998: 1190-92).

All forms of deep-sea fishing from wreck fishing to trawling result in differing impacts on the seabed. Understanding the environmental effects of this industry demonstrates both how undeveloped the management of deep-sea marine archaeology remains in comparison to other areas of marine science and, simultaneously, provides key insights into impacts on the sea bottoms with which shipwrecks interact. These studies have focused on short- and long-term changes to benthic organisms and fish populations.

Impact	Clearcutting	Bottom Trawling
Effects on substratum	Exposes soils to erosion & compress them	Overturns, moves, and buries boulders and cobbles, homogenizes sediments, eliminates existing microtopography, leaves long-lasting grooves
Effects on roots or infauna	Stimulates, then eliminates saprotrophs that decay roots	Crushes & buries some infauna; exposes others, thus stimulating scavenger populations
Effects on emergent biogenic structures & structure formers	Removes or burns snags, down logs, and most structure-forming species above ground	Removes, damages or displaces most structure-forming species above sediment-water interface
Effects on associated species	Eliminates most late-successional species & encourages pioneer species in early years to decades	Eliminates most late-successional species & encourages pioneer species in early years to decades
Effects on biogeochemistry	Releases large pulse of carbon to atmosphere by removing & oxidizing accumulated organic material; eliminates nitrogen fixation by arboreal lichens	Releases large pulse of carbon to water column & atmosphere by removing & oxidizing accumulated organic material; increases oxygen demand
Recovery to original structure	Decades to centuries	Years to centuries
Typical return time	40-200 years	40 days to 10 years
Area covered per year globally	~0.1 million km^2 (net forest & woodland loss)	~14.8 million km^2
Latitudinal range	Subpolar to tropical	Subpolar to tropical
Ownership of areas where it occurs	Private & public	Public
Published scientific studies	Many	Few
Public consciousness	Substantial	Very Little
Legal status	Activity increasingly modified to lessen impacts or not allowed in favor of alternative logging methods & preservation	Activity not allowed in a few areas

*Table 1. A comparison of the impacts of forest clearcutting and trawling
on the seabed (from Watling and Norse, 1998: 1192, table 4).*

The results of the current archaeological study within the Atlas survey zone now indicates that shipwrecks need to be considered an integral component of the marine environment and managed accordingly.

As sources of rich nutrients and sanctuaries for the shelter and nesting of myriad sea life, shipwrecks are key cogs in the food chain for fish and human consumption needs alike. When trawls or nets snag on shipwrecks, their impact is likely to be more devastating long-term on cultural remains than on the seabed or marine life. While biological oases can regenerate over wreckage of any kind, whether scattered or coherent, once wooden hulls and artifacts are dragged, smashed or snapped, their fate and the loss of scientific data is irreversible.

Bottom fishing is one of the most widespread sources of anthropogenic disturbance of seabed communities in the North, Irish and Celtic Seas and within the English

Channel (Kaiser *et al.*, 1998: 354). The ecosystem effects of trawling are well known to affect species diversity, community structure and size composition (Kaiser *et al.*, 2002: 116), primarily:

A. Changes in predator-prey relationships leading to shifts in food-web structures that are not necessarily reversed by reduction of fishing pressure.

B. Effects on abundance and body-size distributions that can result in fauna dominated by small body-sized individuals.

C. Genetic selection for different physical characteristics and reproductive traits.

D. Effects on populations of non-target species (cetaceans, birds, reptiles and elasmobranch fishes) as a result of by-catches or ghost fishing.[2]

E. Reduction of habitat complexity.

Type of Gear	Gear in Contact with Seabottom	Typical Width of Major Disturbing Parts (m ship^{-1})	Towing Speed (knots)	Penetration Depth (cm)
Beam trawl (flatfish)	Trawl shoes, tickler chains, chain mats			
A). Offshore (>12 miles)		12.0 x 2	6	>6
B). Inshore (<12 miles)		4.0 x 2	5	?
Shrimp beam trawl	Trawl shoes, ground rope with rollers	0.2 x 4	4-5	?
Otter trawl	Otter doors	1.5 x 2	3-4	8
	Ground rope	30	3-4	8-10
Industrial trawl				
A). Single	Otter doors	1.5 x 2	3.5	8-10
	Ground rope	25	3.5	?
B). Pair	Ground rope	25	3.5	?
Demersal pair trawling	Ground rope	40	3	?
Mussel dredge	Blade & belly	1.75 x 4	2	5-25
Cockle dredge	Suction head	1.0 x 2	2	≥5
Scallop dredge	Tooth bar & belly			
A). English		0.76 x 16	3	3-4
B). French		2 x 5	3-4	<10
French clam dredge	Blade & belly	0.7 x 2	3-4	<15

Table 2. Summary of the effects for different fishing gears used in the North Sea (from Hall, 1999: 50, table 3.1).

F.   Re-suspension of surficial sediments.
G.   Alteration of benthic community structure.

Trawling and dredges physically disturb the upper layer of sea bottom sediments as they pass, flattening the seabed, exposing shell debris at the surface and buried nutrients to the water column (Tables 1-2). Beam trawlers are typically fitted with tickler chains or a chain matrix attached between the beam and foot rope. Chains are designed to exclude rocks from the gear as they penetrate the upper centimeters of substratum to disturb and fluidize the top layers of sediment and drive flatfish from the seabed and into the net (Duplisea et al., 2001: 1). These inevitably damage the infauna and epifauna. Estimates suggest that some preferred areas of fishing may be visited up to 400 times a year (Kaiser et al., 1998: 354). A typical beam trawler towing two 12m-wide nets at 6 knots can impact about 535 km² of substratum in 2,000 hours in the North Sea (Duplisea et al., 2001: 1, 5).

Shellfish dredges, rock-hopper otter trawls and heavy flatfish beam trawls cause the most extensive disturbance because they are in direct contact with the seabed (Kaiser et al., 2002: 118). The scale of impact is not regular, but is determined by various conditions: the speed of towing, the physical dimensions and weight of the fishing gear, the type of substratum deposits and the strength of currents and tides. Effects on sea bottoms may persist for anywhere between a few hours in shallow waters with strong tides to

decades in deeper areas subject to less natural disturbance (Jennings et al., 2000: 4).

The most dynamic change caused by such fishing gear is to the surface topography. Trawler doors increase the sea bottom roughness through furrowing. Flattening results in the removal of unattached weed, seagrass and coral. Trawling over time can be expected to gradually lower the physical relief of the habitat with potentially deadly consequences for some fish species. The impact of the re-suspension of sediments and fragmentation of rock and biogenic substrata causes a release of nutrients held in the sediment, exposure of anoxic layers and the release of contaminants, which increases biological oxygen demand. Sediment community function, carbon mineralization and biogeochemical fluxes are strongly affected by trawling disturbance (Kaiser et al., 2002: 119-20).

Two food sources are generated for benthic scavenging species by towed fishing gear: dead disarticulated material and exposed and damaged fauna. Interestingly, it is common practice for fishermen to re-trawl an area shortly after being fished due to the exposure of nutrients during the first pass, which attracts a frenzy of fish to the freshly 'plowed' area (Hall, 1999: 60). This has obvious destructive repercussions for newly impacted shipwrecks.

Studies reveal that seabottom form is a major influence on seabed disturbance. The longevity of furrows' vertical disturbance and visibility is dependent on sea bottom sediment profiles. Experiments have demonstrated that on a seabed consisting of mainly coarse sand, such as prevails in some parts of the catchment area of the shipwrecks of HMS *Victory* and the *Marquise de Tournay* (Figs. 43-44), a Bordeaux armed privateer lost in 1757 (Williams and Eltis, 2004: 128) and discovered by Odyssey in 2008, beam trawler tracks may only remain visible for up to 52 hours after a vessel has fished over the site. On sediments with mainly finer particles, tracks completely fade after 37 hours (Fonteyne, 2000: 15).

Absence of fishing furrows on side-scan sonar records from the Atlas shipwreck survey zone can thus in no way be considered to represent an absence of extensive fishing activities. Thus, in a well-known trawl area off southern Portugal, currents contribute to rapid furrow erosion: no marks were detectable across 86.1% of the area examined by a manned submersible down to depths of 300m (Morais *et al.*, 2007: 116). By contrast, scallop dredge tracks can remain visible for up to 2.5 years in maerl habitats (Hall-Spencer and Moore, 2000: 105) and in more compact environments, notably gravels. This may explain the vivid set of scallop dredge furrows graphically registered on side-scan sonars across the center of Odyssey's mid-17th century site with its cargo of elephant tusks, located in a dense shell and gravel environment (Target 580, site T7a35f-5; Figs. 40, 45-47).

Studies indicate that beam trawls will penetrate bottom sediments by depths of 1-8cm, depending on the speed of towing and sedimentological matrix. However, this is highly dependent on seabottom forms. Some tickler chains with an array of 15 chains (weighing around 1.5 tons) only penetrate less than 3cm at speeds of 2.2 knots. Elsewhere, 9.5m-wide beam trawls fitted with 17 tickler chains have disturbed seabeds to depths of 10-20cm. In the case of 12m beam trawls fishing on hard sandy bottoms, tickler chain penetrated to at least 6cm (Fonteyne, 2000: 16-17, 34).

In the northern Irish Sea area of the Isle of Man, gravel sediments are found down to depths of 70m and vary from extremely stony to fine gravel substrata. As with the Western English Channel and Western Approaches, this is an important fishery for great scallops (*Pecten maximus*) and queen scallops (*Aequipecten opercularis*). The annual scallop fishing season lasts from 1 November to 31 May, although queens may be fished all year round. Scallops live in (or are partly buried in) surface sediments and are fished with toothed, Newhaven-type dredges. Toothed dredges scrape through the top 10cm or so of seabed with every pass (Bradshaw *et al.*, 2000: 84).

A single pass of a beam trawl can kill 5-65% of the resident fauna on the seabed for larger invertebrate species, which equates to annual fishing mortality rates of 5-39% in heavily trawled areas (Duplisea *et al.*, 2001: 1). Erect

foliose fauna, which build reef-like structures, are destroyed by towed gear (such as tube worms or the corraline algae, maerl). Studies of mortality rates in the Netherlands by beam trawling for flatfish show that while whelk and hermit crabs are largely unaffected, starfish suffer a 10-30% mortality rate and up to 90% of bivalve *Artica islandica* are killed (Hall, 1999: 53).

Other research into invertebrate species (gastropods, starfish, crustaceans and annelids) detected direct mortality due to a single passage of a trawl varying from about 5% to 40% (Bergman, 2000: 49). Trawling can reduce anthozoa (anemones, soft corals, sea ferns) by 68% and asteroid starfishes by 21%. Repeated chronic dredging is predicted to lead to 93% reductions for anthozea, malacostraca (shrimps and prawns), ophiuroidea (brittlestars) and polychaeta (bristle worms). Single acute dredge events can even lead to 76% population reductions (Kaiser *et al.*, 2002: 123).

Scallop dredges cause mortality rates ranging from 8% on sandy substratas to 25% on gravel (Hall, 1999: 53). One-hour dredge tows by commercial boats equipped with queen scallop fishing gear can kill 27.3-57.0 animals per meter hour of dredging, compared to 4.6-8.9 animals per meter per hour for scallop dredges. This is mainly because more closely spaced teeth collect more animals.

The comprehensive study of trawling and dredges has illustrated that bottom fishing can profoundly disturb the seabed and all organisms – natural and biological – overlying and underlying it. Continuous fishing results in prolonged erosion of the sea bottom. Shipwrecks 'ploughed' by the same fishing equipment should be expected to be similarly impacted, dependant on the nature of deposits (durable or delicate).

The few documented examples of trawlers and gill net fishermen disturbing archaeological deposits at sea include the discovery of the *El Cazador* in the Gulf of Mexico in 1993, lost at a depth of 83-92m in 1784 with a cargo of 450,000 *pesos*.[3] In 1934 the trawler *Muroto*, working out of Cardiff, dredged up a 2nd-century AD Roman pot while fishing on the Porcupine Bank 250km off the west coast of Ireland (Cunliffe, 2002). The Studland Bay protected historic wreck site located off Poole harbor, southern England, a lightly armed Spanish merchant vessel of *c.* 1520-30, was found by a local fisherman whose gear snagged on the site (Gutierrez, 2003; Thomsen, 2000: 69).

The Alderney Elizabethan wreck similarly came to light after a fisherman found a long concreted object tangled in the back-line of one of his lobster pots, which proved to be a musket and the site to be a very rare armed English vessel of the 1590s.[4] The torso and arm of a 2nd century BC bronze statue has recently been recovered from a fisherman's net between the islands of Kos and Kalymnos in the Aegean Sea.

In the Mediterranean, 79 different types of amphoras dating between *c.* 1600 BC and the Crusader period, snagged in fishermen's nets from wrecks located in depths of up to 64m between Ashkelon to the south and Achziv to the north, are on display in the National Maritime Museum, Haifa (Zemer, 1977). Similarly, 70 different amphoras of the 7th century BC to 13th century AD have been caught by fishermen off Turkey and are now in the Alanya Museum (Sibella, 2002).

This paucity of officially documented artifacts snagged in fishing nets most likely stems from fishermen's reluctance to report finds, especially where disturbance or destruction of underwater cultural heritage can carry civil or criminal penalties. Reporting these finds officially requires that the locations be declared, which is something that fishermen avoid whenever possible. Traditionally, they tend to be very protective and secretive about their 'hang lists' featuring the locations of shipwrecks, which are often handed down from generation to generation as a treasured asset.

D. Wreck Fishing

The first public reports of deliberate targeting shipwrecks for fishing with nets emerged in the late 1960s. In the UK the largest offshore wreck fishing fleets are mainly situated along the English Channel between Rye and Falmouth due to the huge concentration of wartime wrecks and the variety of fish that migrate into the Channel's waters from the Atlantic and Biscay region. The size or preservation level of an individual wreck is not considered important: huge catches of various species are equally probable on both small and large sites. Smaller wrecks are considered better fishing grounds for ling and conger eel, while some sites with surviving superstructure are preferred for pollack, cod and coalfish (Arnold, 1996: 11).

Shipwrecks are attractive to deep-sea commercial fishermen because of the high volume of fish populations drawn to nutrient-rich shipwrecks as biological oases. Single catches on the *Lusitania* in the 1970s, for instance, today strewn with snagged and tangled fishing nets, are reported at 477kg (Gammon, 1975: 46). Wrecks are also renowned for unusually large fish seeking shelter, typified by the largest cod caught in British waters (23.8kg), which came from a Devon wreck in 1972. Conger eels caught 40km southwest of Plymouth have weighed up to 46 kg. Until wreck fishing was established, catches of large coalfish were a rarity. Since fishing for these species evolved from angling to commercial wreck fishing, the record for an individual example shot up from 10.3kg to 13.5kg (Gammon, 1975:

15, 16, 19, 23). Some species like whiting and dogfish are almost exclusively found on wreck sites.

The most common types of fish caught on shipwrecks (Arnold, 1996: 20-28; Gammon, 1975: 11, 15) are:

- Black bream.
- Brill: like the banks and scours around wrecks to lie in ambush, well camouflaged on the seabed.
- Seabass: the ultimate predator; loves broken up wrecks for ambushing prey.
- Coalfish: now becoming a rarity as commercial pressure from gill netting hits the population in Channel waters very hard.
- Cod: the main reason why wreck fishing took off; huge cod were very common, but are rapidly dwindling.
- Conger eel: one of most popular predators hunted on offshore wrecks. By far the biggest fish caught on wrecks.
- Ling: the scavenger of wrecks, a powerful eel-like fish. Abundant on deep wrecks from Rye to Falmouth. Grow to extremely large sizes very quickly. Most ling on Channel wrecks weigh an average of 11kg, but exceptional fish over 13.5kg are frequently caught. Extremes of 26.5kg have been landed.
- Pollack: examples in excess of 22.5kg have been taken in gill nets.
- Red sea bream.
- Sharks: use wrecks as a ready-made larder, mostly 48-72km offshore in the Channel during June to September. Lurk in the lee of wrecks.
- Turbot: a flatfish, normally in excess of 9kg when taken on a wreck. Lie on banks around wrecks, especially within large scours made by the tide run.

As fish yields diminish both in the open seas and over shipwrecks in the English Channel, new pressures are being exerted on lost ships. Even in 1996, when Stuart Arnold published *The Art of Wreck Fishing*, wrecks originally visited for deep-sea fishing in the 1960s only held an estimated 5% of the volume of fish harvested in former years. Inshore wrecks located 19-22km from land at depths of up to 40m had been so heavily exploited that "There are very few inshore wrecks that are unknown, and have not been hammered over the years…" (Arnold, 1996: 12).

Consequently, offshore wrecks provide the main area of operation for serious deep-water wreck fishing, with a wider choice of not only numbers of wrecks but also more fish to concentrate on. The optimum time to fish the Channel wrecks has traditionally been between January and October in the Western Approaches, when the gulf stream warms the water, and from March to December in the eastern end of the Channel. Ongoing sea temperature rises, possibly linked to global warming, are changing this traditional timetable.

The locations of many deep-sea shipwrecks are known from UKHO records or can be accessed from the French handbook *Repertoire des Croches et Epaves*. However, as abundant tangled nets of durable synthetic fibers choke sites and make them inaccessible to fishermen without the further risk of losing expensive gear, undiscovered wrecks are being actively sought.

Fishing gill nets can become lost or abandoned for a number of reasons, including the severing of the anchor or surface marker lines by underwater snags during retrieval and conflicts with towed fishing gear. Experiments with gill nets on 11 shipwrecks located along a 100km stretch of coastline in northeast Scotland (Sunderland to Farne Isles) documented that over a two-year period most of the nets remained stretched out throughout the duration of the study, even though their capacity for active fishing was zero due to degradation (broken mesh and bundling) (Revill and Dunlin, 2003).

Although the study concluded that lost nets are an insignificant source of unaccounted fishing mortality, the impact of deep-sea gill net fishing on the archaeological integrity of historical wooden shipwreck is an entirely different matter, with the potential to result in:

A. The decontextualization, inadvertent recovery, loss and probable destruction of artifacts.
B. Snagging and breaking of hull structure, leaving it susceptible to relocation off-site by bottom currents.
C. Dragging of artifacts out of context and off site, leaving them susceptible to loss by current motion.
D. Threats to undiscovered wrecks, actively sought out as former sites become impractical for fishing due to over-exploitation and dense net cover.

3. Fishing Impacts & HMS *Victory* (Site MUN-T1M25c-1)

The shipwreck of HMS *Victory* is one of the three most archaeologically significant sites recorded by Odyssey during the Atlas survey. (The second is a *c.* mid-17th century merchant vessel with a cargo of ivory tusks, iron cannon and manilla bracelet currency; Figs. 45-47. The third is the armed French privateer *Marquise de Tournay*, captured by the British and lost in 1757; Figs. 43-44.) *Victory* was

lost at a depth of around 100m some 100km west of the Casquets (Cunningham Dobson and Kingsley, 2009). The visible wreck site covers an area of 61 x 22m and is characterized by loose scatters of eroded small finds (galley hearth brick, crushed copper vessels), rigging and disarticulated planking scattered between 41 bronze cannon.

Human skeletal material and a skull were discovered below sediments, concentrated adjacent to cannon C10, while further possible remains were identified on the site's surface in association with cannon C22 and C39 (Cunningham Dobson and Tolson, forthcoming). Modern contamination in the form of discarded rubbish is common and includes plastic (Figs. 28, 29), a plastic video cassette tape (Fig. 30), glass bottles (Figs. 19, 27), canvas sheet and a man's black-spotted pink tie (Fig. 19). Although seemingly cosmetic in nature, these finds indicate that *Victory* is far from undisturbed by human impact. For many years bottom currents have and continue to mix such rubbish into the archaeological matrix of the wreckage and to disturb *in situ* remains, adversely affecting the site's coherence.

HMS *Victory* foundered in the Western English Channel, where a fairly smooth sea bottom with a gentle gradient slopes toward the west-southwest into the Western Approaches. In the area of site 25C, coarse sands (0.25-1.0mm diameter) form into large sandwaves intercut by mobile sand ripples (Hillis *et al.*, 1990: 79, fig. 49), from which fresh wreckage is covered, exposed and scoured on an ongoing basis. Beneath the sediment coverage of varying depth is intermittently exposed a sea bottom composed of dense, well-sorted shell fragments and angular flint nodules.

As the sea deepened during the last Holocene transgression (about 10,000 to 7,000 BP), bottom currents deposited a thin and discontinuous veneer of gravelly sand and sandy gravel (generally less than 0.5m thick) over solid formations and channel-fill sediments in the Western Channel. This lag deposit is generally too coarse to be moved by currents (Grochowski *et al.*, 1993: 684). The seabed substrata matrix is dominated by Cretaceous chert flint resulting from seabed or cliff erosion during the transgression and by further cliff erosion during the Holocene adding to the deposit nearshore or fluvial transport during Pleistocene regressions (Hamblin *et al.*, 1992: 82).

Offshore fishing activities are particularly high in the vicinity of the wreck of HMS *Victory* (Table 3). The 4,725 square nautical mile Atlas shipwreck survey covers 34 ICES sub-squares, each measuring about 76.4 x 55.5km. The site is located within a sub-square that contains the highest volume of deep-sea fishing traffic detected anywhere in the survey zone by VMS satellite sightings procured every two hours by the UK Marine and Fisheries Agency between 2000 and 2008: 147,460 sightings, 17.6% of the total.

Vessel Type	Number	% of Total
Beam Trawler	98,580	66.85%
Demersal Side Trawler	190	0.13%
Demersal Stern Trawler	5	0%
Freezer Trawler	420	0.28%
Gill Netter	482	0.33%
Lobster/Crab Potter	10,906	7.4%
Long Liner	114	0.08%
Pair Trawler	2,894	1.96%
Pelagic Stern Trawler	2	0%
Scallop Dredger	16,117	10.93%
Trawler (General)	1,569	1.06%
Unknown	16,051	10.88%

*Table 3. Various fishing forms practiced in the ICES sub-square in which site 25C
(HMS* Victory*) is located, based on VMS satellite data 2000-2008.*

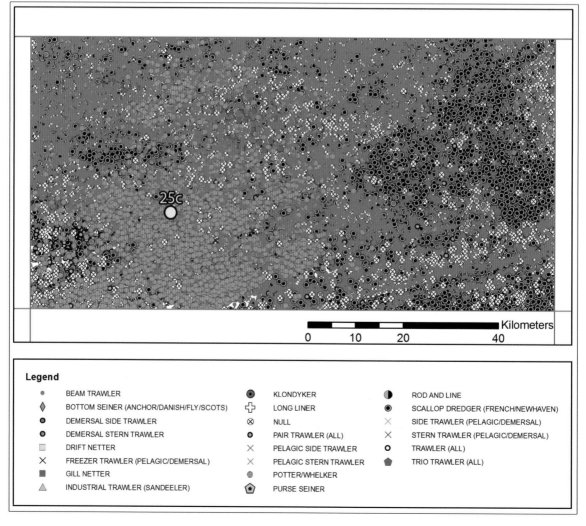

Fig. 12. The wreck of HMS Victory *(site 25C) in relation to VMS satellite sightings of fishing
vessels (2000-2008) within its specific ICES sub-square, Atlas shipwreck survey zone.*

Activities are dominated by beam trawlers (66.85%), scallop dredges (10.93%) and lobster/crab potters (7.4%).

The second highest ratios of fishing within the Atlas survey zone are located in two adjacent sub-squares, accounting for 12.6% and 11% of all fishing activities. These data suggest that 41.2% of all fishing activities are focused in three adjacent sub-squares of the survey region. The wreck of HMS *Victory* lies at the epicenter of this activity. The current analysis is based on total fishing traffic and does not distinguish between steaming and vessels actively fishing. The sample can thus only be considered a generalized indication of net/dredge towing and setting scales within the zones discussed. The filtering of VMS data to focus on fishing hotspots is ongoing.

Twelve separate examples of trawler/wreck fishing impacts have been verified visually on the surface of HMS *Victory*:

1. A series of four distinct sets of fresh beam trawler furrows between 500m and 1000m east-northeast of the wreck site (Figs. 15-16).
2. VMS satellite evidence for the sub-square in which HMS *Victory* lies, covering the period 2000-2008, displays widespread evidence of intensive fishing operations in this area and in the catchment zone of the wreck site (Table 3, Fig. 12). Some 72 fishing vessels have been documented within 1km of site 25C in the same timeframe (65% lobster/crab potters, 29% beam trawlers, 3% scallop dredgers). Statistically, these sightings only represent a very small fraction of the actual fishing activity occurring in and across the wreck site of HMS *Victory*. Average-sized scallop dredges operate at 2.5-3 knots (4.63-5.5km per hour) in the Western English Channel (Dare *et al.*, 1994: 5), while beam trawlers tow at speeds of 4-6 knots (7.4-11.1km per hour) (Duplisea *et al.*, 2001: 1; Fonteyne, 2000: 15). This indicates that positions of VMS records are only potentially accurate to within a maximum geographical area of 11km for dredges and 22.2km for beam trawlers, which are the distances that either form of fishing craft could steam away from a direct shipwreck hit in the two-hour window between satellite detection. Deep-sea trawling has also been active in the study region since at least 1960, far longer than the 2000-2008 sample data available from satellite surveillance.
3. Fishing net mesh snagged between iron concretions towards the southwest flank of the wreck (Fig. 17).
4. Plastic rubbish and fishing cable snagged around the end of a bronze cannon (Fig. 18).
5. Fishing cable snagged on a rectangular iron ballast block towards the southwest of the site (Fig. 19).
6. Thick fishing rope cable snagged on a stone boulder alongside dragged hull remains to the southeast of the wreck (Figs. 21-22).
7. A possible shoe from one end of a beam trawl snagged on a boulder at the southeast of the wreck (Fig. 20).
8. Rope cable snagged between cannon C7 and C8 (Fig. 23).
9. Modern canvas and fishing cable snagged on a deposit of brick, copper and wood on site 25C (Fig. 31).
10. Bronze cannon dragged off-site by trawlers, including C38, C33 and C32, which has been displaced 55m southwest of the wreck (Fig. 14). The marine growth on C32 is notably visible on the underside of the cannon, while the upper side is entirely devoid of any biological material. This indicates that this 4-ton, 42-pounder cannon has been flipped upside down during its recent displacement: until very recently the clean upper side had clearly been embedded long-term in an anaerobic environment, which prevented the growth of marine concretions (Figs. 25-26). The surfaces of all other cannon on the wreck exposed to the water column bear marine growth.
11. A parlor lobster/crab trap on the northeast flank of the wreck (Fig. 24).
12. Scratched parallel scars along both recovered cannon C33 (42-pounder, King George I, 1726) and C28 (12-pounder, King George II, 1734) caused by trawl cable and net friction (Figs. 32-34). These marks are located all along each cannon. Georgian damage, evident as deep gouges along the muzzle of 12 pounder gun C28 and as markings located beneath concretion or the patina of marine growth, are easily distinguished from modern impacts. Trawl scratches visible on cannon C28 includes evidence along the cascable (Fig. 32). Evidence on C33 includes scratches at the foot of one dolphin, right of the royal arms crown and down the middle and lower sides (Figs. 33-34).

4. The Atlas Shipwreck Survey Project: Fishing Impact Overview

The deep-sea fishing impacts evident in the area of HMS *Victory* are far from an isolated case. Between May 2005 and October 2008 Odyssey Marine Exploration's Atlas shipwreck survey visually documented 147 anomalies

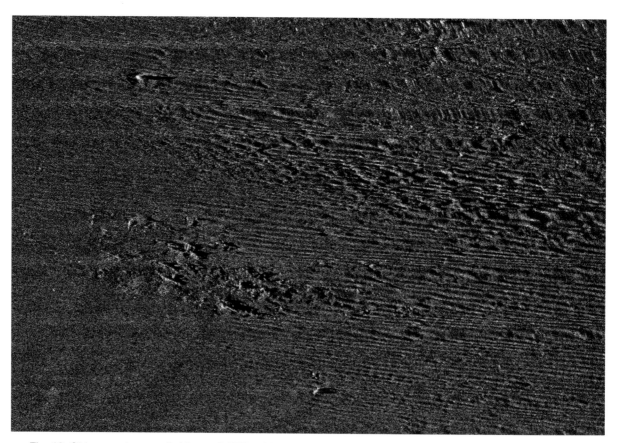

Fig. 13. Side-scan image of shipwreck 25C, with apparent parallel-sided sand ripples running across the site.

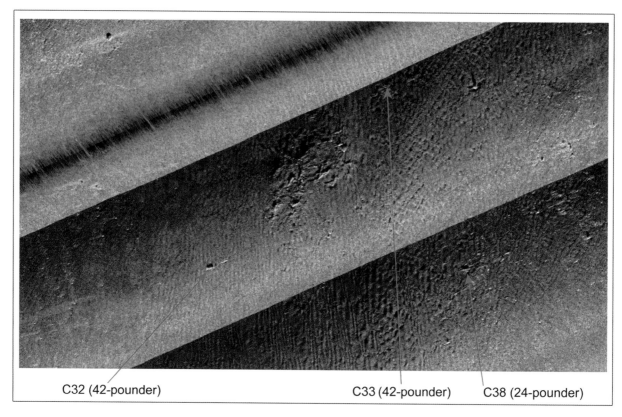

C32 (42-pounder)   C33 (42-pounder)   C38 (24-pounder)

*Fig. 14. Side-scan image of site 25C (February 2009) showing the locations of bronze cannon
dragged off site by trawler impacts, identified by visual ROV inspections.*

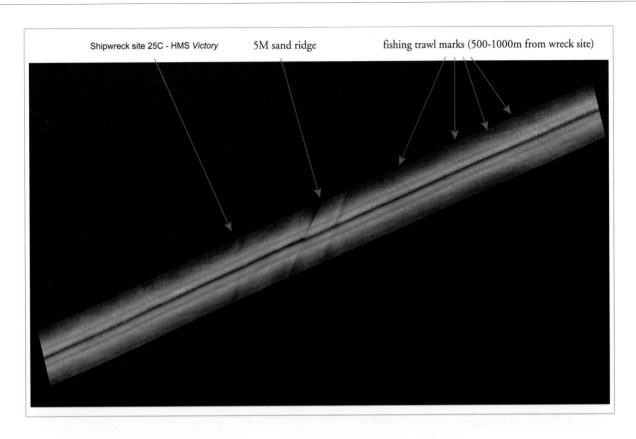

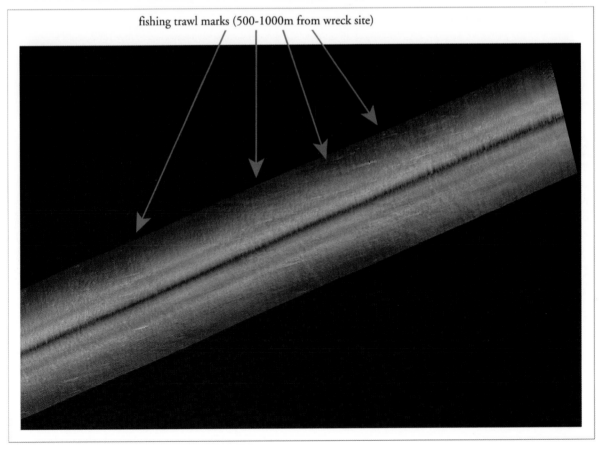

Figs. 15-16. Beam trawler furrows in direct proximity to site 25C, evident on side-scan imagery.

Fig. 17. Green fishing net snagged on wreckage on site 25C.

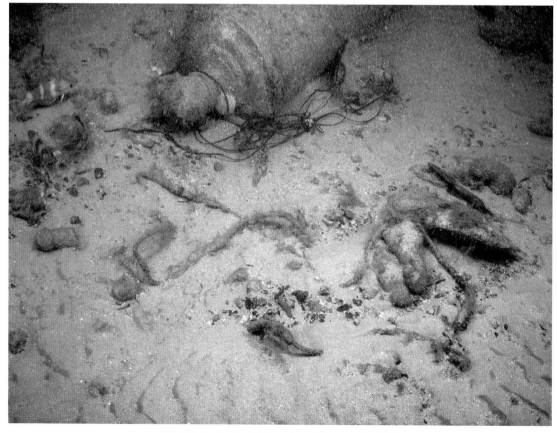

Fig. 18. Partly buried trawler cable on site 25C.

Fig. 19. Snagged fishing net rope, a pink tie and glass milk bottle (in the foreground) on site 25C.

Fig. 20. A possible shoe from one end of a beam trawl snagged on a stone boulder on site 25C.

Figs. 21-22. Fishing cable snagged on a stone boulder on site 25C, with dragged hull remains alongside.

Fig. 23. Fishing cable snagged between cannon C7 and C8 on site 25C.

Fig. 24. A lobster/crab pot on site 25C, evidence of wreck fishing.

Figs. 25-26. The 4-ton 42-pounder bronze cannon C32 with marine growth on the underside, dragged 55m off site and flipped upside down by a trawler or scallop dredge.

Fig. 27. A modern beer bottle under the trunnion of cannon C13 on site 25C and probable trawler scratches along the reinforce.

Fig. 28. Plastic rubbish and sacking in the foreground on site 25C.

Fig. 29. Plastic rubbish on the southern flank of site 25C.

Fig. 30. A plastic video tape cassette on site 25C with iron ballast blocks in the background.

Fig. 31. *Modern canvas (left) and fishing cable (right), snagged on a deposit of brick, copper and wood on site 25C.*

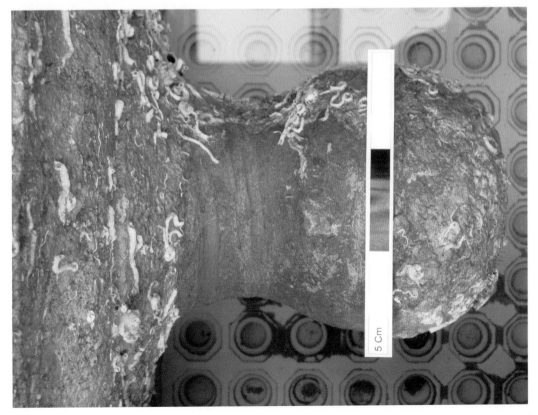

Fig. 32. *Fishing net cable friction damage on the cascable of 12-pounder cannon C28 from the wreck of HMS* Victory *(site 25C). The impact has broken off concretion and exposed a patch of the original bronze surface.*

Fig. 33. Diagonal fishing cable scratches beneath the crown of the royal arms from bronze 42-pounder cannon C33, recovered from the wreck of HMS Victory *(site 25C).*

Fig. 34. Diagonal and horizontal fishing cable scratches on the underside of bronze 42-pounder cannon C33, recovered from the wreck of HMS Victory *(site 25C).*

displaying evidence of mild to extreme trawling/dredging and wreck fishing impacts, ranging from steel wrecks (70; 47%) to wooden wrecks (25; 17%), submarines (7; 5%), geological outcrops (13; 9%), isolated fishing gear on the seabed (19; 13%) and snagged ships' anchors (3; 2%) (Figs. 1-3). This excludes data obtained from side-scan sonar. The wreck sites range from depths of 40-190m, with the majority (58%) concentrated between 90m and 120m.

The character of the fishing industry's impact varies widely. Most conspicuous are extensive sections of commercial gill nets draped across standing steel ships' structures and torn sections of gill and trawl net snagged on wooden wrecks and cannon. Snagged nets have been recorded on 108 wreck sites, from the mid-17th century merchant vessel carrying a cargo of ivory (Figs. 45-47) to World War II submarines (Fig. 7) and steel ships (Figs. 4-6).

This phenomenon results largely from offshore wreck fishing. The scale of the industry has left many sites so densely covered with nets that they have become dangerous to fish without the risk of losing equipment. The over-exploitation of resources on known wrecks has also stripped these biological oases of fish stock in the short-term life cycle, forcing fishermen to seek out virgin wreck sites.

Rock hopper gear identified on 17 wrecks in the Atlas survey zone signifies the omnipresence of a different form of fishing, trawling, denoting the accidental snagging and loss of expensive gear on wreck obstacles. While relatively unproblematic culturally on modern steel vessels, the speed and power exerted by all trawlers (and dredges) is extremely detrimental to delicate wooden wreckage and cultural assemblages. The passage of a beam trawler, for instance, will dislocate articulated and interconnected hull remains and smash and drag – possibly for kilometers – anything *in situ* on the seabed. The relocation 55m offsite and flipping upside-down of a 4-ton bronze cannon on the wreck of HMS *Victory* exemplifies the severe impact of fishing gear. If this is the end-result for such a durable and heavy artifact, little imagination is required to acknowledge the high risk to hulls, small finds and human remains.

As a second example of the threat posed by trawlers, site 2T11w24b-1 (Target 581), is a mid to late 19th century wooden wreck lying at a depth of 124.0m on a shell-rich coarse sand matrix intermixed with scallop shells across a banked seabed. A cargo of white ironstone pottery bowls and plates, some with blue feathering on the rim, lies still partly stacked on its side, having fallen over, on top of a sand ripple. The upper edges have been 'shaved' by a passing trawler/dredge, with vessels partly smashed and dragged out of context. Pottery is scattered across the site alongside an orange rock hopper from the bottom of a trawl net (Figs. 36-37).

This cargo seems to have been relatively recently exposed from beneath its protective sand blanket, but demonstrates the damage to which older ceramic or other delicate cargoes are susceptible. Whether caused by beam trawlers or more destructively by dredges, this process may explain why virtually no pottery other than large bricks is encountered on the surface of any wooden wreck in the survey zone. The interplay of bottom currents on the scattering of pots smashed into sherds in this process remains to be modeled, but is considered to be a core effect of dispersal.

With teeth digging into sea bottoms to extract scallops, dredges are especially destructive to wreck sites. A dredge head snagged and lost on the mid -20th century steel wreck TRI-13a-19Wg-1 (Target 717) at a depth of 72.6m demonstrates the functionality of this form of fishing gear (Fig. 38), designed to literally plough the seabed to extract scallop shells.

Trawler/dredge furrows are common across the Atlas survey zone (Fig. 39). Scallop dredge furrows have been recorded on five side-scan sonar records taken above mid-17th to 19th-century wooden wrecks, and a set of beam trawl furrows was identified adjacent to HMS *Victory* in February 2009. The extensive impacts on site T7a35f-5 (Fig. 40) are manifested on side-scan sonar as parallel-sided furrows produced by a scallop fishing vessel towing 18 dredges per side (pers. comm. Michel Kaiser, May 2009), as well as scratched scars on iron cannon and ballast stones plus net and cable on-site.

Lobster/crab pots have been identified on four wreck sites within the Atlas survey zone, including HMS *Victory* (Fig. 24). Such pots are strung out across the seabed in lines of up to 100 traps. When being pulled in from the surface of wooden wrecks they may snag on and snap hull remains or drag artifacts out of context, leaving them susceptible to being dislocated by bottom currents, scoured and destroyed.

Other distinct signs of fishing activities recorded on the Atlas shipwreck sites include a trawler beam bar (1 site), trawl floats (6 sites), gill floats (33 sites), foot rope (13 sites), trawl rope (8 sites), trawl door (1 site) and steel cable (4 sites), including T7a35f-5, where a length has been caught beneath iron cannon in direct proximity to elephant tusks (Fig. 47). The broken ends of several otherwise intact tusks may be due to snagging.

5. Atlas Shipwrecks: Deep-Sea Fishing Quantification

A total of 838,048 fishing vessels were sighted by VMS (Vessel Monitoring Systems) satellite reconnaissance within the offshore Atlas survey zone between 2000 and 2008. Bearing in mind that the data currently remain

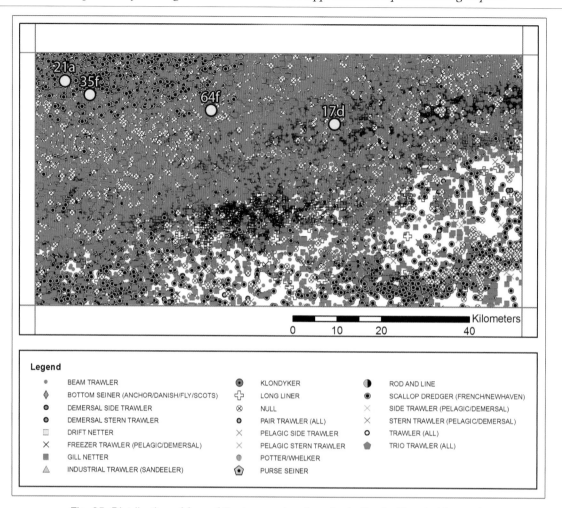

Legend

•	BEAM TRAWLER	◉	KLONDYKER	◑	ROD AND LINE
◆	BOTTOM SEINER (ANCHOR/DANISH/FLY/SCOTS)	✛	LONG LINER	◉	SCALLOP DREDGER (FRENCH/NEWHAVEN)
◎	DEMERSAL SIDE TRAWLER	⊗	NULL	×	SIDE TRAWLER (PELAGIC/DEMERSAL)
◉	DEMERSAL STERN TRAWLER	○	PAIR TRAWLER (ALL)	×	STERN TRAWLER (PELAGIC/DEMERSAL)
□	DRIFT NETTER	×	PELAGIC SIDE TRAWLER	○	TRAWLER (ALL)
×	FREEZER TRAWLER (PELAGIC/DEMERSAL)	×	PELAGIC STERN TRAWLER	⬠	TRIO TRAWLER (ALL)
■	GILL NETTER	●	POTTER/WHELKER		
△	INDUSTRIAL TRAWLER (SANDEELER)	⬟	PURSE SEINER		

Fig. 35. Distribution of four of the ten most archaeologically significant shipwrecks, including wreck site 35F with its ivory cargo, in relation to total VMS satellite sightings of fishing vessels operating in the Atlas shipwreck survey zone (2000-2008).

Fig. 36. A ceramic cargo fallen on one side on a mid to late 19th-century wooden shipwreck (site 2T11w24b-1; Target 581). The top edges of the plates have been 'shaved' by a trawler/dredge. Atlas shipwreck survey zone, depth 124.0m.

Fig. 37. Parts of the ceramic cargo on site 2T11w24b-1 dragged and smashed by a trawler/dredge.

*Fig. 38. A scallop dredge beam bar snagged on an early to mid-20th century steel wreck
(site TRI-13a-19Wg-1; Target 717). This type of fishing gear 'ploughs' the seabed to extract scallop shells and is
highly detrimental to wooden hulls and other archaeological remains. Atlas shipwreck survey zone, depth 72.6m.*

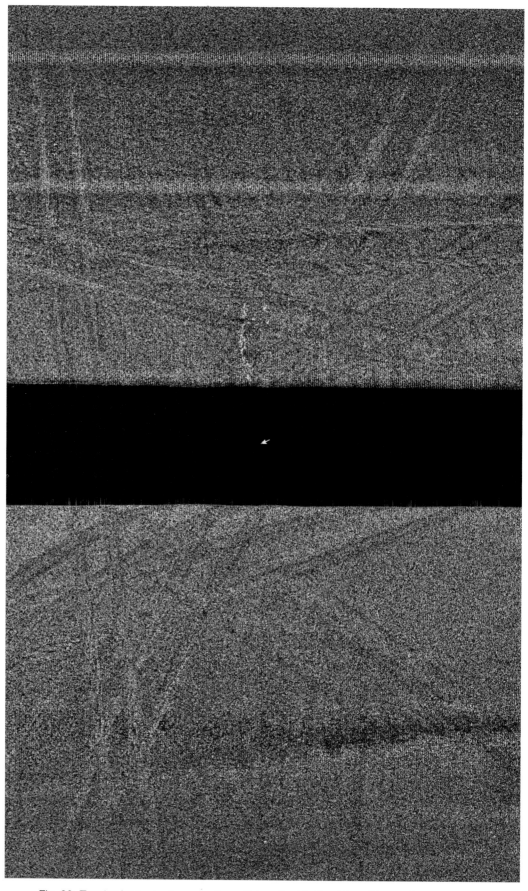

Fig. 39. Trawler furrows criss-crossing a flat seabed in the Atlas shipwreck survey zone.

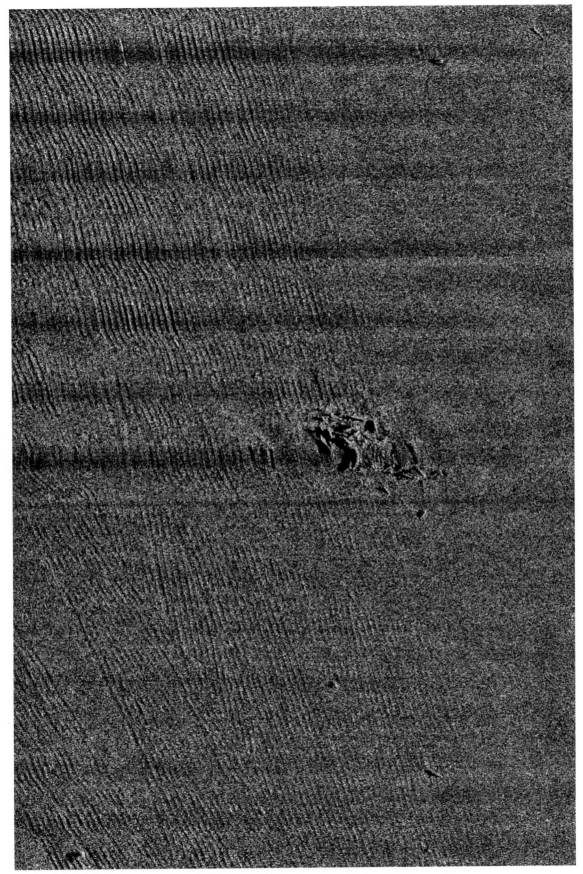

*Fig. 40. Scallop dredge furrows running directly through ivory cargo site T7a35f-5
(Target 580), with cannon visibly dragged off-site.*

unfiltered for steaming versus active fishing actions, this enormous sample currently provides a solid reflection of what types of fishing vessels operate in this part of the English Channel.

Deep-sea fishing is dominated by trawlers, which comprise 58.4% of all activities (490,663 sightings). Of these, beam trawlers are definitively the most active (440,731 sightings; 52.6%), with stern trawlers (27,112 sightings; 3.2%), pair trawlers (10,454; 1.2%), freezer trawlers (4,875 sightings; 0.6%) and side trawlers (5,289 sightings; 0.5%) far less numerous (Figs. 41-42).

Scallop dredges account for a high 15.8% (132,126 sightings) of all activities and gill netters (which focus on wreck fishing) for 7.3% (60,892 sightings). Lobster/crab potters comprise 3.9% of all fishing activities and long liners 2.5% (33,122 sightings). The function of 11.6% of all fishing vessels is undocumented.

VMS observations only monitor the movements of UK boats. An analysis of relative numbers and percentages of fishing activities conducted by different nationalities thus has to rely on the smaller sample of aerial sightings. An examination of fishing vessels operating within the Atlas shipwrecks survey zone identified 73,385 sightings between 1985 and 2008. Of 18 nationalities recognized, the majority of vessels are French (45.5%) and from the United Kingdom (40.5%). Spain represents 9% of activities and Belgium, Denmark, Ireland and the Netherlands 1% each. More obscure vessel registers include Estonia, the Faroes, Lithuania and Russia.

A breakdown of each distinct fishing type by nationality follows:

A. Stern trawling: France (86%), UK (8.7%), Spain (3.4%), Netherlands (0.9%).
B. Beam trawling: UK (89%), followed by Ireland (5.7%), Belgium (3.6%), the Netherlands (0.8%) and France (0.4%).
C. Side trawlers: UK (40.9%), Spain (30.6%), France (23.9%), Denmark (3%), Ireland (1.6%).
D. Pair trawlers: France (56.9%), UK (30.7%), Spain 6.8%, Denmark: 4.9%.
E. Freezer trawlers: the Netherlands (54.6%), Denmark (12.8%), France (11.4%), UK (10.1%), Germany (7.5%) and Ireland (2.2%).
F. Lobster/crab potting: UK (76.5%), followed by France (22.9%).
G. Long liners: Spain (82.4%), UK (10%), France (5.8%), Ireland (0.8%) and Norway (0.4%).
H. Gill netters: UK (90%) followed by France (8.6%).
I. Scallop dredges: UK (89%), Netherlands, (4.4%), Ireland (3.2%), France (2.4%).

This data leave little doubt that the majority of impacts documented by Odyssey across the Atlas survey zone have been caused predominantly by UK fishing vessels. The stern trawling figure apparently dominated by France is possibly a skewed statistic. This category contains 22,205 sightings from aerial reconnaissance. However, within the far larger satellite database, beam trawling massively exceeds stern trawling by 52.6% compared to 3.2%. Since the aerial evidence points to a dominance of beam trawling by the UK (89%), this is a more accurate reflection of this nationality's overall dominance of this industry within the English Channel. France is only highly represented in stern and pair trawling, although this specialty only accounts for 3.2% and 1.2% respectively of the total activities.

UK vessels are also most conspicuous within the scallop dredge industry (89% of all sightings), lobster/crab potting (76.5%) and gill netting (90%). With 2,902 sightings (82.4%), Spain seems to dominate the use of long liners within the survey zone.

6. Conclusion: an End of Innocence

This report has examined a form of shipwreck impact, which, until now, has been almost completely neglected as a major cause of underwater shipwreck destabilization, potential destruction and knowledge loss. Based on the evidence reviewed, the image of pristine deep-sea wrecks displaying superior levels of preservation in contrast to shallow water sites is invalid within the Narrow Seas. In fact it is clear that the opposite is true.

Of 267 shipwrecks recorded in the 4,725 square nautical mile Atlas survey zone by Odyssey Marine Exploration, a total of 112 wrecks have been catalogued with evidence of fishing disturbance on the basis of visual reconnaissance using the Remotely-Operated Vehicle Zeus. A total of 838,048 fishing vessel sightings – both steaming and actively fishing – have been recorded by satellite within the research area for the period 2000 to 2008. Some 73,385 sightings by airplane spotters enable the nationalities exploiting the area – predominantly the UK and France, and less so Spain – to be assessed. To reiterate the observed pattern derived from unfiltered satellite vessel monitoring, deep-sea fishing is dominated by beam trawlers (52.6%), scallop dredges (15.8%) gill netters (7.3%) lobster/crab potters (3.9%) and long liners (2.5%).

Wreck Watch Int. has identified ten sites discovered by Odyssey that warrant further archaeological survey and/or excavation. These shipwrecks would extensively expand our knowledge of the maritime history of the English Channel – in the case of sites MUN-T1M25c-1 (HMS *Victory*) and

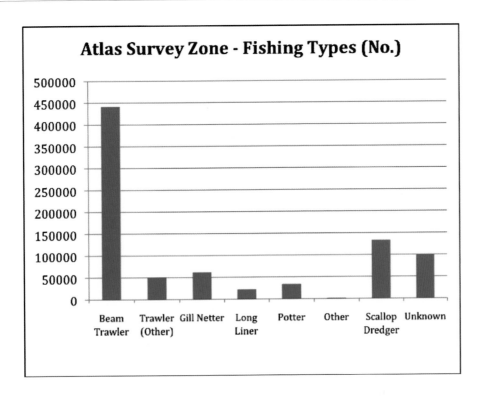

Fig. 41. Fishing activities in the Atlas shipwreck survey zone recorded by VMS satellite, 2000-2008 (nos. of sightings).

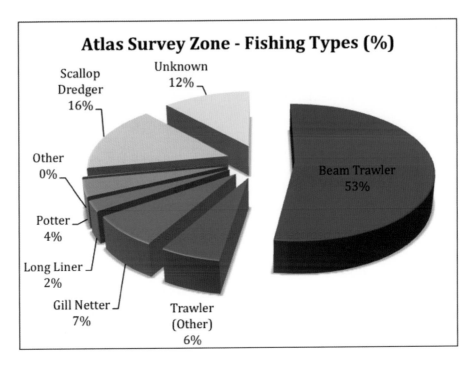

Fig. 42. Fishing activities in the Atlas shipwreck survey zone recorded by VMS satellite, 2000-2008 (%).

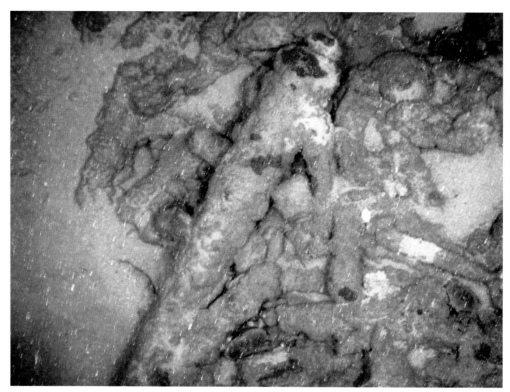

Fig. 43. Dense concretions characterize the surface of the wreck of the French privateer the Marquise de Tournay, *lost in 1757 (site MUN-T1M33c-1; Target 676). Atlas shipwreck survey zone.*

T7a35f-5 (ivory cargo) uniquely so. All of these sites lie in heavily fished waters (Fig. 35). The wrecks of HMS *Victory* and the *Marquise de Tournay* (site MUN-T1M33c-1) within the same ICES sub-square are located at the epicenter of the deep-sea fishing industry within the Western Channel (147,460 sightings).

A variety of sources demonstrate that both sites have been heavily ground down, with trawlers and dredges clearly an active cog in that process. Site MUN-T1M33c-1 has stabilized to some extent due to the profound level of deterioration and dominance of thick concretions on site (Fig. 43), a combination of iron cannon and apparent cargo-related storage units. Unfortunately, on the surface of site MUN-T1M25c-1 delicate organic remains, including human skeletal bones and wooden planking, are currently contextualized and comprise just the latest stratum of archaeology to be exposed and scoured. Consequently, damage to the site will certainly continue.

Attempting to record and recover assemblages from the majority of shipwrecks within the Atlas zone would be a difficult task that is currently beyond the budget or interests of any organization. In this regard the ten most important sites, which constitute 3.7% of all wrecks documented by Odyssey, are archaeological microcosms for the Channel in its totality. If just the wreck of HMS *Victory* and the 17th-century merchant vessel site T7a35f-5 are subjected to further formal archaeological fieldwork, then 0.7% of

the rich maritime heritage discovered so far within the Atlas survey zone could be saved for future generations. Intensive fieldwork on HMS *Victory* would cover a mere 0.4% of all discovered sites, although it is clear that from a heritage and historical perspective its significance warrants exceptional intervention.

Due to the past and ongoing threat from the deep-sea fishing industry, such a managerial position is already a case of damage limitation. The rarity of identified shipwrecks predating 1800 is a serious anomaly and concern. Within the geographical catchment area of the English Channel a 3rd century AD wooden Roman hull is preserved off Guernsey (Rule and Monaghan, 1993). The St. Peter's Port sites include hull sections of nine medieval ships dating from pre-1350 to 1450 (Adams and Black, 2004). The *St. Anthony*, an armed merchant carrack belonging to King John III of Portugal, lost in 1527, has been identified in Gunwalloe Cove, Cornwall.[5] The former Dutch fluit in the East India service, the *Schiedam*, lost on 4 April 1684, lies in the same cove. The currents of Alderney are notoriously dangerous and destructive – amongst the most extreme in the entire English Channel – but nevertheless have preserved remains of an Elizabethan armed dispatch carrier of the 1590s (Davenport and Burns, 1995).

An early 17th century wreck is preserved in Rill Cove, Cornwall (Simpson *et al.*, 1977) and a mid-17th century site at Salcombe off Devon.[6] The wreck of the English East

Indiaman *President*, which foundered in 1684, has been identified near Loe Bar.[7] Lost off Penlee Point, Plymouth, in 1691, the second-rate, 90-gun warship the *Coronation* is another protected UK wreck site.[8] The probable remains of the 70-gun, third-rate *Eagle*, lost on 22 October 1707, are known off Tearing Ledge in the Isles of Scilly (McBride and Larn, 1999). The hull of the 74-gun HMS *Colossus*, wrecked off the Scilly Isles in 1798, is exceptionally intact (Camidge, 2007).

As the coherent hulls of two 19th-century wooden merchant vessels (T7a21a-8 and 2T7a64f-2) within the study region demonstrate, the environment of the Atlas region certainly has the potential to facilitate reasonable preservation. All sites display some level of coarse sands, either mixed with well-sorted gravel or fragmented shell, capable of sustaining anaerobic conditions on wreck sites. Although lost in a similar environment of deep sand to HMS *Colossus* (although coarser), the wreck of HMS *Victory* has apparently suffered far more and appears to have been ground down to the keel line in some areas. Clearly, other scrambling forces are at work in the Atlas zone beyond the typical actions of time and tide.

The chronological pattern of Odyssey's deep-sea wrecks, with an evident rarity of pre-1800 sites, is a distorted archaeological reflection of commercial and military reality. By stark contrast, historical records describe the existence of 1,275 pre-1800 shipwrecks in shallow waters (out to the 30 mile boundary) off Cornwall, Devon, Dorset and the Scilly Isles (this statistic and the below are tabulated from Larn and Larn, 1995). Of these 35 pre-date 1600 (2.7%), 170 date between 1600 and 1700 (13.3%) and 1,070 cluster between 1700 and 1800 (83.9%).[9] This loss timeline is currently the most accurate guide available for appraising the chronological range of wrecks that might be anticipated in the offshore Atlas survey zone, where the rarity of pre-1800 sites is striking.

The paucity of such early wrecks cannot be dismissed as a consequence of selective sealane exploitation by diverse ship types or nationalities (eg. offshore versus inshore sea routes, lighters compared to international merchant vessels). Figures for Dorset's inshore wrecks, for instance, reveal that of 125 mercantile ships lost before 1800 the greater majority (88; 70.4%) were long-distance ships exploiting such far-flung sea lanes as Bordeaux-London, Canary Islands-Hamburg, Genoa-Hamburg, Jamaica-Amsterdam, Le Havre-Baltimore, Leghorn-Amsterdam, Lisbon-London, London-India, Newfoundland-Poole, New York-Liverpool, Sweden-Nantes and Virginia-London. The ships that made these pre-1800 voyages obviously traversed open waters.

This report concludes that arguably the principal reason for the current low level of preservation on the wreck of HMS *Victory* and the rarity of wrecks pre-dating 1800 is a result of fishing impacts in the form of:

1. Direct physical disturbance by beam trawlers and

Fig. 44. Fishing net and plastic next to a concreted iron cannon on the wreck of the Marquise de Tournay.

scallop dredges that cut furrows into the seabed and into shipwreck sites. Although wholly or largely inadvertent, this causes:
- The loosening of archaeological strata.
- The exposure of wrecks to oxygen, leading to direct deterioration of organic remains.
- The decontextualization, inadvertent recovery, loss and destruction of artifacts.
- The snagging and breaking of hull structure, leaving planking susceptible to being washed off-site by bottom currents.
- The dragging of artifacts out of context and off site, leaving them susceptible to loss by current motion.
2. Wreck fishing using gill nets, intentionally or inadvertently on shipwreck sites, which causes the same sets of impact as no. 1 above.
3. Lobster/crab potting intentionally or inadvertently on shipwreck sites, which causes the same sets of impact as no. 1 above (although inadvertent artifact recovery is rare).

The ten shipwrecks that Odyssey considers most archaeologically significant in the survey zone are currently unstable and cannot be left *in situ* without further deterioration and destruction, severe in some cases. If a trawler/dredge

can lift, drag and flip a 42-pounder, 4-ton bronze cannon 55m off-site, then the rest of the artifacts on the wreck of HMS *Victory* have to be considered at high risk, as are the iron cannon on site T7a35f-5 along with the remaining artifacts, including ivory tusks. As Odyssey's experiences on both HMS *Victory* and T7a35f-5 demonstrate, fishermen continue to run lines near and across wrecks of major archaeological significance: for the most part, they are most likely uneducated about the nuances of site formation and the potential for damage.

In addition to the evidence presented by deep scallop dredge furrow scars visible on the side-scan sonar images of site T7a35f-5 (Fig. 40), confirmed by physical scars on some cannon surfaces and ballast stones, Odyssey has observed first-hand evidence of trawling through the site. While the company was surveying the wreck on 25 September 2006, a passing trawler warned the *Odyssey Explorer* to move off station so it could trawl the area. The trawler captain emphatically stated that he had been fishing this seabed for years and had detected no obstructions. This incident demonstrates that the commonly cited argument that fishermen are fully knowledgeable of wreck locations and actively avoid them to protect their gear is incorrect.

Moreover, a very real threat exists to currently undetected wrecks because such sites are being actively sought

Fig. 45. On the badly preserved wreck of a c. mid-17th century merchant vessel, site T7a35f-5 (Target 580), hull remains are only preserved where they are pinned down by iron cannon.

out as fish-rich biological oases as known sites become non-viable due to the over-exploitation of fish resources and dangerous net cover makes access problematic.

Odyssey's results in the Western English Channel and Western Approaches are not isolated. Geophysical research in the Eastern Channel by CEFAS has confirmed that the physical impact of trawlers and scallops feature across a large parts of the area, including the region where aggregate extraction licenses have been granted since 2005 (Vanstaen *et al.*, 2007). The main difference between these two areas of the Channel is the presence of extremely deep sandbanks in the east, 10-30m thick, 3-5km wide and extending across lengths of 30-70km (Reynaud *et al.*, 2003: 364). As the massive scale of offshore aggregate quarrying continues, the impact of newly exposed wreck sites within a large-scale fishing zone will certainly become an extremely complex and expensive underwater cultural heritage managerial issue.

Legislation exists, and is consistently being refined, to protect fishing stocks and commercial interests of fishermen alike, who have their own rich and highly respected maritime traditions within the Narrow Seas. Economically unexploitable by-catch is a major problem within the English Channel, Western Approaches, Celtic and Irish Sea, where one study has demonstrated that an estimated 186 million (72,000 tons) of fish and cephalopods are caught every year,

of which 117 million (24,500 tons) is discarded. Beam trawlers and otter trawlers are together responsible for more than 90% of these discards (Enever *et al.*, 2007).[10]

This inefficiency and damage to the marine environment has been tackled by the imposition of government fishing quotas, the decommissioning of ships and by zoning regulations. Some 17% of the Western Channel's fleet is scheduled for decommission as part of a long-term plan to protect sole stocks.[11] Zoning is largely designed to protect unique and endangered biological formations, such as on Darwin Mounds, an area for the deep-water coral *Lophelia pertusa*, and other deep-water coral sites off the Azores, Madeira and the Canary Islands.[12]

As a discipline, for the most part marine archaeology and cultural heritage managers appear to be unaware of these developments or the threat that deep-sea fishing poses to unique maritime heritage, even though leading scientists have warned that "The seas are undergoing ecological meltdown" (Roberts, 2007: 373). However, it is not necessarily too late for sea life because zoning and marine reserves may allow plant-life and fish species to regenerate and repopulate. Shipwrecks lost at the bottom of the sea do not share that opportunity. Just a single pass from a trawler or dredge can irretrievably destroy unique maritime heritage; unlike fish and plants, substantial knowledge is

Fig. 46. Snagged fishing net on an iron cannon on the c. mid-17th century site T7a35f-5.

permanently lost. Simultaneously, expensive fishing gear can be snagged and lost.

The vast signature of deep-sea fishing registered by Odyssey within the Atlas survey zone makes it clear that the shipwrecks of the Narrow Seas have been subjected to destructive hammer blows on a continuous and extreme basis in some cases. The scale and scope of the impacts to the most archaeologically significant shipwrecks – at the very least – need to be quantified in the near future.

In the absence of any effective political legislation to protect such sites, where does marine archaeology go from here? No viable legal instruments exist to safeguard the world's deep-sea shipwrecks beyond the territorial seas of nations. Even in the case of sovereign immune vessels, no government is likely to willingly monitor and protect an historic ship dozens of miles offshore, even if it was legally possible. Realistically, the protection of shipwrecks stands at the bottom of the food chain in issues of marine studies and conservation. For economic reasons alone, regular satellite or spotter plain supervision of potentially hundreds or even thousands of historical shipwrecks short- or long-term is impractical. Due to such sites' locations far offshore, there is no practical way to prevent the accidental snagging and recovery of wreck structure and artifacts, much less illicit salvage, which AIS (Automatic Identification System) makes a realistic threat.[13] Zoning is entirely unenforceable so far offshore.

This leaves two alternatives. Abandon shipwrecks to the wild natural rhythms of the sea and fisheries in hope rather than intelligent managerial design. Or, alternatively, the fishing industry, other users groups, governments and/ or the private sector should endeavor to pool resources to rescue those shipwrecks of national and international significance. This pattern is most likely to prevail in the future as increasing evidence for comparable scales of fishing impacts to the English Channel and Western Approaches emerges from other oceans. A similar model already exists in the Aggregates Levy Sustainable Fund, which is being put to good effect in the Eastern English Channel to model possible wreck impacts and the erosion of submerged prehistoric landscapes (Dix and Lambkin, 2005; Firth, 2006). Legislation is also in existence for shipwrecks threatened by offshore oil pipelines at Ormen Lange in the Norwegian Sea (Bryn *et al.*, 2007), Nord Stream (Greifswalder Bodden coastal lagoon, Germany) and Mardi Gras, Gulf of Mexico (Ford *et al.*, 2008).

Future research will likely demonstrate that the case of the Atlas survey region is far from unique and in deep seas is actually the rule rather than the exception. The Woods Hole Oceanographic Institution (WHOI) has detected at least two trawl nets and one gill net wrapped around the windlass of the wreck of the schooner *Paul Palmer*, lost in 1913 off Maine.[14] In the Mediterranean Sea, Brendan Foley of WHOI has recalled how "we optically surveyed the sea

Fig. 47. Snagged steel trawler cable on iron cannon on the c. mid-17th century site T7a35f-5, adjacent to elephant tusks with their ends snapped off.

floor off the island of Malta, for centuries a center of maritime commerce. At depths of 500+ meters, we expected to encounter marine life and hoped to discover ancient shipwrecks. Instead, we found only furrows in the sediments, indicating intensive trawling… occasionally we have seen evidence of dragging at depths approaching 1000 meters. It is unlikely that many ancient archaeologically significant sites will survive in areas subjected to trawl fishing."[15] Ballard (2008: 136) has also observed trawl marks in deep waters in depths of 1,000m off Malta, as well as off the Gulf of Naples, Egypt and in the Black Sea. Odyssey has recorded a heavily trawler-impacted mid-19th century merchant vessel 370m beneath the Atlantic Ocean off Jacksonville, carrying a cargo of largely British blue china (Tolson, 2009).

Following Odyssey's three-year non-intrusive shipwreck survey project in the English Channel and Western Approaches, in this sea *in situ* preservation emerges as an inappropriate all-encompassing managerial policy for the protection of maritime heritage, either in the short- or long-term. Incalculable wreck destruction has already occurred and is ongoing. Statistical information indicates that deep-sea fishing and wreck disturbance in the Narrow Seas are predominantly an English problem. Certainly one realistic, responsible policy is to recover elements of the threatened heritage for both the education and enjoyment of future generations.

The comprehensive mapping and planning of sites will help differentiate between heritage-rich shipwrecks with high evidential, historical and communal value (Dunkley, 2008: 24-25), which require the recovery of select archaeological assemblages, those that need to be avoided by fishermen and the greater majority of modern wrecks that are devoid of historical significance and can be exploited by the fishing community (relatively flat wreck sites for beam trawlers and scallop dredges and standing superstructure for netting). The relationship between all user groups (fishermen, ecologists, archaeologists, historians, salvors, sport divers, heritage managers and the marine construction industry alike) is, and needs to remain, respectfully symbiotic.

Acknowledgements

This report owes a vast debt of gratitude to the whole Odyssey team, which has conducted the first comprehensive deep-sea shipwreck survey in the English Channel and Western Approaches: to Greg Stemm for initiating and managing the project and encouraging and facilitating swift publication for our fellow scientists; to Mark Gordon, Laura Barton and John Oppermann for their ongoing support and energetic encouragement; to on-site project managers Tom Dettweiler, Andrew Craig, Ernie Tapanes and Mark Martin.

The primary underwater ROV photographic record on which this report is based was taken under the direction of Directors of Field Archaeology Neil Cunningham Dobson and Hawk Tolson. Neil Cunningham Dobson diligently accumulated the images displaying fishing damage by site from the Atlas survey area, dated the wrecks, identified fishing gear and has strongly facilitated the production of the primary data utilized in this report.

GIS wreck distribution maps were produced with great patience by Gerhard Seiffert. John Griffith processed the hard data obtained by the UK Marine and Fisheries Agency into statistical form and produced the GIS maps in this report. Chief Conservator Fred Van de Walle advised on the bronze cannon lifted from the wreck of HMS *Victory*.

Prof. Michel Kaiser (School of Ocean Sciences, Bangor University), Koen Vanstaen (Cefas) and Prof. Andrew Price (Department of Biological Sciences, University of Warwick) generously commented on the current project and report. For various further support and advice, I am also most grateful to Sir Robert Balchin, Jason Williams, Peter Goodwin and Nick Hall. All errors are of course my own.

Notes

1. These fishing forms are also characterized by the Food & Agriculture Organization of the United Nations: http://www.fao.org/fi/website/FISearch Action.do?dslist=geartype&lixsl=webapps/figis/ shared/xsl/search_result.xsl&kw[0]=name&kv[0]= trawl&refxml=true.

2. Fishing gear tends to be constructed from modern synthetic fibers that are non-biodegradable. This means that snagged or lost gear and torn fragments of net may continue to catch fish indefinitely. This is termed ghost fishing (http://www.jncc.gov.uk/ page-1567). Largely relevant to diveable water depths, this issue is not pertinent to deep-sea shipwrecks, although the ongoing effects of snagged nets of durable nature on site deterioration are in theory a continuous problem.

3. In the absence of published reports, see: http://www. deepimage.co.uk/expeditions/expeditions.htm.

4. See: http://www.alderneywreck.com/node/7.

5. *St Anthony, off Gunwalloe, Kerrier, Cornwall. Designated Site Assessment: Archaeological Report* (Wessex Archaeology, 2007).

6. See:http://www.english-heritage.org.uk/server show/ConWebDoc.6610.

7. *Loe Bar, Penwith (District), Cornwall. Designated Site Assessment. Full Report* (Wessex Archaeology, 2005).

8. *Archaeological Services in Relation to the Protection of Wrecks Act (1973). Coronation Offshore, Penlee Point Plymouth. Designated Site assessment: Full Report* (Wessex Archaeology, 2004).

9. These statistics exclude the 120 Danish galleys lost off Swanage in AD 877, according to the *Anglo-Saxon Chronicles.*

10. Research based on 3,643 hauls from 306 trips aboard commercial fishing vessels (142 different boats) between 2002 and 2005 (Enever *et al.*, 2007).

11. See: http://www.defra.gov.uk/marine/fisheries/fishman/eufleet.htm.

12. See: http://www.jncc.gov.uk/page-1568.

13. By law, all international and passenger ships and vessels in excess of 300 tons are compelled to be equipped with AIS principally for purposes of identifying and locating craft.

14. See: http://www.whoi.edu/sbl/image.do?id=10977&litesiteid=2740&articleId=4958 and http://stellwagen.noaa.gov/maritime/paulpalmer.html.

15. Foley, B., *Impact of Fishing on Shipwrecks*: http://www.whoi.edu/sbl/liteSite.do?litesiteid=2740&articleId=4965.

Bibliography

Adams J. and Black, J., 'From Rescue to Research: Medieval Ship Finds in St. Peter Port, Guernsey', *IJNA* 33.2 (2004), 230-52.

Alward, G.L., *The Sea Fisheries of Great Britain and Ireland* (Grimsby, 1932).

Arnold, S., *The Art of Wreck Fishing* (Seaford, 1996).

Ballard, R., 'Searching for Ancient Shipwrecks in the Deep Sea'. In R.D. Ballard (ed.), *Archaeological Oceanography* (Princeton University Press, 2008), 132-47.

Bergman, M.J.N. and Van Santbrink, J.W., 'Fishing Mortality of Populations of Megafauna in Sandy Environments'. In M.J. Kaiser and S.J. de Groot (eds.), *Effects of Fishing on Non-Target Species and Habitats* (Oxford, 2000), 49-68.

Bradshaw, C., Veale, L.O., Hill, A.S. and Brand, A.R., 'The Effects of Scallop Dredging on Gravelly Seabed Communities'. In M.J. Kaiser and S.J. de Groot (eds.), *Effects of Fishing on Non-Target Species and Habitats* (Oxford, 2000), 83-104.

Bryn, P., Jasinski, M.E. and Soreide, F., *Ormen Lange. Pipelines and Shipwrecks* (Oslo, 2007).

Camidge, K., *HMS Colossus. Survey Report 2007* (2007).

Cunliffe, B., 'People of the Sea', *British Archaeology* 63 (2002).

Cunningham Dobson, N. and Kingsley, S. *HMS Victory, a First-Rate Royal Navy Warship Wrecked in the English Channel, 1744. Preliminary Survey and Identification* (OME Papers 2, 2009).

Cunningham Dobson, N. and Tolson, H., *A Note on Human Remains from the Shipwreck of HMS Victory, 1744* (OME Papers, forthcoming).

Dare, P.J., Palmer, D.W., Howell, M.L. and Darby, C.D., *Experiments to Assess the Relative Dredging Performance of Research and Commercial Vessels for Estimating the Abundance of Scallops (Pectens Maximus) in the Western English Channel Fishery* (Fisheries Research Technical Report No. 96, Lowestoft, 1994).

Davenport T.G. and Burns, R., 1995, 'A Sixteenth Century Wreck off the Island of Alderney'. In M. Bound (ed.), *The Archaeology of Ships of War* (Int. Maritime Archaeology Series, Volume 1, Oxford), 30-40.

Dix, J. and Lambkin. D., 'Modelling Exclusion Zones for Marine Aggregate Dredging'. In *Technical Conference. Marine Aggregate Levy Sustainability Fund. Marine Aggregate Extraction. Helping to Determine Good Practice, July 6 2005, SOAS, London.*

Duke of Edinburgh, H.R.H., *Notes on the Sea Fisheries and Fishing Populations of the United Kingdom* (International Fisheries Exhibition, London, 1883).

Dunkley, M., 'The Value of Historic Shipwrecks'. In I. Radic Rossi, A. Gaspari and A. Pydyn (eds.), *Proceedings of the 13th Annual Meeting of the European Association of Archaeologists (Zadar, Croatia, 18-23 September 2007)* (Zagreb, 2008), 18-28.

Duplisea, D.E., Jennings, S., Malcolm, S.J., Parker, R. and Sivyer, D.B., 'Modelling Potential Impacts of Bottom Trawl Fisheries on Soft Sediment Bioge chemistry in the North Sea', *Geochemical Transactions* 14 (2001), 1-6.

Enever, R., Revill, A., and Grant, A., 'Discarding in the English Channel, Western approaches, Celtic and Irish seas (ICES subarea VII)', *Fisheries Research* 86 (2007), 143-52.

Firth, A., 'Marine Aggregates and Prehistory'. In *Underwater Cultural Heritage at Risk. Managing Natural and Human Impacts* (ICOMOS, 2006), 8-10.

Fonteyne, R., 'Physical Impact of Beam Trawls on Seabed Sediments'. In M.J. Kaiser and S.J. de Groot (eds.), *Effects of Fishing on Non-Target Species and Habitats* (Oxford, 2000), 15-36.

Ford, B., Borgens, A., Bryant, W., Marshall, D., Hitchcock, P., Arias, C. and Hamilton D., *Archaeological Excavation of the Mardi Gras Shipwreck*

(16GM01), Gulf of Mexico Continental Shelf (New Orleans, 2008).

Gammon, C., *Wreck Fishing* (Reading, 1975).

Gray, M.J., *The Coastal Fisheries of England and Wales, Part III: A Review of their Status 1992-1994* (Fisheries Research Technical Report No. 11, Lowestoft, 1995).

Grochowski, N.T.L., Collins, M.B., Boxall, S.R. and Salomon, J.C., 'Sediment Transport Predictions for the English Channel, Using Numerical Models', *Journal of the Geological Society* 150 (1993), 683-95.

Gutierrez, A., 'A Shipwreck Cargo of Sevillian Pottery from the Studland Wreck, Dorset, UK', *IJNA* 32.1 (2003), 24-41.

Hall, S.J., *The Effects of Fishing on Marine Ecosystems and Communities* (Oxford, 1999).

Hall-Spencer, J.M. and Moore, P.G., 'Scallop Dredging has Profound, Long-Term Impacts on Maerl Habitats', *ICES Journal of Marine Science* 57 (2000), 1407-15.

Hamblin, R.J.O., Crosby, A., Balson, P.S., Jones, S.M., Chadwick, R.A., Penn, I.E. and Arthur, M.J., *The Geology of the English Channel* (HMSO, London, 1992).

Hillis, R.R., Gatliff, R.W., Day, G.A. and Edwards, J.W.F., *The Geology of the Western English Channel and its Western Approaches* (HMSO, London, 1990).

Jennings, S., Kaiser, M.J. and Reynolds, J.D., *Marine Fisheries Ecology* (Oxford, 2001).

Jennings, S., Warr, K.J., Greenstreet, S.P.R. and Cotter, A.J.R., 'Spatial and Temporal Patterns in North Sea Fishing Effort'. In M.J. Kaiser and S.J. de Groot (eds.), *Effects of Fishing on Non-Target Species and Habitats* (Oxford, 2000), 3-14.

Kaiser, M.J., Collie, J.S., Hall, S.J., Jennings, S. and Poiner, I.R., 'Modification of Marine Habitats by Trawling Activities: Prognosis and Solutions', *Fish and Fisheries* 3.2 (2002), 114-36.

Kaiser, M.J., Edwards, D.B., Armstrong, P.J., Radford, K., Lough, N.E.L., Flatt, R.P and Jones, H.D., 'Changes in Megafaunal Benthic Communities in Different Habitats after Trawling Disturbance', *ICES Journal of Marine Science* 55 (1998), 353-61.

Larn, R. and Larn, B., *Shipwreck Index of the British Isles. Volume 1: Isles of Scilly, Cornwall, Devon and Dorset* (London, 1995).

McBride, P. and Larn, R., *Admiral Shovell's Treasure and Shipwreck in the Isles of Scilly* (Penryn, 1999).

Morais, P., Borges, T.C., Carnall, V., Terrinha, P., Cooper, C. and Cooper, R., 'Trawl-Induced Bottom Disturbance off the South Coast of Portugal: Direct Observations by the "Delta" Manned-Submersible on the Submarine Canyon of Portimao', *Marine Ecology* 28 (2007), 112-22.

Revill, A.S. and Dunlin, G., 'The Fishing Capacity of Gillnets Lost on Wrecks and on Open Ground in UK Coastal Waters', *Marine Fisheries* 64 (2003), 107-113.

Reynaud, J.-Y., Tessier, B., Auffret, J.-P., Berné, S., De Batist, M., Marsset, T. and Walker, P., 'The Offshore Quaternary Sediment Bodies of the English Channel and its Western Approaches', *Journal of Quaternary Science* 18 (2003), 361-71.

Roberts, C., *The Unnatural History of the Sea. The Past and Future of Humanity and Fishing* (London, 2007).

Rule, M. and Monaghan, J., *A Gallo-Roman Trading Vessel from Guernsey. The Excavation and Recovery of a Third Century Shipwreck* (Guernsey Museum Monograph, 1993).

Sibella, P., *The George McGhee Amphora Collection at the Alanya Museum, Turkey* (INA Quarterly 19, Suppl. 1, 2002).

Simpson, K., Hall, H., Davis, R. and Lam, R., 'An Early 17th Century Wreck Near Rill Cove, Kynance, Cornwall. An Interim Report', *IJNA* 6.2 (1977), 163-66.

Thomsen, M.H., 'The Studland Bay Wreck, Dorset, UK: Hull Analysis', *IJNA* 29.1 (2000), 69-85.

Tolson, H., *The Jacksonville 'Blue China' Shipwreck & the Myth of Deep-Sea Preservation* (OME Papers 3, 2009).

Vanstaen, K., Limpenny, D., Lee, J., Eggleton, J., Brown, A. and Stelzenmuller, V., *The Scale and Impact of Fishing Activities in the Eastern English Channel: an Initial Assessment Based on Existing Geophysical Survey Data* (CEFAS, Lowestoft, 2007).

Walmsley, S.A. and Pawson, M.G., *The Coastal Fisheries of England and Wales, Part V: A Review of their Status 2005-6* (Science Series Technical Report 140, CEFAS, Lowestoft, 2007).

Watling, L. and Norse, E.A., 'Disturbance of the Seabed by Mobile Fishing Gear: a Comparison to Forest Clearcutting', *Conservation Biology* 12.6 (1998), 1180-97.

Williams, G. and Eltis, D., *History of the Liverpool Privateers and Letters of Marque: with an Account of the Liverpool Slave Trade, 1744-1812* (McGill-Queen's University Press, 2004).

Young, A., *Sea Fisheries* (London, 1877).

Zemer, A., *Storage Jars in Ancient Sea Trade* (Haifa, 1977).

9

HMS *Victory*, a First-Rate Royal Navy Warship Lost in the English Channel, 1744. Preliminary Survey & Identification

Neil Cunningham Dobson
Odyssey Marine Exploration, Tampa, USA

Sean Kingsley
Wreck Watch Int., London, United Kingdom

In April 2008, Odyssey Marine Exploration recorded an interesting target in the western English Channel using a side-scan and magnetometer as part of its ongoing Atlas Shipwreck Survey Project. Subsequent visual investigation using the Remotely-Operated Vehicle Zeus, complemented in September and October by a pre-disturbance survey, identified a substantial concentration of wreckage covering an area of 61 x 22m, comprising disarticulated wooden planking, iron ballast, two anchors, a copper kettle, rigging, two probable gunner's wheels and, most diagnostically, 41 bronze cannon.

An examination of the site and its material culture in relation to a desk-based assessment leads to the conclusion that Odyssey has discovered the long-lost wreck of Admiral Sir John Balchin's first-rate Royal Navy warship, HMS *Victory*, lost in the Channel on 5 October, 1744. This preliminary report introduces the results of an archaeological field evaluation, which took the form of a non-disturbance survey and limited small-scale trial trenching, and cumulatively addresses this underlying identification. The prevailing historical orthodoxy that situates the wreck of *Victory* around Alderney and the Casquets is proven to be false.

1. Summary

During ongoing surveys in the western English Channel as part of Odyssey Marine Exploration's Atlas Shipwreck Survey Project, designed to map the archaeological landscape of this zone's international waters, a combined side-scan and magnetometer survey was conducted in April 2008 with a range of 150m. The resultant high-frequency image (410Khz) depicted a clearly disturbed sea bottom across an oval area of 40m, interspersed with linear objects (Fig. 1). The 35-gamma magnetometer profile was suggestive of a wooden wreck with features typifying iron anchors, cannon and ship structure (pers. comm. Ernie Tapanes, November 2008). The crest of a large sand wave was visible some 40m to the northwest.

From the research platform the *Odyssey Explorer*, the Remotely-Operated Vehicle (ROV) Zeus subsequently made 23 dives on site 25C between May and October 2008, which verified the existence of a substantial newly discovered shipwreck:

A. May (two dives) – initial visual verification of the presence of a shipwreck; recovery of a brick fragment from near cannon C4 in order to arrest the wreck site in a US Federal court.

B. June (three dives) – non-disturbance survey, measurement and photography of surface features (type and orientation).

C. September (five dives) – completion of non-disturbance survey of surface features (type and orientation) and non-disturbance photomosaic (2,821 still images taken at an elevation of 2.5m above the seabed).

D. October (13 dives) – limited trial-trenching in an attempt to confirm the identity of the wrecked vessel: exposure of an iron anchor to the northeast to verify the position of the bows; identification and excavation of the wooden rudder to the southwest; trial-trenches focused on the zone between the rudder and the southernmost cannon, C26, where diagnostic small finds belonging to the ship's officers were most likely to be preserved; clearance of sediments around bronze cannon C28 and C33, found to the north of the wreck concentration (beyond the nucleus covered by the photomosaic and pre-disturbance site plan) and their recovery.

Unlike any of the hundreds of other wrecks surveyed by Odyssey Marine Exploration (OME) across several oceans,

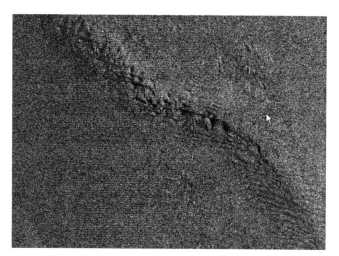

Fig. 1. Side-scan image of site 25C, characterized by a 40m oval area of disturbed sea bottom interspersed with linear objects.

site 25C is characterized by a large number of bronze cannon. Several of the 41 examples feature royal arms indicative of the guns' nationality and date.

Despite both mid-18th century reports and modern theory placing the wreckage of the iconic first-rate Royal Navy warship HMS *Victory*, lost on 5 October 1744, off the Casquets near Alderney in the Channel Isles, the 2008 fieldwork leaves no doubt that site 25C comprises the archaeological remains of this enigmatic loss. *Victory* was the largest warship in the Royal Navy and judged to be the most impressive man-of-war in the world at the time (Clowes, 1966: 108). Launched from Portsmouth dockyard in 1737, she was the flagship of two of the most accomplished and experienced seamen of the age, Sir John Norris, Admiral of the Fleet, and Sir John Balchin, Admiral of the White (Aldridge, 2000; Charnock, 1795b). She went down in a violent storm under the command of Admiral Balchin, aged 74, who was on his way home after successfully liberating a Royal Navy victualling convoy blockaded by the French fleet down the River Tagus (Clowes, 1966: 91; Richmond, 1920: 108).

In September and October 2008, the non-disturbance survey, followed by small-scale trial trenching, largely confined to the stern area of the shipwreck where the most diagnostic artifacts were anticipated to be preserved, produced a master photomosaic of the wreck (Fig. 2) and a pre-disturbance site plan (Fig. 3), photographed all *in situ* material culture and defined the level of site preservation and biological oasis effect in action. For identification purposes, two bronze cannon were recovered, C28 and C33 (Figs. 40-41). The dates, calibre, quantity and English origins of these guns and those on the seabed, cast under King George I (r. 1714-27) and King George II (r. 1727-60), provide robust evidence to recognize site 25C conclusively as HMS

Victory. This identification has been presented to the UK Ministry of Defence, the Royal Navy, the Department of Culture, Media and Sport, and communicated to English Heritage.

This shipwreck is of major historical and archaeological importance as the only first-rate English warship ever discovered underwater and as the only documented Royal Navy wreck seemingly containing its full deployment of bronze cannon. The 42-pounder recovered by Odyssey, cannon C33 (Fig. 41) – the largest contemporary gun used in naval warfare – is the only recorded example in existence. The loss of HMS *Victory* was a tragic event that paved the way for the reorganization of shipbuilding philosophies within the Royal Navy in the subsequent two decades. Contrary to prevailing historical theory, the wreck's discovery in open seas, more than 50km west of the Casquets, immediately exonerates Sir John Balchin and his crew from the accusation of poor navigation on the fateful day of the warship's loss.

This report summarizes the preliminary observations of the archaeological field evaluation (pre-disturbance survey and small-scale trial trenches), which was designed to confirm the wreck's identity, to assess its site formation, current state of preservation and potential longevity, and historical and archaeological significance. The field evaluation ran in conjunction with desk-based documentary research into the vessel, its crew and cargo, including archival research testifying that a large cargo of specie for merchants, as well as a substantial sum of money captured by Balchin as prizes of war, was aboard HMS *Victory* when she went down (see Section 12 below).

The report examines the following themes:

• Marine Environment
• Wreck Destabilization
• Archaeological Features & Site Formation
• Bronze Cannon: Identification & Significance
• Ship Identity: Royal Navy Losses in the English Channel; Bronze Cannon with George I & George II Royal Arms; First-Rate Royal Navy Warship Losses
• Wreck Location: a Case of Mistaken Geography
• HMS *Victory*: Construction
• Naval Operations
• Admiral Sir John Norris
• Admiral Sir John Balchin
• Prizes and Bullion
• The Loss of HMS *Victory* – Poor Design or Ill Winds?

All research on-site and its interpretation remain at a preliminary stage.[1]

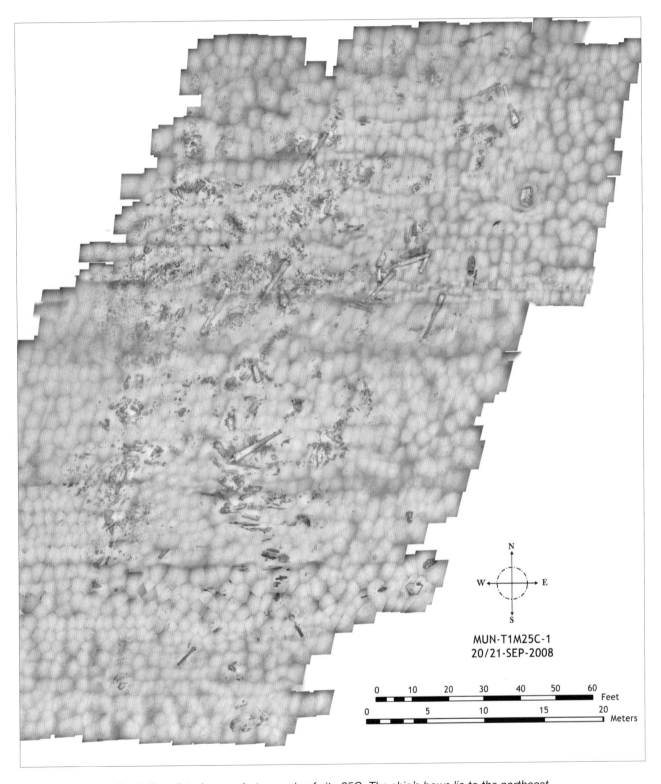

Fig. 2. Pre-disturbance photomosaic of site 25C. The ship's bows lie to the northeast.

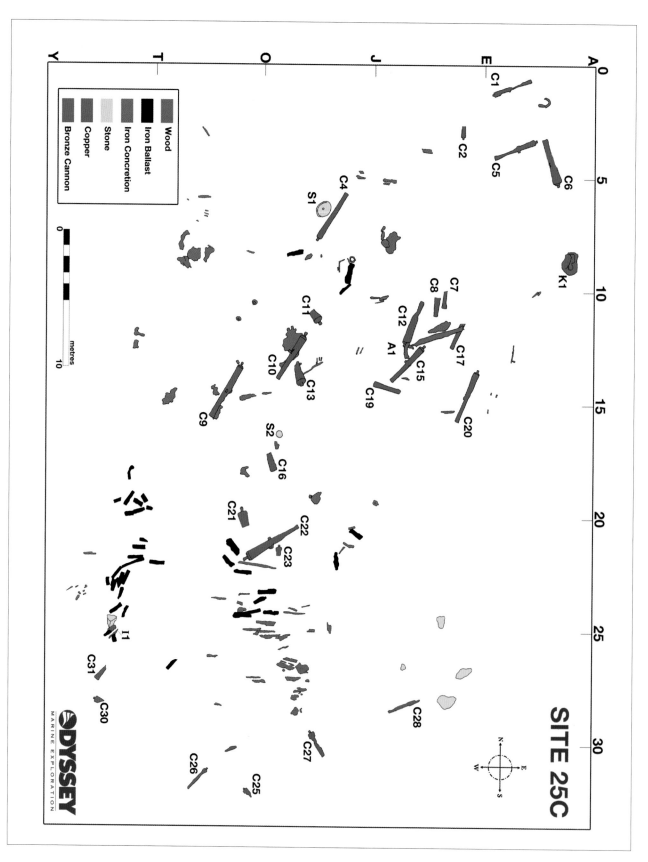

Fig. 3. Pre-disturbance plan of site 25C.

2. Marine Environment

Site 25C lies in the Western English Channel in approximately 100m of water, around 100km west of the Casquets off the Channel Isles, beyond the territorial seas or contiguous zone of any country. The English Channel is a 520km-long funnel-shaped seaway aligned west-southwest to east-northeast. To the west it is 160km-wide and opens into the North Atlantic Ocean; to the east it narrows to 30km wide at Dover Strait. The Channel floor is a smooth, shallow shelf that gently inclines from a water depth of 30m at Dover Strait towards the continental shelf with a gradient of 0.3-0.5% (Gibbard and Lautridou, 2003), reaching 120m at the Western Approaches. The Channel displays a maximum tidal range of 6-10m (Grochowski *et al.*, 1993: 683).

The Narrow Seas are subdivided into three geological zones: the Eastern English Channel, the Central and Western Channel, and the Western Approaches. In the Western Channel where site 25C lies, the sea floor in the central segment and its extension to the southwest are covered by tide-transported sand waves oriented roughly northwest to southeast in a band up to 35km wide parallel to the shelf-break and down to depths of 200m. Their crests are up to 5km long, 1km apart and 7m high (Evans, 1990: 81).

The sandy biolithoclastic layer contains gravely algal skeletal carbonates (0.5-2.5mm thick). The carbonate friction in the superficial sediments is composed of skeletal grains derived from littoral shelf faunas and algae, mainly pelecypods and bryozloans. The sand deposits thicken towards the Western Approaches, where they achieve depths of several tens of meters (Reynaud *et al.*, 2003: 364). The location of site 25C north of the Hurd Deep (Gibbard and Lautridou, 2003: 196) is highly fortuitous due to the

Fig. 4. Encrusted iron anchor ring, A1, next to cannon C15 and C21 to the northeast of the wreck.

presence of sand overlying gravel in this zone. Just to the east, the seabed topography is dominated by pure gravel, which would not have favored the preservation of organic material. These sand waves, conspicuous even in the side-scan image of the seabed (Fig. 1), are highly dynamic and in a constant state of flux, making site 25C susceptible to constant cycles of exposure, scouring and coverage.

The Eastern and Western Channel are separated by a bed-load parting characterized by very high tidal current velocities and by an almost total lack of sand cover over the boulder pavement. To the east, currents and sand transport are directed eastwards towards the Dover Strait; west of the parting, bed-load currents and transport run southwesterly. East and west are thus isolated, non-interactive sedimentological paths (Grochowski *et al.*, 1993: fig. 4; Reynaud *et al.*, 2003: 364). The possibility that gravel dredging in the east may have triggered the exposure of site 25C in the west is thus not feasible.

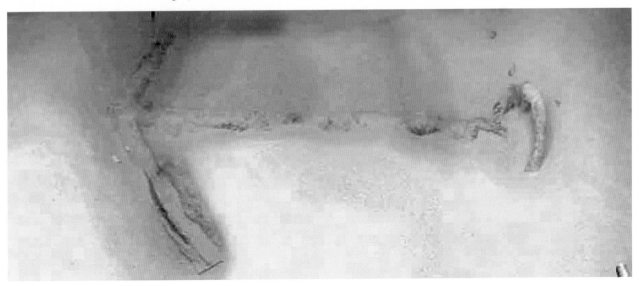

Fig. 5. Intact forged iron anchor, A2, at the northeast tip of the wreck site.

Fig. 6. Copper cylindrical cooking kettle, K1, from the northeast of the wreck. Note the heavy rivets.

3. Wreck Destabilization

Site 25C has been extensively disturbed by beam trawlers and modern pollutants, manifested in the presence of glass bottles, a lobster trap, fishing net, plastic (Fig. 31), cereal boxes, a videotape cassette and other modern contamina-

tion. Of major concern is the orientation of the cannon, some of which ought to reflect their original dispositions at right-angles to the line of the keel. Instead, 59% of the visible guns lie parallel to the postulated longitudinal axis of the keel (Fig. 3). Given the enormous weight of the lower-deck 4-ton 42-pounders, and the extremely high probability that they reached the seabed in their original gun stations, this pattern seems to be the result of trawler cables and nets dragging the site.

Ste 25C lies in an environmental zone that is notorious for trawler disturbance. Trawls equipped with chain mats and 'tickler' chains designed to fluidize the upper layers of sediments and drive flatfish from the seabed into a net weighing about 8,000kg, towed at about 11km per hour, may impact the same area of seabed multiple times each year, destroying 5-65% of the resident fauna and mixing the top 6cm of sediment in a single pass (Duplisea *et al.*, 2001). This points towards a possible disturbance of 24cm of the upper strata of site 25C annually, depending on natural sediment fluidity. Vessel dredges, for instance, exploiting the Fowey-Eddystone scallop fishing ground within a 20 x 8km area off southwest Cornwall use spring-loaded toothbars, each with nine teeth of 8cm length and 7cm spacing. Individual vessels are rigged with between eight and 30 dredges attached to two side beams (Dare *et al.*, 1994: 5).

The physical effects of trawling are equivalent to an extreme bioturbator. As well as destroying and scattering archaeological material, this has major implications for the preservation of concealed deposits abruptly infiltrated by oxygen flow. While departing site 25C in September 2008, just such a trawler was observed running lines that were heading directly for the wreck site.

Although the impact of beam trawling on the marine ecology has been subjected to intensive research and quantification, resulting in the UK Marine and Fisheries Agency paying out £4.7 million in 2007 to break up and decommission fishing boats targeting the Western English Channel,[2] the direct impact on Europe's rich maritime archaeological heritage remains unacknowledged and uncontrolled. The clear evidence of the systematic destruction of shipwreck sites has been largely ignored and gone unpublished. In Odyssey's experience, verified by scientific documentation of numerous sites, wreck destruction is rife in the Channel. With its abundance of fish, octopi, crab and gorgonians, site 25C is a rich biological oasis and thus a great attraction for fishermen, which will undoubtedly result in continued destruction of the shipwreck. To assume that wrecks are unaffected by documented cases of extreme disturbance to the marine ecology is an inaccurate and irresponsible heritage managerial position.

Fig. 7. Gunner's wheel S2 alongside
a cannon ball and cannon C16.

Fig. 8. Gunner's wheel S1 and loose planking
alongside bronze cannon C4.

4. Archaeological Features & Site Formation

The visible surface features of site 25C densely cover an extensive area of 61 x 22m, oriented along a northeast to southwest axis (Figs. 2-3). The seabed topography fluctuates with a maximum altitude of 7m. Some 41 bronze cannon, iron ballast blocks, cupreous artifacts and disarticulated, fragmented planking are interspersed amongst pockets of gravel, flint and small stones protruding from a heavily abraded shell-rich sedimentological matrix.

The wreck site is highly dynamic, covered by ever-shifting sand waves that constantly expose, scour and cover fresh areas of wreckage. Cannon protruding into the sediment at acute angles (Figs. 22-25) suggest that a minimum of 3m of overburden covers the seabed in places and likely conceals extensive wreckage. Visibility on the site varies between 10m and zero at certain stages of the tidal cycle. A current of 0.8 to 1.4 knots was observed running across the seabed.

Some 2,574m-square of site 25C have been surveyed, revealing substantial archaeological deposits. The most

highly conspicuous manifestations are the 41 bronze cannon, which include bores ranging between 4 and 7 inches in diameter, corresponding to 6- and 42-pounder guns. The latter were functionally restricted to the Royal Navy's largest warships, first-rates. Elaborate royal arms of King George I and George II, as well as the founder' dates of 1726 on the 42-pounder cannon C33 and 1734 on the 12-pounder C28, place the wreck site precisely within the timeframe of HMS *Victory*'s construction and operation (see Sections 5 and 6B below).

Apart from the bronze guns, significant artifacts visible on the site's surface include:

1. One iron anchor ring and shank, A1 (grid G12; Fig. 4), and one complete iron anchor to the north-east, A2 (grid C2), signifying the position of the bows (Fig. 5).
2. A copper cooking kettle, K1 (grid B9; Fig. 6).
3. Two probable gunner's stone wheels, S1 and S2, for sharpening bayonets and grinding down shot impurities (grids L6 and N16; Figs. 7-8).
4. Wooden bowls/powder cask lids (grid V24; Fig. 9).
5. A concentration of rectangular iron ballast pigs (predominantly within grids T17-V25; Figs. 11-12).
6. Bronze rigging/pump pulleys, including what resembles a sprocket wheel (grid H10; Fig. 10) from a chain pump used to extract water from the bilge (Goodwin, 1987: 142, fig. 5.13) and a block at the southeastern end of cannon C6 (grid B5; Fig. 13).
7. A possible pewter plate (Fig. 14).
8. A possible sword, I1 (grid V25; Fig. 15).

Fragmented loose wooden planking is predominantly restricted to the south of the wreck (Figs. 3, 16), with the key exception of a probable knee contextualized with galley bricks in grid L9 (Fig. 17). In addition to the northeast-southwest distribution of the cannon, the shipwreck's axis is also suggested by the orientation of the southern planking extending east-west between grids O21-O29 and L25-Q25 (Fig. 3). Since no interconnected sections of hull planking are visible (except for the rudder), these may comprise ceiling or deck planking. Their perpendicular orientation in relation to the conjectured keel line supports the theory that the ship settled on a northeast-southwest axis.

The discovery of a bower anchor to the northeast of the site in grid C2 (Fig. 5), and the badly decomposed rudder some 9m south of cannon B26 (Fig. 19), verifies that the stern lies to the southwest. The rudder, lying on a compass heading of 135 degrees, is approximately 10m long and 1.8m wide, and is held together by seven iron pintle braces, which are the stipulated number for

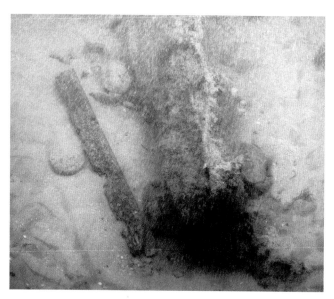

Fig. 9. Disarticulated hull planking and possible wooden gunpowder cask lids or wooden mess bowls.

Fig. 10. Bronze pulley, possibly from the ship's bilge pump system, with a hearth brick behind.

70 to 110-gun Royal Navy warships (Goodwin, 1987: 131).[3] What seems to be the lower end of the rudder is either protected by or repaired with a square casing of lead. The condition of the wood is extremely poor, with surfaces extensively eroded to the extent that the rudder resembles delaminated plywood. It is not possible to distinguish between the back, after, middle and main piece (Steffy, 1994: 298). The iron pintles are almost completely decomposed.

Human bones have been recorded on the surface of site 25C. Clearance of the upper light layer of mobile sand

around the edge of Cannon C10 for recovery exposed what appeared to be a rib bone and a skull 5-30cm below the surface. To the west between the base ring and the right-hand trunnion, and at the end of the muzzle, were further skeletal remains, including rib bones. Sediment removal was immediately stopped after this discovery and the area of the human remains recorded and photographed. ROV Zeus then backfilled the context. Later monitoring by the ROV observed that the area remained covered and protected.

Possible human remains were identified on the site's surface at the cascable end of cannon C22 and the muzzle end of C39. Based on these discoveries, it seems likely that some of the crew were caught at their stations below decks when the *Victory* was chaotically and swiftly wrecked, pinning the seamen beneath shifting cannon. These human remains will be the subject of a pending separate Odyssey report.

A. Anchor A2

Several artifacts and assemblages provide tentative evidence for the ship's form, date and nationality. A trial trench cut around an anchor crown at the northeastern tip of the wreck, just east of cannon C1 in grid C2, exposed a complete forged iron anchor, excluding its wooden stock (Fig. 5). Preliminary indications have provided approximate measurements: crown to ring length 6.90m; diameter of ring 0.91m; and fluke to fluke width 4.4m.

With arms arranged in a v-shaped configuration of about 60 degrees, anchor A2 does not typify French examples with curved arms, but conforms to the 18th-century Royal Navy design, where the relaxed arm angle created less strain on the arm-shank weld in the crown than the acute v-shaped form. HMS *Victory*'s anchors would have been manufactured at Deptford, where a master anchor smith, 12 foreman smiths and 88 hammermen monopolized production in the first half of the 18th century (Jobling, 1993: 92, 93, 95, fig. 10).

Established sizes and weights of Royal Navy anchors for 1745 verify that first-rate Royal Navy warships were equipped with five bower anchors (77 cwt, 19ft 2in), one stream (20 cwt, 13ft 4in) and one kedge (10 cwt, 10ft 4 in) (Curryer, 1999: 56; Lavery, 1987: 35). Site 25C's huge anchor is consistent with an example suitable for a first-rate. If subsequent fieldwork confirms its length of 22.63ft (6.90m), it will comfortably exceed the dimensions of a bower anchor recorded on the wreck of the *Association*, a 90-gun, second-rate Royal Navy warship wrecked off the Scilly Isles in 1707, which measured 18ft 4in (5.6m) in length (Morris, 1967: 49). The dimensions of site 25C's anchor require re-measurement for confirmation, but

Fig. 11. Rectangular iron ballast ingots from the southwest of the site. The pierced metal sheet in the foreground may have been used to nail the ballast physically in situ *within the hull.*

Fig. 12. Rectangular iron ballast ingots from the southwest of the site.

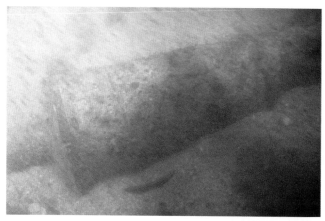

Fig. 13. In the space of a few weeks, some 30cm of sediment was naturally eroded away from a cannon to fully expose a bronze rigging block and galley brick to one side.

currently seem to exceed the length of 21ft 2in (6.45m) for the sheet anchor on Nelson's *Victory*.

B. Copper Kettle

The copper cooking kettle, K1, located towards the northeastern extremity of the wreck (grid B9) correlates with the position of the bows, although it has almost certainly been dragged out of context. Crushed and misshapen, it was originally cylindrical in shape and strongly riveted at the base and rim (Fig. 6). The lid is closed and pierced by a circular hole with a raised rim at its center. A handle points downward to one side.

This shape is typologically distinct from the wide, open cauldron used on the *Mary Rose c.* 1545 (Jones, 2003: pl. 3), but corresponds to the small examples listed on Royal Navy warships of 1750 in T.R. Blanckley's *A Naval Expositor* and which remained the cooking pot of choice into the 1780s. Examples used on first-rates were enclosed by a fire hearth composed of about 2,500 bricks (Lavery, 1987: 197) and dozens of bricks are visible to

the north of site 25C (Figs. 10, 13, 17). A similar kettle has been excavated from the wreck of the English merchant slave ship the *Henrietta Marie*, lost off New Ground reef, Key West, in 1700 (Malcom, 2000), while two large copper fish kettles lost on the first-rate HMS *Royal George* in 1782 were salvaged in 1839 (Codrington, 1840: 72).

After concerns were raised about the weight of brick-lined kitchen galleys on the maneuverability of warships, and worries that copper contributed to scurvy, iron fire hearths started to be preferred from 1757, but only predominated in the Royal Navy after 1780, when Alexander Brodie patented the iron ship's stove. The Navy Board was so impressed by the innovation that they entered into a comprehensive contract with Brodie, giving him a commercial monopoly for English warships (Watson, 1968: 410).

The wreck of HMS *Swift*, lost in 1770 off Patagonia, southern Argentina, was furnished with a similar rectangular iron box, measuring 115 x 75cm, as well as lead sheets to protect the deck from fire and heat. She retained her 44 x 30cm copper cauldron with a fixed handle and Admiralty broad arrow stamped on its upper face (Elkin *et al.*, 2007: 39, 49). Iron fire hearths of the Brodie form have been recorded on the wrecks of HMS *De Braak*, which foundered off Delaware in May 1798, on the 4,968m-deep "Piña Colada" wreck lost off Florida and dated to around 1810 by 14 gold coins wrapped inside a gold box (Sinclair, 2002: 3)[4] and on the early 19th-century Mardi Gras shipwreck off Louisiana (Ford *et al.* 2008: 98-100).

Since copper kettles are associated with cooking galleys, which were positioned at the forward end of the middle deck of three-deckers, well away from the gunpowder magazine, forcing the chimney to pass through two decks before discharging its smoke (Goodwin, 1987: 160; Lavery, 1987: 196), the presence of this artifact on the surface of site 25C seems to reflect the comprehensive deterioration and/or destruction of the upper decks or, at least, their structural collapse to one side of the wreck site. The highly distinct form of the iron Brodie stove recorded on many wrecks post-dating 1770, and absent from site 25C, provides a tentative *terminus ante quem* for site 25C.

C. Gunners' Wheels

Contextualized with bronze cannon C4 (S1; grid L6) and an iron cannon ball and gun C16 (S2; grid N16) lie two circular stone artifacts (Figs. 7-8). These objects are unlikely to be millstones designed for the on-board grinding of grain because the Royal Navy retained victualling yards for this purpose. A marine's standard ration in the Georgian era was 1lb of bread a day. Bread and biscuit

Fig. 14. Bronze cannon and circular pewter plate rim in the foreground.

Fig. 15. Miscellaneous copper artifact and possible iron sword at left.

were baked and packed in bags at the Victualling Office on Tower Hill and at its branch establishments at Portsmouth and Plymouth (Rodger, 1986: 83). When stores needed topping up, warships were serviced by transport ships or overseas yards located at Gibraltar, Port Mahon and other localities (Macdonald, 2006: 60-61).

The stocking of warships with these foodstuffs prior to sailing is verified by the list of stores readied on the first-rate HMS *Royal George* for her voyage into the Mediterranean before she sank off Spithead in 1782. Her victuals included 43 tons of bread (Tracey, 1812: vi).

Site 25C's two circular stone artifacts are more likely to be rare examples of gunners' wheels used to grind down irregularities on shot and to sharpen bayonets. An example is still preserved today on Nelson's flagship, HMS *Victory*, in Portsmouth Historic Dockyard.

D. Iron Ballast

A concentration of about 32 rectangular iron concretions to the southwest of the site (grid T17-V25; Figs. 11-12) appears to be iron ballast blocks used on Royal Navy warships. The exploitation of this medium during the Georgian era remains a matter of some confusion. T.R. Blanckley's *A Naval Expos-*

itor of 1750 explained that "Ballast – is in great Ships generally Beach Stones, and in small Iron, laid in the Hold next the Keelson, in order to keep the Ship stiff, so that they may bear more Sail." This preference is similarly conveyed by the chronicles of Blaise Ollivier, Master Shipwright at France's foremost Royal Dockyard at Brest. Ollivier undertook a secret mission to all of England and Holland's major naval dockyards in 1737, when HMS *Victory* was just being completed in her dry-dock at Portsmouth, to report on methods of shipbuilding by France's maritime rivals. His five-month mission resulted in a 360-page manuscript accompanied by 13 sheets of diagrams and plans.

The shipwright (Roberts, 1992: 167, 169) agreed that the English ballasted ships with what he termed 'earth':

"They stow it in a straight line and parallel to the keel from the main forward bulkhead to the main after bulkhead, and also in a straight line athwartships. They do not use iron kentledge to ballast their ships save for long commissions, and in those ships which have insufficient space in the hold to accommodate earth ballast. I confess that when I saw at Deptford Dockyard that great quantity of kentledge of which I spoke... I believed that the English knew how to make good use of it... I have asked the reason of several officers; they replied that iron ballast stiffens all the movements of the ship, especially the rolling. Upon receiving this reply I enquired as to how the ballast is stowed, and was shown it on either rise of the keelson to larboard and to starboard of this timber. We used to find the same inconvenience in our own ships when we stowed the ballast as the English do, but now that we lay it along the rungheads our ships have an easier motion. The English admit that if iron kentledge did not make the movement of their ships so harsh it would be more advantageous to ballast their ships with kentledge than with gravel or earth, since the weight of the iron is farther removed from the centre of motion, and because the weight of the stores stowed atop the ballast is carried lower down."

Ollivier's argument is inconsistent, however, and contradictory to follow. By his own eye-witness admission (Roberts, 1992: 55), he also reported how he

"found next to one of the docks at Deptford a very great quantity of kentledge which they [Royal Navy] use to ballast their ships. The iron pigs are about 36 inches long and 6 inches square, and with these dimensions they must weight 350 pounds. I will say nothing about this sort of ballast: its usefulness is sufficiently well-known; I wish that no other were employed in the King's ships. The pigs which I saw at Deptford are pierced diagonally by several holes along the edges."

How are we to explain the master shipwright-cum-spy's contradiction in terms? Iron ballast was evidently extremely common at Deptford, much to the disappointment of

Fig. 16. Disarticulated wooden planking to the southwest of site 25C.

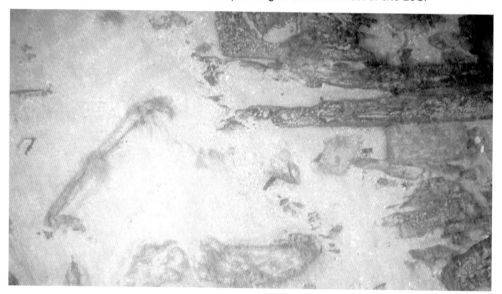

Fig. 17. A possible L-shaped wooden knee associated with galley bricks.

Fig. 18. A wooden spar or stanchion in situ.

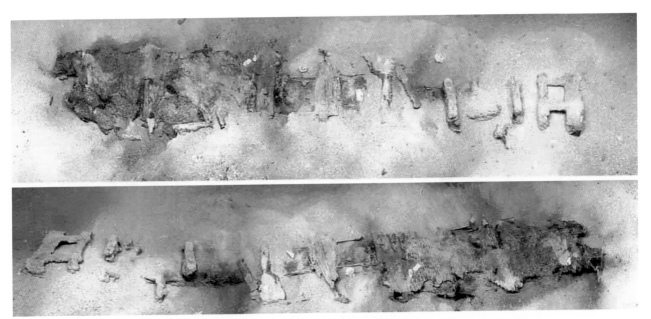

Fig. 19. Photomosaic of the highly deteriorated 10m-long wooden rudder to the southwest of the wreck site (oblique and vertical views).

Ollivier, whose language suggests that the Royal Navy was on the verge of realizing that kentledge offered far greater sailing efficiency than gravel.

Iron ballast on the wreck of HMS *Victory* should not be unexpected. Similar 320lb pig-iron ballast blocks stamped with the English naval board broad arrow, and fixed permanently into the hull to trim the ship, have been recorded on the fifth-rate warship HMS *Fowey*, which was wrecked off Florida in 1748 after seeing service in the English Channel and Gibraltar in 1744 and 1745 (Skowronek *et al.*, 1987: fig. 3). An apparent plate with bolt holes contextualized with the site 25C ballast may comprise part of a similar permanent attachment mechanism (Fig. 11). A reliance on cast iron ballast by the Royal Navy in the 1740s is actually clearly attested by Admiralty shipboard warrants (ADM 106/920/174; ADM 106/920/850).

Kentledge has also been recorded on the wreck of HMS *Pomone*, a fifth-rate, 38-gun frigate lost on the Needles in 1811 and equipped with 37 x 2 cwt iron ballast blocks (3.75 tons) (Tomalin *et al.*, 2000: 18). Analysis of its distribution, and comparisons with Royal Navy plans for the *Artois* (wrecked 1794) and *Barrosa* (lost 1812), suggest that iron ballast was generally laid longitudinally on each side of central members along the keelson in proximity to the ship's well and shot-lockers, but that very little continued aft of the pump and mainmast foot (Tomalin *et al.*, 2000: 17).

As with site 25C's copper kettle and the presence of 42-pounders on the surface of the wreck, this cluster of iron ballast implies that in places HMS *Victory* has broken up to a level beneath its lower deck and below the turn-of-the-bilge. Its presence on the southwest flank of the wreck,

with no trail of archaeology visible to the northwest, raises the possibility that sections of the wreck may remain buried beneath sediments to the northwest. Alternatively, *Victory*'s port side may have collapsed on top of the starboard flank. Neither scenario can be confirmed without complementary core sampling or excavation.

5. Bronze Cannon: Identification & Significance

The 41 cannon dominating the surface of site 25C are currently the most remarkable features of this shipwreck (Figs. 2-3, 20-42). These tools of war were not merely functional. With their elegant dolphins (Fig. 27) and intricate cast design and royal arms, all are exquisite expressions of bronze craftsmanship. A few are entirely exposed above mobile sediments, while the majority are either nearly entirely concealed or plunge into sediments at acute angles (Figs. 22-25). An oxidized patina and light concretion covers most of the cannon.

OME ROV supervisor Gary Peterson, assisted by ROV technician Olaf Dieckhoff, custom-designed a triangular ruler tool for ROV Zeus to measure the precise diameter of the bores and thus determine the guns' types of calibre (Figs. 20-21). The muzzles of 14 cannon were exposed above the sediments, enabling bore measurements to be taken; the trunnion widths of another 11 were measured because by 1716 this cannon element was equal in length to the diameter of the bore (Lavery, 1987: 97). Cannon with bores ranging between 4 and 7 inches diameter were recorded (Table 1).

Fig. 20. ROV Zeus measuring the bore of bronze cannon C33 in situ.

Fig. 21. ROV Zeus measuring the bore of a bronze cannon in situ.

Bore diameter to calibre ratio statistics attributed to Albert Borgard of the Royal Regiment of Artillery, who was active until 1727, preserved in the document *Construction of Brass Gun* (Caruana, 1997: 34, 39), demonstrate that site 25C's cannon correspond to between 6- and 42-pounders (Table 2): three 6- or 12-pounders, three 12-pounders and eight 24-pounders.

Crucially for the site's identification, the six certain and two probable cannon with 7-inch bores correspond to 42-pounder guns – the largest and most prestigious cannon used in European naval warfare. After 1677, this calibre of gun was only employed on first-rate warships in the Royal Navy. Thomas James's *Book of Artillery* relates gun sizes on first-rate Royal Navy warships to deck stations, lengths and weights for the Naval Gun Establishment of 1716 (Table 3), illustrating that first-rate warships carried 28 42-pounder brass cannon on their lower decks, which individually weighed 66 cwt or 3.35 tons (Caruana, 1997: 43).

Contemporary documents standardized the lengths of 42-pounders at 9ft 6in and 10ft. These dimensions were stipulated in 1725 by Colonel Armstrong, Surveyor General of the Ordnance, in John Muller's *A Treatise of Artillery* of 1757, and were the formula relied on for the

complete set of brass cannon manufactured for a 100-gun ship cast by Albert Borgard in the Royal Brass Foundry before 1727 (Blackmore, 1976: 399, 400; Caruana, 1997: 34, 39; Lavery, 1987: 98). For reasons that are not currently explicable, these standards are exceeded by the recovered 42-pounder cannon C33 on site 25C, which measures 3.4m (11.15ft) in length.

The two cannon recovered from site 25C in October 2008 confirm the order of the assemblages' magnitude:

• Cannon C28, 12-pounder (Figs. 40, 42): L. 3.12m, muzzle diam. 11.5cm (4.5in), trunnion diam. 11.5cm, decorated with the royal arms of King George II. Inscribed with the founders name SCHALCH and the date of 1734.

• Cannon C33, 42-pounder (Fig. 41): L. 3.40m, muzzle diam. 17.8cm (7in), trunnion diam. 17.8cm, decorated with the royal arms of King George I. Inscribed with the founders name SCHALCH and the date of 1726.

Most of the cannon lie upside-down, with their top surfaces concealed. Where the upper surfaces of nine examples were recorded underwater (cannon C3, C5, C8, C10, C17, C28, C32, C33, C38), however, all feature along the first reinforce royal arms surmounted by a crown (Figs. 32-38). Within the arms are four subdivided quadrants framed by a circular banner. In the lower left-hand quadrant the profile of a harp is visible, symbolizing the British monarchy's sovereignty over Ireland. In the upper right quadrant the three fleur-de-lys are present. On each side rise two foliate branches (Figs. 32-38). On cannon C5 and C32, the 'ROI' from 'Dieu et mon droit' (God and my right), the legend of the British royal family's divine right to rule, is clearly visible (Fig. 38) with the 'T' excluded from the mould to fit the cannon banner.

These features identify eight of the cannon as cast under King George I of England (r. 1714-27). The 12-pounder gun C28 is almost identical, except for the exclusion of the foliate branches to either side of the arms, which proves that this piece of ordnance was cast under King George II (r. 1727-60). The combination of calibres, plus the 42-pounder bronze guns and royal arms, leaves no doubt that site 25C contains the wreck of an English first-rate warship, whose cannon were manufactured between the second and late sixth decade of the 18th century.

Research into this cannon assemblage clarifies that multiple arms styles co-exist, indicative of production at different times. These manifest in the treatment of the foliate branches:

A. Type 1A (Fig. 32): elaborate swirling twin-leaved branch-

Cannon No.	Royal Arms	Bore Diam. (in.)	Trunnion Diam. (in.)	Type (Pounder)
C1		6		24
C2			4	6/12?
C3	George I	6		24
C4			4.5	12
C5	George I			
C8	George I			
C9		5.5		24
C10	George I	7		42
C12		6.5		42 ?
C13		5.5		24
C17	George I	5.5		24
C19		7		42
C20		5.5		24
C21			6.5	42 ?
C22			5.5	24
C26			4	6/12 ?
C27			4.5	12
C28	George II	4.5	4.5	12
C29		4		6/12 ?
C30		7		42
C31		7	7	42
C32	George I		7	42
C33	George I	7	7	42
C38	George I		6	24

Table 1. List of cannon bore and trunnion diameters on site 25C in relation to gun calibres.

es intercut by an elliptical tripartite foliage motif midway, terminating at the bottom with a convex scroll. A sub-type 1B (Figs. 34-35) is identical except for the absence of the tripartite foliage.

B. Type 2 (Figs. 36-37): less complex single leaved branch, sickle shaped, with a concave lower curve.

C. Type 3 (Fig. 38): elaborate crest with a single leaved branch and no lower scroll, rising upwards to sprout on the outer branch.

From the perspective of ordnance deployment, HMS *Victory* was unique as the last first-rate in the Royal Navy to be armed entirely with brass guns (Lyon, 1993: 39). Site

25C is only one of two first-rates whose ordnance has ever been located underwater. The cannon from the first-rate *Royal George*, wrecked off Spithead in 1782, combined iron and brass ordnance, with the latter almost all melted down following the ship's salvage between 1782 and 1843 (Codrington, 1840: 167). Site 25C contains the wreck of the only known Royal Navy warship equipped with a full complement of bronze ordnance.

At the present state of research, only two other bronze guns of King George I are verified as in existence: an English 13-inch mortar cast in 1726 by Andrew Schalch, master founder at the Woolwich Brass Foundry, bearing the arms of George I on the reinforce and a grotesque mask ornament on its pan (Blackmore, 1976: pl. 65); and an 8-inch howitzer captured at Yorktown in October 1781

Poundage of Gun	42	32	24	18	12	9	6	3	1.5	1
Calibre of the Ball (in.)	6.68	6.10	5.54	5.03	4.40	4.00	3.49	2.77	2.20	1.92
Diam. Of the Bore (in.)	6.97	6.37	5.76	5.24	4.57	4.17	3.65	2.92	2.32	2.03
Length of Gun (ft)	10	10	10	10	9.5	9.5	9	7	6	5.5

Table 2. Bore diameter to calibre ratio statistics preserved in Albert Bordgard's pre-1727 document Construction of Brass Gun *(after Caruana, 1997: 39).*

Deck	No. of Guns	Nature Calibre	Length (ft)	Weight (cwt)
Lower	28	42	10	66
Middle	28	24	10	46
Upper	28	12	9.5	31
Quarter	12	6	9	18
Forecastle	4	6	9	18

Table 3. List of bronze guns on a first-rate Royal Navy warship from Thomas James' Book of Artillery *for naval gun Establishment of 1716.*

and now in the Colonial National Historical Park, Virginia, dating to 1727, with the royal arms of George I on the chase and the coat of arms of John, Duke of Argyll, Master General of Ordnance from 3 June 1725 to 10 May 1740, on the breech (Borresen, 1938: 237, 239; Hogg, 1963: 1629).

The desk-based assessment predicted that a highly conspicuous diagnostic attribute of the wreck of HMS *Victory* would be bronze cannon stamped with the founder's name of Andrew Schalch. The 12- and 42-pounders recovered from the site are clearly marked as having been cast by 'SCHALCH': his name is prominently immortalized along a band circumscribing the first base ring (Fig. 42).

Moreover, site 25C is the only Royal Navy shipwreck discovered with 42-pounder cannon, the most powerful and prestigious guns used in Colonial naval warfare. The gun recovered from the wreck, C33 (Fig. 41), is the sole example in existence on land. The 41 bronze guns so far recorded on the surface of site 25C point towards a realistic expectation of recovering all of her guns (presuming some were not jettisoned). Given the prestigious nature of *Victory's* cannon, and the vessel's status as the pre-eminent warship of the age, it is reasonable to presume that she may have tried to hold on to her cannon, rejecting thoughts of

jettison, until the bitter end.

The significance of site 25C's recorded and anticipated ordnance can be summarized as:

1. The only complete armament of bronze guns from a first-rate Royal Navy warship.
2. The sole intact collection of exclusively bronze cannon from any English man-of-war of any period.
3. The largest collection of bronze guns from a single shipwreck in the world.
4. Extends our knowledge of George I bronze cannon exponentially, also bearing in mind that royal arms were commonly replaced by royal ciphers stamped 'GR' as the standard means of adornment after 1726 (Blackmore, 1976: 17; Borresen, 1938: 237, 239).
5. Site 25C probably contains the largest consignment of bronze guns ever manufactured, and certainly preserved today, under the brilliant eye of master founder Andrew Schalch, the first royal appointee to the Royal Brass Foundry in Woolwich. Schalch was born in 1692 at Schaffhausen, Switzerland, and trained in a cannon foundry at Douai, France. In

were mainly Dutch, Spanish and occasionally English (Caruana, 1997: 51-2). Cannon C29 on site 25C bears a founder's date of 1719, confirming the co-existence on the wreck of HMS *Victory* of an eclectic mix of contemporary and old guns. The diversity of site 25C's cannon will provide the definitive statement on the use of bronze guns within the Royal Navy between the late 17th century and 1744.

6. Ship Identity

The identity of the site 25C shipwreck can be confirmed statistically, and on a purely objective basis, by interweaving three separate strands of research, which interlock to produce a definitive characterization:

A. An examination of all Royal Navy losses in the English Channel. To minimize methodological bias, this approach excludes the historical knowledge about what rates of ships carried 42-pounder bronze guns with George I and George II royal arms. The only condition is that a ship must have 41 guns or more, correlating to the number visible on the surface of site 25C.

B. Identification of site 25C through reference to all Royal Navy ships equipped with a significant armament of 42-pounder bronze guns in combination with King George I and George II royal arms.

C. A survey of the geographical distribution of first-rate Royal Navy warship losses throughout the world's oceans.

A. Royal Navy Losses in the English Channel

Out of 141 first- to fifth-rate Royal Navy ships lost throughout the world's oceans between 1690 and 1810 with 41 cannon or more, only 22 (16%) were lost in British waters (calculated from Winfield, 2007). Of these, only three foundered anywhere near the Channel Isles or in the English Channel:

A. *Victory*, first-rate – 1744, allegedly off the Casquets.
B. *Royal Anne Galley*, fifth-rate – 1721, Lizard Point, Cornwall.
C. *Severn*, fifth-rate – 1804, Granville Bay, Jersey.

The *Royal Anne Galley* is an English Heritage protected wreck site located in about 5m of water off the Lizard Point and can thus be discounted.[5] HMS *Severn* ran aground in Granville Bay, Jersey, and all the crew was saved. Her

Fig. 22. Bronze cannon C30, almost completely buried.

Fig. 23. Bronze cannon C37 almost completely buried (muzzle at right foreground).

1716, aged 24, he was appointed Master Founder at Woolwich, where he remained until 1770, before retiring and dying six year later. Schalch is buried in Woolwich churchyard (Blackmore, 1976: 72). His name should be present on the base ring of the majority of site 25C's Georgian guns.

6. If the comparative data available for the *Royal George*, wrecked in 1782 carrying English, French, Spanish and Dutch guns, some cast as early as 1616 (Caruana, 1997: 51-2), and most dating to around 1630, prove pertinent to *Victory*, then some of her cannon could be virtual museum pieces dating back 150 years and even to the reign of Queen Elizabeth (r. 1558-1603). This assumes that after the Admiralty's logistical shift towards iron guns in 1677, six decades later bronze cannon were becoming increasingly scarce. Thus, the 24-pounders on board the *Britannia* were French, whilst the 12-pounders

fate and location are not disputed and non-controversial. Although the sixth-rate, 276-ton and 94ft-long *Hind* was wrecked relatively near site 25C on a ridge of rocks near Guernsey in 1721, and has not been discovered to date (Hepper, 1994: 31; Winfield, 2007: 243), she was only equipped with 20 guns. Since the surface manifestations of site 25C contain 41 cannon, and the discovery of a King George II cannon associated with a founder's date places the wreck after the year 1734, the *Hind* can be safely excluded from the current equation.

Based on the detected remains of wreckage of Her Majesty's warships in the English Channel and of published historical warship losses, the statistical probability that site 25C is the final resting place of HMS *Victory* is 100% by pursuing this strand of evidence.

B. Bronze Cannon with George I & George II Royal Arms

The reign of King George I (r. 1714-27) witnessed a final flourish in the glorious lifespan of bronze cannon on English warships as the Royal Navy phased them out in favor of iron, primarily due to financial realities. In 1625, brass was already four times more expensive than iron (£8 per hundredweight, compared to £2). When Parliament voted £600,000 for 30 new warships in 1677 – one first-rate, nine second-rates and 20 third-rates – Samuel Pepys calculated that the production of the bronze guns alone would have cost £450,000, leaving an unrealistic sum to cover the expense of building the actual ships. All 30 warships were consequently equipped with iron guns, even the first-rate (Lavery, 1987: 87).

The pivotal moment in the decline of brass guns had arrived, and from now on bronze cannon would be reserved exclusively for the mightiest Royal Navy warships. In 1698, only 11 of 323 ships were equipped with any brass guns at all (Gardiner, 1992: 149) and all-brass ordnance on men-of-war was restricted to flagships and royal yachts. Despite the high cost of bronze gun manufacture, iron's tendency not to overheat and cause muzzles to droop was an additional functional preference.

By the 1716 Naval Gun Establishment, only three first-rates carried 100 brass guns; the four other first-rates were equipped with iron. All rates below had exclusively iron ordnance (Caruana, 1997: 43). At the same time, the 42-pounder bronze gun, formerly considered the Royal Navy's finest and most prestigious weapon, was replaced as a general policy by the 32-pounder demi-cannon. The only ships still equipped with 42-pounders were three first-

rate warships, *Victory*, *Royal George* and *Britannia*. With the naval Gun Establishment of 1723, 32-pounder iron cannon became a permanent fixture on new first-rates (Caruana, 1997: 42, 43, 48, 49, 51).

By the time Blaise Ollivier spied on England's Royal Navy dockyards for the French in 1737, bronze cannon had almost completely disappeared from the Royal Navy's maritime landscape. "I saw no brass guns at the gun wharf at Portsmouth", reported Ollivier (Roberts, 1992: 167), "and there are very few in the stores at Chatham. Recently most of the iron guns have been coated with a varnish, the composition of which is still kept secret by the inventor... It does not melt in the sunshine; I examined it on the hottest days."

One plausible reservation may be expressed over the date of site 25C. HMS *Victory* was launched in 1737 and she foundered in 1744. Both dates fall within the reign of King George II (r. 1727-60). While the majority of the wreck's guns bear the royal arms of George I, and a founder's mark on cannon C29 dates to 1719, only one so far features the arms of George II and dates to 1734. Why do the majority of the cannon not date to the reign of this latter monarch? The majority presence of guns bearing King George I arms is explicable because the construction of *Victory* started in 1726, one year before the death of George I. Thus, it would be logical to assume that the order for her bronze cannon would have been issued this year or even earlier. Accordingly, cannon C33 recovered from site 25C bears a founder's date of 1726 (Fig. 39).

In the early 18th century, ordnance was frequently commissioned when a ship was ordered and was completed long before launching. *Victory* was no different. The bill for her 28 24-pounder gun carriages was submitted eight years before she was launched on 30 September 1729, in accordance with a warrant dated 9 June 1729 (Caruana, 1997: 28). This date provides an obvious *terminus ante quem* for the ordering of the guns destined to lie on these carriages. Royal arms of King George I should thus be expected on the wreck of HMS *Victory*, even excluding the possibility that she was potentially equipped with some antique and newer guns commandeered from naval stores, such as cannon C29 dated to 1719. The presence of the George II cannon on site 25C confirms this mixed ordnance hypothesis.

This separate line of research again leads to the objective conclusion that the only Royal Navy warship equipped with a substantial armament of bronze cannon dating to the reigns of George I and George II, including extremely rare 42-pounder bronze guns, and lost within the English Channel, was the first-rate HMS *Victory*.

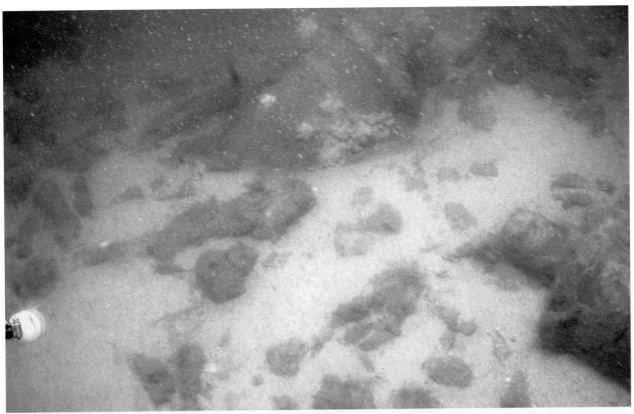

Fig. 24. Bronze cannon plunging into a sand blanket at an acute angle and buried by at least 2m.

Fig. 25. Bronze cannon C10 and C13 protruding from a sandbank at an acute angle.

Fig. 26. Cannon C33 in situ.

Fig. 27. Dolphin handles on cannon C33.

Fig. 28. Cannon C2 in situ. Note the concretion across the muzzle.

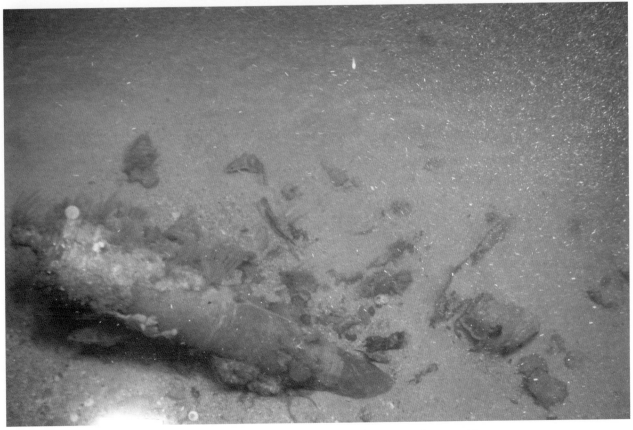

Fig. 29. Cannon in situ. Note the concretion across the cascable.

Fig. 30. Bronze cannon with a broken cascable.

Fig. 31. Bronze cannon in situ. *Note the modern plastic contamination in the background.*

Fig. 32. *Cannon C5 in situ. Crest style 1A.*

Fig. 33. *Cannon C10 in situ.*

Figs. 34-35. Cannon C8 in situ. Crest style 1B.

Figs. 36-37. Cannon C38 in situ. Crest style 2.

Fig. 38. 42-pounder cannon C32 in situ. Crest style 3.

Fig. 39. Founder's date of 1726 along the base ring of cannon C32.

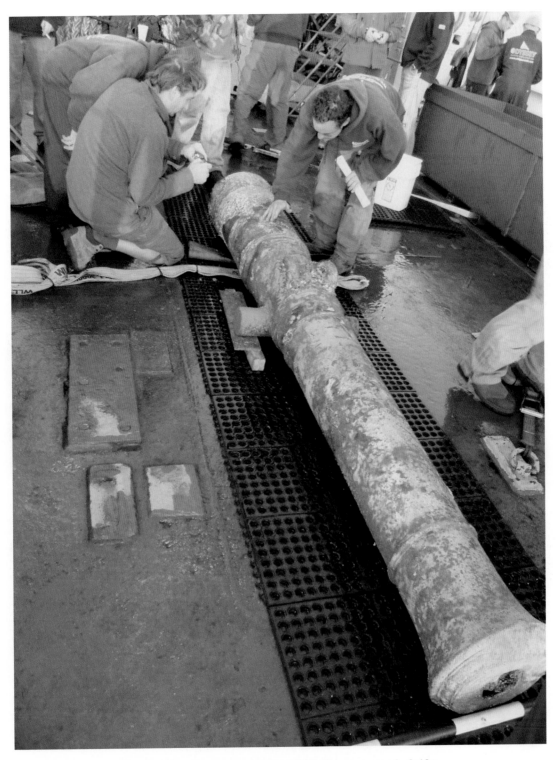

Fig. 40. The 12-pounder cannon C28 after recovery; L. 3.12m.

Fig. 41. The 42-pounder cannon C33 after recovery; L.3.40m.

Fig. 42. The base ring of 12-pounder cannon C28, inscribed 'SCHALCH FECIT', 'Schalch Made It,' and the founder's date of 1734. Andrew Schalch was master founder at the Royal Brass Foundry, Woolwich.

C. First-Rate Royal Navy Warship Losses

According to the above information, the only Royal Navy warships armed with substantial armaments of bronze cannon and 42-pounders, such as are present on the surface of site 25C, were first-rates. Between the start of the reign of King George I in 1714 and 1810, only four first rates were lost in the world's seas (Hepper, 1994; Lyon, 1993; Winfield, 2007):

A. *Ville de Paris* – ex-French prize. Built 1757, taken in the battle of the Saintes, 12 April 1782. 104 guns in 1778-9. Foundered in a hurricane off Newfoundland around 19 September 1782.

B. *Queen Charlotte* – built at Chatham, 1790. Burnt off Livorno (Leghorn), Italy, 17 February 1800.

C. *Royal George* – built at Woolwich, 1752. Foundered off Spithead while being heeled for repair, 29 August 1782.

D. HMS *Victory* – built in Portsmouth, 1726. Wrecked with all hands, allegedly off the Casquets, English Channel, 5 October 1744.

This third distinct line of enquiry again leads to the unavoidable conclusion that the only possible first-rate warship lost in the English Channel within this timeframe was HMS *Victory*.

7. Wreck Location: a Case of Mistaken Geography

The discovery of HMS *Victory* around 100km west of the Casquets in the Channel Isles solves one of Britain's most enduring maritime mysteries. Contemporary accounts of the ship's loss, including first-hand reports from local merchant Nicholas Dobree of Guernsey, reveal that the Admiralty was satisfied that HMS *Victory* foundered off Alderney. Archaeological investigations by Odyssey prove that these accounts were in reality geographically and factually speculative and inaccurate.

The Casquets are the graveyard of the English Channel. This 2.5km-long spread of large rocky islets protrudes 4-10m above the water line, 8km due west of Alderney, and is surrounded by complex 10-knot swirling currents. The *Channel Pilot* guide to the Casquets warns "breakers", "hazardous", "violent eddies" and "use only with local knowledge". No less than 392 wrecks dating between 1278 and 1962 cluster around Alderney, Guernsey and Sark (Ovenden and Shayer, 2002: 8, 19-20). The image of the *Victory* being ripped apart when she struck the Black Rock of the Casquets on 5 October 1744 is both institutionalized within modern history (cf. Ballantyne and Eastland, 2005: 35; Clowes, 1966: 108; Colledge and Warlow, 2006: 374; Dafter, 2001: 22; Lyon, 1993: 39) and everyday life, with her tragic demise appearing on the colorful stamps of Alderney. The artist portrayed the island's lighthouse standing uselessly in the background as the ship sunk.

The deeply entrenched public image of *Victory*'s loss at this location is reflected in *The Biographical Magazine*'s record (Vol. I, 1776: 133) of the life and times of Sir John Balchin, which recalled how:

"The inhabitants of Alderney heard the guns which the admiral fired as signals of distress; but the tempest raged with such uncommon violence, that no assistance could be given. The signal guns were continued during the whole night, but early in the morning the ship sunk, and every person on board perished. She was manned with eleven hundred of the most expert seamen in the royal navy, exclusive of fifty gentlemen of family and fortune, who went as volunteers. Thus one of the most experienced admirals, with eleven hundred and fifty men were lost in a moment, and passed together through the gloomy valley that separates time from eternity."

Eyewitness and physical evidence certainly seemed to place the *Victory* near the Casquets on 5 October. Around 100 warning gunshots were allegedly heard firing by witnesses from Alderney and Guernsey, according to the *Daily Gazetteer* of 22 October, the standard practice for a ship that found itself dangerously close to a reef or other navigational hazard in order to warn other vessels.

The image of *Victory* foundering on the Casquets was strengthened by the discovery of various wreckage marked with the name of the warship. On 19 October *The Daily Advertiser* published the news that the admiralty had been dreading in a letter written by Guernsey merchant Nicholas Dobree, who advised that:

> "This last Week there has been… Pieces of Wreck found upon our Coast; among others, two Topmasts, one 74, the other 64 Feet long, mark'd in white lead VICT; and also a Topsail-Yard, 64 Feet long, mark'd also in white lead Victy; upon the Head of the Naile to the Masts and Yard is the Arrow; to that we greatly fear the *Victory* has been lost upon our Coasts."

Additional wreckage derived from *Victory* included large pump fragments, small gun carriages marked GR (for George Rex), an oar marked '*Victory*' on Sark, and on Alderney the portmanteau of Captain Cotterell (ADM 354/128/81). On 26-29 October 1744, *The Penny London Post* concurred that "Capt. Cottrel's Portmanteau and Lieutenant Billinger's Chest were taken up" on Guernsey. Cotterell was described as "of Wolfe's Regiment of Marines" (*Penny London Post*, 17-19 October 1744). On 5-7 November, the same newspaper reported that "We hear that several Bodies have been taken up on the Alderney-Shore, and one of the Lieutenant of the *Victory*, with his Commission in his Pocket."

The Royal Navy swiftly dispatched the *Falkland* and the *Fly* sloop on a fact-finding mission about this wreckage. The result was seemingly conclusive, with *The Daily Advertiser* of 22 October citing an Admiralty dispatch that confirmed how "in their Cruize they met with several Pieces of Wreck, v.z. several yards, part of a Mast, and part of the carv'd-work Stern, all which believe to belong to the *Victory*; and find, by the People of Alderney, that they heard the firing of 90 and 100 Guns, at the Time she was supposed to be in Distress, so that there is not the least Hopes left of ever hearing of her."

On 3 January 1745 attempts to recover this wreckage were still ongoing, with Nicholas Dobree confirming to the Admiralty by letter (ADM 106/127/1) that "One of the masts, yards and pumps of which I have Given your Honour's advice which have been saved upon our Coast from the unfortunate Wreck of the *Victory* lay still under Some of the Clefts of our Island, the continuall bad weather have Hindered our fishing boats to get said masts etc into our Harbour. I shall soon send you what the salvers demandes for salvage of the same."

A Royal Navy letter of 1 May 1745 addressed to Commander Richard Hughes from Portsmouth Dock also confirmed that "The Warrants (accompanying the same) – Directing the officers to receive two topmasts, some yards and pumps, saved out of the *Victory*; when they are brought from Guernsey to this yard…" (ADM 106/1043/50). Certainly, the local islanders and the

Admiralty were convinced of *Victory*'s fate at the hands of the black rocks of the Casquets.

Site 25C, however, is located around 100km west of the Casquets. The geographical scenario of *Victory* firing her guns off Alderney and then being driven back by the storm so far into the English Channel, of course, is theoretically possible. The logbooks from the *Duke* (ADM 51/282, ADM 52/576), which was accompanying Balchin's fleet back to England, however, verify that the wind was blowing from the west and south-southwest throughout 4 October 1744 and west by north when this warship lost sight of the rest of the fleet. Alderney was only sighted 15 hours later. The absence of any eastern or northeastern winds during this storm makes the scenario of the *Victory* being propelled so far west after striking the Channel Isles physically impossible.

While undoubtedly accurate, Nicholas Dobree's description of some shipboard assemblages from *Victory* being washed up on the Channel Isles from its wreck point has created a false impression of the geography of her loss. There are four reasons to be wary of the merchant's version of events, largely resulting from the high level of rumor surrounding the disappearance of what was perceived to be the greatest warship in the world. Not only are other locations cited as the scene of *Victory*'s possible disappearance, but both contemporary and modern missions to locate her wreckage have detected no incriminating archaeological evidence.

First, part of *Victory*'s stern was also alleged to have washed up on the coast of France (ADM 354/128/81). The *Daily Gazetteer* of 5 November 1744 informed its readers that "They write from Paris, that they have had an Account from the Coast of Normandy, of a great Wreck coming on Shore there, suppos'd to be of some large Ship lost upon the Caskets; whence it seems highly probable, to be the Remains of the *Victory*." Substantial structural components of the ship reaching France would be incompatible with a wreck spot off the Casquets. At the very least, these descriptions reflect how the rumor mill went into overdrive after *Victory*'s loss and generated mixed and inaccurate data.

Secondly, the *Amsterdamsche Courant* of 23 October 1744 reported that "some will have it that it [*Victory*] perished on the coast of Guernsey, others, which represent the most common feelings, that it drifted into the wrong Channel [the Bristol Channel], which today drove up the premium on the insurance of this ship to 15 percent." Meanwhile, *The Daily Advertiser* of 13 October 1744 asserted that "It is generally agreed that Sir John Balchen, in the *Victory*, is drove upon the Coast of Ireland." These reports again reflect general confusion about the location of *Victory*'s demise, and give the first clue that a valuable cargo warranting insurance might have been aboard the ship (see Section 12 below), since warships themselves were not insured.

Thirdly, a faded letter in the Public Records Office, written by Thomas Wilson of the *Deal* on 17 June 1745, reported that despite officially searching for the wreck of the *Victory* on behalf of the Admiralty, she could not be located: "On Thursday last of sailed out of Downs in company with her Majesty's ship Deal" and "proceeded to Farley and not withstanding we had faire weather" and though managed to make "marks bearing and distances for Eight Low Watters could see nothing of your mast... with being conceded under watter or Broke away. Shall leave it to youre Honours better judgment..." (ADM 106/153/255).

Finally, it is not inconceivable that some of the wreckage found around the Channel Isles possibly derived from other Royal Navy warships forced to jettison material during the same storm.

The fact that the *Victory* has eluded the most ardent of surveyors off the Channel Isles, including salvors, fishermen and divers (Ovenden and Shayer, 2002: 22), suggests that the final resting place of the wreck was always likely to lie in a less conspicuous location than the shallow, accessible outcrops surrounding the Casquets. The lack of visual reports of her 100-110 cannon, in addition to the absence of any durable wreckage, notably virtually indestructible ballast and pottery, is suspicious in retrospect.

Based on a letter from Admiral Stuart (ADM 1/909) of 13 October 1744, confirming the last sighting of *Victory* by other warships in her fleet at approximately 30 leagues southeast of the Isles of Scilly, Odyssey Marine Exploration's discovery of site 25C suggests that the warship actually foundered shortly after and not far from the location where her sails were last sighted.

8. HMS *Victory*: Construction

The first timbers for HMS *Victory* were laid down on Portsmouth dock on 6 March 1726, the final year in the reign of King George I. She was nominally a rebuild from the *Royal James*, which was renamed *Victory* in 1691 before being burnt in an accident and dismantled in 1721 (Colledge and Warlow, 2006: 300, 374). What this meant in practical terms remains undefined because the concept of the rebuild was very flexible and could include no recycled timbers, just the need for a replacement vessel replicating the former vessel's architectural lines.

After spending 11 years in dry-dock being constructed – four years more than she ever spent at sea – HMS *Victory* was finally launched on 23 February 1737 (ADM

106/899/198; Fig. 43). She followed in illustrious footsteps, with her 42-gun forerunner battling the Spanish Armada (Ballantyne and Eastland, 2005: 31). Sources disagree about the number of warships named *Victory* that preceded her. Excluding the *Victory* prize ship captured between 1663 and 1667, the fifth-rate, 28-gun *Little Victory* built in Chatham in 1665, the fifth-rate French prize *Victoire* captured in April 1666, and the eight-gun schooner based on the Canadian lakes and burnt down in 1768, the *Victory* launched in 1737 was the fifth and penultimate warship to bear this famous name (Colledge and Warlow, 2006: 373-4; Lavery, 1987: 158, 161, 165, 170; Lyon, 1993: 11, 17, 39, 62).

Victory was built by master shipwright Joseph Allin and cost £38,239 to assemble, plus £12,652 fitting as a flagship. Her dimensions and cannon armament (Winfield, 2007: 4) were:

- Length: 174 feet 9in
- Width: 50 feet 6in
- 1,921 tons
- 850 men
- Lower deck guns: 28 x 42-pounders
- Middle deck guns: 28 x 24-pounders
- Upper deck guns: 28 x 12-pounders
- Quarterdeck guns: 12 x 6-pounders
- Forecastle guns: 4 x 6-pounders

The French master shipwright Blaise Ollivier personally examined *Victory* in her dock at Portsmouth in 1737, described the heights between decks, and wrote a detailed account of her disposition (Roberts, 1992: 126-7, 129), announcing that:

"The ship of 100 guns called the *Victory* which they are building in one of the dry-docks at Portsmouth has the same length, the same breadth and the same depth in the hold as the Royal Sovereign. She has 14 gunports on either side of the gundeck, 15 gunports on the middle deck and on the upper deck, 3 on the forecastle, 7 on the quarterdeck and 2 on the poop... The midship bend of this ship is rounded; her floors are full and have a fair run; she has great fullness at her height of breadth; her capacity is very great, yet her upper works are scarce suitable for her lower body, for she is deep-waisted with much sheer."

Elsewhere, he reported that HMS *Victory* was the only English ship of 100 guns with 15 gunports in the upper deck (Roberts, 1992: 150): the fifteenth port was situated aft between the side counter timber and perpendicular, corresponding to the aftermost gunport on the gundeck. All other Royal Navy warships had 14 gunports. Another unique design feature of *Victory* was the construction of

Fig. 43. A contemporary full hull model of the Victory (1737), probably assembled at the Royal Naval Academy in Portsmouth Dockyard. Photo: © National Maritime Museum Greenwich, SLR0449.

galleries in the poop-royal (Figs. 43-44), which uniquely gave her four tiers of windows, four rows of lights and three elaborately decorated open galleries (Lavery, 1983: 79).

One of several inaccuracies surrounding the loss of HMS *Victory* in 1744 was the size of her crew. The full company of men on-board when she foundered, listed as 880 in her final pay book (ADM 33/380), may be incomplete. The most common figure cited places the number of men lost at 1,100 (*Biographical Magazine*, 1776: 133), which may include marines, soldiers and volunteers not entered into the pay book, but recorded in other documents. Some propositions for the size of *Victory*'s crew rise to an implausible 1,400 men.

9. Naval Operations

After departing dry-dock, *Victory* was commissioned under Captain Thomas Whitney in 1740, with Samuel Faulkner as second captain. Following provocations by Spain and piratical seizures by her privateering nationals, Sir John Norris assumed control of *Victory* at the head of the Channel fleet on 16 July 1740. With 16 warships, Sir John set out

to destroy the Spanish navy (Charnock, 1795a: 356-7). Following the death of Whitney, Faulkner took command as captain in December 1741, before *Victory* became Sir John Balchin's flagship in July 1744 after the retirement of Norris that year (Winfield, 2007: 4).

Despite being considered the largest ship in the navy (Charnock, 1795b: 159) and the finest ship in the world (Clowes, 1966: 108; Dafter, 2001: 22), *Victory* never participated in a major battle and was strangely absent from the only great engagement of her era, the Battle of Toulon on 11 February 1744, when 40 English men-of-war confronted Navarro's Spanish fleet and French warships under De Court (Richmond, 1920: 21; Winfield, 2007: x-xi).

When *Victory* did finally start to punch her weight, she was fighting more for commercial domination than land and liberty. With the opening up of the Indies and Americas, fortunes were being made, and as a pamphleteer of 1672 acknowledged, "The undoubted Interest of England is Trade, since it is that alone that can make us either Rich or Safe, for without a powerful Navy, we should be a Prey to our Neighbours, and without Trade, we could have neither sea-men or Ships"(Rodger, 1998: 172).

The volume of Britain's imports and exports reflected a burgeoning home market and southern England's strategic commercial role as the European center of re-export. British sugar imports rose steadily from 8,176 tons in 1663 to 25,000 tons by 1710. Whereas tea imports to England accounted for £8,000 in 1699-1701 and £116,000 in 1722-24, by 1752-4 they would escalate to £334,000 (Price, 1998: 81). In return, home-grown exports such as woolens, linens, cottons, silks and metal wares to America and Africa were valued at £539,000 in 1699-1701 and £122,000 to East India, but by 1751-54 had leapt to £1,707,000 to America and Africa and £667,000 to East India (Rodger, 1998: 87, 100, 102). The War of Jenkin's Ear against Spain in October 1739, which escalated into the War of the Austrian Succession in 1744, would be dominated by the protection of trade routes.

The most important development in strategic naval thinking in the 18th century was the establishment in the 1740s of the Western Squadron, which guarded the English Channel by maintaining the main fleet out windward in the Western Approaches. Neither France nor Spain had a naval base in the Channel, so any enemy fleet had to come from the west, with an invading force sailing from the ports of Normandy and Brittany. The very real threat of invasion hung constantly in the air. On 3 February 1744, the French fleet did fight ill winds to penetrate the Channel as far as the Isle of Wight, only to be repulsed back to Brest by a large fleet commanded by Admiral Norris on the *Victory* (Charnock, 1795a: 360).

The Channel was England's frontline. Since most of Britain's foreign trade came up and down the Narrow Seas, the ever-cruising fleet was also perfectly placed to cover convoys outward and homeward bound, to watch the main French naval base at Brest and to intercept fleets (Harding, 1999: 185).

It was tied to this strategy that HMS *Victory* was operating in 1744. On 23 April, Sir Charles Hardy had left Spithead at the head of a great convoy protected by the *Victory, Duke, Sandwich, St. George, Princess Royal, Cornwall, Shrewsbury* and *Princess Amelia*, as well as the frigates *Preston* and *Roebuck*. The merchant vessels under his watch held vital victuals and supplies bound for the Mediterranean. Hardy was charged with taking the convoy clear of Brest and its notorious fleet, from where the two frigates would accompany it alone on to Admiral Thomas Matthews at Gibraltar. Matthews was Commander-in-Chief in the Mediterranean and the victuals were essential to provision the allied forces, whose supplies had run dry at the start of April.

The English flotilla arrived at Lisbon on 3 May, and after seeing the convoy safe into the river Hardy headed home, arriving back at Spithead on 20 May (Richmond, 1920: 86, 94). The victualling convoy, however, never made it through the Straits of Gibraltar, but ended up blockaded at Lisbon in the River Tagus by the Brest fleet under the command of de Rochambeau.

With Sir John Norris retired from service, the Royal Navy found itself devoid of experienced admirals suitable of commanding the fleet, and so turned to the remarkable figure of Admiral John Balchin. As of 13 March, aged 74 and following 58 years of service, Balchin was just beginning to enjoy his own retirement and the more relaxed post of Master of His Majesty's Hospital at Greenwich (*The London Gazette*, 13 March 1744).

On 14 July 1744, Sir John, Admiral of the White and newly knighted earlier in the year, was put at the head of a strong squadron of 25 English and eight Dutch warships. Balchin's mission was multi-phased. He was charged with escorting up the Channel a convey of 200 merchant vessels setting out for Newfoundland, New England, Virginia, Maryland, Portugal and the Mediterranean and to see all outward bound trade 100 or 150 leagues into the sea or what seemed safe based on the latest intelligence (Tindal, 1787: 111).

Afterwards, he was required to liberate the victualling convoy intended for Admiral Matthews, which had now been without supplies for three months. The situation was becoming serious enough to turn the entire War of the Austrian Succession in favor of France: the whole campaign in Italy depended on the co-operation of the fleet and, without supplies, the Royal Navy could not aid the allies and the cause with Austria would be lost. Simultaneously, Balchin was to seek intelligence on the strength and movements of the enemy, the number of ships in Brest and the other ports of western France or at sea and to assess their movements. After a six-week cruise, Balchin was to return to Spithead (Richmond, 1920: 104, 108).

If Balchin sighted the Brest fleet, he was given license to blockade it through fears of a pending invasion of England, but was otherwise hoping to clear the English Channel of privateers, an objective that would eventually bear fruit personally around 9 August, when the admiral captured eleven large French San Domingo ships on the way to Lisbon (Richmond, 1920: 107; see Section 12 below).

Meanwhile, the entire elusive Brest fleet had slipped out of port in twos and threes and by 15 July was grouped into 17 sails of 40-70 guns. On 13 August, Balchin learned from Captain Henry Osborn of the *Princess Caroline* that the French were cruising in two strong divisions off Lisbon and Cadiz, the former under de Rochambeau still blockading Matthews' Mediterranean convoy and the latter covering de Torres' long delayed return from the West Indies.

On 24 August, the Admiralty ordered Balchin (Richmond, 1920: 109) "to proceed immediately with the English and Dutch ships under your command off the Rock of Lisbon and to take from thence along with you the said victuallers and storeships as also Captain Osborn and all his majesty's ships of war under his command, and proceed with them to Gibraltar."

Having anticipated these developments, Balchin had already made his way south, arriving off the River Tagus on 30 August, immediately liberating the victuallers and escorting them to Gibraltar. The French squadron of 12 ships retreated to Cadiz with Balchin in hot pursuit and blocking the fleet in port. As *The Daily Advertiser* of 5 September proudly reported back home, "Yesterday it was reported, that the Fleet under Sir John Balchen had fallen in with the Brest Squadron, and that after exchanging a few Broadsides with each other, the latter thought proper to make off."

By 27 September, the English received word that the center of gravity of Mediterranean maritime operations was being transferred from the Gulf of Lyons and west of Italy to the Straits of Gibraltar, where the entire French and Spanish fleet was converging on Cadiz. Balchin's orders were now clearly focused on eradicating the French naval threat (Richmond, 1920: 112), with the Admiralty ordering that:

> "If the Brest squadron shall have joined the French and Spanish squadrons in the Mediterranean… you are, when joined by Vice Admiral Rowley, to endeavour to attack them and to take, sink, burn or otherwise destroy them. And when that service is performed you are to leave a sufficient strength of the fittest and cleanest ships in the Mediterranean under the command of Vice Admiral Rowley and return with the rest to England."

As history would unfold, this final command never reached Balchin. On 9 September 1744, as the admiral took up position to blockade Cadiz and look out for enemy ships arriving from the west, Admiral Grave, the Dutch Commander-in-Chief, informed him that his ships were low on provisions and water. Without the Dutch, Balchin's 17 warships would have been forced to confront 20 enemy craft. So Balchin agreed to accompany the whole fleet home to Spithead.

The 74-year-old admiral left the coast of Galicia on 28 September, but shortly after entering the English Channel on the 3 October a dreadful storm arose, which dispersed the fleet. The *Exeter* lost her main and mizzen mast and was forced to jettison 12 cannon. All of the *Duke's* sails were torn to pieces and her hold under 10ft of water (Beat-

son, 1804: 228; Tindal, 1787: 112). As *The London Gazette* of 6-9 October 1744 chronicled, "Letters from Vice-Admiral Stewart, dated the 7th and 8th Instant, give an Account of his Arrival at Spithead, with all the English and Dutch Men of War of Sir John Balchen's Squadron (except the Admiral's own ship) having seen the Victuallers and Store-Ships, which lay at Lisbon, safely into the Streight's Mouth. Sir John Balchen's ship separated from the rest of the Squadron, in a hard Gale of Wind, in the Mouth of the Channel." Despite the dangers, only the *Victory* and her entire crew were never heard of again.

10. Admiral Sir John Norris

Victory was associated with two of England's most experienced and accomplished commanders. From lowly beginnings as a servant on the *Gloucester Hulk* in 1680 to becoming Admiral of the Fleet in 1743, the highest rank in the Royal Navy, Sir John Norris (Fig. 45) climbed every rung of the maritime ladder during his 54 years of service (cf. Aldridge, 2000; Charnock, 1795a; *The Georgian Era: Memoirs of the Most Eminent Persons who have Flourished in Great Britain, Volume II*, London, 1833, 158-61).

Down the decades, Norris would command over nine warships and earn an uncompromising reputation for having "a natural warmth of temper, which sometimes betrayed him into an extravagance of conduct scarcely to be palliated, and still less defended" after drawing a sword in August 1702 on Captain Ley during a private dispute on the quarter-deck of the *Royal Sovereign* (Charnock, 1795a: 344).

This quality had little long-term effects on Norris' career as his strong character and courage made him many friends in high places. From the moment of joining the *Sapphire* in February 1681, he would enjoy the support of its commander, Sir Cloudesley Shovell, who was making his own strides towards becoming Commander-in-Chief of the British Fleet. Once he tamed his temper, Norris reinvented himself as a fine negotiator in diplomacy. In 1717, he was appointed in a civil capacity envoy extraordinaire and minister plenipotentiary to the Czar of Muscovy, and between March 1718 and May 1730 served as commissioner for the executing office of the Lord High Admiral. In 1723, Norris convoyed King George I from Helvoetsluys to England and in 1730 entertained the King of Sweden on the *Cumberland* in the Baltic.

Norris would gain extensive experience overseas, serving in Newfoundland in 1692 and 1697 as commodore, and between December 1708 and 1730 commanding various squadrons in the Baltic to secure Britain's interests in the timber trade from the threat of Sweden and Peter the

Fig. 44. 'The Loss of HMS Victory, 4 October 1744', by Peter Monamy (18th century).
Photo: © National Maritime Museum, Greenwich, BHC0361.

Fig. 45. Sir John Norris, Admiral of the Fleet, by George Knapton, c. 1735. Photo: © National Maritime Museum, Greenwich, BHC2912.

Fig. 46. Admiral Sir John Balchin, commander of HMS Victory when she was lost on 5 October 1744; by Jonathan Richardson, c. 1695. Photo: kind permission of Sir Robert Balchin.

Great (Kennedy, 1976: 89). Imports of naval stores such as hemp, Stockholm tar, wooden planks and masts from the Baltic increased four-fold between 1688 and 1714 (Rodger, 2004: 191).

Norris made his fortune relatively early in life. For seizing two French frigates in 1690, he earned £1,000 in prize money. Five years later onboard the fourth-rate *Carlisle* between Pantellaria and Tunisia, he captured the French *Content* and shared in its prize value. En route to Newfoundland and during two cruises after arriving in 1697, Norris took several further prizes worth over £40,000. Finally in 1705, he was appointed to command the *Britannia* in support of the cause of Arch-duke Charles in the Mediterranean fleet under his old, powerful friend Shovel. Norris' attack on Fort Montjioc so impressed the Arch-duke that he was recommended in correspondence to Queen Anne, honored with a knighthood and presented with 1,000 guineas.

From 10 March 1707, when he was promoted to Rear-Admiral of the Blue, to 1710, Norris made rapid promotion: Rear-Admiral of the White in January 1708, Vice-Admiral of the White in the same month, Vice-Admiral of the Red in December 1708, Admiral of the Blue in November 1709 and in 1710 he became Admiral-in-Chief in the Mediterranean. Norris would have to wait 22 more years until being elevated to Admiral of the White in January 1732 and Vice-Admiral of Great Britain that April. In 1743, he achieved the greatest honor in the Royal Navy, Admiral of the Fleet, the highest rank in the service.

Norris served on *Victory* throughout his later career, most notably at the head of 16 warships in the Channel fleet against Spanish pirates on 16 July 1740. His bold reputation was confirmed in February 1744, when from the Downs on *Victory* at the head of a fleet of 25 Royal Navy warships and 24 frigates he forced back to Brest the French that had pierced the Channel as far as the Isle of Wight (SP 36/63) – with a little help from a sea storm that wrecked and grounded part of the invading fleet assembled at Dunkirk (Beatson, 1804: 42, 173). Appropriately, this act of heroism was the last time that Admiral Sir John Norris commanded a warship.

In March 1744, having served for 54 years, Norris requested permission from George II to relinquish command of the Channel, stating that he had "served the Crown longer as an admiral than any man ever did..." The king accepted his decision (ADM I/4112). Despite his nickname of 'Foul-Weather Jack', so called because superstitious sailors foretold a storm every time the commander took to the sea, the timing of his departure from active service would prove prophetic in relation to *Victory*'s downfall that year. His memorial in a church at Hempsted Park recalls that "there never breathed a better seaman, a greater officer, a braver man, a more zealous Wellwisher to the present Establishment, nor consequently a truer Englishman, than this Sir John Norris" (Aldridge, 1965: 173, 182).

11. Admiral Sir John Balchin

After Norris' timely retirement, the longest serving naval commander of his age replaced him (Fig. 46). Born on 2 February 1670, John Balchin took a commission in the Royal Navy aged 15.[6] By the time he retired in 1744, Sir John had dedicated 58 years of service to the Royal Navy – 34 more years than Nelson. His life and deeds are predominantly chronicled in four sources: the *Biographical Magazine* (1, 1776: 132-34), *The Lives of the British Admirals, Part 1* (London, 1787), J. Charnock's *Biographia Navalis* (London, 1795), and L. Stephen (ed), *Dictionary of National Biography Volume III* (London, 1885). Complementary facts are also present in the English newspapers, notably *The Daily Advertiser* and *Penny London Post*. Sir John Balchin's full timeline is provided in Appendix 1.

From working the waters of the West Indies to twice being captured by the French and exonerated during court martial, Balchin would command 13 warships. On 12 October 1702, on the *Vulcan* fireship he participated in the capture and burning of French and Spanish ships at Vigo in the War of the Spanish Succession and between 1703 and 1707 got his first taste of patrolling the English Channel and North Sea on the *Adventure* and *Chester*.

In October of that year, after a brief station along the Guinea coast, Balchin was part of a small squadron convoying a fleet to Lisbon, including a thousand horses for the campaign in Spain, which was captured in the Channel by the French force of Forbin and Duguay-Trouin. Exchanged in September 1708, Balchin returned to England on parole, but was fully acquitted by a court-martial on 27 October.

In August 1709, he was appointed to the *Gloucester*, a new ship of 60 guns when lightning struck twice. Just after clearing land off Spithead on 26 October 1709, Balchin was again captured by Duguay-Trouin and tried that December by court-martial for the loss of the *Gloucester*. Balchin's warship was found to have taken on Duguay's own ship, the 74-gun *Lis*, for more than two hours, while another fired at her and three other ships prepared to board her. *Gloucester*'s foreyard was shot in two, the head-sails were rendered unserviceable, and she had received great damage to the yards, masts, sails and rigging. The court concluded that Captain Balchin had discharged his duties valiantly and fully acquitted him.

Between 1710 and 1715, Captain Balchin was appointed to the 48-gun *Colchester* for Channel service and cruised between Portsmouth, Plymouth and Kinsale for almost five years. In February 1715, he transferred to the 40-gun *Diamond* for a voyage to the West Indies and the suppression of piracy. Balchin started sailing new waters in 1717, commanding the *Orford* in the Baltic under Sir George Byng. A year later he captained the 80-gun *Shrewsbury* off Sicily in the defeat of the Spanish under Sir George, before accompanying his own noble predecessor, Sir John Norris, into the Baltic on the 70-gun *Monmouth* in the three successive summers of 1719, 1720 and 1721, once more in 1727, and with Sir Charles Wager in 1726.

Balchin was dispatched to Cadiz and the Mediterranean in 1731 on the *Princess Amelia* as second-in-command under Sir Charles Wager to take possession of Leghorn and place Carlos on the throne of Naples. In the war against Spain in 1740 he commanded a squadron of six sails in the Mediterranean sent without success to intercept the homeward-bound Spanish fleet of treasure ships returning from Vera Cruz to Spain. Later that year, Balchin commanded the squadron in the Channel.

A Post Captain by the young age of 27 in the Nine Years' War, he made commander by 1701, Rear-Admiral of the Blue in 1728, Rear-Admiral of the White a year later, Rear-Admiral of the Red in 1732 and Vice-Admiral of the White in 1734. In 1739 Balchin was appointed Vice-Admiral of the Red and was promoted to Admiral of the White on 9 August 1743.

After retiring in March 1744, knighted, and given command of Greenwich Naval Hospital, he was rushed back into service two months later after Sir Charles Hardy's victualling convoy with vital naval supplies for the Mediterranean fleet was blockaded by the French down the River Tagus at Lisbon. Having dispersed the Brest fleet of de Rochambeau and captured at least 11 prizes, Balchin was en route back to England when the *Victory* was caught in a violent storm in the English Channel on 3 October. Aged 74, the greatest commander of the period perished with at least 880 men and the finest warship in the world, allegedly off the Casquets near Alderney.

King George II recognized Balchin's heroic service to king and country by settling a pension of £500 a year on the admiral's wife for the duration of her lifetime (*The Biographical Magazine*, Vol. I, 1776). His deeds were also commemorated and memorialized by the erection of an elegant monument in Westminster Abbey, executed by Peter Scheemakers in fine marble, displaying a bust of Sir John surrounded by a sarcophagus, flanked by naval trophies, the Balchin family arms and an anchor above a scene of the commander battling storm waves. An inscription beneath this bittersweet scene reads:

"To the Memory of Sr JOHN BALCHEN Knt. Admiral of the White Squadron of his MAJESTY'S Fleet Who in the Year 1744 being sent out Commander in Chief of the Combined Fleets of England & Holland to cruise on the Enemy was on his return Home in his MAJESTY'S Ship the VICTORY, lost in the Channel by a Violent Storm, From which sad Circumstance of his Death we may learn that neither the greatest Skill, Judgement or Experience join'd to the most firm unshaken resolution can resist the fury of the winds and waves, and we are taught from the passages of his Life which was fill'd with Great and Gallant Actions but ever accompanied with adverse Gales of Fortune, that the Brave, the Worthy, and the Good Man meets not always his reward in this World. Fifty Eight Years of faithfull and painful Services he had pass'd when being just retired to the Government of Greenwich Hospital to wear out the Remainder of his Days, He was once more, and for the last time call'd out by his KING & Country whose interests he ever preferr'd to his own and his unwearied Zeal for their Service ended only his Death which weighty misfortune to his Afflicted Family became heighten'd by many aggravating Circumstances attending it, yet amidst their Grief had they the mournful Consolation to find his Gracious and Royal Master, mixing his concern with the General lamentations of the Publick, for the Calamitous Fate of so Zealous so Valiant and so able a Commander, and as a lasting Memorial of the Sincere Love and Esteem born by his Widow to a most Affectionate and worthy Husband, this Honourary Monument was erected by Her."

History records that Sir John Balchin was an admiral of great experience, sound judgment, tenacious memory and intrepid courage. Having fought for the rights of the humble seaman, he was especially popular below decks. By his own testimony, his greatest pleasure in his life was the honor of the British flag. His notorious reputation as a brilliant commander and dangerous foe was recognized internationally, to such an extent that the enemy dreaded even the name of the ship which Balchin commanded. Upon his tragic death, "The whole nation expressed a deep and generous concern for this terrible misfortune" (*The Lives of the British Admirals, Part 1, London*, 1787, 33).

12. HMS *Victory* – Prizes & Bullion

The movements of HMS *Victory* off Lisbon and Gibraltar between mid-August and late September 1744 are only chronicled in broad terms. Various historical accounts, however, leave no doubt that Sir John Balchin actively sought out prizes during his final mission, which was standard practice for Royal Navy commanders, but also may have taken on a commercial venture for the personal gain of himself and his crew. Specific and circumstantial historical sources indicate that Balchin engaged in the recognized practice of carrying merchants' specie back to England. Lisbon was the bullion capital of Europe and the Mediterranean world, its commerce and currency were blockaded in port, and Balchin would have welcomed the chance to profit from his last command, adding a significant measure of wealth to his retirement fund.

In peacetime, bullion was predominantly ferried from Lisbon to Falmouth in English packet-boats in the regular postal service. For instance, 61 consignees sent £28,844 to Falmouth by packet-boat on 2 January 1741 and by 1764-69 these vessels carried an average of £895,061 bullion annually. The currency transported consisted mainly of Portuguese coin, predominantly gold *moedas* minted from the mines of Brazil, but also some silver *crusados* (Fisher, 1971: 95, 99, 103).

Shipments of gold to England were an open secret, with bills of lading signed at the Public Coffee House in Lisbon, leading an English Envoy in 1734 to criticize merchants who publicly discussed shipments and "with as little Secresie send it on board, as they do a Chest of Oranges" (Tyrawly to Newcastle, 17 April 1734; SP 89/37). By 1742, the single, double and quadruple *moedas* was so prevalent in Britain that it was renowned as "in great measure the current coin of the Kingdom" (Vallavine, 1742).

The prospect of profitable freights to England encouraged warships to pass by Lisbon for little other strategic reason, and Royal Navy captains and commanders had a track record of involvement in the bullion trade. Sir John Norris, the *Victory*'s former commander, certainly participated in this commerce. As Milner, the English consul in Lisbon, wrote to the Lord Treasurer on 19 October 1711, "The fleet wth Sr John Norris... carried away large sums, several houses sending twenty to forty thousand pd a house & all some" (SP 89/21). Three years prior to the *Victory*'s loss, Lord Tyrawly advized that "there is not an English Man of Warr homeward bound from almost any Point of the Compass that does not take Lisbon in their Way home... every Body knows that [they] have no other Business in life here but to carry away Money" (Tyrawly to Newcastle, 7 January 1741, SP 89/40).

In 1758, the English consul to Lisbon observed that "the Merchants here would always give preference to Ships of Warr... for the Freight of... Specie home" (Franklin to Pitt, 20 August 1758; SP 89/51). Because of the perceived guarantee of security, warships could charge freight of 1% of the transported bullion's value, as opposed to 0.25-0.5% charged by the Falmouth packets. As H.E.S. Fisher emphasizes in *The Portugal Trade. A Study of Anglo-Portuguese Commerce 1700-1770* (London, 1971: 99), "From Lisbon bullion was also shipped on homeward-bound English men-of-war, both frigates and ships of the line. Strongly armed as well as possessing diplomatic immunity from search, they were almost ideal for bullion carriage and it was in fact common for captains to supplement their incomes in this way."

No ship in the world would have been considered a safer transport in 1744 than the *Victory*. After the lengthy French blockade of the River Tagus, there was undoubtedly a backlog of bullion shipments in Lisbon, and merchants would have welcomed an offer by Balchin for safe transport to England.

The onset of war and the danger of transport compounded the demand for willing warships to enter this commercial maritime arena. Without them, the economy would have frozen up: during the War of Austrian Succession, for instance, a merchant fleet and its escorts from England were delayed by nearly a year. In July 1740, English houses of commerce in Lisbon had received no supplies from England for nine months, with the result that their warehouses were "quite drained of all sorts of Goods particularly the Woolen" (Tyrawly to Newcastle, 23 July 1740; SP 89/40).

Between 1743 and 1744 exports of general commodities to Portugal fell from £1,145,000 to £889,000 and imports from Portugal to England declined by a half from £466,000 to £212,000 (Whitworth, 1776: 27-8). By 1745-6, England was witnessing a period of severe financial crisis.

The notion that Sir John Balchin, plucked out of retirement at the tender age of 74, chose to profit from his presence in Lisbon, seems to be confirmed by the *Amsterdamsche Courant* of 18/19 November 1744, which describes how a huge sum of money was being carried by his flagship when she foundered: "People will have it that on board of the Victory was a sum of 400,000 pounds sterling that it had brought from Lisbon for our merchants." This would equate to approximately 4 tons of gold coins. The presence of this high-value commercial cargo presumably explains why the *Amsterdamsche Courant* of 23 October reported that concerns over the disappearance of the *Victory* "today drove up the premium on the insurance of this ship to 15 percent." Warships *per se* were not insured; only the carriage of a commercial cargo would warrant such a development.

Research indicates that merchants' bullion from Lisbon was probably not the sole high-value cargo on *Victory* when she was wrecked. The seizure of prizes was rife across Europe in the 18th century. By the Convoys and Cruizers Act of 1708, the net sum of any prize was divided by eight.

The captain of the capturing ship received three-eighths, but if operating under orders, then one of those eighths went to the flag officer, presumably the admiral: flag officers generally ensured that ships in their fleet operated under their direction. Another eighth was divided equally amongst the lieutenants, the captain of the marines and the master. A further eighth went to the warrant officer, boatswain, gunners, carpenters, purser, chaplain, surgeon, master's mate, junior officers and the quartermaster. The petty officers – boatswain's mate, gunner's mate and tradesmen (caulkers, ropemakers, sailmakers) – received a further eighth, while the remainder was split between the rest of the crew (Hill, 1998: 201; Rodger, 2004: 522).

Since the start of war with France in March 1744 and 14 August that year, English ships had taken £3 million worth of prizes (*Daily Post*, 20 August 1744). Towards the end of August 1744, Balchin successfully captured over a dozen prizes, a significant percentage of the sale of which would have gone into his own estate should he have survived the storm of 5 October. An added professional incentive for the admiral was the legal stipulation that the monetary shares of any officers and seamen who went absent without leave, as well as those officers, seamen, marines and soldiers who failed to make a claim within three years, had their prize money forfeited to the Royal Hospital at Greenwich, where Balchin was governor (Horne, 1803: 70). For Balchin, prizes made both personal and professional good sense.

Some of the commodities seized were relatively basic. *The London Gazette* of 21-25 August 1744 reported how under Balchin's orders the *Hampton Court* and a Dutch warship escorted six French prizes bound from Cape François and St. Domingo in to Spithead on 22 August. The prizes contained cargoes of sugar, indigo and coffee. However, this source fails to provide the complete picture. *The Daily Advertiser* of 23 August 1744 contributes the following facts: "Letters from on board the Sunderland, Man of, belonging to Sir John Balchen's Squadron, dated the 18th instant, in the Latitude 45.56, mention, that they had taken six Ships from Martinico, and were in Pursuit of four more, which they were in Hopes of coming up with; and that Ship which the Sunderland boarded had a great Quantity of Money on board..." Within a few days Balchin took five more French Ships from Martinico, which were escorted into Portsmouth (*The Daily Advertiser*, 27 August, 1744).

Supplementary details of what Balchin's officers recovered from these French prizes appeared in *The Penny London Post* of 31 August - 3 September, which gleefully announced how "In rummaging the Tessier, a Martinico Ship, taken by the Hampton Court and the Chester Men of War, there have been found conceal'd in the Ballast 28,000 Dollars and two Casks of Gold, reckon'd 25,000 l." Similarly, "On examining the Le Lux del Francis, a French Prize, taken by his Majesty's Ships the Dreadnought and Hampton Court, there was found conceal'd in the Ballast five Bags of Dollars, valued at 12000l" (*The Penny London Post*, 17-19 September 1744). Both the *Dreadnought* and *Hampton Court* were part of Balchin's fleet that had accompanied him down to Lisbon (Richmond, 1920: 106). *The London Evening-Post* of 4-6 September received further information that "We hear there were found on board one of the St. Domingo Ships, that struck to the Dutch Men of War along with Admiral Balchen, above 60,000 Pieces of Eight."

Despite the time lag between these three dispatches reaching London, it is reasonable to presume that all of the French vessels were part of the same Martinico convoy. The historical veracity of Balchin's fleet capturing so many high-value prizes is born out by the swift reaction of Holland, which dispatched Commodore Baccherst to London to represent the Dutch squadron sailing with Sir John Balchin's fleet and to settle a dispute about the taking of the Martinico ships (*The Daily Advertiser*, 31 August 1744). The Dutch were evidently not willing to be squeezed out of their entitlement to a share of the prize money.

Alongside these 11 prizes, Balchin's fleet – presumably under his orders – also captured two other enemy craft. The *Jersey* took two Spanish ships bound from Bordeaux to Toulon and carried them to Gibraltar (*Daily Post*, 3 September 1744), while on 28-30 August *The London Evening-Post* informed its readers that "The Princess Amelia, Capt. Jandine, took a French Felucca of Malta, bound for the Streights from the Levant, who took out 1,000 l. in Specie; and the Ship, ransomed for 70,000 Livres, is since taken by the Oxford Man of War."

The possible magnitude of the windfall to which Sir John Balchin was entitled lies beyond the parameters of this paper, but it is conceivable that the extremely generous sum of £500 that King George II bestowed on the admiral's wife as an annual pension (*The Biographical Magazine*, Vol. I, 1776) took this financial situation into consideration. What is of immediate concern to the shipwreck of HMS *Victory* is the destination of the specie. The fact that *The London Gazette* of 21-25 August only referred to cargoes of sugar, indigo and coffee amongst the prizes brought home by the *Hampton Court* correlates with the assumption that the large sums of money cited above did not accompany her. If they had, this fact would have been loudly trumpeted in the press.

Any specie or bullion from Lisbon, or other valuables and prize money that might have been seized or carried on a commercial basis, would have undoubtedly been taken

aboard the *Victory* – the largest floating strongbox in the Royal Navy. Such entrepreneurial ventures rarely entered the annals of formal book-keeping in the first half of the 18th century. Ultimately, the enigma of Admiral Balchin's high-value cargo will only be confirmed through excavation of site 25C.

13. The Loss of HMS *Victory* – Poor Design or Ill Winds?

From the very beginning of her life, HMS *Victory* had a reputation for being "very high-sided and consequently 'leewardly', a factor which probably contributed to her wrecking" (Winfield, 2007: 4). It is worth reiterating the professional opinion about this first-rate of Blaise Ollivier, Master Shipwright at France's foremost Royal Dockyard at Brest, whose undercover visit to Portsmouth in 1737 (Roberts, 1992: 126-7) concluded that "she has great fullness at her height of breadth; her capacity is very great, yet her upper works are scarce suitable for her lower body, for she is deep-waisted with much sheer." No less a luminary than Sir John Norris, Admiral of the Fleet, who served on *Victory* between 1740 and 1744, also complained that this warship had poor sailing capabilities caused by her height and treble balconies, according to a letter of 14 April 1740 sent by Sir Jacob Acworth, Surveyor of the Navy, to Joseph Allin, Master Shipwright at Portsmouth (Ballantyne and Eastland, 2005: 33).

This reputation certainly stuck to *Victory* through her lifetime and would be identified as the underlying cause of her loss at sea. As Hervey's early history of the Royal Navy concluded (1779: 258), "The loss of this ship has been imputed to a defect in its construction, and many complaints were at that time made concerning the principles on which the men of war were built, and the conduct of the surveyor general of the navy." In an almost identical vein, Beatson (1804: 228) agreed that "The loss of the Victory has been generally imputed to a defect in her confirmation, she being reckoned too lofty in proportion to her breadth. Many complaints of a like nature were made about this time, against the principles on which the British ships of the line were then built."

The problem was supposedly rectified in the build of the *Royal George* in 1752, which was described as "The first attempt towards emancipation from the former servitude", and was "at that time, deemed the paragon of beauty, and considered as the *ne plus ultra* of perfection in the science of marine architecture" (Charnock, 1800: 138). A contemporary report of the *Royal George*'s sinking off Spithead in 1782, however, suggests that her height remained problematic and her hull somewhat rotten. *A Description of the Royal George With the Particulars of her Sinking* (Portsmouth, 1782) revealed that "The Royal George was far from being a sound ship that she could not have rode the seas more than another year. Her timbers had long been rotten, and her whole frame was patched up for present purposes." One of her carpenters announced that hardly a peg would hold together in her hull.

Even though *Victory* (launched 1737, lost 1744) was far younger than the *Royal George* (launched 1756, wrecked 1782) when she foundered (after seven years compared to 26), the problem of *Victory's* disproportionate height to width ratio may have been compounded by a similar poor state of health. The severe decay that the British fleet suffered in warships' timbers in the 1730s and 1740s is an established fact. The general longevity of most ships of line in the 18th century was about 12-16/17 years. Warships including *Victory*, launched between 1735 and 1740, however, enjoyed only an average of 8.9 years until they required a major repair (Wilkinson, 2004: 76).

Ollivier's observation, whilst spying on the Royal Navy's yards when HMS *Victory* was in dry-dock, that the English stored timbers unsystematically, heaping old wood on newly cut planks, thus introducing dry and wet rot into warships, isolated one element of the problem. At Deptford he complained about how the timber "is used with but little care; much of the sapwood is left on, and I saw many frames, timbers of the stern and transoms where there were two or three inches of sapwood already half rotted on one or two of their edges" (Roberts, 1992: 54). The rotting of English men-of-war was compounded by the Admiralty's failure to act on the Navy Board's concerns that warships in harbor were not being ventilated around the bulkheads and strakes of gun decks (Wilkinson, 2004: 82-83).

The problematic sourcing of timber for wooden knees is also theoretically significant. During the reign of King George II, the procurement of timber reached crisis levels. Towards the end of the Seven Years War (1756-63), Roger Fisher, a specialist on wood supply, observed that "Indeed, so great has the consumption been that one of the most eminent timber dealers in the county of Sussex now living, has declared to me, that there is not now, as he verily believes, more than one tenth part of the full grown timber, standing or growing, as there was when he entered into business, forty-five years ago" (Marcus, 1975: 12).

This deficiency was not merely a matter of bad management, but one of partial environmental determinism and a failure by the Admiralty to react appropriately. The first 40 years of the 18th century witnessed a succession of mild winters. A sustained positive phase in the North

Atlantic Oscillation created unusually high pressure and a strong westerly airflow that resulted in the decadal temperature rising by 0.6 degrees centigrade above normal between 1730 and 1739 – when *Victory* was being built. Consequently, cut timbers contained more sap than in typical growth cycles, making the seasoning process longer if not impossible. Wood was rotting instead of seasoning (Wilkinson, 2004: 85, 88-89).

All of these factors could have had a cumulative effect on the hull of HMS *Victory*, and her service record hints that all was not well with her structure. By October 1744, she had notably suffered numerous accidents and may have been as badly patched up as the *Royal George* would be later. Admiralty records leave the impression that from the start, the construction and operation of *Victory* experienced deep-set problems:

A. In the absence of a Parliamentary vote for shipbuilding during the reign of King George I, the practice of great re-builds along the lines of previous warships prevailed (Rodger, 2004: 412). *Victory* was nominally a re-build of the *Royal James*, renamed *Victory* in 1691, which arguably introduced design flaws from the very beginning by combining old and new shipbuilding principles. After *Victory's* loss in 1744, the Royal Navy notably abandoned the concept of the re-build.

B. The fact that it took 11 years to build and launch *Victory* between 1726 and 1737 reflects the complex logistics involved in constructing such a voluminous first-rate. Oddly, by comparison, the first-rate *Royal George* took just under four years to build and launch. The reasons for the delay – suspicious or not – remain obscured.

C. As early as 4 March 1737, Mr. Ward requested plate to rebuild *Victory* (ADM 106/895/30), which was granted on 17 March 1737 (ADM 108/899/233).

D. The re-fitting of *Victory* for sea on 26 January 1740 (ADM 106/920/38) included the need to insert new large wooden knees (ADM 106/920/80). The request to fell New Forest timber for knees, cheeks and standards for the *Victory* was reiterated on 25 February 1740 (ADM 106/920/94), with correspondence of 28 February confirming that no suitable timber was available (ADM 106/920/99). This suggests that *Victory* required serious repairs within two years of being launched.

E. A warrant for the cleaning and graving of *Victory* for Channel service was issued on 18 February 1740 (ADM 106/938/86).

F. On 17 April 1740, *Victory* docked for another re-fit for Channel service (ADM 106/920/174).

G. On 18 July 1740, *Victory* lost her head and spritsail yard and anchored off Bembridge Head (ADM 106/921/41). She was taken to Portsmouth to have a temporary figure-head installed (ADM 354/112/137), docking on 24 July (ADM 106/921/57).

H. A letter of 4 September 1741 requested the repair of defects in *Victory* (ADM 106/939/121).

I. 2 November 1741, *Victory* was refitted at Portsmouth (ADM 354/116/1).

J. On 25 February 1744, *Victory* was damaged during a fierce storm (SP 36/63), although this comment on the ship's fate was subsequently retracted (SL 36/63). Yet on 28 February 1744, Sir John Norris requested anchor stocks, stoops, bolts and treenails for *Victory* (ADM 106/987/51).

The length of time that *Victory* spent being built, and the reality that re-fits were deemed necessary already in March 1737 (the year she was launched) and January 1740, when new knees had to be inserted, leaves the question of *Victory*'s seaworthiness open to debate. In the absence of oak timber of sufficient size and suitability for ship construction, she was almost certainly constructed in part of unseasoned timber. The amount of time she spent in and out of dock would also have compounded any problem of rot, given the above concerns that warships were not being adequately ventilated.

Yet in the final analysis, the height-to-width ratio of *Victory* may have directly been responsible for her downfall. While the rest of the fleet of early October 1744 made it safely home to England, only HMS *Victory* was wrecked. Top heavy, she may have tended to roll amidst the storm waves of the English Channel. Her center of gravity may well have been too high to conquer the elements.

14. Conclusion

All of the available archaeological and historical data clarify that the only possible shipwreck which site 25C could represent is HMS *Victory*. No other Royal Navy first-rate warship equipped with over 41 bronze cannon featuring the royal arms of King George I, King George II and carrying 42-pounder guns was wrecked anywhere remotely near the English Channel. *Victory* measured

53 x 15m, which fits very closely with the dimensions of site 25C – 61 x 22m – allowing for collapse and scattered material culture.

Site 25C represents the only scientifically surveyed first-rate Royal Navy warship in the world. Chronologically, *Victory* is the only English man-of-war whose wreck has been surveyed or excavated dating between 1706, when the third-rate, 50-gun *Hazardous* foundered in Bracklesham Bay (Owen, 1988), and 1747, when the fourth-rate, 50-gun *Maidstone* was lost on rocks off Noirmoutier, France (de Maisonneuve, 1992). All other 18th-century Royal Navy warship wrecks are third- to sixth-rates: *Fowey* (fifth-rate, lost Florida 1748; Skowronek *et al.*, 1987); *Invincible* (third-rate, lost in Solent 1758; Bingeman and Mack, 1997); *Swift* (sloop-of-war, sunk Patagonia, Southern Argentina, 1770; Elkin *et al.*, 2007); *Sirius* (sixth-rate, lost Norfolk Island, Australia, 1790; Stanbury, 1998); and *Colossus* (third-rate, wrecked on Scilly Isles 1798; *HMS Colossus Survey Report October 2001*; Camidge, 2003; 2005).

The shipwrecked remains of HMS *Victory* can be anticipated to contain a wealth of archaeological data that are capable of addressing numerous key historical issues, including:

1. Final resolution about how, where and why this famous first-rate was lost (poor construction, inferior design, rotten timber?).

2. Exoneration of Admiral Balchin, the captain, officers and crew from the charge that *Victory* foundered on the rocks of the Casquets through faulty navigation. Instead, it is likely that they were victims of an appalling storm, possibly combined with problematic ship design.

3. Exoneration of Guernsey's lighthouse keeper, who was charged with letting the lights go out and of thus contributing to the wrecking of *Victory* (ADM 6/134).

4. Analysis of a critical period in ship construction before the English Navy turned to coppered hulls in 1761 (Marcus, 1975: 8). The two decades after the loss of *Victory* triggered a revolution in shipbuilding philosophy.

5. Recovery of the largest surviving collection of bronze guns and 42-pounders from any warship in the world.

6. A unique window into the life of Georgian society, revealing what exotic domestic ceramic wares the commander and captain used, compared to the crew's everyday dining utensils. The decades preceding the Industrial

Revolution witnessed a sharp rise in semi-exotic material consumption within the "middling classes" (Berg, 2007: 32-36). The small finds from the wreck would provide a fascinating vignette of this pivotal era.

7. Closure for the descendants whose minimum of 880 ancestors died in the tragedy of *Victory*'s loss, excluding an unknown number of marines and soldiers and 50 volunteers born into Georgian England's noblest families.

8. Recovery of a significant collection of bullion and specie from the period.

The discovery and scientific recovery of HMS *Victory* offer enormous opportunities for archaeological and historical research and mainstream education. At the time of her loss, *Victory* was considered to be the finest and most powerful ship in the world (Clowes, 1966: 108; Dafter, 2001: 22) and her demise had far-reaching consequences on the Royal Navy and public. Bringing the ship – and the life of its officers and crew – back to life will remind the world of the period that launched the greatest naval empire and of the dedication and brilliance of the men that forged that seaborne realm.

Meanwhile, the shipwreck of HMS *Victory* at site 25C is currently endangered. She lies within heavily exploited fishing grounds, where beam trawlers equipped with iron-toothed dredges plough up the seabed. The severe impact on the marine ecology is a subject of renowned gravity. Contrary to prevailing perceptions of wreck management that favor archaeological preservation *in situ*, such a policy on site 25C will result in the wholesale destruction of the contextualized remains of the *Victory*. Research into this shipwreck offers a unique opportunity to secure critical insights into deep-sea site formation processes, degradation histories and the potential for heritage to survive in this heavily used body of water, which will enable future preservation strategies to be developed for other shipwrecks at risk in the English Channel.

The ship has already been ground down to the level of her ballast, well below the lower gundeck. Cannon have been dragged off-site. The human remains of some dedicated gunners, who served *Victory* and lost their lives for England's military stability, run the risk of being crushed by trawlers, ploughed away into oblivion or lost in nets. From both the archaeological and human perspective, this unique heritage – the warship whose loss paved the way for Nelson's iconic *Victory* and the Battle of Trafalgar – deserves and demands to be saved for future generations.

Acknowledgements

The authors wish to extend their sincere gratitude during the June-September 2008 fieldwork season to the vision and support of Greg Stemm (Co-founder and Chief Executive, Odyssey Marine Exploration), Ernie Tapanes and his search team, whose hawk-eyed professionalism identified site 25C as a special target in the first place, and to the industry and excellence of: Tom Dettweiler, Andrew Craig and Mark Martin (Project Mangers); Jesus Perez, Gary Peterson, Eric Peterson (ROV Supervisors); David Dettweiler, Jeff Thomas, Roberto Blach, Jose Rodriguez, Olaf Dieckhoff and Paul Money (ROV Technicians); Jim Gibeaut, Chris Heke, Kris Allen and Ryan Wells (Surveyors); Gerhard Seiffert (Data Manager), Fred Fretzdorff, Dave Kamm and Tom Money (Data Loggers); Ernie Tapanes, Daniel Adams, Kris Allen, Jim Gibeaut, John Graziano, Brett Hood, Tom Money, Jamie Sherwood, Terry Snyder, Ryan Wells and Clay Wolthers (Search Operations); Fred Van de Walle (Chief Conservator).

This article has benefited from early archival research by John Griffith, Mark Mussett, Patrick Lize and Dr David Hebb, and from the comments of Simon Davidson and Rif Winfield. This report was laid out by Melissa Kronewitter.

For their constant enthusiasm and support at Odyssey Tampa, our ongoing gratitude is extended to Mark Gordon, Laura Barton and John Oppermann. Special thanks are extended to Jason Williams (President, JWM Productions) and the Discovery Channel.

Notes

1. This report is based on primary data collated in the field by and discussed by Neil Cunningham Dobson (Odyssey Principal Archaeologist) in his *The Legend Project. Initial Survey Summary. Site MUN-TIM25C-1* (OME, 2008). The desk-based historical and archaeological research and interpretation was conducted by Dr. Sean Kingsley (Wreck Watch Int., London).
2. http://www.mfa.gov.uk/news/press/070830.htm.
3. Anchor A2 and the rudder were exposed during the limited trial trenching and thus are not depicted on the pre-disturbance photomosaic or site plan, which were produced prior to this phase.
4. http://web.mit.edu/deeparch/www/events 2002conference/papers/Sinclair.pdf.
5. See *Advisory Committee on Historic Wreck sites. Annual Report 2006* (2007: 38) and http://www.english-heritage.org.uk/server/show/ConWebDoc.14031.
6. The spellings Balchin and Balchen are used interchangeably within the popular and academic literature.

Sir Robert Balchin has advized us that the 'e' inaccurately crept into the admiral's name due to his tendency to sign his letters with a flourishing hand, making the 'i' resemble and 'e'. In this report we adhere to Balchin's original spelling as given at birth.

Bibliography

Aldridge, D.D., 'Admiral Sir John Norris 1670 (or 1671)-1749: His Birth and Early Service, his Marriage and his Death', *Mariner's Mirror* 51 (1965): 173-92.

Aldridge, D., 'Sir John Norris, 1660?-1749'. In P. Le Fevre and R. Harding (eds.), *Precursors to Nelson. British Admirals of the Eighteenth Century* (London, 2000), 129-50.

Ballantyne, I. and Eastland, J., *Warships of the Royal Navy. HMS Victory* (Barnsley, 2005).

Beatson, R., *Naval and Military Memoirs of Great Britain, 1727 to 1783. Vol. I* (Edinburgh, 1804).

Berg, M., *Luxury and Pleasure in Eighteenth-Century Britain* (Oxford University Press, 2007).

Bingeman, J.M. and Mack, A.T., 'The Dating of Military Buttons: Second Interim Report Based on Artefacts Recovered from the 18th-Century Wreck Invincible, Between 1979 and 1990', *IJNA* 26.1 (1997), 39-50.

Blackmore, H.L., *The Armouries of the Tower of London. I. The Ordnance* (London, 1976).

Blanckley, T.R., *A Naval Expositor (1750)* (Jean Boudriot, Rotherfield, 1988).

Borresen, T., 'The Markings of English Cannon Captured at Yorktown', *The Journal of the American Military History Foundation* 2.4 (1938), 235-39.

Camidge, K., *HMS Colossus. Progress Report 2003* (2003).

Camidge, K., *HMS Colossus. CISMAS Debris Field Survey 2005* (2005).

Caruana, A.B., *The History of English Sea Ordnance 1523-1875. Volume II: 1715-1815. The Age of the System* (Jean Boudriot Publications, Rotherfield, 1997).

Charnock, J., *Biographia Navalis; or Impartial Memoirs of the Lives and Characters of the Officers of the Navy of Great Britain from the Year 1660 to the Present Time, Vol. II* (London, 1795a).

Charnock, J., *Biographia Navalis; or Impartial Memoirs of the Lives and Characters of the Officers of the Navy of Great Britain from the Year 1660 to the Present Time, Vol. III* (London, 1795b).

Charnock, J., *An History of Marine Architecture Including an Enlarged and Progressive View of the Nautical Regulations and Naval History, Both Civil and Military, of All Nations, Especially of Great Britain. Vol. III* (London,1800).

Clowes, W.L., *The Royal Navy. A History from the Earliest Times to 1900, Volume Three* (London, 1966).

Codrington, Sir E., *A Narrative of the Loss of the Royal George at Spithead, August 1782; Including Tracey's Attempt to Raise her in 1783, Her Demolition and Removal by Major-General Pasley's Operations in 1839-40-41-42&43, including a Statement on her Sinking Written by her then Flag-Lieutenant, Admiral Sir C.P.H. Durham* (London, 1840, 7th ed.).

Colledge, J.J. and Warlow, B., *Ships of the Royal Navy: the Complete Record of all Fighting Ships of the Royal Navy* (Chatham, 2006).

Curryer, B.N., *Anchors. An Illustrated History* (London, 1999).

Dafter, R., *Guernsey Wrecks. Shipwrecks around Guernsey, Alderney and Sark* (Tonbridge, 2001).

Dare, P.J., Palmer, D.W., Howell, M.L. and Darby, C.D., *Experiments to Assess the Relative Dredging Performance for Research and Commercial Vessels for Estimating the Abundance of Scallops (Pectens maximus) in the Western English Channel Fishery* (Fisheries research Technical Report No. 96, Lowestoft, 1994).

Duplisea, D.E., Jennings, S., Malcolm, S.J., Parker, R. and Sivyer, D.B., 'Modelling Potential Impacts of Bottom Trawl Fisheries on Soft Sediment Biogeochemistry in the North Sea', *Geochemichal Transaction* 14 (2001), 1-6.

Elkin, D., Argueso, A., Grosso, M., Murray, C., Vainstub, D., Bastida, R. and Dellino-Musgrave, V., 'Archaeological Research on HMS Swift: a British Sloop-of War Lost off Patagonia, Southern Argentina, in 1770', *IJNA* 36.1 (2007), 32-58.

Evans, C.D.R., *The Geology of the Western English Channel and its Western Approaches* (HMSO, London, 1990).

Fisher, H.E.S., *The Portugal Trade. A Study of Anglo-Portuguese Commerce 1700-1770* (London, 1971).

Ford, B., Borgens, A., Bryant, W., Marshall, D., Hitchcock, P., Arias, C. and Hamilton D., *Archaeological Excavation of the Mardi Gras Shipwreck (16GM01), Gulf of Mexico Continental Shelf* (New Orleans, 2008).

Gardiner, R., *The Line of Battle. The Sailing Warship 1650-1840* (Conway Maritime Press, London, 1992).

Gibbard, P.L. and Lautridou, J.P., 'The Quaternary History of the English Channel: an Introduction', *Journal of Quaternary Science* 18 (2003), 195-99.

Goodwin, P., *The Construction and Fitting of the Sailing Man of War* (Conway Maritime Press, London, 1987).

Grochowski, N.T.L., Collins, M.B., Boxall, S.R. and Salomon, J.C., 'Sediment Transport Predictions for the English Channel, Using Numerical Models', *Journal of the Geological Society* 150 (1993), 683-95.

Harding, R., Seapower and Naval Warfare 1650-1830 (London, 1999).

Hepper, D.J., *British Warship Losses in the Age of Sail 1650-*

1859 (Jean Boudriot Publications, Rotherfield, 1994).

Hervey, F., *The Naval History of Great Britain; From the Earliest Times to the Rising of the Parliament in 1799* (London, 1779).

Hill, R., *The Prizes of War. The Naval Prize System in the Napoleonic Wars, 1793-1815* (Stroud, 1998).

Hogg, O.F.G., *The Royal Arsenal. Its Background, Origin and Subsequent History Volume 1* (Oxford University Press, 1963).

Horne, T.H., *A Compendium of the Statute Laws and Regulations of the Great Admiralty Relative to Ships of War, Privateers, Prizes, Re-captures and Prize-Money* (London, 1803).

Jobling, H.J.W., *The History and Development of English Anchors ca. 1550-1880* (MA Thesis, Texas A&M University, 1993).

Jones, M., (ed.), *For Future Generations. Conservation of a Tudor Maritime Collection. The Archaeology of the Mary Rose, Volume 5* (Portsmouth, 2003).

Kennedy, P., *The Rise and Fall of British Naval Mastery* (London, 1976).

Lavery, B., *The Ship of the Line. Volume I: the Development of the Battlefleet 1650-1850* (Conway Maritime Press, London, 1983).

Lavery, B., *The Arming and Fitting English Ships of War 1600-1815* (London, 1987).

Lyon, D., *The Sailing Navy List. All the Ships of the Royal Navy Built, Purchased and Captured 1688-1860* (Conway Maritime Press, 1993).

Macdonald, J., *Feeding Nelson's Navy. The True Story of Food at Sea in the Georgian Era* (London, 2006).

Maisonneuve, De., B., 'Excavations of the *Maidstone*, a British Man-of-war Lost off Noirmoutier in 1747', *IJNA* 21.1 (1992), 15-26.

Malcom, C., 'The Copper Cauldrons aboard the Henrietta Marie', *The Navigator: Newsletter of The Mel Fisher Maritime Heritage Society* (2000), 15.2.

Marcus, G.J., *Heart of Oak. A Survey of British Sea Power in the Georgian Era* (Oxford University Press, 1975).

Mehl, H., *Naval Guns. 500 Years of Ship and Coastal Artillery* (London, 2001).

Morris, R., *Island Treasure* (London, 1967).

Ovenden, J. and Shayer, D., *Shipwrecks of the Channel Islands* (Guernsey, 2002).

Owen, N.C., 'HMS *Hazardous* Wrecked 1706. Pre-Disturbance Survey Report 1987', *IJNA* 17.4 (1988), 285-93.

Price, J.M., 'The Imperial Economy 1700-1776'. In P.J. Marshall (ed.), *The Oxford History of the British Empire. Volume II. The Eighteenth Century* (Oxford University Press, 1998).

Reynaud, J.-Y., Tessier, B., Auffret, J.-P., Berné, S., De

Batist, M., Marsset, T. and Walker, P., 'The Offshore Quaternary Sediment Bodies of the English Channel and its Western Approaches', *Journal of Quaternary Science* 18 (2003), 361-71.

Richmond, H.W., *The Navy in the War of 1739-48. Volume II* (Cambridge University Press, 1920).

Roberts, D.H. (ed.), *18th Century Shipbuilding. Remarks on the Navies of the English & the Dutch from Observations Made at their Dockyards in 1737 by Blaise Ollivier, Master Shipwright to the King of France* (Jean Boudriot Publications, Rotherfield, 1992).

Rodger, N.A.M., *The Wooden World. An Anatomy of the Georgian Navy* (London, 1986).

Rodger, N.A.M., 'Sea-Power and Empire, 1688-1793'. In P.J. Marshall (ed.), *The Oxford History of the British Empire. Volume II. The Eighteenth Century* (Oxford University Press, 1998), 168-83.

Rodger, N.A.M., *The Command of the Ocean. A Naval History of Britain, 1649-1815* (London, 2004).

Skowronek, R.K., Johnson, R.E., Vernon, R.H. and Fischer, G.R., 'The Legare Anchorage Shipwreck site – Grave of HMS *Fowey*, Biscayne national Park, Florida', *IJNA* 16.4 (1987), 313-24.

Stanbury, M., 'HMS Sirius 'reconstructed… Pygmy Battle Ship' or 'Appropriate' 6th Rate Vessel?'. In M. Bound (ed.), *Excavating Ships of War* (Oswestry, 1998), 217-29.

Steffy, J.R., *Wooden Ships and the Interpretation of Shipwrecks* (Texas A & M University Press, 1994).

Tindal, N., *The Continuation of Mr. Rapin's History of England; From the Revolution to the Present Times, Vol. XXI* (London, 1787).

Tomalin, D.J., Simpson, P. and Bingeman, J.M., 'Excavation Versus Sustainability In Situ: a Conclusion on 25 Years of Archaeological Investigations at Goose Rock, a Designated Wreck-site at the Needles, Isle of Wight, England', *IJNA* 29.1 (2000), 3-42.

Tracey, W., *A Candid and Accurate Narrative of the Operations Used in Endeavouring to Raise his Majesty's Ship Royal George, in the Year 1783; with an Account of the Causes and Reason which Prevented the Success* (Portsea, 1812).

Vallavine, P., *Observations on the Present Condition of the Current Coin of the Kingdom* (London, 1742).

Watson, W.N.B., 'Alexander Brodie and His Firehearths for Ships', *Mariner's Mirror* 54.4 (1968): 409-412.

Whitworth, C., *State of the Trade of Great Britain, Part II* (London, 1776).

Wilkinson, C., *The British Navy and the State in the Eighteenth Century* (Woodbridge, 2004).

Winfield, R., *British Warships in the Age of Sail, 1714-1792* (Minnesota, 2007).

Appendix 1. Admiral Sir John Balchin – A Timeline

• 1692 – lieutenant of the *Dragon* and then the *Cambridge*.
• 25 July 1697 – appointed captain of the 32-gun *Virgin*.
• 12 October 1702 – on the *Vulcan* fireship participated in the capture and burning of French and Spanish ships at Vigo in the War of the Spanish Succession. Balchin brought home the *Modere* prize of 56 guns.
• 1703-1707 – accumulated enormous experience patrolling the English Channel and North Sea on the *Adventure* and *Chester*.
• 10 October 1707 – after a brief station along the Guinea coast, Balchin was part of a small squadron captured in the Channel by a French force commanded by Forbin and Duguay-Trouin while convoying a fleet to Lisbon, including a thousand horses for the campaign in Spain.
• September 1708 – Balchin returns to England on parole, is tried and fully acquitted in court-martial on 27 October.
• August 1709 – appointed to the *Gloucester*, a new ship of 60 guns.
• 26 October 1709 – after just clearing land off Spithead, captured for a second time by Duguay-Trouin.
• 14 December 1709 – tried a second time by court-martial for loss of the *Gloucester*. Balchin's warship was found to have taken on Duguay's own ship, the 74-gun *Lis*, for more than two hours, while another fired at her, and three other ships prepared to board her. *Gloucester*'s foreyard was shot in two, the head-sails were rendered unserviceable, and she had received much damage to the yards, masts, sails, and rigging. The court concluded that Captain Balchin had discharged his duties very well, and fully acquitted him.
• 1710-1715 – Captain Balchin appointed to the 48-gun *Colchester* for Channel service and cruised between Portsmouth, Plymouth, and Kinsale for almost five years.
• February 1715 – Transferred to the 40-gun *Diamond* for a voyage to the West Indies and the suppression of piracy (returned May 1716).
• May 1716 – appointed to the 70-gun *Orford* in the Medway until February 1718.
• 1717 – commanded the *Orford* into the Baltic under Sir George Byng.
• February-December 1718 – captained the 80-gun *Shrewsbury* off Sicily in the defeat of the Spanish under Sir George Byng. The *Shrewsbury* was commanded by Vice-admiral Charles Cornwall, second in command in battle off Cape Passaro on 31 July.
• May 1719 – Balchin appointed to the 70-gun *Monmouth*,

in which he accompanied Admiral Sir John Norris to the Baltic in the three successive summers of 1719, 1720 and 1721.
• 1722-1725 – commanded the *Ipswich* guardship at Spithead.
• February 1726 – again appointed to the *Monmouth* for the yearly cruise up the Baltic with Sir Charles Wager in 1726 and in 1727 with Sir John Norris.
• October 1727 – sent to reinforce Sir Charles Wager at Gibraltar, besieged by the Spaniards; returned home January 1728.
• 19 July 1728 – promoted to Rear-admiral of the Blue.
• 1729 – appointed Rear-admiral of the White.
• 1731 – dispatched to Cadiz and the Mediterranean on the *Princess Amelia* as second-in-command under Sir Charles Wager to take possession of Leghorn and place Carlos on the throne of Naples.
• 1732 – appointed Rear-admiral of the Red.
• February 1734 – appointed Vice-admiral of the White and commanded a squadron at Portsmouth for a few months.
• 1739 – appointed Vice-admiral of the Red.
• 1740 – in the war against Spain commanded a squadron of six sails in the Mediterranean to intercept (without success) the homeward-bound Spanish Assogues fleet of treasure ships returning from Vera Vruz to Spain.
• Late 1740 – Balchin commands squadron in the Channel.
• 9 August 1743 – promoted to Admiral of the White.
• March 1744 – knighted and appointed governor of Greenwich Hospital, with a pension of £600 a year during his lifetime.
• 1 June 1744 – Balchin is restored to his active rank as Admiral of the White.
• 28 July 1744 – sailed from St. Helen's to liberate Sir Charles Hardy from the French blockade of the River Tagus.
• 14 August to 31 August 1744 – Balchin arrives at the River Tagus, liberates Sir Charles' convoy and proceeds to Gibraltar in search of the Brest fleet.
• 18 August 1744 – at Gibraltar, *Victory* sees the 26 store-ships safely into the Mediterranean.
• 28 September 1744 – Balchin leaves the coast of Galicia for England.
• 3 October 1744 – entire fleet is dispersed by a violent storm.
• 4 October – final sighting of HMS *Victory*.
• 10 October 1744 – the entire English fleet arrives home at St. Helens apart from HMS *Victory*.

A Note on Human Remains from the Shipwreck of HMS *Victory*, 1744

Neil Cunningham Dobson & Hawk Tolson

Odyssey Marine Exploration, Tampa, USA

During preparations to recover a bronze cannon for identification purposes from the shipwreck of HMS *Victory* (site 25C), lost in the western English Channel on 5 October 1744, a human skull and ribs were exposed around cannon C10. As the site survey continued, further surface deposits believed to be skeletal material were recorded around cannon C22 and C39.

The presence of these human remains was unexpected because of their rarity on wreck sites of all dates and forms not buried in anaerobic mud or clay. The discovery contributes an interesting layer of complexity and interpretative data to the site's formation. The human bones were photographed and then re-buried, and further fieldwork was restricted to contexts devoid of this sensitive material, pursuant to an agreement with the MOD and Royal Navy.

This report briefly summarizes the locations and extent of the human bones on site 25C's surface and presents comparative archaeological data to clarify the infrequency with which they are generally encountered on shipwrecks. Sources demonstrate that while small quantities of human bones can be expected on shipwrecks, especially in mud environments and on complex sites that trap and seal deposits, in general the image of shipwrecks as 'grave sites' is an inaccurate and misleading distortion of archaeological reality.

1. Human Bones on Site 25C

One of the objectives of the survey of site 25C in the western English Channel in October 2008 was to select a bronze 42-pounder cannon for recovery. This strategy was designed to confirm its dimensions and the nature and date of its royal arms, and thus to help identify the shipwreck definitively as remains of a first-rate Royal Navy Georgian warship. Only the most prestigious first-rates carried 42-pounders after the 1716 Naval Gun Establishment. This procedure, combined with a study of the 41 guns on the site's surface dated to between 1719 and 1734, and a geographical analysis of the wreck's location, has led to the conclusion that site 25C contains the long-sought shipwreck of Admiral Sir John Balchin's HMS *Victory*, lost in the English Channel on 5 October 1744 (cf. Cunningham Dobson and Kingsley, 2009).

Cannon C10 (Fig. 1) was judged to be a suitable candidate for recovery because it lay horizontally on the surface of the site and appeared to be relatively free of sediment cover and concretion. Most of the cannon are largely concealed or plunge into the sediments at acute angles. Situated just north of the site's center in grids M12-N14, this cannon was lying level on the seabed with the crest and dolphins facing upwards. It was 95% uncovered, which would have made the rigging of the *Odyssey Explorer*'s recovery straps a relatively straightforward process and would have caused minimum disturbance to any adjacent or underlying archaeological contexts.

During the removal of the upper loose layer of mobile sand around the bottom edge of cannon C10's westerly trunnion, human remains were encountered. What was later identified as a complete probable human rib bone was found lying on the surface adjacent to the westerly flank of the cascable, close to the cannon base ring (Fig. 2). The bone was yellow in color, while the exposed end was black. It did not appear to be *in situ* and had apparently been moved from its original resting place naturally or by human intervention.

As the ROV continued to investigate the context beneath and adjacent to the lower surface of the cannon at the cascable end, a smooth black oval object was uncovered between 5 and 30cm below the sediment (Fig. 2). On close inspection, the object proved to be the top of a human skull embedded in what appeared to be a black organic layer. Other than the absence of the mandible, no damage to the skull was apparent. The upper teeth retain their white color and all are apparently intact (Fig. 3).

To the right of the skull, parallel to the western side of cannon C10, between the base ring and the trunnion, further skeletal remains were observed. Blackened rib bones protruded vertically out of the sediment alongside what seemed to be additional components of the same skeleton articulated beneath the gun. More surface deposits of human remains were identified at the muzzle end of cannon C10 (Fig. 4).

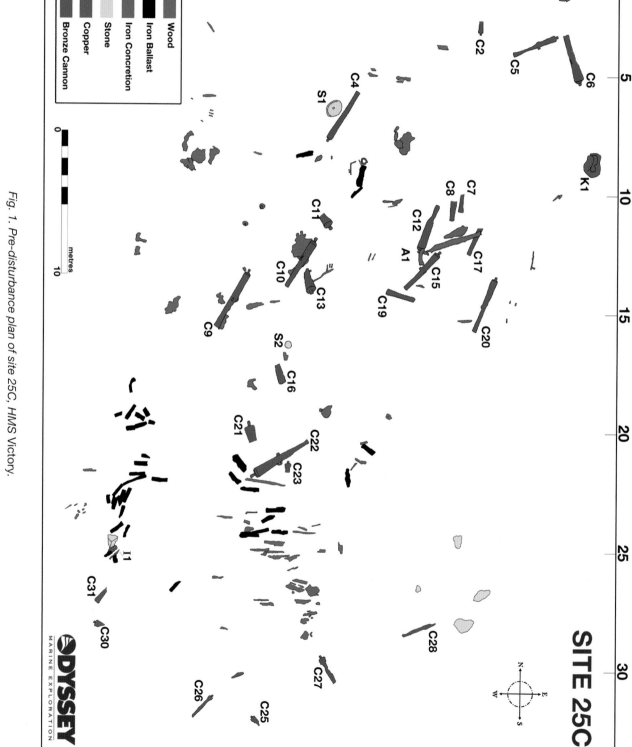

Fig. 1. Pre-disturbance plan of site 25C, HMS Victory.

Fig. 2. The exposure of a human skull and rib bones around the cascable end of cannon C10.

Fig. 3. Detail of the human skull associated with cannon C10.

Fig. 4. Surface deposits of human bone at the muzzle end of cannon C10.

Following the exposure of the skull, all operations were immediately halted. The skull was photographed and then placed back in its original position. Supplementary photographs and video were taken of the area surrounding the skull and cannon. ROV Zeus then re-buried the remains in their original positions. Later surveys confirmed that the skull remained covered and protected.

Additional surface deposits of probable human remains were subsequently discovered at the cascable end of cannon C22 (Fig. 5), whose trunnion diameter of 5.5cm suggests the gun is a 24-pounder, and at the muzzle end of C39, which is located outside the main wreck nucleus. Surface deposits were records between cannon C9 and C10 (Fig. 6).

Even though small-scale trial-trenching to the south of the wreck between the rudder and cannon C26 did not expose any further human remains, based on these discoveries the presence of other disarticulated and articulated human remains should be anticipated on site 25C. The presence of elements of a skeleton beneath cannon C10, a lower deck 42-pounder, seems to reflect the fate of a crew member who was pinned down by the gun as it was torn out of its station when HMS *Victory* sank violently.

2. Shipwrecks & Human Bone Preservation

The preservation of human bones on shipwreck sites is an undeveloped research area in underwater archaeology. Such assemblages are unusual on shipwrecks of all site-formation types and periods, despite the loss of life that often accompanied many maritime tragedies. As Arnaud *et al.* (1980: 53) emphasize, "In submarine archaeology, the discovery of human bone remains is a very rare event." For this reason, the subject receives no individual treatment within Robinson's classic *First Aid for Underwater Finds* (1998) or Pearson's *Conservation of Marine Archaeological Objects* (1988: 53-4), where the rarity of human bones compels the subject to be restricted to observations of carved animal bone.

This state of affairs results from the reality that the vast majority of shipwrecked sailors and crew members either managed to escape a foundering vessel or, after perishing in or near it, their bodies drifted free of the wreckage as water replaced any pockets of air below decks. Contemporary salvage or structural collapse over time can also release and scatter remains after the event (Mays,

Fig. 5. Surface deposits of possible human bone at the cascable end of cannon C22, with a wooden stanchion at right.

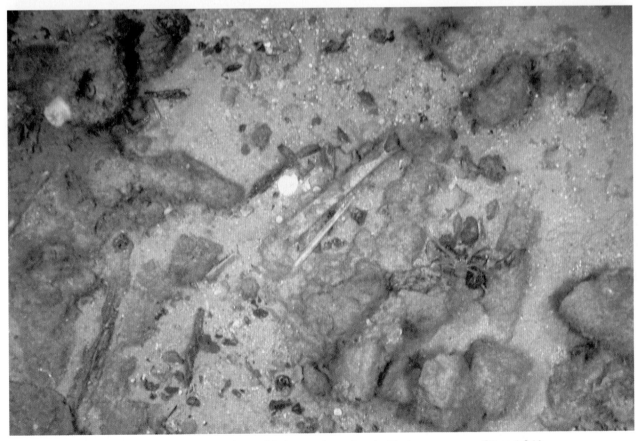

Fig. 6. Surface deposits of possible human bone located between cannon C9 and C10.

2008: 127). The majority of shipwreck sites where human remains have been preserved lie on shallow coastal shelves in temperate climatic zones. As the 90 human skeletons buried beneath hearths in the submerged Pre-pottery Neolithic C village of Atlit, Israel, demonstrate, only when bones are comprehensively and tightly sealed will large assemblages remain well preserved (Kingsley, 2008: 80).

Forensic studies demonstrate that in most marine environments a human corpse will be reduced to skeletal form in less than three weeks, although some degree of articulation may prevail for as long as 18 months. Following the loss of soft tissue, skeletal surfaces are abraded by current-driven sediments. Physical transport of the remains by currents may result in their impact with hard surfaces to cause additional breakage and dispersal. Biological activity involving boring, encrusting and scavenging further degrades bones, resulting in advanced deterioration within 12 years, even in cases of the most durable skeletal parts (Mays, 2008: 125).

As a result, the vast majority of human bones on shipwrecks are only preserved if and when a victim became trapped below decks, such as beneath cannon and cargo. This prevents dispersion until a sealing layer may be deposited to preserve bone within an anaerobic environment. Therefore, the degree of preservation will depend on how quickly the remains become sediment-inundated and whether such burial seals out oxygen – the main reason that mud and clay are superior to sand for this purpose (Mays, 2008: 125; Gregory, 1995: 65).

Limited skeletal remains typify wrecks located in sandy and hard mud environments, as opposed to fluid mud contexts like the *Mary Rose*, *Kronan* and *Vasa*, where human bones should be expected and are common (Mays, 2008: 127). The survival of soft tissue only survives in the most rare of warm or mineral-rich springs and cold, oxygen-depleted environments (Lenihan, 1987: 328), such as on the 17th-century *La Belle* shipwreck in Matagorda Bay, North America (Bruseth and Turner, 2005: 118-19).

Within these limits, the gross preservation of bones from marine shipwreck sites can be quite good, as exemplified in the rapidly buried contexts of the *Kronan*, *Vasa* and *Mary Rose*. Three incomplete skeletons have been recovered from two Mediterranean wrecks off southern France dated to the 10th centuries AD and were sufficiently well preserved to have facilitated examination of their calcium/phosphorus ratio, which was found to be nearly the same as in fresh samples (Arnaud *et al.*, 1980). In fact, bone preservation on some wreck sites has been sufficiently effective to permit mitochondrial DNA extraction and analysis, as in the case of two human bones found on the *Wanli*, a European merchant vessel wrecked in the 1630s in 43m off Dungun, Malaysia (Ariffin *et al.*, 2007: 30). The outstand-

ing preservation of the mud-inundated *Mary Rose* skeletal assemblage enabled isotope tests to assess the diet and origin of her crew members (Bell *et al.*, 2009: 166).

Research into the deterioration of unburied animal bones in a seawater environment has been conducted in relation to the *Swan*, a Cromwellian shipwreck lost off western Scotland in 1653, where samples were studied in close proximity to the wreck. These were examined at regular intervals over a one-year period and correlated with physical, chemical and biological parameters measured during the experiment. When removed from the site after 52 weeks, the human bones exhibited widespread softening and the precipitation of phosphates, which negatively affected their structural stability. After drying, they "became extremely light, brittle, and chalky" (Gregory, 1995: 62-63). Results of the experiment concluded that biodeterioration is the most significant effect on bone in seawater. The process commences with attacks by bacteria and fungi, which leads to the establishment of macro flora and fauna (kelp, boring crustacea and mollusca) on the bone's surfaces. This, in turn, establishes pathways by which additional biological, chemical, and physical deterioration can occur (Gregory, 1995: 65).

Arguably the major obstacle to optimum preservation is not chemical reactions, however, but scrambling processes in the marine environment. These scatter and intermix human bones from shipwrecks, primarily through current transport.

3. Optimum Skeletal Preservation

The *Mary Rose* is often inappropriately heralded as a prime example of why shipwrecks should receive the status of a marine 'grave'. When Henry VIII's warship sank in 1545, only 30 of her 200 sailors, 185 soldiers and 30 gunners survived. The remains of 92 fairly complete skeletons have been recovered, accounting for no less than 43% of the entire crew. However, the environmental circumstances surrounding the ship's preservation are extraordinary, not typical. As the *Mary Rose* sank very rapidly, her anti-boarding netting covered all of the exposed decks, tragically trapping the crew inside. The four tides a day in the Solent swiftly inundated the vessel and her contents in deep silt, which engulfed the ship's exterior and interior. A hard shell seabed naturally deposited in the late 17th or early 18th century then sealed all the Tudor levels *in situ* (Stirland, 2005: 66, 76, 79). Without this unique combination of circumstances the ship's hull structure and skeletal assemblage would not have been so remarkably preserved.

A similar environmental scenario characterizes the 1,553 pieces of human bones from 25 individuals excavated from the *Vasa*, wrecked in 1628. When King Gustavus Adolphus of Sweden's warship was lost on her maiden voyage, she foundered in sight of land and about half of her crew was able to swim to shore.[1] Well-preserved human bones were similarly recovered from the silty, mud-inundated wreck of *La Belle*, an expedition ship of Robert Cavelier, Sieur de La Salle, which grounded hard on the muddy bottom of Matagorda Bay in 1686, where it eventually collapsed inwards and was buried. One complete skeleton was found in the remains of an accommodation/store room, and elements of another in an aft cargo hold. Both are believed to be the remains of crewmen who died before the sinking, most likely of thirst. The skeleton found in the accommodation/store room still contained "almost the entire brain" within the skull (Bruseth and Turner, 2005: 115-18).

In addition to fluid mud environments, bones are also exceptionally well-preserved in the deep, icy waters of freshwater bodies such as Lake Superior, where skeletal remains and soft tissue have been effectively preserved on at least three modern wrecks: the package freighter *Kamloops*, where the entire crew of 22 died of drowning or hypothermia in December 1927 (Lenihan, 1987: 328); the bulk freighter *Emperor*, where 12 out of 33 were lost in 1947 (Lenihan, 1987: 185); and the bulk freighter *Edmund Fitzgerald*, where the entire crew of 29 perished in November 1975.[2] In all three cases, a process known as adipocere formation or saponification swiftly converted the soft tissues "into a soft waxy-type substance, frequently compared to soap" (Lenihan, 1987: 328). The *Fitzgerald* remains, which were located outside the hull, are much more degraded than those from the other vessels, where the bones were found inside.

4. Realities of Human Remains on Shipwrecks: Managing Expectations

Other shipwrecks where small numbers of human bones have been recorded provide a more balanced reflection of preservative parameters. When the Royal Navy frigate *Dartmouth* was wrecked off Scotland in 1690, all but six of the 130-man crew was drowned (Martin, 1978: 31). Yet the only human remains uncovered during the excavations were a few bones associated with one shoe found trapped under a cannon (Adnams, 1974: 271). Osteological investigations of more than 200 human bones excavated from HMS *Pandora*, which foundered off the north coast of Queensland on the Great Barrier Reef in 1791, identified just three of the 35 drowned crew members (Steptoe and Wood, 2002).[3] Some 60% of the bones of a lone male were recovered from a crew of 60 on the Cromwellian vessel the *Swan*. This male appeared to have been trapped below decks when the vessel

sank off Duart Point, Scotland, in 1653.[4]

The rarity of human bones on both merchant vessels and Colonial-period warships is exemplified by the wreck of the *Orient*, which was blown up in action against England in 1798 off Aboukir Bay, Egypt, during the Battle of the Nile. Although only 60 of the *Orient*'s 1,040 crewmen survived the explosion, only a single mandible has been discovered during excavations, leading the research team to conclude that "Underwater archaeologists rarely find actual human remains – typically not even bone can withstand the salt water, marine life, and other destructive elements" (Foreman *et al.*, 1999: 54, 140, 204).

In what was the greatest loss of life in a single event during the War of 1812 between US forces and Britain on the American Great Lakes, 53 men from the combined crews were drowned in Lake Ontario during the capsizing of the *Hamilton* and *Scourge* (Cain, 1983: 111). Again, only the skeletal remains of a single individual have been identified during remotely-operated vehicle surveys of the site.[5]

5. Conclusions

The discovery of human remains on the surface and beneath light sediment cover on wreck site 25C was not anticipated. Odyssey has investigated hundreds of shipwrecks during the Atlas Project within the English Channel and this is the first occurrence of human remains. Their presence is the result of what seems to be the *Victory*'s rapid sinking, combined with the movements of the ship's crew below decks. One possible cause of death may have been a sailor being crushed beneath bronze cannon that had broken free of their gun stations. However, it is not impossible that these tragic souls simply drowned and that currents and trawler action relocated the bones, which became trapped and wedged in place alongside durable artifacts. The bones' exposure is the result of the dynamic mobile sediments and currents that constantly cover and uncover the site, working in tandem with scrambling caused by beam trawlers. By contrast, bones are unlikely to be preserved on sites characterized by solid sea bottoms (rock or hard substrata), where they are not sealed within anaerobic contexts.

Even though Odyssey Marine Exploration only expects to find on site 25C a very small percentage of the skeletal remains of the approximately 900-1,100 seamen, marines and volunteers who lost their lives on HMS *Victory* in 1744, the destruction and inadvertent snagging in nets of these human bones by intensive trawler activity in the western English Channel is a very real and immediate threat. On the basis of the results of the current fieldwork, recovery of HMS *Victory*'s skeletal assemblage should be classified as rescue archaeology.

Recovery and study of site 25C's skeletal remains may provide crucial information on the following subjects:

- Demography
- Disease
- Genetics
- Diet
- Professional functions (repetitive strain disorders)
- Surgery practices
- Forensic taphonomy in deep waters

Ultimately, any human remains from the wreck of HMS *Victory* will contribute immensely to the understanding of daily life in the Georgian navy. Some 107 skeletons of a motley crew of Royal Navy pensioners have recently been excavated and studied at the site of the Royal Hospital at Greenwich. These veterans of Britain's wars with the Dutch, Americans, Spanish, the French Republic and Napoleon display a wide variety of pathological conditions from multiple fractures to rickets, tuberculosis, syphilis, scurvy, cancer, as well as amputations and craniotomies. The Royal Hospital assemblage dates between 1749 and 1856 (Boston *et al.*, 2008). HMS *Victory*'s skeletal assemblage will push back this chronology and thus expand our knowledge of life at sea in Georgian Britain.

However, first and foremost, any plans for the ultimate disposition of the remains of HMS *Victory*'s sailors is a question which must be left entirely up to the Royal Navy and the MOD, and perhaps the families of the deceased that can be located. Whichever approach is utilized, whether re-interment at sea, returning them to land for burial, or using them for scientific study, any actions must be conducted in a manner that appropriately respects the brave sailors and the lives that they lost for their country.

Notes

1. See: http://www.bruzelius.info/Nautica/Medicine/Wasa-skeletons.html.
2. See: http://www.shipwreckmuseum.com/fitz.phtml.
3. See also *HMS Pandora: Human Remains*: http://www.qm.qld.gov.au/ features/pandora/human.
4. Martin, C., 'Resurrecting the Swan: Archaeology of a Cromwellian Shipwreck, 1653', *History Scotland Magazine*: http://www.historyscotland.com/features/resurrecting theswan.html.
5. *Hamilton and Scourge Project*: http://www.hamilton-scourge.hamilton.ca/home.htm.

Bibliography

Adnams, J.R., 'The Dartmouth, a British Frigate Wrecked off Mull, 1690', *IJNA* 3.2 (1974), 269-74.

Ariffin, S.H.Z., Wahab, R.M.A., Zamrod, Z., Sahar, S., Abd Razak, M.F., Ariffin, E.J. and Senafi, S., 'Molecular Archaeology of Ancient Bone from 400 Year Old Shipwreck', *Asia Pacific Journal of Molecular Biology and Biotechnology* 15.1 (2007), 27-31.

Arnaud, G., Arnaud, S., Ascenzi, A., Bonucci, E. and Graziani, G., 'On the Problem of the Preservation of Human Bone in Sea-Water', *IJNA* 9.1 (1980), 53-65.

Bell, L.S., Lee Thorp, J.A. and Elkerton, A., 'The Sinking of the Mary Rose Warship: A Medieval Mystery Solved?', *Journal of Archaeological Science* 36 (2009), 166-73.

Boston., C., Witkin, A., Boyle, A. and Wilkinson, D.R.P., *'Safe Moor'd In Greenwich Tier'. A Study of the Skeletons at the Royal Hospital Greenwich* (Oxford Archaeology Monograph 5, Oxford, 2008).

Bruseth, J.E. and Turner, T.S., *From a Watery Grave: The Discovery and Excavation of La Salle's Shipwreck, La Belle* (Texas A&M University Press, 2005).

Cain, E., *Ghost Ships - Hamilton & Scourge: Historical Treasures from the War of 1812* (New York, 1983).

Cunningham Dobson, N. and Kingsley, S.A., *HMS Victory, a First-Rate Royal Navy Warship Wrecked in the English Channel, 1744. Preliminary Survey & Identification* (OME Papers 2, Tampa, 2009).

Foreman, L., Phillips, E.B. and Goddio, F., *Napoleon's Lost Fleet: Bonaparte, Nelson and the Battle of the Nile* (New York, 1999).

Gregory, D., 'Experiments into the Deterioration Characteristics of Materials on the Duart Point Wreck Site: an Interim Report', *IJNA* 24.1 (1995), 61-65.

Kingsley, S., 'From Carmel to Genesis: A Neolithic Flood for the Holy Land?', *Bulletin of the Anglo-Israel Archaeological Society* 26 (2008), 75-93.

Lenihan, D.J. (ed.), *Submerged Cultural Resources Study: Isle Royale National Park* (Southwest Cultural Resources Center Professional Papers Number 8, Santa Fe, 1987).

Martin, C.J.M., 'The *Dartmouth*, a British frigate Wrecked off Mull, 1690. 5. The Ship', *IJNA* 7.1 (1978), 29-58.

Mays, S., 'Human Remains in Marine Archaeology', *Environmental Archaeology* 13.2 (2008), 123-33.

Pearson, C., *Conservation of Marine Archaeological Objects* (London, 1988).

Robinson, W., *First Aid for Underwater Finds* (London, 1998).

Snow, E.R., *Great Atlantic Adventures* (New York, 1970).

Steptoe, D.P. and Wood, W.B., 'The Human Remains from HMS Pandora', *Internet Archaeology* 11 (2002).

Stirland, A.J., *The Men of the Mary Rose. Raising the Dead* (Stroud, 2005).